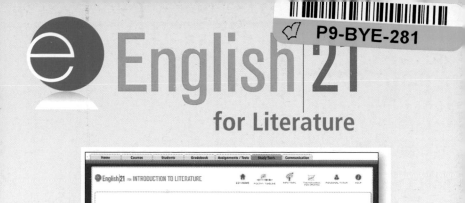

# English 21
## for Literature

www.thomsonedu.com/english21

## Supporting students through every step of the writing process

More than just the largest compilation of online resources ever organized for literature courses, English21 supports students through every step of the writing process, from assignment to final draft. This complete support system weaves robust, self-paced instruction with interactive assignments to engage students as they become better prepared and more effective writers.

**OPEN HERE TO LEARN MORE ABOUT HOW English21 CAN WORK FOR YOU!**

www.thomsonedu.com/english21

## REVISE AND EDIT

An **Interactive Handbook** with animations, over 250 interactive writing exercises, 360 grammar activities, and student paper workshops related to grammar and writing support students in the revising and editing of their papers.

## EXPLICATE

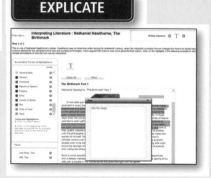

An extensive **Media Library**, featuring over 700 multimedia assets, includes a wealth of audio clips (42), video clips (32), stories (11), poems (389), plays (8), essays (58), and images (203). To help students annotate works and generate evidence for their papers, all media can be read through Wadsworth's unique note-taking tool, *The Explicator*.

Unlike traditional note-taking, *The Explicator* empowers students with a state-of the art analysis tool that allows them to examine and annotate both traditional texts as well as non-traditional texts, including images, video clips, and audio clips, acting as a bridge between reading and writing.

---

### Also available: English21 *Plus* for Literature

English21 *Plus* includes all of the features mentioned above plus access to Wadsworth's **InSite for Writing and Research™**, a groundbreaking, all-in-one electronic portfolio and peer review application. **InSite** also includes an originality checker powered by **Turnitin®**, a rich assignment library, and an electronic grademarking system.

THOMSON

**InSite**
For Writing and Research™

turnitin

# The Literary
# Experience

## ESSENTIAL EDITION

# The Literary Experience

## ESSENTIAL EDITION

**Bruce Beiderwell**
*University of California, Los Angeles*

**Jeffrey M. Wheeler**
*Long Beach City College*

**THOMSON**

**WADSWORTH**

Australia • Brazil • Canada • Mexico • Singapore
Spain • United Kingdom • United States

## THOMSON
### WADSWORTH

The Literary Experience, Essential Edition
Bruce Beiderwell / Jeffrey M. Wheeler

Publisher: Lyn Uhl
Development Editor: Marita Sermolins
Assistant Editor: Lindsey Veautour
Technology Project Manager: Stephanie Gregoire
Executive Marketing Manager: Mandee Eckersley
Marketing Assistant: Kate Remsberg
Marketing Communications Manager:
    Stacey Purviance
Signing Representative: Bill Brisick
Associate Content Project Manager:
    Jessica Rasile

Print Buyer: Sue Carroll
Permissions Editor:
    Margaret Chamberlain-Gaston
Permissions Research: The Permissions Company
Text Designer: Garry Harman
Photo Manager: Sheri Blaney
Photo Researcher: Francelle Carapetyan
Cover Designer: Cabbage Design Company
Compositor/Production Service:
    Newgen–Austin
Cover/Text Printer: Thomson West

Thomson Higher Education
25 Thomson Place
Boston, MA 02210-1202
USA

For more information about our products,
contact us at:
Thomson Learning Academic Resource Center
1-800-423-0563

For permission to use material from this text
or product, submit a request online at
http://www.thomsonrights.com
Any additional questions about permissions
can be submitted by e-mail to
thomsonrights@thomson.com

Library of Congress Control Number:
2007935088

ISBN-13: 978-1-4282-3050-7

ISBN-10: 1-4282-3050-5

Credits appear on pages 395–401, which constitute
a continuation of the copyright page.

# Brief Contents

# Contents

# Preface

## LITERARY ANALYSIS THAT GROWS FROM THE STUDENT'S READING EXPERIENCE

Books *about* literature sometimes create barriers to the very subject they intend to explore. The "about" may suggest that there is some special knowledge separate from the primary texts and the immediate experience of those texts that is somehow supposed to be mastered. The result is both disheartening and familiar. Students, for example, will sometimes say they love to read but that they hate to write about what they have read. Or they might resist "talking about" what they've read because talk seems somehow removed from whatever they've felt as they read. Literary study quickly becomes centered on definitions, on correct answers, on knowledge that can often be acquired without even reading a literary text (how many students have written on, say, *Great Expectations* after reviewing only a study guide to that novel?). *The Literary Experience* starts by recognizing that the experience of a text comes first. Critical questions, terminology, and theory are introduced not as the "real subject" (the things that will be on the test) but as means to deepen and clarify the reading of a text.

## AN ORGANIZATION BASED ON INTERPRETIVE QUESTIONS OF INCREASING COMPLEXITY

In *The Literary Experience*, you will find literary selections and discussion of literary elements grouped in a way that facilitates the discussion that leads to thoughtful writing about texts. The organization is both organic and progressive: the opening chapters address the sorts of basic questions and essential elements that one encounters in nearly any text (questions of story, character, theme, and so on). These are elements that we need to identify in order to make sense of a text. From there, the book moves to elements involved in constructing a text (like coherence, interruption, symbol). These elements emphasize the rhetorical impact of the text, the relationship between the text's structure and an audience's reaction to that structure. The final chapters move to matters outside of the text (context, genre) to help us to think about how we experience any text not just as an isolated encounter but also as part of a larger culture.

## A CRITICAL VOCABULARY THAT SPRINGS FROM A STUDENT'S OWN EXPERIENCE

Every chapter opens with framing questions that have been carefully crafted to show students they already ask crucial questions themselves—if not about literature, then about the things in life upon which literature is built. Rather than focusing discussions narrowly on the formal elements, the chapters address feelings, thoughts, and problems that arise from an active engagement with a text. The questions that lead into the chapter discussions serve as a starting place that is grounded in a meaningful and concrete critical issue.

The Essential Edition of *The Literary Experience*, then, leads students to encounter new words in familiar contexts. As teachers, we all seek to help students acquire a vocabulary that extends and deepens their understanding. Understanding a specialized word involves using it in ways that can lead one to a more engaged, nuanced, and powerful reading. Furthermore, command of such a word gives one the power to articulate the sorts of complex intellectual and emotional responses that works of art engender. For instance, the discussion of rhythm leads a student to consider the effect of silence in the film *Jaws*, the uses of pauses in poetry, and the motion created by language choices in prose. Such an active and thoroughly internalized acquisition of key words is consistent with a process oriented approach to reading and writing. No literature class is ever definitive. Often a student finds a class most fulfilling by leaving with a reading list longer than the one that completed the term. But perhaps the student achieves a bigger sense of what literary experiences might mean. For example, the student may begin to look at a painting or a television show in new and enlivening ways by bringing knowledge from the classroom back to what lies outside.

## LITERARY ELEMENTS: TEACHING ACROSS GENRES

The most common arrangement for an introductory literature class has three main divisions: fiction, poetry, and drama. They do contain most of the elements that *The Literary Experience* includes, but because they emphasize an element like plot in a story, rhythm in a poem, or setting in a play, they may suggest that any one element operates exclusively in a single genre. By isolating poetry in concentrated units, for example, students may be led to respond to a poem only in the constricting, artificial context of other poems. Furthermore, what is gained in such a study may be unnecessarily contained by the "poetry unit." It is useful to remember that the pleasures of rhythm are available to children long before they are able to read and long, long before they think of poetry as a "genre." Similarly, issues of plot or character do not arise only in the study of prose fiction. And setting is hardly a concern specific to the theater.

We mix genres to make the teaching of literature consistent with actual literary experience. After all, we read to explore feelings and ideas; we make connections among ideas without the constraints of genre; we do not seek to understand formal elements for their own sake. A reader's experience of a poem may be enhanced by reading a story that influenced it, by remembering a film that explores a similar theme, by looking at a painting that was produced at the same time, or by seeing a photograph that captures the poem's setting. Our mixing does more than simply create variety; it deepens our literary experience by enabling us to draw connections among genres instead of creating the impression that each genre is distinct and has its own set of literary terms.

The literary elements that we discuss spring from the interpretive questions that students ask about any text, beginning with plot: What is happening and why do we care? Of course, organizing this book around "elements" as opposed to genres suggests its own kind of arbitrariness. We've been careful to cross-reference elements within chapters in order to emphasize that a response to any given text (and the writing that it generates) isn't bound by a chapter heading. The recurring elements emphasize the fact that this critical vocabulary is not some arbitrary list; it enables us to develop deeper analysis. The *Making Connections* boxes in each chapter break through the problems that often arise from a simple "elements of" approach to teaching literature. The look ahead–look back nature of this feature explicitly crosses from the consideration of the chapter's featured element to specific aspects of other works from other chapters or from the world of literature at large.

## READING IS WRITING / WRITING IS READING

*The Literary Experience* emphasizes the importance of the student's writing throughout. Writing is presented as a means to explore and discover—as an extension of reading, not an assignment tagged on to reading. Students need to understand that their writing is important for something more than assessment. Because we believe that writing can be a means to deepen understanding, we do not divide "understanding" and "reading" from the activity of writing. All are part of a coherent, rich experience. Therefore, there is no large "writing about literature" section standing entirely separate from the rest of the text at the beginning or the end. Woven throughout are brief discussions that underscore what is ever present: an understanding of writing's centrality. For example, each chapter contains the following components.

- A *Note to Student Writers* that draws lessons from literary texts or the study of literary texts that can be applied to critical writing. Some of these notes offer specific generative suggestions (what kinds of questions prompt the development of ideas or the definition of a thesis?); some explain the logic of common conventions (why use the present tense when recounting the action of a narrative?); some call attention to crucial rhetorical features that critical writers must master (how does one acknowledge a position and then turn strongly against it?).

- *Experiencing Literature* sections through which we demonstrate for students how they might interact with a piece of literature and what sorts of questions they can ask about a particular element as they engage a text.

- *Modeling Critical Analysis* section that ends every chapter and serves to show students how to incorporate what they have learned in the chapter and previous chapters as well as show them how to translate their critical reading into writing.

This new Essential Edition of *The Literary Experience* orients students to literary study by helping them understand how questions they often ask as they read (for example, "what happened?") can lead to sophisticated analyses. All versions of *The Literary Experience*—the Comprehensive Edition, the Compact Edition, and the Essential Edition—prompt students to view writing as an extension of reading. All enable them to acquire and use a precise critical vocabulary, and all help them define reading as a broad-ranging intellectual and emotional activity. The Essential Edition is the pedagogical and philosophical core of the whole enterprise without the anthologies found at the end of every chapter in the larger editions. Instructors who select readings to explore a single highly defined theme or to represent a particular historical period or specific literary movement will find that this edition is indeed *essential*, for it grounds students in the most basic concerns of any critical reader and writer. The Essential Edition should complement any college literature course taught at any level. It offers students a set of adaptable tools that enable them to move into thoughtful engagement with any text, and it provides instructors with a solid analytical framework to assist in the transition from specific themes or text into more general principles of literary study.

# SUPPLEMENTS

In order to further engage students in literature, *The Wadsworth Original Film Series* is available to be packaged with *The Literary Experience*. This DVD includes three short films, including Eudora Welty's "A Worn Path," John Updike's "A&P," and Raymond Carver's "Cathedral." This DVD also includes interviews with the authors themselves. In addition to the *Wadsworth Original Film Series* DVD, three films are also available on DVD or VHS to be packaged with *The Literary Experience*. These separate DVDs contain Alice Walker's "Everyday Use," Langston Hughes "Salvation," or Tillie Olson's "I Stand Here Ironing." Each adaptation is followed by author interviews. Some instructors may find the films to be a useful conversation starter.

## Instructor's Manual

To aid in the task of teaching with this text, the *Instructor's Manual* is an all-in-one resource containing a brief introduction to each chapter that examines the literature examples, images, and film references used to further explain how the featured pieces work within the element as well as what other pieces in the book exemplify that element. Because the manual was developed for the Comprehensive and Compact Editions of *The Literary Experience*, it also includes support for features of these titles that may be useful in a more general way to supplement instructors using this book. Those features include: "Cultural Context" for every literature piece appearing in the anthologies; a "Discussion" section, with at least a paragraph about how the work fits into the element and one about how it fits into the theme and how the piece relates to other elements and themes in the book; an expansion of the questions that are currently in the book and how the piece would work with the "Experiencing Literature through Writing" questions; and sample syllabi created by authors Bruce Beiderwell and Jeffrey Wheeler. In addition, the *Instructor's Manual* contains a bonus resource in "A Guide to Using Film"—a detailed chapter-by-chapter guide to give instructors advice on how to use film references currently in the book, along with new films, coupled with in-depth summaries and specific scene suggestions—to be used in the classroom. All the films are tied to in-class discussion questions and writing prompts to engage students' interests.

# ACKNOWLEDGMENTS

A book this thick requires the work of many more people than we could ever list on a title page or even here in the acknowledgments. The following reviewers have looked at different incarnations of the chapters that you find here. Their careful reading, insightful questions, and generous advice have made the book more useful and more teachable.

Donald Andrews, *Chattanooga State Technical Community College*
Melissa Barth, *Appalachian State University*
Joseph Bathanti, *Appalachian State University*
Janet Beck, *Appalachian State University*
Betty Bettacchi, *Collin County Community College*
Jacqueline Blackwell, *Thomas Nelson Community College*
Amy Brazillier, *Red Rocks Community College*
Barbara L. Brown, *San Jacinto College Central*
Glenda Bryant, *South Plains College, Levelland*
Larry Carlson, *College of Charleston*
Laura Carroll, *Abilene Christian University*
Patricia Cearley, *South Plains College, Levelland*
Karen Chaffee, *Ulster County Community College*
Helen Chester, *Milwaukee Area Technical College*
Sherry Chisamore, *Ulster County Community College*
Basil Clark, *Saginaw Valley State University*
Mike Compton, *University of Memphis*
Denise Coulter, *Atlantic Cape Community College*
Christy Desmet, *University of Georgia*
Tammy DiBenedetto, *Riverside Community College*
Scott Douglass, *Chattanooga State Technical Community College*
Joy M. Eichner-Lynch, *Contra Costa College*
Jo Nell Farrar, *San Jacinto College*
Jane Focht-Hansen, *San Antonio College*
DeLisa Ging, *Northern Oklahoma College*
Diana Gingo, *University of Texas, Dallas*
Paul Goodin, *Northern Kentucky University*
Gary Harrington, *Salisbury University*
Dawn Hayward, *Delaware County Community College*
Ana Hernandez, *Miami Dade Community College*
Gillian R. Hettinger, *William Paterson University*
Kathy Houghton, *Erie Community College*
Rebecca Housel, *Rochester Institute of Technology*
David Johansson, *Brevard Community College*
Ken Johnson, *Georgia Perimeter College*
Jan McArthur, *Delgado Community College*
Miles McCrimmon, *J. Sargeant Reynolds Community College*
Linda McGann, *South Plains College, Levelland*
Thomas Gerard McNamee, *Eastern Oregon University*

Richard Middleton-Kaplan, *Harper College*
Rod Val Moore, *Los Angeles Valley College*
Michael Morris, *Eastfield College*
Mona Narain, *University of Texas, San Antonio*
Jeffrey N. Nelson, *University of Alabama, Huntsville*
Chris Partida, *North Harris Community College*
Peggy Peden, *Nashville State Community College*
Jan Prewitt, *Emporia State University*
Geri Rhodes, *Albuquerque TVI Community College*
Richard Rosol, *Quinnipiac University*
Steve Sansom, *North Harris Community College*
Cary Ser, *Miami Dade Community College*
Michael Sollars, *Texas Southern University*
Donald R. Stinson, *Northern Oklahoma College*
Constance Strickland, *Wesley College*
Raven Sweet, *University of Memphis*
Andrea Kaston Tange, *Eastern Michigan University*
Tom Treffinger, *Greenville Technical College*
Edward P. Walkiewicz, *Oklahoma State University, Stillwater*
Mark Woods, *Jefferson Community College*

Also special thanks to the following for their guidance:

Wilson Chen, *Benedictine University*
Suzy Holstein
Dennis Lynch, *Michigan Technological University*
Thomas Lochhaas
Linda Venis, *University of California, Los Angeles*
Shari Zimmerman, *Hofstra University*

We'd like to thank in particular Diana Gingo of the University of Texas, Dallas, who has offered thoughtful responses throughout our writing process and who has written the Film Guide for the book.

Much of our inspiration comes from the lively and informed conversations that we have had with the faculty at UCLA's Writing Programs and in the English Department at Long Beach City College. Good colleagues make for good teaching. Special thanks to Teddi Chichester, George Gadda, Sonia Maasik, Gina Shaffer, Velvet Pearson, Hiro Sasaki, Frank Gaspar, and Ron DiCostanzo.

It has been a great pleasure to work with the entire Thomson Wadsworth team on this project. Initially, Bill Brisick encouraged us to submit our proposal for a "very short book" teaching students to write about literature. Aron Keesbury, Senior Acquisitions Editor, liked that proposal but didn't let a positive first reading stop him from pressing for something better; he helped mold *The Literary Experience* into a very different and much more ambitious text and anthology. The Essential Edition is a return to our original vision while continuing to expand that vision beyond our anticipations. Development Editor Marita Sermolins guided the production of the book, looked at every draft, chased after every permission, and helped us to keep track of all of the pieces of this huge enterprise. Lindsey Veautour helped with the trimming and tightening that has made this edition truly essential. Samantha Ross led a group that has done far more than just check for typos in the manuscript—as did her successor Lianne Ames, who worked on both the comprehensive and compact versions, and Jessica Rasile, who we thank for her work on this, the Essential Edition of *The Literary Experience*. Bill Coyle of Salem State College has written the author headnotes. And Jessie Swigger of the University of Texas, Austin, has authored the *Instructor's Manual*. All of their good work in the final stages of the process built upon the efforts of those who have helped us get started and continue through to the end. Kate Edwards has taken our text and shown how it is marketable. Guided by their comments, we have rewritten and rethought the project; any remaining mistakes can only be the result of our own oversight.

Throughout the process, we have aimed to make a book worthy of the good students in our lives: Samuel Beiderwell, Renata Gusmão-Garcia, Chloe Wheeler, and Blake Wheeler. Finally, we must thank those who have lived with this project as it has developed: Ivna Gusmão and Laura Scavuzzo Wheeler They have heard about each proposal, each phone call, and every review, and they have been our first editors and proofreaders. Their support is deeply appreciated.

# Introduction to the Elements of Literature

## How Do We Know What Terms to Use When We Talk about Our Experience with Literature?

THEODOTUS: The fire has spread from your ships. The first of the seven
wonders of the world perishes. The library of Alexandria is in flames.
CAESAR: Is that all?
THEODOTUS (*unable to believe his senses*): All! Caesar: will you go down to
posterity as a barbarous soldier too ignorant to know the value of
books?
CAESAR: Theodotus, I am an author myself; and I tell you it is better that
the Egyptians should live their lives than dream them away with the
help of books.

(*Caesar and Cleopatra*, George Bernard Shaw)

As unlikely as it might seem, the conversations that we have about literature—the very words we use to approach texts—are profoundly influenced by
historical chance. Consider, for example, the book that has been among the
most influential works of literary criticism in western civilization: Aristotle's
*Poetics*. The version of that work that survives is only a partial discussion. It is
possible we should blame Julius Caesar for what is missing: Caesar, in the
midst of his affair with Cleopatra, is reputed to have ordered his troops to set a
strategic fire in the port of Alexandria that spread to Alexandria's great library
and destroyed its collection. One of the books that may have been in that
library was the only surviving copy of Aristotle's treatise on comedy. Scholars

since have bemoaned the loss of such an important text. If that treatise had survived, the shape of literary studies might be very different today.

What if Caesar had ordered his men to be more careful with their torches? We might privilege Aristophanes instead of Sophocles. Students might be more likely to read *Much Ado about Nothing* than *Hamlet*. But of course we do *not* have Aristotle's seminal text on comedy and we manage pretty well without it. We sometimes try out the terms that Aristotle uses for tragedy to see which are most useful in the discussion of comedy. We still talk about character and plot, but we modify the discussion for this other genre. In his discussion of tragedy, Aristotle suggests that in comedy character is more important than plot, but it is up to us to continue the discussion, to make sense of that claim with our own examples. And then we can try out the same terms as they might relate to fiction or poetry or film.

The methodical approach Aristotle uses to examine dramatic productions is the same approach he takes to examine natural organisms, social structures, and philosophical systems. For Aristotle, everything in the world can be treated as a text to read. By classifying the parts of the thing that he is examining, he establishes a method of presenting his own perspective and of advancing his own argument. But by establishing distinct and well-defined categories, he sets up a system that others can use. Essentially, Aristotle establishes the groundwork for conversations that will follow. His clear definitions of the parts of drama give us a vocabulary to talk about what we have seen. More than two thousand years after he set up these categories, most discussions of drama still refer to and build upon Aristotle's vocabulary.

## DEVELOPING A FLEXIBLE CRITICAL VOCABULARY

The advantage of a specialized vocabulary is that it helps us to identify parts of a whole with precision. In the study of anatomy, for instance, it is important to be able to distinguish among the various internal organs; the lungs, heart, and liver may all work together but they serve very different functions. Creating a vocabulary makes it possible to see and to discuss the intricacies of a subject. But the vocabulary isn't the thing itself; it is a tool that helps us understand the thing—the object of our study.

Because Aristotle gave us an especially rich and useful vocabulary, we often look for complications and moments of discovery when we begin to analyze drama, just as we locate the heart and lungs when we think about anatomy. But having such a perceptive guide may blind us to other aspects of the drama. We might find the parts of the play that Aristotle points out because we have words to describe them; we might miss parts of the play that Aristotle's vocabulary doesn't address. Still, we can argue that the loss of Aristotle's treatise on comedy, though unfortunate, helps us to push the boundaries that his terms set for us. As we establish definitions for the elements of comedy, we develop a process to identify the elements of any other sort of expressive art that we might want to discuss.

In this book, we foreground the process through which we establish and define elements of literary texts and the literary experience. Because Aristotle's text is so old and well established, it is easy to think about his elements of poetics as absolute and complete rather than arbitrary and useful. But systems only come alive when we realize they are both arbitrary *and* useful. The words that Aristotle uses to describe the elements of drama are the ones we begin with when we describe any expressive art, yet when we discuss poetry, for example, we discover that we need to adapt, elaborate, and invent. As we describe "new" elements, we develop a fuller vocabulary to describe general elements like word choice or rhythm. To understand that each of these elements is a tool for articulating the complex ideas presented in expressive arts, we find it helpful to break the traditional boundaries of genre. Using a symbol like a flag, for instance, to represent something other than itself (a country, a cause, patriotism, warmongering) is something that we often discuss when we study poetry because attention to the use of individual words is generally part of the discipline that we teach when we teach poetry. In reality, though, all forms of expressive arts use symbols. In fact, all of these genres share a set of common elements. By examining that single element across genres, a student can learn to manipulate that term more effectively and to use that term outside of the confines of this textbook.

The goal of this book is to help each of you to engage with Aristotle and with anyone else who has ever been interested in discussing their experience with a work of art. Furthermore, it seeks to enable you to express yourself when you read a book or see a film that moves you in some way. When you contribute to this discussion, others should be able to pick up the threads of your ideas to continue weaving further discussions. So we want you to acquire a critical vocabulary that helps you read, respond, and communicate something important about texts, a vocabulary that also enables others to respond to your reading. But we don't want to reduce literary study to a vocabulary lesson; we want you to discover and test the value of particular words as you experience a poem, play, story, or film.

## CRITICAL WRITING AS CONVERSATION

Aristotle's approach to literature hasn't had such influence simply for abstract reasons: as we have suggested, his criticism has enabled people to communicate effectively about how they respond to literary texts. Imagine for a moment a fairly typical movie-going experience. Assume that you've gone with a friend to see a campus screening of Paul Haggis's *Crash*. As the final credits come to a close and you begin to move toward the exit, a conversation might begin with a basic question: "Did you like it?" This is an easy discussion to start, and also an easy one to end if the answer is simply "yes" or "no." But that will not likely be enough. If you hated the movie, you might say, "The characters were all just walking stereotypes that got jumbled together in a bunch of impossible coincidences." If you liked it, you might respond, "All the coincidences made me think about the stereotypes that exist in real life and affect how we think and act." Either way, you are beginning to establish criteria for your discussion. You suggest that to meet your standards a good film must adhere to a certain order, must fairly represent or comment upon life, or must purposefully employ familiar elements (of plot, of character, of structure, and so on).

Now imagine you stop at a coffee shop on campus and you find a group of friends seated around a table who have just seen the same movie. You join them and discover that they are in the midst of their own discussion about *Crash*. You probably do more listening at first than speaking; after all, you need to know what ground they've covered and what direction they've taken. But at some point, you find an opportunity to fit your own opinions into the public conversation. One of the people at the table found the film boring and shallow: "All the twists and turns of the story make it seem complicated, but when you get right down to it the only thing the film gives us is a bunch of clichés about tolerance." You catch at that complaint because it allows you to pick up on and contribute something of your own to the conversation:

> Yeah, this film ran through just about every stereotype around and strung together an unbelievable string of events. But somehow the whole thing seemed new to me. The energy was different—more than just "don't make stupid assumptions about people." The film kept me off-balance. I wasn't always sure where I was supposed to stand in relation to even some of the obvious stereotypes. It all got me to thinking about how hard it is to tell the difference between revealing racism and reinforcing it.

Note that our imagined talk has moved to a point. If you are challenged to back up your interpretation, you will do so by reference to the film. We have moved beyond simply liking or disliking. We are contextualizing, putting the film into categories based on our previous experience in film and in other studies. As we call up these familiar categories, we are able to conduct further analysis and continue the conversation.

Our imagined coffee shop meeting links conversations with reading and writing. The talk recounted in the sample dialogue just above represents a process of thinking through the literary experience. Note how these few sentences begin to define and follow a point as one would do in a paper. The passage even displays some of the rhetorical gestures common in writing; note, for example, that the speaker opens with a concession and then moves to a counterpoint that carries through to the end. The key term for both conversation and composition is *process*. As you discuss *Crash* (or any other work of art) with your friends, you will likely learn something. You'll clarify—indeed—discover ideas. You'll test arguments and, when you find them weak, you'll revise or discard them.

## CRITICAL WRITING AS AN EXTENSION OF READING

Critical writing is often seen as merely an assignment—something to "get through" not something to grow from. But once we understand how writing takes a place as part of a whole literary experience we can begin to make writing seem less alien. Writing (like conversation) grows from alert, engaged, informed, and active reading. Literary texts ask—even demand—such a powerful idea of reading. Consider what occurs (what you feel, what you think) as you read the following short poem.

**Langston Hughes** (1902–1967)

# Harlem (1951)

What happens to a dream deferred?

Does it dry up
like a raisin in the sun?
Or fester like a sore—
And then run?
Does it stink like rotten meat?
Or crust and sugar over—
like a syrupy sweet?

Maybe it just sags
like a heavy load.

*Or does it explode?*

There is no script for your response to this (or any) poem. You might feel anger or frustration; you might sympathize with the speaker or want to argue with him. You might be confused by the questions posed. "Harlem" prompts us to describe, question, interpret, and feel. And whatever line of thought we follow, we search for words to clarify and deepen the experience. At some point, if we wish to move forward, we make writing part of our reading. In brief notes, journal entries, or exchanges over e-mail with other readers we actively seek words that register our sense of the text. Critical writing, then, emerges from active reading; indeed, it is part of active reading.

We can apply the same notions to our experience of any work of art. We hear, we see, we feel, we think—we experience. We try to explain and enrich our experience of a text through our own words. When we appreciate this connection between *our* reading and *our* writing (our viewing and our writing, our seeing and our writing, our listening and our writing) we can begin to appreciate what is involved in the discipline of literary criticism and how rewarding that discipline can be. Reading, after all, isn't just a matter of decoding letters on a page. At the broadest level, reading prompts reflection, interpretation, and discussion. We read a poem or a story of course, but we also read the look on a friend's face in a moment of crisis. We read paintings or a piece of music. We read movies. We receive complex signals in everyday life from various sorts of "texts"; we sort them out, give them shape, and set them in context of related signals. Things we read become a living part of our experience. The act of reading and writing are vitally connected: *to write about a work of art is to extend the very process that characterizes our reading.*

If we think of writing as an activity through which we gain understanding and deepen experience, we can realize a broad vision of what it means to write critically. We can appreciate the great importance of a narrowly specialized vocabulary. We can see how writing together with reading becomes a single creative process. Writing sharpens and enriches reading. Writing helps us see things we might have missed. Writing leads to discovery. *The Literary Experience* will consistently link critical writing, critical reading, and critical conversation. It will help you to write by helping you read more perceptively. It will help you to read by engaging you as a writer.

*The Literary*
*Experience*
ESSENTIAL EDITION

# 1 Scene, Episode, and Plot

## What Happened, and Why Do We Care?

At some level, we're all storytellers. We have a need and a desire to give meaning to the raw experience of our lives by selecting and arranging details. When we recount something that happens to us, we're likely to leave out things that don't quite fit. We may even slightly modify what did happen in order to achieve a truth or power that goes beyond plain facts. We're attentive to dramatic design. We lead into our stories, build to a point of crisis, and finish forcefully. Our motives for crafting stories are complex and varied. We might want to give a satisfying close to a difficult period of our lives so that we can "move on"; in this respect, we are often the audience for our own stories. On other occasions, we want to make sure actions add up to some clear message or moral for the person we're speaking to (think of a parent telling a child a story that begins, "When I was your age . . . "). There is also a great pleasure in putting a string of events together so that those events become a unified story—a skillfully constructed work of art.

The drive to give artistic shape to experience is so strong that it often works with very little prompting. Much conversation involves exchanging stories. We listen to a friend tell a story and then tell another in response. Our intense need for—as well as our deep pleasure in—stories shows in the fact that we build them from the slightest bits of raw material that come our way: a small incident at work, a disagreement with a friend, an observed odd behavior of a stranger in line at a convenience store. We can even work something up from a single image. In fact, we often do work from something that small. A photograph, for example, captures feelings of a particular moment, but that moment often suggests to our imaginations a time before and a time after. We'll often build a narrative from the evidence a single picture provides, despite the obvious limitations of that

Edouard Boubat, *Rendez-vous at the Café La Vache Noire*, Paris (1957)

evidence. This building involves both our creative and our critical intelligence. We assess how details fit together to suggest actions that surround the picture. For example, look closely at the photograph above.

It's quite possible to tell a very brief story "around" Boubat's photograph *Rendez-vous at the Café La Vache Noire*. Some obvious questions may come quickly to mind that force us to respond in terms of narrative. What has brought the woman to the café? What is happening at the moment caught by the camera? What will unfold? How does the story end? We can't, of course, *know* the answers, but Boubat's photograph offers specific features that prompt us to speculate. Consider, for example, the woman's expression and body language. She looks out to the street with perhaps both expectation and anxiety. She seems uncomfortable waiting; she holds her purse with both hands. Notice, too, that behind her at the bar are only men. Reflected in the glass is the world before her that lies outside. What story do you make from such observations?

## INCIDENT, SCENE, AND SEQUENCE

In the brief discussion of Boubat's photograph, we have touched upon the notions of incident and scene. **Incident** suggests a specific, small action. **Scene** is closely related to but more expansive than incident. In a dramatic work, a scene might be understood simply as the entrance and/or exit of important characters from the stage. A scene may also be defined by mood (a crying scene, a comic scene, a revenge scene), function (a transitional scene, an expository scene, an anticipatory scene), or even place (an outdoor scene, a bedroom scene, a courtyard scene). But the term is usually employed more broadly still and is not limited to dramatic productions. A scene may be thought of as a coherent action within a larger structure of action. In this sense, a scene should convey a particular conflict that is subordinate to some larger conflict.

Incidents and scenes (if left to stand alone) are fragments. They are the bits and pieces that can be arranged to build a plot. **Plot** refers to the meaningful fabric of action. It suggests structure. At the most basic level, this means that a plot has a beginning, middle, and end; it represents a whole action. More specifically, an author provides **exposition** (context), then conveys **rising action** (action that leads to a decisive point), a **climax** (the decisive point), **falling action**, and **resolution** or **denouement** (a French word meaning "the untying of a knot"). Plots, then, are usually highly crafted actions. The **sequence** of scenes that make up a plot is not a random sequence or a mere series of conflicts. It's a carefully laid out set of scenes that grow from **conflict** and make sense together. Perhaps one action causes another, or relates thematically to another, or counterpoints another. The author's careful arrangement of action in plot may be especially evident in **foreshadowing** (preparing the reader for action that is to come) and **flashback** (a return to past action). Both of these strategies illustrate how plot requires that we think of scenes in relation to one another.

## Experiencing Literature through Plot

To sharpen our sense of plot's importance and *meaning*, we'll examine two brief pieces that upset or cut short our expectations. The two poems that follow ask us to consider what meaning we draw from plots by refusing to give us any plot in the usual sense. Both ask us to be self-conscious about the degree to which we actively shape stories. Can any significant piece of life be contained by a well-thought-out story? Can we assign a beginning, middle, and end to experience? Are lives as neat as that? Do we (as natural storytellers) impose order on chaos? If so, are stories a way to make experience significant? Robert Pinsky's "Poem with Lines in Any Order" centers us on these problems. Pinsky makes us think about many things, including our own active, participatory role in giving shape and meaning to events. Are we all plot makers in a world that has no master plot?

Robert Pinsky (1940– )

# Poem with Lines in Any Order (2004)

Sonny said, *Then he shouldn't have given Molly the two more babies.*
Dave's sister and her husband adopted the baby, and that was Babe.
You can't live in the past.
Sure he was a tough guy but he was no hero.
Sonny and Toots went to live for a while with the Braegers.                         5
It was a time when it seemed like everybody had a nickname.
Nobody can live in the future.
When Rose died having Babe, Dave came after the doctor with a gun.
Toots said, *What would you expect, he was a young man and there she was.*
Sonny still a kid himself when Dave moved out on Molly.                              10
The family gave him Rose's cousin Molly to marry so she could raise the
    children.
There's no way to just live in the present.
In their eighties Toots and Sonny still arguing about their father.
Dave living above the bar with Della and half the family.

The first thing most readers do once they finish this poem is to go back and
play with the sequence of lines to make something more satisfying. But is this
what Pinsky is asking for? His title might encourage us to take the lines (and
the experiences they represent) as truly random. Is it possible that Pinsky is
asking us to accept chaos and reflect upon our tendencies to give events a beginning, middle, and end? Or perhaps he is suggesting that plots can be split into as many shapes as there are people to give them shape. Then again, maybe these lines aren't really random at all. There is a thread woven through the poem that makes us think about how we relate (or fail to relate) story to actual experience: "You can't live in the past" (line 3);

## Making Connections

Szymborska's "ABC" and Pinsky's "Poem with Lines in Any Order" also inevitably raise questions about "character." Who are the characters here? Our sense of character arises largely out of seeing characters behave in the context of meaningfully ordered events. As you read about character in Chapter 2, think back on these two poems and ask yourself how much your sense of character depends upon plot.

"Nobody can live in the future" (line 7); "There's no way to just live in the
present" (line 12). That is, there is no way to live if we accept everything as a
jumbled mess of random signals and fail to give shape and meaning to the
events that happen around us: we seek some order in order to live.

Wislawa Szymborska also deftly toys with notions of sequence in "ABC"—a poem that reminds us of how artificial and arbitrary our storytelling can be. Szymborska doesn't present lines "in any order" as Pinsky does. By making the order unfold in alphabetical sequence, she leaves us struck by a sense of arbitrariness; the sequence is played out on a grid that has no necessary or organic relationship to experience. Szymborska is also blunt in marking off the limits of what we know or can know. If, like the narrators of the poem, we can't "find out" about things that are important to us, can we create richly interwoven plots? Can we find meaning?

**Wislawa Szymborska** (1923– )

# ABC (2004, trans. Stanislaw Baranczak and Clare Cavanagh)

I'll never find out now
what A. thought of me.
If B. ever forgave me in the end.
Why C. pretended everything was fine.
What part D. played in E.'s silence.                                    5
What F. had been expecting, if anything.
Why G. forgot when she knew perfectly well.
What H. had to hide.
What I. wanted to add.
If my being around                                                    10
meant anything
to J. and K. and the rest of the alphabet.

# EPISODE, IMPRESSION, AND FRAGMENT

Some important thematic implications of a fully developed, carefully designed plot are challenged by writers with simple strategies of abbreviation. If a writer thinks that the real world can't be captured within a traditional plot, then some reduced form of narration becomes an attractive choice. An **episode** suggests a single, continuous, and brief action that stands alone. An episode within a large story or novel refers to a specific action that could be detached from the larger plot. Some novels are built from a string of episodes. This tumbled-out-one-thing-after-another sequence of actions constitutes an **episodic narrative** or an **episodic novel**. Episodic narratives tend to be open rather than closed. An **open ending** is one that leaves essential matters largely unresolved. Mark Twain's *Adventures of Huckleberry Finn* nicely illustrates an episodic, open narrative.

Huck recounts a string of adventures and at the end "lights out" to the territory ahead for what will be further adventures. Any sequel (and Twain did write one for Huck) will add episodes but will never "wrap up" Huck's experience. The reader may be left unsure about what happens to important characters, or what significance to draw from the action, or how "whole" the action was. A **closed ending** more aggressively wraps up the various strands of action. It communicates a relatively final conclusion. Popular detective stories are probably the clearest example of strongly closed fictions.

An episode can be thought of as a means to purposefully abbreviate plot. Plot, as we've mentioned, involves both writer and reader in a careful putting together of incidents and scenes. It challenges us to find patterns, discover relationships, and distinguish primary from secondary. Some modern writers, wary of the control implied by fully developed plots (as some painters are wary of fully realized representations of objects), deliberately cut stories short; they may feel that the **fragment** they offer readers more honestly represents the confusing, unstable world in which we live. Or at least they believe that the fragment more accurately registers the way we experience life. A deliberate emphasis on episode as opposed to plot is related to the notion of an **impression**. It's useful to think about what we mean by that word and by impressionism or impressionist. An impression brings us back to the immediate feeling created by a picture or a painting.

When critics first labeled the painter Claude Monet an "impressionist," they were not praising him. Many early viewers thought that Monet failed to make complete sense of—or achieve an ideal vision of—the subjects he painted. For example, some critics complained that Monet diminished his subjects by attending so closely to the particular qualities of light (conditioned by weather, the time of day, the season) that surrounded the subjects. In regard to Monet's *Portal of Rouen Cathedral in Morning Light* (p. 7), one criticism may have been: "Why is he painting the fog when he should be painting the church?" We could imagine Monet answering, "Because it was foggy on the day that I sat before the church" or "Fog is the main thing I saw when I painted that day" or "Because I wished to capture the ephemeral nature of fog." Monet might have asked his own questions in response to the complaint: "Why should I paint something that supposedly lies behind what I *actually* see at a particular moment? Why do you assume the church and not the fog is the real subject of my painting?"

There is an important idea here that relates very much to the vision of artists working with other materials (words, film, sound). An impression is of the moment. It is bound by time, subject to changing conditions. An impression is essentially subjective. It registers what an individual saw or felt at a single point in time. It is a sensation—something seen, felt, smelled. An impression is not a statement or an ideal; nor is it an absolute, fixed eternal truth. It is not a generalization. An impression is *not* a plot.

Claude Monet, *Portal of Rouen Cathedral in Morning Light* (1894)

## Experiencing Literature through Impression and Episode

What Monet was doing with paint meshes with what Stephen Crane oftentimes did with words. Crane didn't believe that the world he knew allowed for long, carefully wrought, richly plotted fictions. He worked in short forms and often deliberately reduced his sense of scale. He registered impressions through the experiences of individual characters and believed that those subjective impressions were as close as he could get to "truth." The title of the story that follows deliberately announces his sense of limits. Crane uses the indefinite article *an*, not the definite article *the*. He promises to deliver a single fragment of experience, one bit from many that could have been selected. He also explicitly presents an "episode." We don't expect great length. We don't expect a complex weaving together of incidents. Because of his title, we don't seek to make this one episode more than a particular episode that occurs at a particular time and place. The life of the main character before the episode or after isn't really Crane's interest. Yet the shock of loss one feels upon reading this work is sufficient to justify it as art.

Stephen Crane (1871–1900)

# An Episode of War (1899)

The lieutenant's rubber blanket lay on the ground, and upon it he had poured the company's supply of coffee. Corporals and other representatives of the grimy and hot-throated men who lined the breastwork had come for each squad's portion.

The lieutenant was frowning and serious at this task of division. His lips pursed as he drew with his sword various crevices in the heap, until brown squares of coffee, astoundingly equal in size, appeared on the blanket. He was on the verge of a great triumph in mathematics, and the corporals were thronging forward, each to reap a little square, when suddenly the lieutenant cried out and looked quickly at a man near him as if he suspected it was a case of personal assault. The others cried out also when they saw blood upon the lieutenant's sleeve.

He had winced like a man stung, swayed dangerously, and then straightened. The sound of his hoarse breathing was plainly audible. He looked sadly, mystically, over the breastwork at the green face of a wood, where now were many puffs of white smoke. During this moment the men about him gazed statue-like and silent, astonished and awed by this catastrophe which happened when catastrophes were not expected—when they had leisure to observe it.

As the lieutenant stared at the wood, they too swung their heads, so that for another instant all hands, still silent, contemplated the distant forest as if their minds were fixed upon the mystery of a bullet's journey.

The officer had, of course, been compelled to take his sword into his left hand. He did not hold it by the hilt. He gripped it at the middle of the blade, awkwardly. Turning his eyes from the wood, he looked at the sword as he held it there, and seemed puzzled as to what to do with it. In short, this weapon had all of a sudden become a strange thing to him. He looked at it in a kind of stupefaction, as if he had been endowed with a trident, a scepter, or a spade.

Finally he tried to sheathe it. To sheathe a sword held by the left hand, at the middle of the blade, in a scabbard hung at the left hip, is a feat worthy of a sawdust ring. This wounded officer engaged in a desperate struggle with the sword and the wobbling scabbard, and during the time of it he breathed like a wrestler.

But at this instant the men, spectators, awoke from their stone-like poses and crowded forward sympathetically. The orderly-sergeant took the sword and tenderly placed it in the scabbard. At the time, he leaned nervously backward, and did not allow even his finger to brush the body of the lieutenant. A wound gives strange dignity to him who bears it. Well men shy from this new and terrible majesty. It is as if the wounded man's hand is upon the curtain which hangs before the revelations of all existence—the meaning of ants, potentates, wars, cities, sunshine, snow, a feather dropped from a bird's wing; and the power of it sheds radiance upon a bloody form, and makes the other men understand sometimes that they are little. His comrades look at him with large eyes thoughtfully. Moreover, they fear vaguely that the weight of a finger upon him might send him headlong, precipitate the tragedy, hurl him at once into the dim, gray unknown. And so the orderly-sergeant, while sheathing the sword, leaned nervously backward.

There were others who proffered assistance. One timidly presented his shoulder and asked the lieutenant if he cared to lean upon it, but the latter waved him away mournfully. He wore the look of one who knows he is the victim of a terrible disease and understands his helplessness. He again stared over the breastwork at the forest, and then, turning, went slowly rearward. He held his right wrist tenderly in his left hand as if the wounded arm was made of brittle glass.

And the men in silence stared at the woods, then at the departing lieutenant; then at the wood, then at the lieutenant.

As the wounded officer passed from the line of battle, he was enabled to see many things which as a participant in the fight were unknown to him. He saw a general on a black horse gazing over the lines of blue infantry at the green woods which veiled his problems. An aide galloped furiously, dragged his horse suddenly to a halt, saluted, and presented a paper. It was, for a wonder, precisely like an historical painting.

To the rear of the general and his staff a group, composed of a bugler, two or three orderlies, and the bearer of the corps standard, all upon maniacal horses, were working like slaves to hold their ground, preserve their respectful interval, while the shells boomed in the air about them, and caused their chargers to make furious quivering leaps.

A battery, a tumultuous and shining mass, was swirling toward the right. The wild thud of hoofs, the cries of the riders, shouting blame and praise, menace and encouragement, and, last, the roar of the wheels, the slant of the glistening guns, brought the lieutenant to an intent pause. The battery swept in curves that stirred the heart; it made halts as dramatic as the crash of a wave on the rocks, and when it fled onward this aggregation of wheels, levers, motors had a beautiful unity, as if it were a missile. The sound of it was a war chorus that reached into the depths of man's emotion.

The lieutenant, still holding his arm as if it were of glass, stood watching this battery until all detail of it were lost, save the figures of the riders, which rose and fell and waved lashes over the black mass.

Later, he turned his eyes toward the battle, where the shooting sometimes crackled like bush-fires, sometimes sputtered with exasperating irregularity, and sometimes reverberated like the thunder. He saw the smoke rolling upward and saw crowds of men who ran and cheered, or stood and blazed away at the inscrutable distance.

He came upon some stragglers, and they told him how to find the field hospital. They described its exact location. In fact, these men, no longer having part in the battle, knew more of it than the others. They told the performance of every corps, every division, the opinion of every general. The lieutenant, carrying his wounded arm rearward, looked upon them with wonder.

At the roadside a brigade was making coffee and buzzing with talk like a girl's boarding school. Several officers came out to him and inquired concerning things of which he knew nothing. One, seeing his arm, began to scold. "Why, man, that's no way to do. You want to fix that thing." He appropriated the lieutenant and the lieutenant's wound. He cut the sleeve and laid bare the arm, every nerve of which softly fluttered under his touch. He bound his handkerchief over the wound, scolding away in the meantime. His tone allowed one to think that he was in the habit of being wounded every day. The lieutenant hung his head, feeling, in this presence, that he did not know how to be correctly wounded.

The low white tents of the hospital were grouped around an old schoolhouse. There was here a singular commotion. In the foreground two ambulances interlocked wheels in the deep mud. The drivers were tossing the blame of it back and forth, gesticulating and berating, while from the ambulances, both crammed with wounded, there came an occasional groan. An interminable crowd of bandaged men were coming and going. Great numbers sat under the trees nursing heads or arms or legs. There was a dispute of some kind raging on the steps of the schoolhouse. Sitting with his back against a tree a man with a face as gray as a new army blanket was serenely smoking a corncob pipe. The lieutenant wished to rush forward and inform him that he was dying.

A busy surgeon was passing near the lieutenant. "Good morning," he said, with a friendly smile. Then he caught sight of the lieutenant's arm, and his face at once changed. "Well, let's have a look at it." He seemed possessed suddenly of a great contempt for the lieutenant. This wound evidently placed the latter on a very low social plane. The doctor cried out impatiently: "What mutton-head had tied it up that way anyhow?"

The lieutenant answered, "Oh a man."

When the wound was disclosed the doctor fingered it disdainfully. "Humph," he said. "You come along with me and I'll 'tend to you." His voice contained the same scorn as if he were saying: "You will have to go to jail."

The lieutenant had been very meek, but now his face flushed, and he looked into the doctor's eyes. "I guess I won't have it amputated," he said. "Nonsense, man!" Nonsense! Nonsense!" cried the doctor. "Come along, now. I won't amputate it. Come along. Don't be a baby."

"Let go of me," said the lieutenant, holding back wrathfully, his glance fixed upon the door of the old school house, as sinister to him as the portals of death.

And this is the story of how the lieutenant lost his arm. When he reached home, his sisters, his mother, his wife, sobbed for a long time at the sight of the flat sleeve. "Oh, well," he said, standing shamefaced amid these tears, "I don't suppose it matters so much as all that." ■

The main action of Crane's "An Episode of War" occurs out of the blue. The soldiers are *not* in the midst of battle. They are in the midst of the most mundane of activities: rationing out the company's supply of coffee. The bullet comes as a surprise. The men don't spring into action in response. They gawk, feel awkward, seem a little awed that one among them has been injured. The wounding doesn't fit into a larger action—it is a random event, a horrifying reminder that danger is ever present and that the most momentous events are not scripted. Life matching up with art seems almost ridiculously accidental: "An aide galloped furiously, dragged his horse suddenly to a halt, saluted, and presented a paper. It was, for a wonder, precisely like an historical painting." It seems appropriate that Crane leaves his story open at the end. We have a strong impression of the moment he returns home, but a limited sense of how that moment will be played out in his family life ahead. By not attempting to strongly close the story, Crane suggests the most solid truths are limited ones.

## TENSION, RELEASE, AND RESOLUTION

At some level, a grandly plotted story is like a great musical piece: it builds **tension**, releases tension, and achieves resolution. To put it another way, plots prompt us to think of (and feel) oppositions and alternatives. Will he stay or run? Will she tell or remain silent? Do they know, or are they still unaware of what is unfolding? The tension created and sustained by such questions produces a momentum that requires release. Tension and release (as we've suggested earlier) also lead to the desire for resolution: we want things more or less pulled together in most stories. The careful working together of various strands may lend a narrative great emotional force. Plots involve us in actions and in the fates of characters; plots encourage us to keep turning the pages. Plot can also help communicate a compelling worldview by giving larger shape, meaning, or purpose to action. But short of such grand effects, plot offers the sheer pleasure of artful management. We appreciate the craft involved in a well-made story.

Arthur Conan Doyle's Sherlock Holmes stories have long offered readers pleasure in the plot. Michael Chabon, a contemporary novelist, writes in the essay "The Game's Afoot" that "Conan Doyle found a way to fold several stories, and the proper means of telling them, over and over into a tightly compacted frame, with a proportionate gain in narrative power. [The Sherlock Holmes stories] are storytelling engines, steam driven, brass-fitted, but among the most efficient narrative apparatuses the world has ever seen. After all these years, they still run remarkably well."° "As Scandal in Bohemia" is one of these smooth-running engines. As you read the story, consider the distinction Holmes makes between "seeing" and "observing." For him, seeing is a mere matter of physical perception. Observing, though, is making sure that what we see registers fully. It is a neat distinction for a detective and one that also works well for a student of literature.

Doyle's "A Scandal in Bohemia" gives us an especially good chance to consider the point Chabon makes about Doyle's folding several stories together. The "folding" is what distinguishes a plot from a mere string of events. We're left with a strong sense of unity and closure with the Doyle story, because all the parts mesh so well. As Chabon points out, the meshing is so fine that we might not notice that Doyle has several stories working together. The King initially tells a story to Holmes: Irene Adler has a compromising picture that may influence world events. Holmes later tells a story to Watson: The detective went in disguise to Adler's neighborhood and became a participant in her elopement and marriage to Godfrey Norton. Watson recounts to us the trick Holmes pulls to uncover the picture's hiding place (after Holmes had spelled out to Watson what was to occur): the false injury, the smoke bomb, the cry of fire. Irene Adler tells a story to Holmes in her remaining letter: She was (despite forewarnings) taken in by him but saw through his deception just in time. And Watson again reports to us on how Holmes and the King respond to Adler's poise. All of these stories work together to give us a sense of a unified action that begins, builds, and closes. We have one plot woven of many incidents told from multiple perspectives and aimed at (seemingly) different audiences. Observing all of this complexity in "A Scandal in Bohemia" prepares us well for how subtly plots may operate.

---

° *The New York Review of Books* (vol. LII, no. 3; February 24, 2005, p. 14)

# MULTIPLE AND REFLEXIVE PLOTS

The layers that make up a Sherlock Holmes story suggest a number of fresh possibilities for constructing plots. The layers can be more than an efficient engine; they can suggest the complex textures of "real" life. And the layers do not need to add up to a unified story or a simple chronological plot (in which action links to action in clear sequence, like beads on a string). We often discover that as a single work unfolds, we process multiple stories or **multiple plots**. We get a sense in many narratives that plots are there for us to discover, to construct. A cliché such as "there are always two sides to a story" becomes inadequate because we realize that two sides are hardly enough to account for the complexity we routinely contend with in both life and art. We're often prompted to consider how one story becomes something quite different if we simply shift a point of emphasis. A **subplot** (that is, a subordinate or secondary plot) might give us insight into what happens in the major action it parallels. A subplot might also flesh out for us some aspect of character. In *Hamlet*, for example, we might consider the tensions between Laertes and Hamlet as forming an instructive subplot to the conflict that unfolds between Hamlet and Claudius.

Many writers, particularly more recent writers, convey a high degree of self-consciousness in their work. That is, they are aware of, as well as interested in, the philosophical, psychological, and dramatic potential inherent in plot. Such self-consciousness can become a kind of strategy; readers are reminded as they read to think about the plot as a plot. We sometimes call such plots **reflexive plots**; the way in which a story is constructed becomes the very thing we are forced to think about, to reflect upon.

*Memento* (2000), a film directed by Christopher Nolan, is an exceptionally good example of a **reflexive** or **self-conscious narrative**. Nolan (who adapted the film from "Memento Mori," a short story by his brother, Jonathan Nolan) literally runs his plot backward. The main character—Leonard Shelby (played by Guy Pearce)—is a man who has no short-term memory as a result of a blow to his head. He remembers who he is (his name, his family, his life before his injury) but cannot hold in his mind the simplest moment-to-moment experiences. Leonard forgets not only his keys but his car. He forgets people he has met within minutes of leaving their presence; he forgets where he lives or how he got to whatever place he happens to be; he forgets why he is doing what he is doing; and he forgets very quickly what he has just done.

Nolan gives us the last action first—a brutal killing—and then moves backward to help us understand how and why things came to that end. Shelby, despite his forgetfulness, is motivated by revenge. He seeks to kill the man who raped and murdered his wife and who took his memory. His detective work, though, can move forward only through a painstaking process of note taking. Because he cannot remember any clue he uncovers, he must write

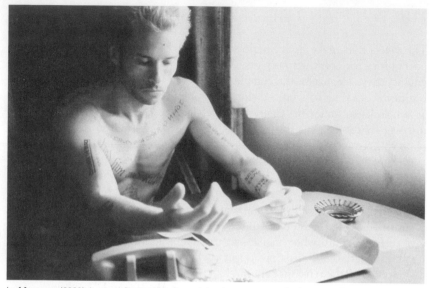

In *Memento* (2000), Leonard Shelby (Guy Pearce) develops a system of using notes, Polaroid pictures, and tattoos to help him remember crucial information.

down everything. He even tattoos crucial information on his own skin. And of course, once he consults his notes, the situations that prompted the writing have been forgotten. By telling the story in this fashion, Nolan demands that the viewers put many of the pieces together for themselves. He also makes us aware that the main character has fashioned a rather different plot than the actual truth. We're then left to think about truth, limits, motives, not just "what" happens but why "what" happened. In a sense, the plot in this case is the meaning or theme of the story.

## A Note to Student Writers: Critical Reading and Understanding

The impulse to tell stories isn't all that different from the impulse to talk and write about the stories we encounter as readers and viewers. Critical reading isn't just passively absorbing a story; it involves participating in the creation of the story as it unfolds. As we read, we anticipate events and link incidents. We discuss, interpret, and evaluate. Sometimes we question, complain, and even "fix" the story. When we begin to write in response to literature, we press such impulses forward more forcefully still. In some ways, critical writing becomes its own kind of narrative. To analyze is to break something into pieces so that we can understand how it all fits together. A critical essay involves this breaking down and fitting together. Writing a critical essay makes a story *ours*. The process of writing critically forces us to understand what happens and why.

One seemingly simple thing you can do to get a grip on essential features of a text is to summarize the action that unfolds in a work you are reading. You'll find it is often a helpful exercise. Summary forces you to read closely and shrink the text to the barest essentials. Such a basic recounting can oftentimes open up what might seem puzzling works. Even when we don't think of a work primarily in terms of events, there is usually some core action that we must understand. For example, Marge Piercy's "Unlearning to not speak" is a short poem that relates types of incidents that don't necessarily add up to a fully realized story. The poem's total effect might seem to convey a mood (desperation and anger) and an appeal (speak up!). But neither the mood nor the appeal will make much sense if we can't recount what happens in the poem.

**Marge Piercy** (1936– )

# Unlearning to not speak (1973)

Blizzards of paper
in slow motion
sift through her.
In nightmares she suddenly recalls
a class she signed up for                               5
but forgot to attend.
Now it is too late.
Now it is time for finals:
losers will be shot.
Phrases of men who lectured her                         10
drift and rustle in piles:
Why don't you speak up?
Why are you shouting?
You have the wrong answer,
wrong line, wrong face.                                 15
They tell her she is womb-man,
babymachine, mirror image, toy
earth mother and penis-poor,
a dish of synthetic strawberry ice cream
rapidly melting.                                        20
She grunts to a halt.
She must learn again to speak
starting with I
starting with We
starting as the infant does                             25
with her own true hunger
and pleasure
and rage.

; referred to in the fourth line set up a succession of incidents that create a
, or experience that is more than a single action. But Piercy gives us many particulars
to work with. The girl in the poem feels desperate, unconfident, overpowered by the stern
male authorities who teach not so much a subject as a set of attitudes about status and
gender. We get quick hints of larger incidents that we need to flesh out for ourselves. A girl is
thrown on the defensive by the instructor's questions. Why is it so difficult for her to respond?
We can imagine a situation in which the questions are not fair, not even real. The questions
don't arise from a subject or an intellectual problem; they arise from an established prejudice.
The problem is being a girl. In the minds of the male teachers, the girl is too shy, too dumb, too
pushy, too weak, too whatever. As the poem progresses, we learn that she has been
disempowered by this education. Piercy suggests that by getting back to something that
predates her education, some more elemental sense of personal need, desire, and identity,
the girl can "unlearn to not speak." The poem's most basic action might be summarized as
follows: The girl's male teachers routinely put her down in class until finally she realizes, out of
frustration, anger, need, and joy, that she must stand up to speak her own mind.

## MODELING CRITICAL ANALYSIS:
## JAMAICA KINCAID, GIRL

Jamaica Kincaid's "Girl" hardly seems to have a plot. Plots are, after all, made
up of incidents and scenes that work together. A plot isn't a list of observations but a carefully arranged sequence of events. "Girl" for the most part
seems to "list" demands an older woman (a mother?) makes on a young girl:
do this, don't do that, do things this way, don't do things that way. And "Girl"
packs everything into one very long sentence. How can a single sentence,
however long, develop a plot?

**Jamaica Kincaid** (1949– )

# Girl (1983)

Wash the white clothes on Monday and put them on the stone heap; wash
the color clothes on Tuesday and put them on the clothesline to dry; don't
walk barehead in the hot sun; cook pumpkin fritters in very hot sweet oil; soak
your little cloths right after you take them off; when buying cotton to make
yourself a nice blouse, be sure that it doesn't have gum on it, because that way
it won't hold up well after a wash; soak salt fish overnight before you cook it; is
it true that you sing benna in Sunday school?; always eat your food in such a
way that it won't turn someone else's stomach; on Sundays try to walk like a
lady and not like the slut you are so bent on becoming; don't sing benna in
Sunday school; you mustn't speak to wharf-rat boys, not even to give directions; don't eat fruits on the street—flies will follow you; *but I don't sing benna*

*on Sundays at all and never in Sunday school*; this is how to sew on a button; this is how to make a buttonhole for the button you have just sewed on; this is how to hem a dress when you see the hem coming down and so to prevent your-self from looking like the slut I know you are so bent on becoming; this is how you iron your father's khaki shirt so that it doesn't have a crease; this is how you iron your father's khaki pants so that they don't have a crease; this is how you grow okra—far from the house, because okra tree harbors red ants; when you are growing dasheen, make sure it gets plenty of water or else it makes your throat itch when you are eating it; this is how you sweep a corner; this is how you sweep a whole house; this is how you sweep a yard; this is how you smile to someone you don't like too much; this is how you smile to some-one you don't like at all; this is how you smile to someone you like completely; this is how you set a table for tea; this is how you set a table for dinner; this is how you set a table for dinner with an important guest; this is how you set a table for lunch; this is how you set a table for breakfast; this is how to behave in the presence of men who don't know you very well, and this way they won't recognize immediately the slut I have warned you against becoming; be sure to wash every day, even if it is with your own spit; don't squat down to play marbles—you are not a boy, you know; don't pick people's flowers—you might catch something; don't throw stones at blackbirds, because it might not be a blackbird at all; this is how to make a bread pudding; this is how to make doukona; this is how to make pepper pot; this is how to make a good medicine for a cold; this is how to make a good medicine to throw away a child before it even becomes a child; this is how to catch a fish; this is how to throw back a fish you don't like, and that way something bad won't fall on you; this is how to bully a man; this is how a man bullies you; this is how to love a man, and if this doesn't work there are other ways, and if they don't work don't feel too bad about giving up; this is how to spit up in the air if you feel like it, and this is how to move quick so that it doesn't fall on you; this is how to make ends meet; always squeeze bread to make sure it's fresh; *but what if the baker won't let me feel the bread?*; you mean to say that after all you are really going to be the kind of woman who the baker won't let near the bread? ■

It is useful to think of the many stories, the many plots, suggested by Kincaid's list of impressions, memories, and incidents. Kincaid triggers multiple associa-tions about growing up that readers can fill in, indeed must fill in. She, like Marge Piercy in "Unlearning to not speak" (p. 15), seems to depend upon the reader's ability to elaborate upon the smallest hints and create full scenes, or even stories. We can imagine how thickly textured the girl's life is with reprimands. For example, if she joins other children for a game of marbles, she can be scolded for squatting like a boy. Such gender lessons, of course, are part of larger assumptions about status and power. The girl is not a boy and must always remember what that fact means. It means that any sign of independence quickly becomes a marker of moral or social inadequacy. It means that the girl must control signs because she controls little else: how to "behave in the presence of men," how to hide who she is, "how to make a good medicine to throw away a child before it even becomes a child."

Kincaid, again like Piercy, gives readers some means to structure the whole. If we look at "Girl" carefully, we'll note some important interruptions and repetitions. On two occasions, we have a break in the voice—the person on the receiving end of all the instructions speaks for herself. The first time this happens (about a third of the way into the piece), the woman steams ahead without a pause. The girl has spoken, but the woman hasn't listened or hasn't thought any back talk is worth responding to. The second break (marked by italics, as the first is) occurs at the end of the piece. Here the girl questions the real-world application of the advice: "*what if the baker won't let me feel the bread.*" The older woman's response returns again to the strategy of diminishment that has been part of the whole story: What kind of woman is this girl bent on becoming? The older woman sees nothing but bad ahead, but readers are more likely to imagine the girl's youthful independence more than any presumed natural deficiency.

## Using Plot to Focus Writing and Discussion

- What happens over the course of the text?
- How do things change from the opening scene?
- What events lead to this conclusion?
- Is this a conclusion that you expected? What led you to this expectation? What details in the opening of the text shape your expectations?
- Why do events unfold here in the order that they do? Is this a chronological account of events, or is there some other ordering principle?
- Are there events that we do not learn about? How are these undiscovered details significant?
- How has the author made this story interesting?

# 2 Character

## Who Is Involved, and Why Does It Matter?

In Paul Thomas Anderson's film *Punch Drunk Love* (2002), the main character, Barry Egan (Adam Sandler), pulls aside his brother-in-law, Walter, at a family party. Barry wants to know if it's "normal" to break spontaneously and uncontrollably into tears. Walter responds awkwardly by asking Barry if there is "something wrong" or if these feelings just match the inner experience of "other people." Barry answers in a blank monotone: "I don't know if there is anything wrong because I don't know how other people are." It's a powerful moment in the film because it captures a sense of helpless loneliness, of profound disconnection. At some level, we recognize the uncomfortable truth that none of us knows for certain how other people are (how they feel or why they act as they do). And that fact suggests the frightening thought that none of us really *knows* other people.

It's a thought everyone confronts and almost no one fully accepts. We stubbornly seek to break from the boundaries of self and understand people around us. We can surely listen more openly and attentively than Walter does to Barry. We observe mannerisms and vocal tones. We "put ourselves in another person's shoes." We think about how our individual experience fits larger patterns of behavior. We use our own experience and our own feelings as a checkpoint against what we see in others. All of these efforts to realize how "other people are" demand much of our imaginative intelligence; we exercise close observation, shrewd analysis, and patient reflection. Such exercise reminds us that literary experience *is* experience; to put it another way, there is no need to distinguish literary experience from "life experience." Our fascination with stories is strongly rooted in our everyday desire to know people, to understand the motives that underlie action or to grasp the feelings that show in words and gestures. If we lose a belief in the possibility of such knowledge, we go blank, like poor Barry.

# BUILDING CHARACTER

In describing their own creative process, some writers make character (quite simply, people or figures in a story) a primary force. Vividly imagined characters can, in effect, speak to the writers who create them. A turn in a plot might result from an author's sense that a main character demanded that turn. For example, did Jim in Mark Twain's novel, *Adventures of Huckleberry Finn*, scold Huck for playing a cruel practical joke on him because Mark Twain wanted to establish Jim—a slave—as an adult man with a full claim to respectful treatment? Or was it that Twain felt absolutely compelled to give Jim his say? To put it another way, did Twain discover in the act of creation that the character he had come to know would not put up with a boy's foolish pranks?

We would need to ask Mark Twain about his writing process, but it's certainly clear that characters can come alive for authors as well as readers. Experiencing a literary text, whether we are reading it or writing it, involves a close engagement with characters outside ourselves. This experience makes our world bigger. If we do not (as readers or writers) conceive of characters as people we can know, these characters will seem artificial, unconvincing, and uninteresting.

Of course, we must also imagine situations (usually points of conflict) that define characters. Usually, those situations involve some clear point of conflict. In fact, the word **protagonist** (the main or leading character) comes from the Greek for "the first one to battle." If the battle is against another character, the opponent is the **antagonist**. These words, because they capture a crucial defining tension are in some ways more useful than terms such as *main* and *secondary character*. It's also important to remember that although a protagonist is usually the hero or heroine and the antagonist may be a villain, the terms are not synonymous, for a hero or heroine may not be the central actor in a narrative; we could easily imagine a story with both a hero and a heroine, but not a story with two protagonists. **Hero** and **heroine** also introduce in common usage positive moral or social qualities (just as *villain* suggests evil or malice). *Protagonist* and *antagonist*, strictly speaking, center us on how characters function in a narrative action, not how they affirm the author's values.

## Experiencing Literature through Character

Michael Chabon's highly regarded novel *The Amazing Adventures of Kavalier & Clay* gives us two vividly realized characters who need to create a character of their own. Sammy and Joe (Chabon's main characters) have a contract to produce a comic book; in the following scene, they begin, understandably enough, by trying to imagine a new superpower upon which to build a new superhero. But this line of thinking goes nowhere: Sammy and Joe get stuck on the wrong questions. Only when they change their approach to building character does their project come alive.

**Michael Chabon** (1963– )

## from The Amazing Adventures of Kavalier & Clay (2000)

"Who is he," Joe said.
  "Who is he, and what does he do?"
  "He flies."
  Sammy shook his head. "Superman flies."
  "So ours does not?"
  "I just think I'd . . . "
  "To be original."
  "If we can. Try to do it without flying, at least. No flying, no strength of a hundred men, no bulletproof skin."
  "Okay," Joe said. The humming seemed to recede a little. "And some others, they do what?"
  "Well, Batman—"
  "He flies, like a bat."
  "No, he doesn't fly."
  "But he is blind."
  "No, he only dresses like a bat. He has no batlike qualities at all. He uses only his fists."
  "That sounds dull."
  "Actually, it's spooky. You'd like it."
  "Maybe another animal."
  "Uh, well, yeah. Okay. A hawk. Hawkman."
  "Hawk, yes, okay. But that one must fly."
  "Yeah, you're right. Scratch the bird family. The, uh, the Fox. The Shark."
  "A swimming one."

"Maybe a swimming one. Actually, no, I know a guy works in the
Chesler shop, he said they're already doing a guy who swims. For Timely."

"A lion?"

"Lion. The Lion. Lionman."

"He could be strong. He roars very loud."

"He has a super roar."

"It strikes fear."

"It breaks dishes."

"The bad guys go deaf."

They laughed. Joe stopped laughing.

"I think we have to be serious," he said.

"You're right," said Sammy. "The Lion, I don't know. Lions are lazy.
How about the Tiger. Tigerman. No, no. Tigers are killers. Shit. Let's see."

They began to go through the rolls of the animal kingdom, concentrating naturally on the predators: Catman, Wolfman, the Owl, the Panther,
the Black Bear. They considered the primates: the Monkey, Gorillaman, the
Gibbon, the Ape, the Mandrill with his multicolored wonder ass that he used
to bedazzle opponents.

"Be serious," Joe chided again.

"I'm sorry, I'm sorry. Look, forget animals. Everybody's going to be thinking of animals. In two months, I'm telling you, by the time our guy hits the
stands, there's going to be guys running around dressed like every damn animal
in the zoo. Birds. Bugs. Underwater guys. And I'll bet you anything there's going
to be five guys who are really strong, and invulnerable, and can fly."

"If he goes as fast as the light," Joe suggested.

"Yeah, I guess it's good to be fast."

"Or if he can make a thing burn up. If he can—listen! If he can, you
know. Shoot the fire, with his eyes!"

"His eyeballs would melt."

"Then with his hands. Or, yes, he turns into a fire!"

"Timely's doing that already, too. They got the fire guy and the water
guy."

"He turns into *ice*. He makes the ice everywhere."

"Crushed or cubes?"

"Not good?"

Sammy shook his head. "Ice," he said. "I don't see a lot of stories in ice."

"He turns into electricity?" Joe tried. "He turns into acid?"

"He turns into gravy. He turns into an enormous hat. Look, stop. Stop.
Just stop."

They stopped in the middle of the sidewalk, between Sixth and Seventh
avenues, and that was when Sam Clay experienced a moment of global
vision, one which he would afterward come to view as the one undeniable

brush against the diaphanous, dollar-colored hem of the Angel of New York to be vouchsafed to him in his lifetime.

"This is not the question," he said. "If he's like a cat or a spider or a fucking wolverine, if he's huge, if he's tiny, if he can shoot flames or ice or death rays or Vat 69, if he turns into fire or water or stone or India rubber. He could be a Martian, he could be a ghost, he could be a god or a demon or a wizard or monster. Okay? It doesn't *matter*, because right now, see, at this very moment, we have a bandwagon rolling. I'm telling you. Every little skinny guy like me in New York who believes there's life on Alpha Centauri and got the shit kicked out of him in school and can smell a dollar is out there right this minute trying to jump into it, walking around with a pencil in his shirt pocket, saying, 'He's like a falcon, no, he's like a tornado, no, he's like a goddamned wiener dog.' Okay?"

"Okay."

"And no matter what we come up with, and how we dress him, some other character with the same shtick, with the same style of boots and the same little doodad on his chest, is already out there, or is coming out tomorrow, or is going to be knocked off from our guy inside a week and a half."

Joe listened patiently, awaiting the point of this peroration, but Sammy seemed to have lost the thread. Joe followed his cousin's gaze along the sidewalk but saw only a pair of what looked to be British sailors lighting their cigarettes off a single shielded match.

"So . . . " Sammy said. "So . . . "

"So that is not the question." Joe prompted.

"That's what I'm saying."

"Continue."

They kept walking.

"How? is not the question. What? is not the question," Sammy said.

"The question is why."

"The question is *why*."

"Why," Joe repeated.

"Why is he doing it?"

"Doing what?"

"Dressing up like a monkey or an ice cube or a can of fucking corn."

"To fight crime, isn't it?"

"Well, yes, to fight crime. To fight evil. But that's all any of these guys are doing. That's as far as they ever go. They just . . . you know, it's the right thing to do, so they do it. How interesting is that?"

"I see."

"Only Batman, you know . . . see, yeah, that's good. That's what makes Batman good, and not dull at all, even though he's just a guy who dresses up like a bat and beats people up."

"What is the reason for Batman? The why?"

"His parents were killed, see? In cold blood. Right in front of his eyes, when he was a kid. By a robber."

"It's revenge."

"That's interesting." Sammy said. "See?"

"And he was driven mad."

"Well..."

"And that's why he puts on bat's clothes."

"Actually, they don't go as far as to say that," Sammy said. "But I guess it's there between the lines."

"So we need to figure out what is the why."

"What is the why?" Sammy agreed. ∎

Chabon does double duty in this wonderfully vivid scene. He's telling us something about the creation of character; he's letting us into a secret of his art. Building character isn't about mere features or characteristics; it's about the underlying *why* that makes the choice of features or characteristics apt. To use Chabon's (or Sammy's) own example, Batman isn't a compelling, dark, and menacing hero simply because black bat suits and ominous stares are cool, but because this character's outfit and bearing express the barely controlled rage that resides within him. The *what* (the bat) builds from the *why* (a brutalizing childhood experience). Maybe Christopher Nolan, the director of *Memento*, read Chabon's book: in the latest movie version of the Batman story, Nolan makes *why* the film's premise. The film's title underscores the point: *Batman Begins*. Nolan has been quoted as saying that Batman was interesting largely because he isn't, in the usual sense, a superhero; he's just a "guy who does a lot of push-ups." But what is really interesting is that he is driven to do those push-ups. The motivation—the why—is generative. Nolan, like Sammy, believes the beginning provides the why that gives emotional substance to the costumes and toys that took over some of the earlier, less successful versions of the character.

## PRESENTING CHARACTER

Chabon has a second thing going in the previous excerpt: he is building two richly imagined and freshly presented new characters—Sammy and Joe. Chabon's method of **characterization** (the technique of creating a sense of character) seems almost invisible; it is as if he simply allows the characters to present themselves. Sammy and Joe come alive primarily from **dialogue**; we hear them speak and observe them interacting. Chabon resists, for the most part, the temptation to swoop in like some authorial superhero and tell us everything about these characters directly. We're allowed to listen in and observe things for ourselves, much as we do when we watch a play. We might notice that Sammy consistently takes the lead in the conversation. He's the one dissatisfied with the usual run of superheroes. He's the one who, in his frustration of not breaking from the superficial formulas, presses boring ideas to ridiculous conclusions (for example, Lionman's "super roar" breaks dishes). Sammy is the one who is more drenched in comic-book lore and knowledge of comic-book competitors. Sammy fills Joe in on the essentials about Batman. He knows what's going on in the business—what the rivals are working on. He is also the one who first grasps the basic problem. Sammy realizes that they need to change the question. Joe speaks less, but Chabon manages to make him come alive too. Joe may not be brilliant, but he is persistent (he's the one who keeps bringing Sammy back by telling him to "be serious"). And he is smart enough to listen to his cousin and not allow the flash of insight to get away. He prods him just as it seems that Sammy's moment of inspiration dims. He even first comes up with the crucial word *why*, even if he doesn't fully grasp its importance.

### A Note to Student Writers: Leading Questions

Sammy's insight is one that critical writers would do well to consider. A "what" question could be a good starting place for description and summary, but "whats" don't lead easily into analysis. "Why" questions lead more powerfully into developing ideas. They help us think through distinctions, explain impressions, and support assertions. So when you feel stuck on "what," try formulating critical questions around "why" and see if those questions help you press your ideas forward. And although Sammy insists that "how," like "what," is "not the question," critical writers may generate a great deal from "how" questions that turn attention to the artist's craft as opposed to the character's behavior.

## PICTURING CHARACTER

Listening in on a conversation, catching a tone of voice or a turn of phrase, helps us know Sammy and Joe. But we can see character emerge as a physical presence and through gestures as well. We interpret character from a dense

**Making Connections**

Consider how we often read character in everyday life through specific observation of things the person owns or buys. For example, we might speculate about the person in front of us at the grocery store on the basis of items that person has in the shopping cart. If we notice that same person a few minutes later in the parking lot, our first impression might be reinforced or revised by the car the person drives. Writers manage such impressions very carefully. Remember that they are really the ones who choose the groceries and the cars for their characters.

fabric of visual clues: clothes, posture, facial expressions, physical size, age, and so on. We must also consider how those clues fit with other elements within our field of vision. Where is a scene taking place? What seems to be the situation? How do the characters interact?

## Experiencing Film and Literature through Character

The film still shown here from *Gone with the Wind* (1939) catches a moment when Mammy (played by Hattie McDaniel) is helping the heroine, Scarlett O'Hara (Vivien Leigh), dress. It's a picture loaded with information that helps us understand character. Of course, there is the obvious: Mammy is a servant (a slave actually, although we wouldn't necessarily know that if we had only this photograph). Scarlett is the served. Mammy is black; Scarlett, white. Mammy is enormous; Scarlett, trim. The clothes accent the size differences: Mammy's bluntly cut and buttoned-up housemaid's uniform contrasts sharply with Scarlett's elaborate yet delicate underclothes. The size difference is underscored further by the fact that Mammy is tightening a corset on the already very slender Scarlett. There can't be any doubt who has been sent the gift on the bed, or who sleeps in the bed. Scarlett quite literally owns this world.

The various bits of information from the photograph, along with the most minimal background information (the names of the two characters and knowledge that the scene is set in the pre-Civil War South), might lead us to fairly simple insights about these characters if it weren't for some more subtle signals. However subservient Mammy must ultimately be, subservience isn't what comes through here. Mammy is talking in an animated manner and Scarlett is listening, even though she hardly seems happy with what she is hearing. Furthermore, Hattie McDaniel's Mammy is not just big—she's substantial. She fills more than a large physical space within the frame. She expresses authority and strength. Scarlett, for her part, is hardly compliant. Vivien Leigh communicates Scarlett's impetuous willfulness. The way she

Vivien Leigh and Hattie McDaniel in *Gone with the Wind* (1939)

holds the bedpost against Mammy's tug on her corset strings suggests the forceful push/pull nature of her complex relationship with human "property."

The role that Hattie McDaniel played was, at the time of the film in 1939, one of a very narrow range of roles available for black actresses. That contemporary social reality lends further, troubling dimensions to the picture. McDaniel was to become the target of some who felt that her portrayal too expertly realized the essentially racist vision of the book and film. It's certainly a sad note that no black actor or actress from the film could attend the premiere in Atlanta, Georgia, with the rest of the principal actors. And to enlarge the affront, McDaniel's photograph was deleted from a publicity program to be distributed at that grand event (her prominence in that program insulted some local officials). Yet she won an Academy Award for her portrayal of Mammy (a first for an African American); she also had the satisfaction of knowing that playing a servant paid much better than actually working as one (McDaniel was a maid not long before coming to Hollywood).

The complexities of the situation that Hattie McDaniel finds herself in provide the African American poet Rita Dove a rich study in character. What does it feel like to be oversized but invisible? An award winner who cannot be a "star"? An actress who must play only the limited roles she has

Hattie McDaniel accepting her Academy Award
at the Coconut Grove in 1940

tried to escape with mixed success in life? The poem "Hattie McDaniel Arrives at the Coconut Grove" pictures the night of the Academy Awards in 1940 with greater complexity than the photograph of Hattie McDaniel could possibly capture. We see in Dove's poem a method of characterization that builds from the outside (from what we see around the character, not from what the character says). We get only one line from McDaniel herself amid much description; Dove sets the scene and helps us see McDaniel the actress dressed very unlike Mammy the film character. We also get some relevant cultural, historical, and biographical information. Finally, we get the poet's reflections on Hattie McDaniel: questions, speculation, identification, and finally, judgment.

**Rita Dove** (1952– )

# Hattie McDaniel Arrives at the Coconut Grove (2004)

late, in aqua and ermine, gardenias
scaling her left sleeve in a spasm of scent,
her gloves white, her smile chastened, purse giddy
with stars and rhinestones clipped to her brilliantined hair,
on her free arm that fine Negro                                    5
Mr. Wonderful Smith.

It's the day that isn't, February 29th,
at the end of the shortest month of the year—
and the shittiest, too, everywhere

except Hollywood, California,                                                            10
where the maid can wear mink and still be a maid,
bobbing her bandaged head and cursing
the white folks under her breath as she smiles
and shoos their silly daughters
in from the night dew . . . What can she be                                              15
thinking of, striding into the ballroom
where no black face has ever showed itself
except above a serving tray?

Hi-Hat Hattie, Mama Mac, Her Haughtiness,
the "little lady" from Showboat whose name                                               20
Bing forgot, Beulah & Bertha & Malena
& Carrie & Violet & Cynthia & Fidelia,
one half of the Dark Barrymores—
dear Mammy we can't help but hug you crawl into
your generous lap tease you                                                              25
with arch innuendo so we can feel that
much more wicked and youthful
and sleek but oh what

we forgot: the four husbands, the phantom
pregnancy, your famous parties, your celebrated                                          30
ice box cake. Your giggle above the red petticoat's rustle,
black girl and white girl walking hand in hand
down the railroad tracks
in Kansas City, six years old.
The man who advised you, now                                                             35
that you were famous, to "begin eliminating"
your more "common" acquaintances
and your reply (catching him square
in the eye): "That's a good idea.
I'll start right now by eliminating you."                                                40

Is she or isn't she? Three million dishes,
a truckload of aprons and headrags later, and here
you are: poised, between husbands
and factions, no corset wide enough
to hold you in, your face a dark moon split                                              45
by that spontaneous smile—your trademark,
your curse. No matter, Hattie: it's a long, beautiful walk
into that flower-smothered standing ovation,

so go on
and make them wait.                                                    50

Dove's final lines suggest a deep appreciation and sympathy for Hattie
McDaniel. The great smile was both a "trademark" and a "curse." But
Dove's speaker doesn't end on that note of ambivalence. Hattie is to enjoy
her moment, and Dove wants the reader to enjoy it with her.

## FEELING FOR CHARACTER

The desire to know something about others isn't built on an abstract curiosity.
We must *want* to know about a character. A character must matter to us. If
Sammy felt that the *why* of Batman didn't justify the *what*, he would likely
have found the character unbalanced (too violent) or just plain silly (bat suits
and bat gadgets). He wouldn't think of Batman as a creative touchstone. Of
course, we don't usually need to accept the kind of unlikely *what* that comes
with a superhero. Most artists build from more mundane materials; many
artists work from subjects quite literally close to home: family, friends, jobs,
and so on. The simplest *whys* can lead to a rich and deeply involving sense of
character: Why did she ask him to lunch? Why did he behave so coldly? Why
did they eat so little? Why did she insist on paying the bill?

### Experiencing Literature through Character

Concern for character often grows from immediate personal concerns. Cathy
Song in the poem "Picture Bride" reflects on the distant past of a grandmother. How can the younger woman, the poem's speaker, connect with a
grandmother over time and dramatically changed circumstances? How does
the old woman encompass for the speaker a still-living history? Why is it
important to rescue a sense of the older woman's past? Everything in the
poem is driven by a powerful sense of **identification**. The grandmother was a
year younger than the poet when she moved from home to a new land and an
arranged marriage. The poet realizes the profundity of that move. She sorts
through her own feelings, her own situation, and wonders how that young
woman (that young woman who became the old woman who is the poet's
grandmother) must have felt when she—at the poet's age—came to an
unfamiliar land and looked in the face of a stranger she knew was to be her
husband? This act of imagining also lends weight to the poem's speaker. It is
not just the grandmother whom we meet in this poem. The speaker becomes
a character as well.

Cathy Song (1955– )

# Picture Bride (1983)

She was a year younger
than I,
twenty-three when she left Korea.
Did she simply close
the door of her father's house                                    5
and walk away. And
was it a long way
through the tailor shops of Pusan
to the wharf where the boat
waited to take her to an island                                   10
whose name she had only recently learned,
on whose shore
a man waited,
turning her photograph
to the light when the lanterns                                    15
in the camp outside
Waialua Sugar Mill were lit
and the inside of his room
grew luminous
from the wings of moths                                           20
migrating out of the cane stalks?
What things did my grandmother
take with her? And when
she arrived to look
into the face of the stranger                                     25
who was her husband,
thirteen years older than she,
did she politely untie
the silk bow of her jacket,
her tent-shaped dress                                             30
filling with the dry wind
that blew from the surrounding fields
where the men were burning cane?

Song suggests the character of both the grandmother and the granddaughter
through questions. Perhaps she cannot cross a gulf between past and present
with flat statements. Too much specific knowledge has been lost over the years;
the grandmother's youth has become too distant. But enough detail remains to

give substance to the questions. And the speaker of the poem can identify closely because the speaker is what the grandmother once was: a young woman.

Robert Hayden also reflects on family in "Those Winter Sundays." His speaker concretely remembers his father and doesn't need to imagine or project from bits of information others have collected. Nor does he ask questions about what his father felt or who he was; his knowledge is limited but firm. Hayden tells a brief story that unfolds a sense of a quiet, uncomplaining man who expresses feelings through hard work and everyday acts of attention. The picture of the father comes through clearly. We get a sketch of a character who is defined by his steadiness. At the end we're left thinking of the second character in the poem. The question that rounds off Hayden's poem is self-reflective. It causes us to think of the son who only as an adult begins to appreciate the depth of his father's love.

**Robert Hayden** (1913–1980)

# Those Winter Sundays (1966)

Sundays too my father got up early
and put his clothes on in the blueback cold,
then with cracked hands that ached
from labor in the weekday weather made
banked fires blaze. No one ever thanked him.      5

I'd wake and hear the cold splintering, breaking.
When the rooms were warm, he'd call,
and slowly I would rise and dress,
fearing the chronic angers of that house,
Speaking indifferently to him,      10
who had driven out the cold
and polished my good shoes as well.
What did I know, what did I know
of love's austere and lonely offices?

The father and son in Hayden's poem introduce in miniature a broad distinction critics often make between character types in novels and plays: static and dynamic. **Static characters** do not change in the course of the story; **dynamic characters** do change. It is useful to further distinguish character types within these categories. Some static characters become objects of criticism; they foolishly resist what seems an appropriate or necessary change. Hayden's father is not this sort of static character. He is unchanging in a way that suggests steadiness, firmness of purpose, clarity of essential values. The father's static quality results from the unrelentingly hard world he must deal with; it's not a personality defect. Some dynamic characters change as a result of specific knowledge; they simply adjust behavior on the basis of new information. Other dynamic characters change at the deepest level of being; they undergo a revolution in their way of seeing and approaching the world. "Those Winter Sundays" is too brief a piece to communicate a full sense of what knowledge the son comes to, but it does suggest a profound insight on the nature of mature love that could hardly leave the son unchanged.

## CHARACTER AND FUNCTION

So far, we've discussed character in terms of knowing or understanding others. We've used words like *motivation, sympathy,* and *identification.* The assumption is that we engage with characters as we engage with people. But we need to acknowledge that characters in literary texts serve a wide range of functions; they are not always in a work for us to "know" as we might hope to know a person.

Many people take the lead of the novelist E. M. Forster and distinguish between **round characters** and **flat characters**. Round characters (according to Forster) possess a complex psychology—layers of complex and perhaps even conflicting motivations. Flat characters are one-dimensional; they may possess a vivid trait but not a substantial identity. These terms can sometimes be useful in making broad distinctions among character types, but *round* and *flat* will be misleading words if we use them to signal a fixed artistic value. It would be a mistake, for example, to assume that round characters are "well drawn" and flat characters are "poorly conceived."

Characters must always be viewed in relation to a whole work. We don't ask only who they are but how they function. For example, we recognize many characters for roles that have become familiar over innumerable works (the shady gambler, the annoying little brother, the meddlesome mother-in-law). Such **stock characters** (the flattest of the flat) do not demand much of us, nor do they leave us with a feeling that we've enlarged our range of experience. But this is not to say that they are, from an artistic standpoint, failures. In such cases, the character's complexity is not the issue; what matters is, does the character fit within a plan for the whole? A stock character might be used to help move a plot forward or perhaps provide a bit of information necessary for a larger purpose. Some simple characters serve to bring out qualities in major characters; they act as **foils** that show off the relatively complex dimensions others possess.

More important still, we must remember that psychological insight isn't the only means to depth or the only type of depth. Some characters embody ideas (or ideals) more than recognizable behaviors. They may seem more satiric than realistic, more fanciful than grounded, more mythic than human. Distinctions such as these are about kind, not quality. A flat character may actually allow us (in some works at least) to access profound feelings. Occasionally, the character's supposed "narrowness" or one-dimensionality may be better described as intensely concentrated.

The father in Judith Ortiz Cofer's "My Father in the Navy: A Childhood Memory" isn't "real" in the same sense that a fully realized independent character is real. In the mind of the speaker, the father possesses no psychological depth or even independent existence. In this poem, that is hardly a problem, for the speaker's father, the angel who appears magically to herald a new day, helps us appreciate the longings of the child—the child's desire for a family's wholeness, for a strongly reassuring presence. The father is beautifully realized, not as a person but as an image a child holds. If the poet chose to give him "depth," the poem's subject would shift: it would no longer be the same intensely felt "childhood memory."

**Judith Ortiz Cofer** (1952– )

# My Father in the Navy:
# A Childhood Memory (1987)

Stiff and immaculate
in the white cloth of his uniform
and a round cap on his head like a halo,
he was an apparition on leave from a shadow-world
and only flesh and blood when he rose from below        5
the waterline where he kept watch over the engines
and dials making sure the ship parted the waters
on a straight course.
Mother, brother and I kept vigil
on the nights and dawns of his arrivals,        10
watching the corner beyond the neon sign of a quasar
for the flash of white our father like an angel
heralding a new day.
His homecomings were the verses
we composed over the years making up        15
the siren's song that kept him coming back
from the bellies of iron whales
and into our nights
like the evening prayer.

The character who is most "rounded" here is the speaker. We feel and understand the rich desire of the child for the father. We can also appreciate the great power that the child feels the father possesses. If we complain that Cofer has not developed the father's character, we've missed what Cofer *has* accomplished in the character of the daughter.

## MODELING CRITICAL ANALYSIS: JAMAICA KINCAID, GIRL

We mentioned in the previous chapter that Jamaica Kincaid's "Girl" (p. 16) defies any easy discussion of plot; it would seem that the story is more purely a character sketch. But a moment's reflection raises interesting critical issues. The title directs us to the girl as a point of focus, as the main character. But the story itself is almost entirely delivered by the woman who orders and instructs the girl. Only two short lines are spoken directly by the girl. Much of what we actually read isn't about the girl at all but about behaviors and duties that are pressed upon her. How is it that her character emerges? Is the girl the main character?

Kincaid from the very start opens with commands. Having the speaker aggressively load on obligations puts the reader, in effect, in the same position as the girl: we are at the receiving end of all the orders. One result is that we can sympathize with the girl. We can feel the weight of being a girl in a culture that is both demanding and restrictive of girls. A sense of character then emerges not from a look inside the girl or from the girl's words but from a visceral understanding of how outside forces (social rules, customs, and expectations) control the girl's experience of the world.

It is in that context that we may see her brief interruptions as admirable—perhaps even heroic. The main speaker projects an identity upon the girl, but the girl resists. She doesn't, she objects, sing *"benna on Sundays"*; she does question an order that does not match her own understanding of the way the world works. Of course, the question she asks at the story's end—*"what if the baker won't let me feel the bread"*—is quickly thrown back against her: "you mean . . . you are really going to be the kind of woman who the baker won't let near the bread?" This question rhetorically functions more as an accusation or as a judgment upon the girl. But as strongly as we might feel its sting, we hold steady and have some reason to think the girl will too. The girl is one who claims some sense of self against the identity put upon her from the outside.

It's also important to note that the girl is not the only character we get to know. The older woman who acts as mentor, boss, judge, and mother has internalized the many lessons that she gives so readily. The fact that she knows how to wash, sew, plant, cook, nurse, iron, and so on suggests that hers has been a life spent doing things for others. But she hasn't accepted a life lived wholly at the whims of those more powerful than she. She knows how to use the few powers she has: "this is how you smile to someone you don't like too much; this is how you smile to someone you don't like at all; this is how you smile to someone you like completely." She knows how to "bully" a man and how it can happen that a man bullies her. She is a character who has managed to achieve some independence in a highly restricted world. For example, near the end, she tells the girl how to love a man but also tells her to not feel too bad if those instructions don't work. It seems that the woman acknowledges limitations built into her society but finds ways to circumvent some of those limitations. And it seems she wants the girl to have that survivor's knowledge too.

## Using Character to Focus Writing and Discussion

- Who are the characters in the story?
- How is each introduced? What are their names?
- What are their physical characteristics? What are their personalities?
- What details help us identify a particular character even when that character is not identified by name?
- Which characters (if any) are better developed than other characters in the text?
- What changes (if any) do we see in the characters?
- What contrasts or tensions, if any, do we see among characters?
- Which character gains our sympathy or support within the narrative? Does this sympathy lead us to feel unsympathetic for any other character?
- How do the characters function within the narrative? How important is any single character to moving the plot forward? How important is any single character to our knowledge of other characters within the narrative?
- How does any single character exhibit a value system that influences the ways that we receive the narrative?

# 3 Theme

## What Does This Text Mean?

## Is There One Right Way to Read This Text?

Theme can be seen as central to the experience of literature and film. We want texts to *mean* something. We tend to value depth, complexity, and relevance. We presume that the greatest works of art reward us because they express significant and lasting themes. At some level, each of the elements addressed in the chapters of this book contributes to the shaping of meaning and, for that reason, demands attention. Yet an insistent search for theme can also be viewed as an avoidance of the literary experience. If we translate a poem into a statement, we risk losing the very qualities that made it a poem. If we neatly summarize a story's "message," we may miss out on a range of complex emotions that the story could inspire. If we bring a narrow sense of purpose to our reading, we will fail to engage the work of art on its own terms.

These different perspectives on theme might seem irreconcilable on many counts.

| | |
|---|---|
| This chapter on "theme" is essential; it's central to the concerns of everything in this book. | This chapter on "theme" is redundant; it's covered in every chapter. |
| Themes are "in the text" for readers/writers to identify as given. | Themes are defined by readers/writers to make sense of or deepen a text. |
| A theme is an idea. | A theme is an echo of an idea. |
| Works of art communicate meaning. | Works of art surpass meaning. |

Fortunately, we don't need to reconcile everything in life or in literary study. When we're made conscious of oppositions, the resulting tension can be productive. We can be sensitive to theme without becoming a "theme hunter." We want you to attend to meaning without deadening the immediate sensory or emotional force that literature and film convey. To achieve and maintain such a delicate critical balance, we'll need to think carefully about how we write about theme, what we mean by theme, and what we mean by "meaning."

## THEME AND THESIS

It's useful to start thinking about theme by reflecting upon the demands we must satisfy as critics. In an essay, theme suggests "thesis"—a key assertion that guides the entire presentation, an assertion that is woven through the whole. A thesis in an analytical paper should be clearly defined and assertive. It should be a statement that a writer can (and must) back up. This notion of argument is harder to grasp than one might think. It's common for inexperienced writers to arrive at a thesis that is really nothing more than a preview of topics to be discussed in the course of the essay. Consider the following example of what we might call a generic thesis:

> To understand our reaction to the wounded lieutenant in "An Episode of War," we must consider Stephen Crane's management of plot, character, and point of view.

This kind of statement makes no real argumentative claim and therefore doesn't function as a purposeful lead. You could remove the words that identify the object of attention and substitute almost any author and title:

> To understand our reaction to X in "Y," we must consider Z's management of plot, character, and point of view.

A formulaic lead like this is sure to result in an equally formulaic essay that checks off the topics for discussion in a paragraph-by-paragraph fashion without helping anyone see how the paragraphs work together. A critical writer needs to do more than this.

What exactly is our reaction to the wounded lieutenant in Crane's story? Why do we react in that way? How is it that Crane is able to make us respond as we do? Questions like these might lead to a workable, argumentative, and engaging thesis as well as a richer and more coherent sense of the story's meaning. They first of all help us establish a critical issue: Crane presents the lieutenant for the most part from the outside. We see him as others see him.

Only occasionally do we see from the lieutenant's eyes, and even then it usually seems that we're getting a mere report of what he sees. Such observations prepare for an argument, an assertion, a thesis (not a list of points "to discuss"):

> Crane's seemingly objective presentation of the episode actually intensifies our sympathy for the lieutenant, because that objectivity makes us feel the wounded man's helplessness.

The previous sentence, of course, can't stand alone. It needs to be defended and explained. A **thesis**, like a **theme**, can be thought of as a main idea, a motivating idea, or a structuring idea.

Relating theme and thesis in these ways highlights the function of repetition in both art and criticism. A thesis in a critical essay is sustained by transitions that echo the main line. A pattern of key words or subordinate linked assertions helps sustain an argument. Such repetition is also clearly part of how theme plays out in literature and film. If you watch George Lucas's original *Star Wars*, you can't help noticing the rousing score by John Williams that blasts through the opening credits and establishes the tone for the battle between good and evil that lies at the heart of this production. If you listen even casually, you will also notice that each major character in the film has his or her own music to accompany whatever action is going on. Darth Vader's theme is, of course, menacing. The deeply ominous notes accentuate his threatening visual presence. Music guides us with other characters as well. As the rebels fly off to blow up the Death Star, individual pilots may be indistinguishable in their orange suits and helmets, but the music helps us recognize Luke Skywalker and smile in relief when the *Millennium Falcon* swoops in (with its own music) to help knock Darth Vader off his course. The theme music permeates the film with each variation building upon another, adding in the various characters' themes as they enter alliances or conflicts, until the climax or decisive point, which recapitulates the sounds from the opening in a final theater-rattling combination of brass and cymbals.

## THEME AND MORAL

Concentrating on theme sometimes leads us to a narrowed sense of what a text might mean. Our experience of a work often feels much larger than the paper that attempts to explain the experience in terms of meaning or message. Perhaps our tendency to isolate, extract, and narrowly restate a single theme from a literary text arises from our familiarity with certain kinds of "easy" works. For example, the simplest children's stories often have a lesson to teach. They may wrap up a message neatly at the end with an explicit moral—a concluding statement that specifies what lesson we are to draw from the narrative. Charles Perrault provides such a structure for his 1697 version of the tale "Little Red Riding Hood." Perrault doesn't want his readers to miss the point, so after narrating the story, he spells out the moral for them.

**Charles Perrault** (1628–1703)

# Little Red Riding Hood (1697)

Once upon a time there was a little village girl, the prettiest that had ever been seen. Her mother doted on her, and her grandmother even more. This good woman made her a little red hood which suited her so well that she was called Little Red Riding Hood wherever she went.

One day, after her mother had baked some biscuits, she said to Little Red Riding Hood: "Go see how your grandmother is feeling, for I have heard that she is sick. Take her some biscuits and this small pot of butter." Little Red Riding Hood departed at once to visit her grandmother, who lived in another village. In passing through a wood she met old neighbor wolf, who had a great desire to eat her. But he did not dare because of some woodcutters who were in the forest. He asked her where she was going. The poor child, who did not know that it is dangerous to stop and listen to a wolf, said to him: "I am going to see my grandmother, and I am bringing some biscuits with a small pot of butter which my mother has sent her."

"Does she live far from here?" asked the wolf.

"Oh, yes!" said Little Red Riding Hood. "You must pass the mill which you can see right over there, and hers is the first house in the village."

"Well, then," said the wolf. "I want to go and see her, too. I'll take this path here, and you take that path there, and we'll see who'll get there first."

The wolf began to run as fast as he could on the path which was shorter, and the little girl took the longer path, and she enjoyed herself by gathering nuts, running after butterflies, and making bouquets of small flowers which she found. It did not take the wolf long to arrive at the grandmother's house. He knocked: Toc, toc.

"Who's there?"

"It's your granddaughter, Little Red Riding Hood," said the wolf, disguising his voice, "I've brought you some biscuits and a little pot of butter which my mother has sent you."

The good grandmother, who was in her bed because she was not feeling well, cried out to him: "Pull the bobbin, and the latch will fall."

The wolf pulled the bobbin, and the door opened. He threw himself upon the good woman and devoured her quicker than a wink, for it had been more than three days since he had last eaten. After that he closed the door and lay down in the grandmother's bed to wait for Little Red Riding Hood, who after awhile came knocking at the door. Toc, toc.

"Who's there?"

When she heard the gruff voice of the wolf, Little Red Riding Hood was scared at first, but, believing that her grandmother had a cold, she responded: "It's your granddaughter, Little Red Riding Hood. I've brought you some biscuits and a little pot of butter which my mother has sent you."

The wolf softened his voice and cried out to her: "Pull the bobbin, and the latch will fall."

Little Red Riding Hood pulled the bobbin, and the door opened. Upon seeing her enter, the wolf hid himself under the bedcovers and said to her: "Put the biscuits and the pot of butter on the bin and come lie down beside me."

Little Red Riding Hood undressed and went to get into bed, where she was quite astonished to see the way her grandmother was dressed in her nightgown. She said to her: "What big arms you have, grandmother!"

"The better to hug you with, my child."

"What big legs you have, grandmother!"

"The better to run with, my child."

"What big ears you have, grandmother!"

"The better to hear you with, my child."

"What big eyes you have, grandmother!"

"The better to see you with, my child."

"What big teeth you have, grandmother!"

"The better to eat you."

And upon saying these words, the wicked wolf threw himself upon Little Red Riding Hood and ate her up.

MORAL
One sees here that young children,
Especially young girls,
Pretty, well brought-up, and Gentle,
Should never listen to anyone who happens by,
And if this occurs, it is not so strange
When the wolf should eat them.
I say the wolf, for all wolves
Are not of the same kind.
There are some with winning ways,
Not loud, nor bitter, or angry,
Who are tame, good-natured, and pleasant
And follow young ladies
Right into their homes, right into their alcoves.
But alas for those who do not know that of all the wolves
the docile ones are those who are most dangerous.

Perrault's moral fits neatly at the end of this familiar tale, and there is some satisfaction at having a tidy reason for a gruesome story of a girl being devoured. The moral justifies the terror: with Perrault's rationale, this story serves as a lesson to any girl who might be seduced by the flattery of a charming young man. But on closer examination, the moral seems to tag on a simpler message than the story itself encourages. Perrault's fable in its entirety suggests a tension between the civility that has been taught this "Pretty, well brought-up, and Gentle" girl and the wolf who is able to use that very sign of class to trick the girl: he speaks politely and engages her in a civil conversation during which he gains the information he needs in order to trap her later. The poor girl is a model of goodness; she goes to visit her sick grandmother, and it is her concern for her grandmother's seemingly worsening condition that leads to her demise. Yet Perrault's moral, in effect, shakes a disapproving finger at her. What wrong does she commit that leads her to such a dismal end? It seems Perrault wants Little Red Riding Hood to be knowing and suspicious as well as innocent and polite. Can a proper young girl possess, within Perrault's view of things, all of these qualities? The moral offers clear advice and a stark warning, but the story itself suggests anxiety over the conflicting signs of goodness and the power of proper manners to hide evil.

None of this is to say that Perrault's explicit message is incongruous with his narrative. He does pick up on elements within the story to draw his conclusion. He does emphasize Little Red Riding Hood's childish innocence and the wily ways of the wolf. But should we go on to impugn all wolves (as Perrault does) for the offense of this particular wolf? Can't there be good, polite wolves (or at least good, polite young men)? Is Perrault suggesting the subversive notion that manners are a dangerous obligation for girls/women and useful tool for boys/men? It seems possible that a good reader of this tale could complicate Perrault's own explicit thematic statement. Couldn't you argue that the theme of the story concerns the unjust moral and social burdens women and girls must bear in a patriarchal society?

The varied interpretive possibilities of "Little Red Riding Hood" suggest that theme doesn't need to be boiled down to a moral even when a moral is offered. When we write about the narratives we read, we should work to be less absolute than Perrault. His moral ends any conversation that we might have about the meanings of the story. One goal of conversation should be to open up ideas and possible interpretations of the story. Finding a moral is satisfying, but it often requires us to overgeneralize about the text in question. It can even be a way to avoid the demands that complex works of literature pose. James Thurber makes some fun of stories with easy morals with his twisted take on the old story.

James Thurber (1894–1961)

# The Girl and the Wolf (1939)

One afternoon a big wolf waited in a dark forest for a little girl to come along carrying a basket of food to her grandmother. Finally a little girl did come along and she was carrying a basket of food. "Are you carrying that basket to your grandmother?" asked the wolf. The little girl said yes, she was. So the wolf asked her where her grandmother lived and the little girl told him and he disappeared into the wood.

When the little girl opened the door of her grandmother's house she saw that there was somebody in bed with a nightcap on. She had approached no nearer than twenty-five feet from the bed when she saw that it was not her grandmother but the wolf, for even in a nightcap a wolf does not look any more like your grandmother than the Metro-Goldwyn lion looks like Calvin Coolidge. So the little girl took an automatic out of her basket and shot the wolf dead.

Moral: It is not so easy to fool little girls nowadays as it used to be. ■

Calvin Coolidge, known as "Silent Cal," served as thirtieth president of the United States (1923–1929).

Since the founding of the Metro-Goldwyn-Mayer studios in 1924, there have been five different lions used as mascots for the studio. This image shows "Jackie," who was used from 1928 to 1956.

Thurber plays with the conventional story and claims to bring it out of the world of make-believe. We still have a talking wolf prone to developing disguises, but the character of the girl has, comically, changed. This allows Thurber to offer the generalizing moral about "little girls nowadays." The result pokes fun at our tendency to attribute morals to stories; it also teases our conventional notion of Little Red Riding Hood's innocence and passivity as well as the innocence and passivity of any "well-brought up" girl. Thurber's turn against our expectations challenges our tendency to settle easily for morals in the works that we read.

Consider how the following report of a girl-devoured-by-wolf story compares to those of Perrault and Thurber. It doesn't offer a moral so explicitly as either of these, but one could argue the moral remains strongly implied. How does that implied moral work? Does it question the value of a moral, or does it ask us to think about why we construct morals to stories?

# Girl Devoured by Wolf

Yesterday, in a nearby village, a wolf which had somehow entered the house ate an old woman and her young granddaughter. The girl's name has been withheld pending notification of her mother, but neighbors report that shortly before her death she was seen wearing a "little red riding hood."

Investigators at the scene of the murders suspect that the wolf entered the old woman's bedroom by pulling at a simple bobbin mechanism at her door. They found traces of the wolf's hair in the bed as well as in a nightcap lying by the side of the bed. A basket containing some biscuits and a small pot of butter, apparently a gift brought by the girl to her grandmother, was overturned and strewn about the room.

Citizens are asked to be on the lookout for a wolf described as having big arms, big legs, big ears, big eyes, and big teeth. Authorities warn children not to talk to any wolves as there has been a rash of incidents in the community in recent months. ∎

## Experiencing Literature through Theme

Critical writers explore the gray area between a plain statement of meaning, such as a moral, and the more ambiguous reactions that a story inspires. Theme resides in this gray area and cannot be easily extracted from the text. We can think of a literary or filmic theme as an abstract expression made concrete through the carefully patterned fabric of key words, sounds, images, and so on. The content of the expression and the mode of expression must be understood together. For instance, consider the following poem by Marge Piercy.

Marge Piercy (1936– )

# A Work of Artifice (1982)

The bonsai tree
in the attractive pot
could have grown eighty feet tall
on the side of a mountain
till split by lightning.                                   5
But a gardener
carefully pruned it.
It is nine inches high.
Every day as he
whittles back the branches                                10
the gardener croons,
It is your nature
to be small and cozy,
domestic and weak;
how lucky, little tree,                                   15
to have a pot to grow in.
With living creatures
one must begin very early
to dwarf their growth:
the bound feet,                                           20
the crippled brain,
the hair in curlers,
the hands you
love to touch.

We can all agree that Piercy's poem is "about" the oppression of women, surely an important matter. But the compelling qualities of this poem do not reside in theme so narrowly defined. Consider this: If we register only what the poem is about, if we write about what Piercy writes about, we'll find ourselves as restricted as the bonsai tree; we'll be dealing with abstract ideas and remain one step away from the poem itself. A critical writer who uses the poem to generalize about sexual oppression in our society may fail to account for (or even address) what makes "A Work of Artifice" distinctive. And such a critic will almost certainly rehash familiar ideas in ways that will reduce the power of Piercy's language to the language of summary or statement.

But if we consider how meaning is embodied by the text, we may press forward to a deeper level of appreciation and insight. How does Piercy project and explore a tension between the "natural self" and the artificial, constructed self of our culture? Why does she "whittle" back the lines of the poem (note that the longest line concerns the tree's potential growth)? How does she engage the reader in an increasingly personal and forceful relationship with the bonsai tree? Why does she juxtapose something as foreign and debilitating as "bound feet" with the relatively familiar and seemingly innocuous "hair in curlers"?

Clearly, identifying a message is not necessarily the same thing as writing critically about theme. Mere identification stifles development. Responsive audiences seek to extend analysis. Definition provides one way to elaborate productively upon theme. You could, for example, pause in Piercy's poem over words like *whittles*, *croons*, and *pruned* in order to consider both what those words denote (what they signify, what they mean literally) and what they connote (what they suggest, what they imply emotionally). You could also pause over the words you use in response to the text. At times, modifying a general word will help you establish a clearer sense of theme. The subject of Piercy's poem, for example, is not simply "oppression." We have previously used the term *sexual oppression*, but we can press harder still on this point of meaning: sexual oppression in this poem is *insidious, subtle, deceptive, manipulative,* and *pervasive*. Oppressive male power finds expression under the guise of *kindness, gentleness, concern*. Ironically, that power is justified as "natural," whereas the entire poem accentuates its "artifice." Such careful thinking upon the meanings of words can enrich your sense of what constitutes theme.

## MULTIPLE THEMES IN A SINGLE WORK

Much of what we've discussed in this chapter involves our approach to texts as much as it does the texts themselves. Responsiveness to theme (like any kind of aesthetic responsiveness) requires active engagement with the work. We read for a variety of purposes, and those purposes may well include social or religious instruction. But when we read *exclusively* for a particular kind of instruction, we're not really reading literature—no matter what the quality of the work before us. To put it a slightly different way, a work can become literature only when it is used as literature. Such an active model of reading means that we must be willing to think of theme in the plural. As we suggested earlier, even Perrault's simple tale suggests possibilities that are not contained in the moral. We can underscore important qualities of theme by three statements and three related questions:

1. Themes emerge as problems or questions more often than as specific lessons or morals. How does a work challenge us?
2. Themes tend to be suggestive and open ended. Why does a work matter to us more than a clear summary of its theme?
3. Themes are inevitably a matter of interpretation. Why must we support our reading with evidence from the text?

Some works force us to reflect on such concerns by making us question the validity of common interpretive clues or signs of authority. We tend, for example, to separate literature from news stories because literature is artistically shaped. The events reported by journalists are considered raw accounts driven by reality. But if we give the matter greater thought, we realize that anytime that anyone writes up "facts," some degree of ordering comes into play—usually a good deal more than we like to admit. Stories from the newspaper or television news do more than inform the public; they express and shape values, opinions, and attitudes. They may not be literature, but neither are they merely records of what "really happens." What if we bring a literary sensibility to these everyday materials? We might then be alive to a richer, more complex range of possible meanings.

## Experiencing Literature through Theme

Maxine Hong Kingston's "The Wild Man of the Green Swamp" addresses these matters directly. From the very start, Hong Kingston makes us think of the way we select, tell, and understand stories. We are led to question how we know what we know as we read conflicting reports on the Wild Man from eyewitnesses, officials, doctors, ship's officers, journalists, and an interpreter. Behind all of these voices is the narrator, who patches together the reports with no comment on their credibility.

**Maxine Hong Kingston** (1940– )

# The Wild Man of the Green Swamp (1977)

For eight months in 1975, residents on the edge of Green Swamp, Florida, had been reporting to the police that they had seen a Wild Man. When they stepped toward him, he made strange noises as in a foreign language and ran back into the saw grass. At first, authorities said the Wild Man was a mass hallucination. Man-eating animals lived in the swamp, and a human being could hardly find a place to rest without sinking. Perhaps it was some kind of a bear the children had seen.

In October, a game officer saw a man crouched over a small fire, but as he approached, the figure ran away. It couldn't have been a bear because the Wild Man dragged a burlap bag after him. Also, the fire was obviously manmade.

The fish-and-game wardens and the sheriff's deputies entered the swamp with dogs but did not search for long; no one could live in the swamp. The mosquitoes alone would drive him out.

The Wild Man made forays out of the swamp. Farmers encountered him taking fruit and corn from the turkeys. He broke into a house trailer, but the occupant came back, and the Wild Man escaped out a window. The occupant said that a bad smell came off the Wild Man. Usually, the only evidence of him were his abandoned campsites. At one he left the remains of a four-foot-long alligator, of which he had eaten the feet and tail.

In May a posse made an air and land search; the plane signaled down to the hunters on the ground, who circled the Wild Man. A fish-and-game warden "brought him down with a tackle," according to the news. The Wild Man fought, but they took him to jail. He looked Chinese, so they found a Chinese in town to come translate.

The Wild Man talked a lot to the translator. He told him his name. He said he was thirty-nine years old, the father of seven children, who were in Taiwan. To support them, he had shipped out on a Liberian freighter. He had gotten very homesick and asked everyone if he could leave the ship and go home. But the officers would not let him off. They sent messages to China to find out about him. When the ship landed, they took him to the airport and tried to put him on an airplane to some foreign place. Then, he said, the white demons took him to Tampa Hospital, which is for insane people, but he escaped, just walked out and went into the swamp.

The interpreter asked how he lived in the swamp. He said he ate snakes, turtles, armadillos, and alligators. The captors could tell how he lived when they opened up his bag, which was not burlap but a pair of pants with the legs knotted. Inside, he had carried a pot, a piece of sharpened tin, and a small club, which he had made by sticking a railroad spike into a section of aluminum tubing.

The sheriff found the Liberian freighter that the Wild Man had been on. The ship's officers said that they had not tried to stop him from going home. His shipmates had decided that there was something wrong with his mind. They had bought him a plane ticket and arranged his passport to send him back to China. They had driven him to the airport, but there he began screaming and weeping and would not get on the plane. So they had found him a doctor, who sent him to Tampa Hospital.

Now the doctors at the jail gave him medicine for the mosquito bites, which covered his entire body, and medicine for his stomachache. He was getting better, but after he'd been in jail for three days, the U.S. Border Patrol told him they were sending him back. He became hysterical. That night, he fastened his belt to the bars, wrapped it around his neck, and hung himself.

In the newspaper picture he did not look very wild, being led by the posse out of the swamp. He did not look dirty, either. He wore a checkered shirt unbuttoned at the neck, where his white undershirt showed; rounded by men in cowboy hats. His fingers stretching open, his wrists pulling apart to the extent of the handcuffs, he lifted his head, his eyes screwed shut, and cried out.

There was a Wild Man in our slough too, only he was a black man. He wore a shirt and no pants, and some mornings when we walked to school, we saw him asleep under the bridge. The police came and took him away. The newspaper said he was crazy; it said the police had been on the lookout for him for a long time, but we had seen him every day. ■

Only in the final paragraph of the story do we learn why we've been left with so little guidance as to what to make of all the reports: the narrator is a schoolchild who (like most any child) passes along statements without critically reflecting upon them. We would argue that Hong Kingston uses this narrator to mock the smug, self-satisfied language of established authority; through the child she reveals its judgmental cruelty. For example, the narrator does not think that the Wild Man looks wild in the newspaper pictures yet still calls him the Wild Man because that is the only name used in the media. In other words, the narrator has been taught to reject his or her own instincts and, like most people, doesn't judge on what he or she sees so much as on what he or she is told to see. As a result, a real man becomes a dehumanized "wild man." The narrator is not even mature enough to contest the statements of the authorities when those statements are inconsistent with the narrator's firsthand experience: the narrator sees the second "Wild Man" every day, but the newspaper reported that the police had been looking for this dangerous creature a "long time."

Of course, Hong Kingston doesn't actually tell us all of this. She requires us to go beyond her naïve narrator's understanding. And in going beyond the child, we go beyond the attitudes of the dominant culture depicted in this story. Perhaps one of Hong Kingston's themes is that too many people passively accept too many stories from too many dubious sources. It is not just a child, after all, who reports of a Wild Man in the swamp; the newspapers pick up the story and the name itself from the people who live near the Green Swamp. And it is not a child who presses the Wild Man to suicide; the unsympathetic authorities bear that responsibility. But we can't blame only those authorities, for the child's naïve narration leads us to question our own habits of acceptance. Even though Hong Kingston does not paste a moral at the end of her story, the story may inspire us to ask whether we too often read the world in a childish way when we experience it through the limiting lens of media. This is not *the* theme of the story, but it is *a* theme that the story addresses.

---

**Making Connections**

Read the newspaper or watch the evening news, and find one example of a story that focuses on people who are homeless, poor, new immigrants, or "foreigners." How does the presentation encourage a particular interpretation or judgment (its language, its emphasis, its point of view)? Does it imply or even state a moral?

---

# WHEN THE MESSAGE IS UNWANTED

Writers and filmmakers create worlds for us to enter and, for a time, live within. Literary works and films may well ask us to step into unfamiliar territory and see things in context of the artist's vision. To some extent, this involves a willing surrender. We approach works of art receptive to the notion that they may offer us something new, that they may widen our experience or deepen our powers of sympathy and empathy. These are compelling reasons to seek the experience of art. Inevitably and appropriately though, we remember where we entered. We test any new imaginative construction against the ways we've already come to understand the world. We assess the vision, the world, of one artist in relation to our previous experience—including our previous literary experience. We consider our values. Receptivity and openness do not require a total submission to an author's worldview. One's critical intelligence can and should operate along with one's imagination. Although we may discover that the literary work compels us to modify our sense of things, we need not assume that that is the necessary outcome.

Leni Riefenstahl's famous documentary *Triumph of the Will* (1935) serves as a case in point. The film, commissioned by Adolph Hitler, celebrates the glories of Germany's Third Reich and the power of Hitler. Riefenstahl's visual imagination, her sense of structure, her command of the technical dimension of filmmaking all are displayed to grand effect. But what is the world to which we're asked to submit? *Triumph of the Will* opens with gorgeous aerial shots clouds, churches and other grand buildings, city streets unfolding beneath the camera's eye. We also see from our lofty vantage point soldiers marching. An airplane appears alongside us. Interspersed throughout are shots of crowds—not unruly threatening crowds but crowds thrilled by the very things we have seen. The effect is intended to bring the viewer into a world poised at a moment of greatness. Riefenstahl want us to share the excitement—to be one among the many.

From our perspective, critical resistance in this case—not surrender— becomes an essential response. A plane lands, and Adolph Hitler emerges to the adoration of the masses. Riefenstahl makes the grand buildings, the beautiful shots from the sky, the disciplined soldiers, adoring crowds, and sleek aircraft all work to aggrandize the 1934 Nazi Party Congress and, of course, the party's leader. *Triumph of the Will* seeks our assent to National Socialism, to militaristic power, to presumptions of cultural and racial superiority, to far-reaching imperialistic ambitions. The truly extraordinary skill involved in this effort is at the service of a worldview that cost the lives of millions.

The example of *Triumph of the Will* may lead us to a dismal thought about works of art. If we can't trust novels, poems, films, or plays to communicate something good or true, then we should feel no compunction about dismissing them out of hand. No one wants to be manipulated. But we should remember

Director Leni Riefenstahl went to great lengths to create a dramatic impact as she filmed *Triumph of the Will* at the 1934 Nuremberg Nazi Party Rally.

that if we're open to art, no single work stands alone—separate from other works of art and separate from history. Viewed in the context of our complete experience (both life experience and literary experience), Riefenstahl's motives cannot hide. Of course, one could argue that those motives hid well in Germany of 1935 to contribute to a historical nightmare. But those who enthusiastically embraced *Triumph of the Will* were not fully engaged by a work of art; they were eager and ready to accept power and effective expressions of power.

One possible theme of Maxine Hong Kingston's "The Wild Man of the Green Swamp" is worth recalling here: Bring your whole person to the act of reading. The child narrator of her tale can't quite do that and uncritically repeats what the newspapers say even when it's clear that he or she has seen something different. The narrator's childlike puzzlement gives us room to draw out the theme and consider what that theme might mean to us now. In a similar way, our attention to thematic aspects of Perrault's fairy tale allows us to move beyond his moral and to think about the issues that the moral raises for us. How do such stories, for example, make girls/women morally responsible for boys'/men's behavior?

## A Note to Student Writers: Discovering What You Want to Say

Many students feel that their own critical writing is disconnected from the imaginative texts they are asked to write about. Misperceptions about theme are sometimes the source of such dissatisfaction. Students sometimes assume that the right answer to an assignment is the key to success; this assumption leads to an emphasis on product, which often amounts to a statement of *what* the work "really" means. But success more likely comes to the student who takes the right *approach* to an assignment; this understanding emphasizes process, which usually involves an exploration of *how* the work achieves meaning.

Good critical writing involves discovery and the rewriting that discovery makes necessary. Interaction with your own writing involves a healthy messiness. We suggest you take notes, ask questions, make lists and then reflect upon your notes, answer your questions, and organize your lists. Be active as a writer before you actually get to the point at which you are "writing the paper." Amid the conflicting demands of a typical course schedule, you might think it unrealistic to do so much in preparation for one paper in one class. But think of this suggestion from another angle: The writer who tries to get to the last thought first (and reduce a literary text to a simple theme) will often get stuck because the literary text doesn't cooperate. So instead of spending time frozen at the keyboard in a futile hope for *the* answer, try spending time testing responses and ideas at the keyboard in a search for answers. You'll find that the more patient route is not necessarily slower and is almost certainly more rewarding.

# MODELING CRITICAL ANALYSIS: JAMAICA KINCAID, GIRL

Jamaica Kincaid's "Girl" (p. 16) allows for a fairly simple thematic summary. The story concerns a culture that presses significant limitations upon girls. A girl's life is proscribed by numerous duties and rules. Many are put in the negative: it is as difficult to keep up with all the prohibitions as it is to keep up with demands. But "Girl" is hardly a simple story. Kincaid embodies a cultural mind-set in the concrete attitudes of a particular person. To put it another way, Kincaid registers the heavily layered and burdensome effects of abstract ideas on an individual. Yet the experience of reading "Girl" cannot be captured by identifying a theme of oppression. "Girl" also subtly confronts and defies the very social limitations it depicts.

From the start, Kincaid makes it clear that a girl in the world she presents has little time for anything we might call her "own." On Monday, do this; on Tuesday, do that. Many of these insistent instructions, of course, concern practical matters. The girl must know how to clean, how to cook, how to sew, how to iron, how to tend the vegetable garden, and so on. By putting the whole list in an unbroken stream of a single sentence, Kincaid makes us not only understand but feel the girl's situation. Duties and demands cascade upon her. Even Sundays are no relief, for when the girl is free of active duties, she must be hyperconscious of the things she should not do. The girl apparently bears, on behalf of her sex, an especially heavy moral burden. Seen from the outside through the eyes of one schooled in the culture, a girl can hardly avoid moral condemnation. In relation to behavior between girls and boys, it would seem girls are always to blame. Kincaid's girl will be seen, from the slightest lapse of decorum, as a "slut." And to be seen that way is to be that way. The girl is defined by others before she can define herself.

As powerfully as these social demands press upon the girl, Kincaid also helps us appreciate how girls/women seek to gain on occasion some edge in the grossly imbalanced system within which they must operate. The title directs attention to the girl who is spoken to, not the apparently older woman who speaks. Although we might take this to suggest how thoroughly acculturated one becomes in an unjust social system (women are taught to perpetuate injustices upon women), we have signs that the woman has found ways to gain her own real if limited power. She instructs the girl, for example, in how to "bully a man." She offers warning insight of how a man bullies a girl. She includes, almost casually, information on how to abort an unwanted child in a long list of other more mundane "how-to" items. It would seem that the woman has learned in her own life (probably in part from other older women) how to make decisions separate and secret from the men seemingly in power. And toward the end of her list, the older woman tells the girl "how to spit up in the air if you feel like it." Here we get the first and only sign that the woman knows the girl may *feel* like doing one thing or another that has no relation to the comfort or benefit of the men around her. With it comes the sense that some things can be done purely on feeling if one is astute enough to dodge the consequences.

It's worth finally attending to the two lines in which the girl herself speaks. Neither represents a decisive claim against the demands and judgments made upon her, but both register a real if faint resistance. The girl is not an altogether passive subject. Her first break against the woman's instructions is a complaint: *"but I don't sing benna on Sundays at all and never in Sunday school."* The girl here contests the woman on a point of fairness or of accuracy. She won't wholly accept the way another person sees her. The second is a question: *"but what if the baker won't let me feel the bread?"* In this instance, the girl interjects a concern that the woman's advice isn't covering the real situations she will face or has faced already. The girl, it seems, understands very well practical life difficulties and wants to gain some insight on how to meet those difficulties. If we attend carefully to all the signals Kincaid gives us, we will find that "Girl" is about more than the prohibitions and injustices built into a male-dominated society; it is also about resourceful and (in context) valiant individual responses to such prohibitions and injustices.

## Using Theme to Focus Writing and Discussion

- How does this work challenge us?
- What does it ask us to think about?
- As you read the work, what details stand out? Look for words, images, or ideas that seem to fit together, and arrange these details into lists.
- The labels that you develop for these lists could be your initial themes for this work.
- What patterns do you find among the details that you have listed?
- Do any of these patterns seem to conflict with other patterns? For instance, in Perrault's story, we find references to proper deportment, yet the moral warns us against false appearances.
- What significance do you see in the conflict or the congruence of these emerging themes?
- How does your identification of these themes help you see aspects of the text that you did not see before you identified the theme?

# 4 Point of View

## How Do We Know What We Know about What Happened?

We may say that a storyteller *relates* a story to us. That verb helps us think about how any narration of a story not only adds coherence to a series of random events but also gives the audience a relationship to the events, a position in relation to what has happened.

Anyone who has ever experienced some sort of misunderstanding among friends or family members is quite aware of the idea of perspective. Everyone involved has a different version of the events. We spend much time recounting each of our individual perspectives; comparing what we perceived with what someone else saw; searching for the source of the problem within these narratives; and hoping that by unfolding our different narratives, we might bring ourselves back to some semblance of the harmony that existed before the misunderstanding. It is often the person who wasn't there who gets to hear all of the accounts and to judge the merits of the different perspectives. This form of storytelling can be quite tense, and the implications can be far-reaching precisely because everyone involved has some relation to the story. Authors frequently take advantage of the intensity of feeling that comes with a particular point of view: perspective is always part of a narrative.

## PERSPECTIVE

**Point of view** is a term that comes from the study of art and from an interest in making figures on a page seem lifelike. The point of view refers to an actual point or hole that is used to establish the position of objects within a composition. The Dürer woodcut depicts two artists who are using a mechanical method to establish point of view. They have fixed their point to the wall on the right. By stretching a string from that point to the lute that they are about to draw, the artists note where the string passes through the frame of the picture to determine precisely where the object should appear when they swing their white canvas back into the frame.

The artists depicted in the woodcut will make the scene seem real by setting all objects onto the canvas in strict relation to the viewpoint that they have arbitrarily selected. In Western art, the movement to utilize and to codify theories of perspective came during the fifteenth century, when there was a great interest in humanism and the general acknowledgment that human observations tend not to be objective; we notice things that interest us, and we define them not as they actually are but in relation to ourselves.

In a two-dimensional work of art, the sense of depth that perspective gives is an illusion. The artist distorts the objects within the field of vision to make the scene appear just as it would to that single eye "seeing" the picture. The most common "trick" in representing perspective is to make parallel lines converge as they move away from the vantage point. For instance, in the Dürer woodcut, we know that the walls of the room are parallel; the fact that

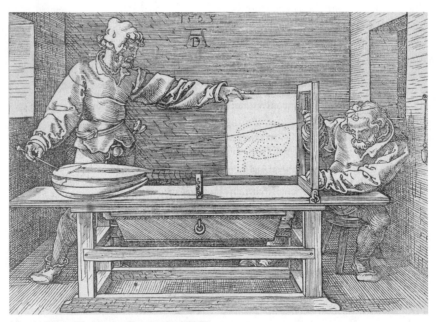

Albrecht Dürer, *Working on Perspective* (1525)

they come together behind our artists is a trick of perspective to indicate increasing distance from our point of view.

Artists of the Renaissance made much more elaborate versions of Dürer's simple exercise. They constructed mathematical models to create the illusion of depth, such as Masaccio creates in *Trinity*. Below, you can see his completed painting with lines drawn in to illustrate Dürer's strings and the distortions that come with perspective. On page 58 is a sketch of the side view (or depth) that is represented by the illusion of perspective in Masaccio's painting, with the strings stretched to their full length.

In the ensuing centuries, the term *point of view* has come to be used much more widely. Often, we hear the term used to mean simply an opinion. But thinking more strictly about the peculiar distortions that come from any specific perspective helps us see narrative issues more clearly. It helps us go beyond the order of events that the narrator has arranged for us and consider how the narrator's interests, personality, motives, and background are an important part of the story.

For example, in the poem that follows, Dorothy Parker writes from the perspective of Penelope, the wife of Odysseus, who waits for twenty years for her husband to return from the Trojan War. Penelope is a literary character from Homer's *Odyssey*; more specifically, we know her from the point of view of her husband, Odysseus, for whom Penelope is symbolic of the stable home

Masaccio, *Trinity* (1427–1428)

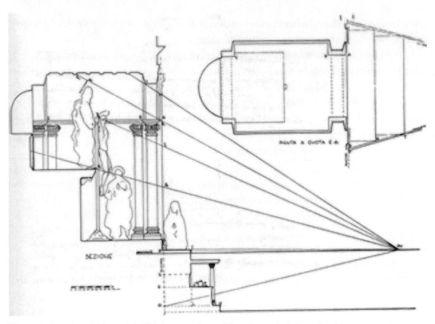

Plan and elevation of Masaccio's *Trinity* according to Piero Sanpaolesi, Brunelleschi

that he longs for throughout his adventures with warriors, gods, and monsters. Even when the story's narrative focuses on her house, Penelope is generally up in her room out of the action. Parker's poem shifts this focus.

**Dorothy Parker** (1893–1967)

# Penelope (1928)

In the pathway of the sun,
In the footsteps of the breeze,
Where the world and sky are one,
    He shall ride the silver seas,
        He shall cut the glittering wave.        5
I shall sit at home, and rock;
Rise, to heed a neighbor's knock;
Brew my tea, and snip my thread;
Bleach the linen for my bed.
        They will call him brave.        10

This poem neatly divides the character of the wandering Odysseus (lines 1–5) from the patience of Penelope (lines 6–9). Penelope echoes the language of the epic poem in her description of her husband's journey. In contrast, her own twenty years of rocking and household chores are much less glamorous, but the final line challenges us to rethink our understanding of the famous story. Parker's poem helps us see Penelope's perspective, but it also points to the fact that the conventions of heroism celebrated in a poem such as the *Odyssey* give little acclaim to the quiet heroism of Penelope, whose endless waiting requires a formidable endurance without the grand adventures that Odysseus enjoys.

---

### A Note to Student Writers: Distinguishing Author from Speaker

You must accurately signal perspective in the narratives you analyze. Although an author of a poem or story may on occasion speak directly from personal feelings and convictions, it is generally best to distinguish the **poet** or **author** from the **speaker**. Although Parker is the author of "Penelope," she is not the speaker. Authors imagine, create, and give life to speakers. Authors use speakers to achieve particular effects. Note that the previous paragraph refers to "Parker's poem" but highlights Penelope as the speaker. In some cases, this distinction is absolutely necessary (an author who relates a story through a cruel and manipulative speaker wouldn't like to be identified as one with the speaker).

---

# THE NARRATIVE EYE

In 1818, Caspar David Friedrich created two paintings that work together as a pair. Their contrasts are pronounced. One uses cool blue colors; the other uses warm oranges. In one, a man stands on top of rugged rocks; in the other, a woman stands amid softer vegetation. But the composition of the two paintings is quite similar. At the center of each, Friedrich gives us the back of a single character: we share something of the characters' point of view. In one picture, we see rocks, mountains, and fog. In the other, we see a brilliant sunrise at daybreak. But we also see the characters who stand before these landscapes. By placing people in the **foreground** of the pictures, Friedrich changes everything. Each landscape is significant because of the character who experiences that landscape and who, therefore, defines it for us. Without the human figures, there would be scant connection between Friedrich's fog and his morning light. And we would not have some important interpretive clues. For example, we would not be prompted to think of how Friedrich defines masculine and feminine in terms of nature.

These paintings remind us again of issues vital both to visual arts and to literary texts in general. The people from whose points of view we are seeing are fictions created by artists. As much as we feel that we are getting the man's

Caspar David Friedrich, *Wanderer above the Sea of Fog* (1818)

Caspar David Friedrich, *Woman in the Morning Light* (1818)

or the woman's **perspective**, that we see from their vantage point, in Friedrich's paintings, we are actually standing behind each of them. Our perspective is the artist's perspective, but the artist makes us feel empathy for these characters in the foreground, and thus we forget that the artist is manipulating our reaction. In addition, it is clear that there is no getting around point of view in a work of art. Even if Friedrich removed the man and the woman from his paintings, we'd still be seeing from a perspective the artist has controlled. So always ask yourself as you read literature: Through whose eyes do I see? How might that point of view influence what I'm seeing and hearing? How does perspective shape my understanding of events?

## RELIABLE AND UNRELIABLE NARRATORS

As readers, we must think hard about point of view because it strongly shapes the meaning, authority, and power we draw from fiction. We often cannot understand stories unless we understand how they are told. What is the source of a story? What prompts its telling? How much does the teller know? Can the narrator be trusted? We can begin to respond to such questions by broadly classifying narrative points of view as either third-person or first-person narration.

### Third-Person Narrators

In **third-person narration**, the narrator is outside the story and refers to all characters by name or as "he," "she," or "they." An **omniscient narrator** moves freely about in time and space. In many cases, an omniscient narrator may move freely in and out of the minds of the characters. A narrator that breaks into a story to guide the reader's judgment is called an **intrusive narrator**.

At the beginning of A *Christmas Carol*, Charles Dickens employs a narrator who can't quite let the story get going. This narrator digresses upon conventions of language (why do we use "door-nail" to epitomize death?) and conventions in literature (what makes Hamlet's father a remarkable character in Shakespeare's play?) as he strives to convey the simple fact that Scrooge's partner, Marley, is dead.

**Charles Dickens** (1812–1870)

from A **Christmas Carol** (1843)

Marley was dead: to begin with. There is no doubt whatever about that. The register of his burial was signed by the clergyman, the clerk, the undertaker, and the chief mourner. Scrooge signed it. And Scrooge's name was good upon

'Change, for anything he chose to put his hand to. Old Marley was as dead as a door-nail.

Mind! I don't mean to say that I know, of my own knowledge, what there is particularly dead about a door-nail. I might have been inclined, myself, to regard a coffin-nail as the deadest piece of ironmongery in the trade. But the wisdom of our ancestors is in the simile; and my unhallowed hands shall not disturb it, or the Country's done for. You will therefore permit me to repeat, emphatically, that Marley was as dead as a door-nail.

Scrooge knew he was dead? Of course he did. How could it be otherwise? Scrooge and he were partners for I don't know how many years. Scrooge was his sole executor, his sole administrator, his sole assign, his sole residuary legatee, his sole friend, and sole mourner. And even Scrooge was not so dreadfully cut up by the sad event, but that he was an excellent man of business on the very day of the funeral, and solemnized it with an undoubted bargain.

The mention of Marley's funeral brings me back to the point I started from. There is no doubt that Marley was dead. This must be distinctly understood, or nothing wonderful can come of the story I am going to relate. If we were not perfectly convinced that Hamlet's Father died before the play began, there would be nothing more remarkable in his taking a stroll at night, in an easterly wind, upon his own ramparts, than there would be in any other middle-aged gentleman rashly turning out after dark in a breezy spot—say Saint Paul's Churchyard for instance—literally to astonish his son's weak mind. ■

This intrusive narrator stands outside the action and refers to Scrooge in the third person but is also aware of Scrooge's thoughts (Scrooge is aware of Marley's death but not "dreadfully cut up by the sad event"). This narrator guides the reader's judgment by talking about the convention of ghost stories, pointing out to the reader that the story that follows will fit into that tradition. This narrator establishes a presence as a chatty and personable companion to lead us through a story about a character who is altogether less humane than our guide.

An author who restricts the third-person narration to the consciousness of one or more characters employs a **limited narrator** or **limited omniscient narrator**. An **objective narrator** reports, records, or shows only what could be seen or heard by an outside observer. Authors who use an objective narrator do not comment on the action. Neither do they get inside the minds of any of the characters (at least not directly). Many of Ernest Hemingway's short stories use an objective narrator. An objective narrator is sometimes called an **impersonal narrator**. The following excerpt from Hemingway's "Hills Like White Elephants" serves as a good example of objective or impersonal narration:

The hills across the valley of the Ebro were long and white. On this side there was no shade and no trees and the station was between two lines of rails in the sun. Close against the side of the station there was the warm shadow of the building and a curtain, made of strings of bamboo beads, hung across the open door into the bar, to keep out flies. The American and the girl with him sat at a table in the shade, outside the building. It was very hot and the express from Barcelona would come in forty minutes. It stopped at this junction for two minutes and went on to Madrid. ▪

In this account, in stark contrast to the selection from Dickens, the narrator offers only facts that anyone might observe about this scene. There are no excursions into the peculiarities of the English language or thoughts about the way these characters might think about each other. Especially after reading Dickens, we might say that this narrator has no personality, but the sparse descriptive style that Hemingway uses here has its own peculiarities. What does the narrator notice? The hills, the lack of shade, the string of beads to keep out the flies, and the train schedule. These are all things that any observer might see, but look carefully at another detail. The first character is called "the American." There is not a name, just the nationality. The second character is "the girl"—again no name, and now only a vague indicator of age. How can this objective narrator tell that this is an American rather than someone from somewhere else? Is "girl" the same as "woman"? And what does the narrator fail to describe? The time of day, the relation between these two people, what they are wearing, why they are here. The few details that the narrator has chosen to notice discreetly lends a personality to this impersonal voice and helps us see that even objectivity comes from a particular point of view.

## First-Person Narrators

Such particularity is easy to note in some cases. A **first-person narrator** speaks from within the story and can know only what the imagined "I" knows ("I looked back just as he rounded the corner and saw him pick up the wallet"). Just like a jury member who decides how much to value the testimony of an eyewitness, readers of first-person narratives consider evidence of reliability. Ultimately, readers must define where the author stands in relation to the events the author's narrator recounts.

In the Sherlock Holmes stories, Dr. Watson faithfully chronicles the adventures of the detective. His characteristics as Holmes's audience and as the self-conscious recorder of what happens influence what we get to see of Holmes. We see only what Watson sees. He may be on the scene (sometimes performing some duty to help Holmes solve the crime), or he may have to trust the account that Holmes gives him. He acts as an appreciative audience to Holmes's theatrical deductive work, and we have to wonder whether his admiration of Holmes might ever make him change the scene to Holmes's advantage or to interpret events in complimentary ways. Still, all in all, we accept him as a **reliable narrator** within his limits.

An author may, of course, speak directly through a character to register his or her own deepest values. But first-person narrators often express an author's moral perspective indirectly or ironically. For example, the first-person narrator could be a child who reports "facts" without understanding them. Or the first-person narrator could even be a dishonest, self-serving, cruel character. Such narrators are **unreliable narrators**. To further complicate matters, readers must also consider how involved a first-person narrator is in the story. Some first-person narrators are **detached observers** (perhaps Nick Carraway in *The Great Gatsby*); others play the central role in the story they will tell (Huck in *Adventures of Huckleberry Finn*). Sometimes, instead of hearing the polished version of a story that such a narrator might deliver to an audience, we hear it as though it were the narrator's own often rambling, jumbled thoughts, that is, the narrative appears to be a **stream of consciousness** (Bloom in James Joyce's *Ulysses*).

### Experiencing Literature through Point of View

In "The Vacation," Wendell Berry describes a video camera as an objective narrative instrument, but he also suggests the limits of such an apparatus.

**Wendell Berry** (1934– )

# The Vacation (1997)

Once there was a man who filmed his vacation.
He went flying down the river in his boat
with his video camera to his eye, making
a moving picture of the moving river
upon which his sleek boat moved swiftly                                5
toward the end of his vacation. He showed
his vacation to his camera, which pictured it,
preserving it forever: the river, the trees,
the sky, the light, the bow of his rushing boat
behind which he stood with his camera                                  10
preserving his vacation even as he was having it

so that after he had had it he would still
have it. It would be there. With a flick
of a switch, there it would be. But he
would not be in it. He would never be in it.                        15


This poem is about narration: Berry tells the tale of a man who can see his
vacation only through the point of view of his camera. But this poem about
narration is also narrated. What sort of narrator does Berry use? Berry's
narrator tells a story. The narrator is not a person in the story but does
have access to the thoughts of the man with the camera, as well as to
knowledge that the man does not have and to a future that the man is not anticipating. Berry uses this narrator to judge the man and to comment on the problem of allowing a recording device to substitute for actual experience. Without directly stating so, Berry's narrator suggests that the man pays a price for trying so hard not to lose any of his vacation.

### Making Connections

An author uses a variety of techniques to give us a character who seems real and consistent, even in inconsistencies. Character is discussed in Chapter 2. It is important to note that the narrator of a work can be considered another character, but this character may seem to be hidden.

## FILM FOCUS AND ANGLES

A film also expresses a narrative voice—a point of view. The building block
of any film is the smallest element: the single **frame**. In analyzing the
**composition** of a painting or of a single frame, we can learn something
about point of view by considering how the characters and all of the other
elements are arranged within the frame. The objects in the **foreground** will
demand special attention. A foregrounded subject can be further prioritized
by **shallow focus**, a technique that brings a specific plane into clear focus
and leaves the rest of the picture out of focus.

In this frame from *The Magnificent Ambersons* (1942) on page 66, the couple
in the foreground (Anne Baxter and Tim Holt) commands our attention, and
the rest of the room is clearly less important. The shot itself focuses on the
couple rather than on anything else in the room. It is clear that there is
something else going on, but the shot indicates that whatever this other activity
may be, it is not central to this scene. In **deep focus**, objects remain clear as they
grow more distant; in deep focus, the cinematographer achieves a greater **depth
of field** and forgoes concentration on a specific subject.

In the frame from *Citizen Kane* on page 66, we can see part of the effect
that Orson Welles has achieved as the camera pulls away from the window

*The Magnificent Ambersons* (1942). Objects in the foreground command our attention.

*Citizen Kane* (1941)

*Trapped* (1949). The high-angle shot in this scene suggests the power of law enforcement over James Todd.

*Nosferatu* (1922). The low-angle shot lends the subject power over the viewer.

through which we watch young Kane playing in the snow. As the camera begins to settle on Kane's mother and the other people inside the house, we can still see the window and the young boy whose future is being determined by events inside the house.

The angle from which a picture is taken also contributes to the overall impression we get when we see a scene. A **high-angle shot** (a picture taken from above the subject) may communicate a sweeping feel or may place the viewer in a strong position in relation to the subject.

In the frame from *Trapped* (1949) on page 67, the high angle of the shot suggests the power that the law enforcement officials hold over James Todd, who is holding his hands in the air. We see the scene from the point of view of the man with the gun in the foreground rather than of Todd. Such an effect can be exaggerated by the degree of the angle (an **extreme high-level shot** or an **aerial view**).

An **eye-level shot** (camera and subject at the same height) generally suggests greater immediacy by putting the viewer right with the subject. A **low-angle shot** (the camera set below the subject) may lend the subject of the picture power over the viewer.

For example, in the frame on page 67, we look up to the vampire in the film *Nosferatu*. Of course, the degree of the angle is important here as well. In this case, it emphasizes the deformity of the figure. Just as a filmmaker or a painter must choose where to place the camera or where to stand when making a painting, an author must choose where to stand to transfer perceived reality into words. This decision impacts our perception of the entire narrative as we read.

Henry Taylor's poem "After a Movie" uses the cinematic motif to show the point of view of a person who leaves a movie and looks at the world with an eye still used to the dark world of the movie theater. Notice how the person sees real scenes as though they were frames from a film.

**Henry Taylor** (1942– )

# After a Movie (1996)

The last small credits fade
as house lights rise. Dazed in that radiant instant
of transition, you dwindle through the lobby
and out to curbside, pulling on a glove
with the decisive competence                                          5
of the scarred detective

or his quarry. Scanning
the rainlit street for taxicabs, you visualize,

without looking, your image in the window
of the jeweler's shop, where white hands hover                    10
above the string of luminous pearls
on a faceless velvet bust.

Someone across the street
enters a bar, leaving behind a charged vacancy
in which you cut to the dim booth inside,                         15
where you are seated, glancing at the door.
You lift an eyebrow, recognizing
the unnamed colleague

who will conspire with you
against whatever the volatile script provides ....               20
A cab pulls up. You stoop into the dark
and settle toward a version of yourself.
Your profile cruises past the city
on a home-drifting stream

through whose surface, sometimes,                                 25
you glimpse the life between the streambed and the ripples,
as, when your gestures are your own again,
your fingers lift a cup beyond whose rim
a room bursts into clarity
and light falls on all things.                                   30

   The character in this poem views the world as though he were one of the
characters in the film that has just ended: "the scarred detective / or his
quarry." He sees the world as if it were carefully arranged for this scene. He is
not an actor who knows ahead of time what the "volatile script provides." But
he has adopted the consciousness of the fictional character who works within
the conventions of film. Instead of just looking across the street, his eyes work
like a camera, "Scanning / the rainlit street." In a jeweler's shop window, his
own reflection shows in the foreground, but the character sees like a camera
through that reflection to focus on the string of pearls. Not until the final lines
of the poem is the character able to regain his natural point of view when "a
room bursts into clarity / and light falls on all things."

## Experiencing Film through Point of View

Alfred Hitchcock dramatizes the problem of limited point of view in *Rear
Window* (1954), the story of photographer L. B. Jefferies (Jimmy Stewart),

who is confined to his apartment as he recuperates from a broken leg. To pass the time, Jefferies looks out his window into the windows of the apartments that face his, and he sees scenes from the lives of his neighbors. He would seem to be an impartial observer, and he believes that he is detached from the lives that he is observing; these are not people he knows. But as he watches, he becomes involved in the stories that unfold. He becomes a narrator creating his own order from the fragmented scenes that he observes. As the film progresses, Hitchcock suggests that Jefferies may have become more involved in these stories than in his own life.

While looking out over his neighborhood, Jefferies comes to believe that the man in an opposing apartment has killed his wife and somehow disposed of the body. Jefferies's suspicion arises only from odd things that he sees from his window, yet he eventually draws his nurse, Stella (Thelma Ritter), and his girlfriend, Lisa Fremont (Grace Kelly), into his obsession. Jefferies also calls in his friend Doyle (a police detective played by Wendell Corey) to check out the "evidence," but Doyle dismisses Jefferies's theories. The pursuit of the murderer is left to a man who can't get out of his apartment, a beautiful society woman, and a plainspoken practical nurse.

*Rear Window* is very cleverly scripted, but its pleasures cannot be expressed by a summary of action. Hitchcock establishes in the film's opening

*Rear Window* (1954)

shot what becomes the film's essential dynamic. The audience looks from an apartment window across to adjacent apartments; the audience, in effect, inhabits the apartment from which the view is shot. After the camera pans over the neighborhood, it turns back to reveal the viewer we have already been linked to (we have seen through his eyes): L. B. Jefferies, broken leg and all. The exchange between looking at and being looked at will underlie everything that follows.

Hitchcock highlights the particularity of point of view in this film by carefully framing individual shots. The border that the camera (and screen) establishes includes the very window frames that Jefferies sees through (both his own windows and his neighbors'). By calling attention to frames, Hitchcock suggests that we always shape what we see. In other words, we construct reality much like we compose a picture; we arrange what we perceive so that it fits together or "adds up" in a way that makes sense to us. Such thoughts lead us to realize that no person's vision is complete; therefore, no person's interpretation of actions can be absolutely trustworthy. Much of the suspense of *Rear Window* arises from the thought that Jefferies may not be seeing all that he needs to see. Perhaps truth requires that he see the very things the frames cut off.

Hitchcock's specific emphasis on window frames keeps us particularly aware that we are not only looking from one apartment but also peering into the private apartments of others. Frames in this respect can be seen as boundaries we are not supposed to cross. For example, that Jefferies is a bit disappointed when the newlywed wife thinks to close the blinds to her bedroom window. If Jefferies is a "Peeping Tom," as his nurse at first claims, we who watch movies (at least this movie) seem no better; we, after all, are eager to see everything he sees across the square. Therefore, the thrill Jefferies and the audience get from discovery is compromised by the knowledge that the thrill does not arise from a praiseworthy pursuit of truth and justice. We all become fascinated by seeing things others would choose to hide from us.

## SHIFTING PERSPECTIVES

The medium of film offers a ready alternative to the problem of a limited perspective. Almost every film offers a variety of camera angles to give us a sense that we see what is really happening. When a television network covers a sporting event, it places cameras around the arena to offer some sense of full coverage of the event. When a referee in a football game makes a call, he does so from his unique place on the field, from his observation of that play, and from his memory of what he has observed. He might confer with the other referees to confirm his call; meanwhile, the network will quickly review the play from each of its cameras, and those of us who are watching may feel as though we have a better idea of what really happened than those who have made the official call. There is a sense that the more one sees, the more likely one is to see things "correctly," but every person has a different interpretation of events; the person who hears all the different stories may or may not feel better informed than those who were actually there. The pursuit of "correctness" gives way to an interest in exploring the different approaches made possible by each point of view. Each new view deepens the experience, even if it does not resolve anything.

Just as camera angles alter the way an event is perceived, authors shift the perspective within a narrative to give particular depth to the story. In Stevie Smith's "Not Waving but Drowning," the poem shifts from an objective narrator to the voice of a dead man to those who are watching and back again to the dead man.

**Stevie Smith** (1902–1971)

# Not Waving but Drowning (1957)

Nobody heard him, the dead man,
But still he lay moaning:
I was much further out than you thought
And not waving but drowning.

Poor chap, he always loved larking                           5
And now he's dead
It must have been too cold for him his heart gave way,
They said.

Oh, no no no, it was too cold always
(Still the dead one lay moaning)                             10
I was much too far out all my life
And not waving but drowning.

A central image of the poem is the difficulty posed by different perspectives: what might have looked like playful waving was actually a cry for help. The tragedy within this image is that the observers, who are aware of the man and his waving, might have offered help, but they were unable to interpret his gesture. As we hear from the man, we learn that there was a much larger communication problem. The observers characterize him as one who enjoys "larking," and even after his death, they assume that the cause of death was cold water. The dead man is still trying to correct their misperception—his "no no no" desperately tries to shake the survivors out of the nearly comical rhythm of the poem and of their confidently wrong explanations. He claims to have been out "too far" all of his life. The image of the drowned man trying to

talk with those who get to interpret his life could stand for anyone in any sort
of circumstance who has gotten "too far out."

## Experiencing Literature through Perspective

In the following poem, Philip Levine confronts issues of perspective at several
different levels. He sets his own poem against the context of "famous photographs" that Charles Sheeler took in Dearborn's Ford factories in the late 1920s
and early 1930s. The photograph here is an example of Sheeler's style in this
series. The machine is a massive presence, but the man who makes this machine
work is smaller than most of the machine's pieces. By referring to Sheeler's
photographs, Levine situates his own personal narrative and sets up a contrast
between the famous "dwarfed" men in the photographs and Mrs. Strempek
working with her trowel across the street in a house now "long gone to fire."

Charles Sheeler, *River Rouge Plant Stamping
Press* (1927)

**Philip Levine** (1928– )

# Photography 2 (1999)

Across the road from Ford's a Mrs. Strempek
planted tulip bulbs and irises even though

the remnants of winter were still hanging on
in gray speckled mounds. Smoking at all times
she would kneel, bare legged, on the hard ground                    5
and half smile when I passed coming or going
as she worked her trowel back and forth for hours
making a little stubborn hole and when that
was done making another.
          When Charles Sheeler
came to Dearborn to take his famous photographs              10
of the great Rouge plant he caught some workers,
tiny little men, at a distance, dwarfed
under the weight of the tools they thought
they commanded. When they got too close
he left them out of focus, gray lumps with white              15
wild eyes. Mainly he was interested in
the way space got divided or how light
changed nothing.
          Nowhere does Mrs. Strempek
show up in all the records of that year,
nor do the few pale tulips and irises                        20
that bloomed in the yard of her rented house
long gone to fire. For the first time I was
in love that spring and would walk the long mile
from the bus stop knowing it was useless,
at my feet the rutted tracks the trucks made,               25
still half frozen. Ahead the slag heaps
burning at all hours, and the great stacks
blackening the sky, and nothing in between.

Look carefully at the perspectives that Levine offers in his poem. Then, examine the perspective that Sheeler offers in his photograph. How does Mrs. Strempek compare to the nameless worker in the photograph? How do the two narrators (Levine's "I" and Sheeler's photographic point of view) treat these characters differently? Why does Levine position his own spring of first love between the images of a smoking woman planting bulbs and the Ford employees?

In Frank Gaspar's poem "It Is the Nature of the Wing," the narrator strives to become conscious of multiple perspectives and is fully aware of the fragmentary nature of each one. Yet the narrator sees every distraction as potentially enlightening.

Frank X. Gaspar (1946– )

# It Is the Nature of the Wing (2004)

The problem is being a fragment trying to live out a whole life.
From this, everything follows. Or the problem is being
fractured and preoccupied with one's own mending, which
lasts as long as you do and comes with its legion of distractions.
Just now, when a lovely-throated motor comes gliding up                          5
the street to one driveway or another, I can tell you
there is a certain kind of safety in a fact like that. It is so
solid you can lean on it in your bad hours. It can lift you, too,
from your despair, which is of no consequence, which can
be measured against the dropping flowers of the wisteria,                        10
which fall because of their nature and essence, and stain
the redwood planks of the small deck in the back of the house.
That doesn't mean those used-up blossoms feel at home
under everyone's feet or at the mercy of my stiffened broom.
Didn't Plato say it is the nature of the wing to lift what is heavy?              15
He was speaking of love again, I can remember that much, and
then love was a ladder, too, but lifting again, always upward.
Then it is possible to love Plato for his faith, which is so strong
he becomes difficult and obdurate in the late nights. He is
hardly distracted by a passing car. He is fixed on something                     20
beautiful, and why not? When I step out onto the porch, there
is nothing shining in the sky. Oh, and the wisteria blooms have
fallen some more and are like a sad carpet. And some small
insects are dancing in the garage's yellow lamp. They don't hear
the little bats squeaking. It's all right. You could even say they                25
look happy, they look joyful. Surely they are beautiful in their
ignorance and danger. See how they hold your head and command
your eye? Looking upward? Looking toward that homely light?

The narrator begins by noticing the unconsciousness of machinery, the
motor (a fragment of the car that is actually moving up the street). He
moves on to grasp at the perspective of wisteria blossoms (which may not
feel at home under our feet), Plato (an attempt to understand the line that
Gaspar uses as his title), and insects by the garage. The narrator simultaneously fails in his quest not to be distracted from the larger questions that
consume him and succeeds by using these seemingly distracting perspectives
to help him look "upward" toward some larger philosophical understanding
of unattainable ideas such as love and faith.

An awareness of perspective helps us as readers see how authors manipulate our attention. Point of view controls the degree of sympathy we may have toward a character; it guides our judgment of the actions of characters; it contributes to our interpretation of the whole work. An awareness of technique gives us a greater appreciation of the craft that goes into the literary production and enriches our conversations about what we are reading.

## MODELING CRITICAL ANALYSIS: ROBERT BROWNING, MY LAST DUCHESS

One of the most famous first-person narrators in poetry is the duke who tells the story of his late wife in Robert Browning's "My Last Duchess." The poem takes place in the ducal palace of Ferrara, Italy, during the Renaissance. The duke is speaking admiringly about a painting of his wife (now deceased) that he commissioned the artist "Frà Pandolf" to paint. Through the duke's description of the painting and the manner in which the image was painted, we begin to learn something of the character of this "last Duchess" and of the duke himself. We gradually learn that the duke is speaking to an emissary for the man whose daughter might become the next duchess.

**Robert Browning** (1812–1889)

# My Last Duchess (1842)

*FERRARA*
That's my last Duchess painted on the wall,
Looking as if she were alive. I call
That piece a wonder, now: Frà Pandolf's hands
Worked busily a day, and there she stands.
Will't please you sit and look at her? I said                    5
"Frà Pandolf" by design, for never read
Strangers like you that pictured countenance,
The depth and passion of its earnest glance,
But to myself they turned (since none puts by
The curtain I have drawn for you, but I)                         10
And seemed as they would ask me, if they durst,
How such a glance came there; so, not the first
Are you to turn and ask thus. Sir, 'twas not

Her husband's presence only, called that spot
Of joy into the Duchess' cheek: perhaps                                    15
Frà Pandolf chanced to say "Her mantle laps
Over my Lady's wrist too much," or "Paint
Must never hope to reproduce the faint
Half-flush that dies along her throat": such stuff
Was courtesy, she thought, and cause enough                               20
For calling up that spot of joy. She had
A heart—how shall I say?—too soon made glad,
Too easily impressed; she liked whate'er
She looked on, and her looks went everywhere.
Sir, 'twas all one! My favour at her breast,                             25
The dropping of the daylight in the West,
The bough of cherries some officious fool
Broke in the orchard for her, the white mule
She rode with round the terrace—all and each
Would draw from her alike the approving speech,                          30
Or blush, at least. She thanked men,—good! but thanked
Somehow—I know not how—as if she ranked
My gift of a nine-hundred-years-old name
With anybody's gift. Who'd stoop to blame
This sort of trifling? Even had you skill                                35
In speech—which I have not—to make your will
Quite clear to such an one, and say, "Just this
Or that in you disgusts me; here you miss,
Or there exceed the mark"—and if she let
Herself be lessoned so, nor plainly set                                  40
Her wits to yours, forsooth, and made excuse,
—E'en then would be some stooping, and I choose
Never to stoop. Oh sir, she smiled, no doubt,
Whene'er I passed her; but who passed without
Much the same smile? This grew; I gave commands;                         45
Then all smiles stopped together. There she stands
As if alive. Will't please you rise? We'll meet
The company below, then. I repeat,
The Count your master's known munificence
Is ample warrant that no just pretense                                   50
Of mine for dowry will be disallowed;
Though his fair daughter's self, as I avowed
At starting, is my object. Nay, we'll go
Together down, sir. Notice Neptune, though,
Taming a sea-horse, thought a rarity,                                     55
Which Claus of Innsbruck cast in bronze for me!

Browning presents the poem as a speech from the duke. That speech is never interrupted by a question or a response. The duke has something to say but has no interest in hearing from someone else. In showing his gallery, the duke offers a self-portrait, perhaps a calculated self-portrait. It's essential to note that the "I" of "My Last Duchess" is emphatically not Robert Browning. Author and speaker must be kept distinct. As the speaker's conversation unfolds, so do his relations with the scene itself. He tells about "my last Duchess" and the artist who rendered her, and in so doing, the duke reveals much about himself. We pick up on his jealousy and his unrestrained frustration at what he perceives to be the lack of respect that his dead wife showed to him. As the duke finishes talking about this painting (in the middle of line 47) and moves on to the next artwork in his collection, we get the poetic equivalent of a widening shot so that we can suddenly see the audience listening to the talking duke. In this revelation, we learn more about the duke's sense of morality. He feels no qualms about having given "commands" that stopped "all smiles" from his wife. Whether he means to warn his future wife of his intolerance for any sort of indiscretion, whether he is simply brutally honest about his past, or whether he is so self-involved as to be unaware of the repugnance of his attitudes and actions, we cannot help feeling that the emissary would be wrong to let the next marriage go forward.

By creating this account from the perspective of the duke, Browning also puts us into the position of the emissary, who is gradually discovering the character of a potential future member of the family. Though we begin by appreciating art and the duke's storytelling, we ultimately realize that the seemingly learned man who is talking about art is, at best, a boor, and, at worst, a murderer without a conscience.

## Using Point of View to Focus Writing and Discussion

- Who is speaking? How do we know?
- How does this speaker's position influence our view of events?
- If the narrator is not a character in the action, whose point of view influences our understanding of events?
- What values or limitations impact this narrator's presentation?
- How many, if any, of these limitations did the author intend to include? For instance, we may see limitations such as a view of women's place in society that indicate the author's cultural bias rather than something that the author created as part of a character in the story.
- How do we encounter any other point of view in this narrative?
- What details in the narrative help us understand the speaker?
- What, if anything, can we see that contradicts the account that we hear from our narrator?

# 5 Setting

## Where and When Does This Action Take Place?

## Why Does It Make a Difference?

Setting may be thought of in narrow terms as the physical and temporal **background** to a story. In the theater, the word *setting* refers specifically to how items are arranged on a stage. Actors move about the stage in relation to these items. Normally, our attention is focused primarily on the actors. There is nothing wrong about such restrictive ideas of the word when one wants a restricted idea, but this chapter will define **setting** more expansively as the total environment within which narrative actions take place. The characters' general living conditions as well as the time and place in which they live constitute setting.

Such a broad use of the word *setting* also suggests its great importance. Reflect for a moment on an especially powerful event in your life. It's likely that you remember that event not only as an action but as an action grounded in a particular time and place. It would be hard to narrate the action without describing where and when the action unfolded. Or put the case in reverse: Reflect for a moment on a significant place in your life. It's likely that the place will provoke you to feel, to remember, to tell stories. Setting is not merely background—or at least not necessarily only background. Setting can function as part of a literary text's whole effect.

## PLACE AND TIME

Place and time function together in our lives as well as in literary texts. We often anticipate the importance of our memories by taking pictures of grand occasions (graduation, birthdays, moving to a new home, and so on). Most of us strive to catch not only people on film but the physical environments closely tied to the people's experience. A common sign of the way we link place and action is displayed every time a vacationer sets out to write a message on a postcard.

The front of the postcard shows an idealized picture of the place where the writer is visiting; the back of the card allows the writer to report on what has happened in that place. The writer may describe what he or she has been doing or might tell about the monuments that are pictured on the front of the card. Even though the results are often banal ("The weather is beautiful; wish you were here"), the linking of action and character with setting makes postcards a pleasure to receive. Skilled authors who can take us fully into another place or time offer far deeper pleasures.

In his famous personal essay "Once More to the Lake," E. B. White shows what it is like to recall old events through the act of revisiting a place. A complex sense of time past, present, and (through the son) future emerges from the description. White registers specific details and makes it clear those details count for something. He writes of how similar the lake (where he had vacationed with his father) still is when he returns years later with his son, but he also comments on the differences that have come about due to progress: "[T]he road under our sneakers was only a two-track road. The middle track was missing, the one with the marks of the hooves and the splotches of dried, flaky manure. There had always been three tracks to choose from in choosing which track to walk in; now the choice was narrowed down to two." The

distinction here between trails carved by horses and trails kept clear by automobiles is subtle, but White uses the difference in the place to help him describe the narrowing options of his own life as he has grown older. The most disconcerting difference for him is the fact that his son has now taken his place, performing his role in the memories that White associates with the lake.

White's setting is hardly mere background; it is an integral part of the meaning that unfolds in the narrative. It exerts a power over the action of the story. The nature of the place is dynamic; it changes over time in ways that chart White's own progress through life. An appeal of setting within fiction is that, as in White's memoir, it brings the past to life—it makes the past meaningful to the present moment.

---

### A Note to Student Writers: Descriptive Summaries

E. B. White is coauthor with Richard Strunk of a classic writing guide still widely used. In *Elements of Style*, Strunk and White emphasize the importance of concrete, specific images to vivid descriptive writing. In the previous passage, White wants to be sure we see the tracks cut in the dirt road, for he knows that if we don't get a very solid feel for the reality of the place, none of the ideas or emotions that have grown from the place will be compelling. Readers need something they can access through touch, sight, or sound.

Critical writers can learn something from this emphasis on the concrete. It's important to establish a very clear sense of a text to be analyzed before jumping into an analysis. We've said that "why" and "how" questions help one think analytically, but it's worth remembering that a simple "what" question often needs to come first. A "what" question won't likely lead you to a thesis, but it may help you clarify your sense of a topic. It's useful to think of summary as a kind of description. And like any good description, summary must build on well-selected and clearly presented details that can be checked against the reader's/viewer's own experience.

---

## Experiencing Literature through Setting

Sometimes, setting makes other elements of narrative (character and action) decidedly secondary; setting can be the primary force of meaning and emotional effect. In "February Evening in New York," Denise Levertov embeds a brief scene involving two characters in the middle of a richly textured impression of a specific place and time. We're forced to read character and incident in context of feelings created by the enormous energy of city life in New York.

# February Evening in New York (1959)

As the stores close, a winter light
  opens air to iris blue,
  glint of frost through the smoke,
  grains of mica, salt of the sidewalk.
As the buildings close, released autonomous                5
  feet pattern the streets
  in hurry and stroll; balloon heads
  drift and dive above them; the bodies
  aren't really there.
As the lights brighten, as the sky darkens,                10
  a woman with crooked heels says to another woman
  while they step along at a fair pace,
  *"You know, I'm telling you, what I love best*
  *is life. I love life! Even if I ever get*
  *to be old and wheezy—or limp! You know?*                15
  *Limping along?—I'd still ..."* Out of hearing.
To the multiple disordered tones
  of gears changing, a dance
  to the compass points, out, four-way river.
Prospect of sky                                            20
  wedged into avenues, left at the ends of streets,
  west sky, east sky: more life tonight! A range
  of open time at winter's outskirts.

Notice that unlike many poems we have seen in this book, this poem has no
spacing after any of the syntactical or stanzaic breaks in its lines. Everything
crowds together as we read, just as the New York sidewalks grow packed as
stores close and people are "released." The sentences that begin with "as"
also grow progressively longer (four lines, five lines, then seven lines).
Impressions pile upon impressions. The importance of setting to this poem
is so great that Levertov has the setting reflected in the poem's structure. In
the density of this poem's impressions, we're encouraged to read the lines of
the "woman with crooked heels" as indicative of a larger encompassing
energy that subsumes even the sky that is barely "wedged into avenues" for
the viewer who looks to the ends of the streets.

   Setting can also take a central function in sections of extended narratives. The following passage is taken from Theodore Dreiser's *Sister Carrie*, a

very long novel published in 1900 and acknowledged for its groundbreaking **realism**—a mode of depiction that builds on close, accurate attention to specific historical and social settings. In this selection, eighteen-year-old Carrie Meeber has arrived alone in Chicago, and through her eyes we see a place that is as unfamiliar to us (as a modern audience) as it is to her, a newcomer to the city. The narrator is telling us about Carrie and about the Chicago that she sees. This narrator reveals the social pressures that work upon Carrie through a description of the department store she moves through. As you read, note the ways in which the setting is essential to our understanding of Carrie's character.

**Theodore Dreiser** (1871–1945)

## from Sister Carrie (1900)

At that time the department store was in its earliest form of successful operation, and there were not many. The first three in the United States, established about 1884, were in Chicago. Carrie was familiar with the names of several through the advertisements in the "Daily News," and now proceeded to seek them. The words of Mr. McManus had somehow managed to restore her courage, which had fallen low, and she dared to hope that this new line would offer her something. Some time she spent in wandering up and down, thinking to encounter the buildings by chance, so readily is the mind, bent upon prosecuting a hard but needful errand, eased by that self-deception which the semblance of search, without the reality, gives. At last she inquired of a police officer, and was directed to proceed "two blocks up," where she would find "The Fair."

The nature of these vast retail combinations, should they ever permanently disappear, will form an interesting chapter in the commercial history of our nation. Such a flowering out of a modest trade principle the world had never witnessed up to that time. They were along the line of the most effective retail organisation, with hundreds of stores coordinated into one and laid out upon the most imposing and economic basis. They were handsome, bustling, successful affairs, with a host of clerks and a swarm of patrons. Carrie passed along the busy aisles, much affected by the remarkable displays of trinkets, dress goods, stationery, and jewelry. Each separate counter was a show place of dazzling interest and attraction. She could not help feeling the claim of each trinket and valuable upon her personally, and yet she did not stop. There was nothing there which she could not have used—nothing which she did not long to own. The dainty slippers and stockings, the delicately frilled skirts and petticoats, the laces, ribbons, hair-combs, purses, all touched her with individual desire, and she felt keenly the fact that not any of these things were in the range of her purchase. She was a work-seeker, an outcast without employment, one whom the average employee could tell at a glance was poor and in need of a situation.

It must not be thought that any one could have mistaken her for a nervous, sensitive, high-strung nature, cast unduly upon a cold, calculating, and unpoetic world. Such certainly she was not. But women are peculiarly sensitive to their adornment.

Not only did Carrie feel the drag of desire for all which was new and pleasing in apparel for women, but she noticed too, with a touch at the heart, the fine ladies who elbowed and ignored her, brushing past in utter disregard of her presence, themselves eagerly enlisted in the materials which the store contained. Carrie was not familiar with the appearance of her more fortunate sisters of the city. Neither had she before known the nature and appearance of the shop girls with whom she now compared poorly. They were pretty in the main, some even handsome, with an air of independence and indifference which added, in the case of the more favoured, a certain piquancy. Their clothes were neat, in many instances fine, and wherever she encountered the eye of one it was only to recognize in it a keen analysis of her own position—her individual shortcomings of dress and that shadow of manner which she thought must hang about her and make clear to all who and what she was. A flame of envy lighted in her heart. She realised in a dim way how much the city held—wealth, fashion, ease—every adornment for women, and she longed for dress and beauty with a whole heart.

Department store interior, ca. 1900

On the second floor were the managerial offices, to which, after some inquiry, she was now directed. There she found other girls ahead of her, applicants like herself, but with more of that self-satisfied and independent air which experience of the city lends; girls who scrutinised her in a painful manner. After a wait of perhaps three-quarters of an hour, she was called in turn. ■

The place in this instance defines the character. We understand and feel Carrie's insecurity through the environment within which she lives. Her excitement, fear, envy, and ambition, as well as her social status and educational background, all become apparent as things we both know and experience through her engagement with the department store and all it contains.

## THE ROLE OF PHYSICAL OBJECTS

Objects can also serve as props to activate the memory and retrieve the past. Well-chosen details can bring alive the social and emotional conditions of a character's environment. In Kazuo Ishiguro's novel *Remains of the Day* (1989), the narrator is Mr. Stevens, a butler whose identity is linked to the prestigious house that he has long served; however, Stevens has had the misfortune to move through his career as the upper class declines both economically and morally. In one scene, while on a journey away from Darlington Hall (the place where he has spent almost all of his adult life), Stevens considers taking a side trip to the English village of Mursden. Because his entire life is bound within a very narrow social world, he assumes that the reader is as fluent in the details of butlery as he is. The fact that we are not so fluent contributes to our understanding of how contained a life Stevens has led. Note the ways in which Ishiguro's butler, addressing the reader directly, evokes a sense of place and time through describing household details.

**Kazuo Ishiguro** (1954– )

## from Remains of the Day (1989)

Perhaps "Mursden" will ring a bell for you, as it did for me upon my first spotting it on the road atlas yesterday. In fact, I must say I was tempted to make a slight detour from my planned route just to see the village. Mursden, Somerset, was where the firm of Giffen and Co. was once situated, and it was to Mursden one was required to dispatch one's order for a supply of Giffen's dark candles of polish, "to be flaked, mixed into wax and applied by hand." For some time, Giffen's was undoubtedly the finest silver polish available, and it was only the appearance of new chemical substances on the market shortly before the war that caused the demand for this impressive product to decline.

As I remember, Giffen's appeared at the beginning of the twenties, and I am sure I am not alone in closely associating its emergence with that change of mood within our profession—that change which came to push the polishing of silver to the position of central importance it still by and large maintains today. This shift was, I believe, like so many other major shifts around this period, a generational matter; it was during these years that our generation of butlers "came of age," and figures like Mr. Marshall, in particular, played a crucial part in making silver-polishing so central. This is not to suggest, of course, that the polishing of silver—particularly those items that would appear at table—was not always regarded a serious duty. But it would not be unfair to suggest that many butlers of, say, my father's generation did not consider the matter such a key one, and this is evidenced by the fact that in those days, the butler of a household rarely supervised the polishing of silver directly, being content to leave it to, say, the under-butler's whims, carrying out inspections only intermittently. It was Mr. Marshall, it is generally agreed, who was the first to recognize the full significance of silver—namely, that no other objects in the house were likely to come under such intimate scrutiny from outsiders as was silver during a meal, and as such, it served as a public index of a house's standards. And Mr. Marshall it was who first caused stupefaction amongst ladies and gentlemen visiting Charleville House with displays of silver polished to previously unimagined standards. Very soon, naturally, butlers up and down the country, under pressure from their employers, were focusing their minds on the question of silver-polishing. There quickly sprang up, I recall, various butlers, each claiming to have discovered methods by which they could surpass Mr. Marshall—methods they made a great show of keeping secret, as though they were French chefs guarding their recipes. But I am confident—as I was then—that the sorts of elaborate and mysterious processes performed by someone like Mr. Jack Neighbours had little or no discernible effect on the end result. As far as I was concerned, it was a simple enough matter: one used good polish, and one supervised closely. Giffen's was the polish ordered by all discerning butlers of the time, and if this product was used correctly, one had no fear of one's silver being second best to anybody's.

I am glad to be able to recall numerous occasions when the silver at Darlington Hall had a pleasing impact upon observers. For instance, I recall Lady Astor remarking, not without a certain bitterness, that our silver "was probably unrivalled." I recall also watching Mr. George Bernard Shaw, the renowned playwright, at dinner one evening, examining closely the dessert spoon before him, holding it up to the light and comparing its surface to that of a nearby platter, quite oblivious to the company around him. ■

The claim that something as mundane as silver polish might be as significant as our narrator suggests would seem preposterous until we see how much this particular product had an impact upon the work that Stevens did. Inspired by an obscure place-name that is familiar to him only from its association with a household product, Stevens tells us much about a time and a social condition that is unfamiliar to us. The idea that butlers might share the social pretensions of their master, the fact that there was competition among household staffs, and the possibility that it might play out in the glow of silver all help put us into another world. That world becomes more grounded in reality through Stevens's reflections upon a specific consumer product.

### Making Connections

In Chapter 4, we considered point of view. In this passage from *Remains of the Day*, Ishiguro develops a distinct point of view through the voice of his narrator. He uses Stevens's lengthy reflections on silver polish to create for us a certain view of class and propriety. We see the setting from the perspective of the butler, and we understand that what Stevens reports is controlled by his years of service to the upper class.

This element of setting also contributes to our understanding of the delicate psychological state that Mr. Stevens is in throughout his journey. The imaginative "detour" he takes to Mursden is clearly motivated by his need to find a stable reference point. Stevens's car trip from one part of England to another moves him far from his sense of home. Coming upon a town associated with something he knows well helps him maintain some sense of comfort and confidence in an unfamiliar place. Reflecting so much on this particular commercial product makes him feel that he has in fact been connected to this new, wider world—even if he hasn't *lived* in that world.

Stevens's silver polish is real enough, but it's hardly familiar to us. The fact that we don't know anything about the product contributes to our sense that the world he inhabits is passing. When a product mentioned or shown in a narrative *is* familiar to us, we may grow suspicious: we might dismiss a scene that includes a brand-name item as mere product placement—an advertisement embedded in the work. Although we are often right to be cynical (corporations routinely pay to have their products show up in movies, for example), we should not fail to see how everyday products can be integrated meaningfully into a narrative and may contribute significantly to the way setting functions. Movies illustrate the point nicely. For example, think of the ways familiar items scattered over a tabletop might function in relation to a larger action within a film. In a horror movie, the familiarity might help us identify with the world presented and therefore make impending disasters feel more threatening. In a domestic drama, we might define our relation to characters through the items on the tabletop: a can of Mountain

Dew would say one thing, an open bottle of Jack Daniels another, and a Perrier still another. If a character in a comedy pulls a shiny, late-model Mercedes SUV into a McDonald's drive-thru and orders a Diet Coke, Big Mac, and fries—supersized—we'll pick up a general satiric comment on contemporary American culture. If a character in a detective story parks his 1962 Chevy Impala in front of a Foster's Freeze (a California chain particularly popular in the early days of fast food), we'll be located in a very specific *milieu*—a French word that literally means "center" or "middle" and is used to designate particular social, temporal, and physical surroundings.

*Mise-en-scène* (another French term) suggests what is quite literally put into the scene. It originally referred to the staging of plays: the arrangement and inclusion of furniture, backdrops, stray items, and props that make up the environment within which characters act. In a similar fashion, film critics use the term *mise-en-scène* to describe what is captured within a shot. The concept applies to any constructed work of art that places objects in a scene. It is useful to remember that details of setting are selected, framed, and foregrounded with a purpose in mind. Objects don't just happen to be part of a setting.

## IMAGINARY PLACES

Art is always about bringing imagination to life. So far, we've treated setting in terms of how artists lull us into accepting a setting as real—as identifying it as a place and time we can recognize and relate to. On some occasions, setting functions much differently. In Edgar Allan Poe's "Ulalume—a Ballad," we quickly get lost in both time and space. Even the place-names we have are confusing: "It was hard by the dim lake of Auber, / In the misty mid region of Weir." You can scan a map very closely and not find Auber or Weir. Poe hasn't consulted an atlas, for he doesn't so much want to identify his setting as to use setting to evoke a sensation. Auber and Weir are the names of two landscape painters of the period. Poe is not asking us to accept the reality of these places; he is asking that we associate his poem with feelings we might have in relation to other artistic works. Here, as is often the case in gothic pieces, **atmosphere** (feelings evoked in the reader through setting) prevails over concrete matters of time and space. Poe's setting radically disconnects us from everyday life.

Many other works seek to create through setting an interplay between the real and the fanciful. This problem becomes interesting in the directions that a playwright gives to describe the setting of a play. Unlike fiction, in which the entire setting appears in the text of the story, the play provides only the dialogue. To produce a play, set designers, who follow the instructions the playwright gives in the introduction to the play, will build the actual stages on which the actors will perform. They make the imaginary setting described in the printed play into some realized place. In *The Glass Menagerie*, Tennessee Williams describes specific realistic features of the Wingfield apartment, where the play takes place, including a fire escape that is a part of the set. But that detail, which is a rather straightforward instruction for a set designer, is interesting to Williams because it is "*a structure whose name is a touch of accidental poetic truth, for all of these huge buildings are always burning with the slow and implacable fires of human desperation.*" He describes a real object that a stage carpenter might build as he shows that his interest is in the meaning that he finds in that object. He sets the action in a specific, real place, but his explanation is of its symbolic value rather than of its real details. To describe the setting, he insists that this play is set in "*memory and is therefore nonrealistic. Memory takes a lot of poetic license. It omits some details, others are exaggerated, according to the emotional value of the articles it touches, for memory is seated predominantly in the heart. The interior is therefore rather dim and poetic.*" *Dim* is an adjective that is instructive for those who try to translate these directions into a real stage; *poetic* is a bit more problematic and open to a far greater range of possible meanings. This playwright emphasizes the imaginary nature of the real place that is to be created on the stage.

Movies again may serve to illustrate the importance of setting. The level of planning that goes into each frame of film (and every aspect of setting) becomes clear when we look at the storyboards that directors draw long before they begin to shoot a film. Because filming requires so many artists working together, the director will plan out each shot in advance. To tell the story, the director determines where the action will take place and what camera angles will be necessary to track that action. Looking at the storyboards helps us appreciate the tremendous planning and work that often goes into creating everything we see. Initial storyboards quite literally sketch the basic elements of a setting. By the time that we see the final product, the production team has fleshed out that sketch to give it exactly the desired look and feel.

## Experiencing Film through Setting

The following sequence includes a detailed sketch from the storyboards and the corresponding shot from two scenes of Jean-Pierre Jeunet's *Amélie* (2001). Jeunet is known to be one of the most conscientious planners in the film business; these sequences demonstrate that planning a film consists of far more than just writing dialogue. Look at the director's evolving ideas

Storyboards and film stills from *Amélie* (2001)

about the angles from which we see the characters. Notice that the director has an idea of how the details of the set should emphasize the action. As you look at the details of each shot, describe the setting. When does the action take place? What sorts of places are these? How do the details that we see here suggest a set of larger details that we cannot see?

*Amélie* is a film that creates a distinct world that is real in all of its details but does not quite feel like any real world we know. Even in these two shots, one can see something of this effect. The yellow quality of the lighting suggests that the scenes are set in some past time. The serious girl who is examining the stuffed monster is working in an environment that helps emphasize her young professionalism. The woman sits in a bath that is elegant enough to have come out of the latest design catalogue, and the careful arrangement of light and flowers is at odds with her ordinary appearance. Jeunet seems to want us to look at the world with a fresh perspective—to observe subtle beauties that are somehow obscured by their familiarity. The little things that don't quite mesh catch our attention and make us see in unaccustomed ways.

Jeunet's sort of visual playfulness is pressed to a further extreme in *Babe: Pig in the City* (1998). Director George Miller and his team create a city skyline for Babe to look out upon that is a composite of the world's most famous cities. The setting here is a wildly inventive mixture/blending of images that are simultaneously familiar and disorienting. Take a look at the still from the film, and try to identify as many famous structures as you

*Babe: Pig in the City* (1998)

can. What have the set designers done to make the buildings fit together in this particular cityscape? What sort of effect does this cityscape achieve? To what extent does it seem real? Where does the fantastic aspect begin? Why would the filmmakers favor a composite skyline over a real one?

Also consider the effect on the audience of framing the shot with the back of Babe's (the pig's) head looking out at the city. The main character is in the position (along with the audience) of taking it all in.

**Making Connections**

Look back to the Friedrich paintings in Chapter 4 (p. 60). It may seem strange to set this movie still in comparison to famous nineteenth-century paintings, but Miller employs a similar technique in *Babe: Pig in the City*. Setting is felt not only as a place but as a particular character's experience of place. The audience joins in that experience by looking, in effect, over the shoulder of the character. Setting isn't just background.

---

### A Note to Student Writers: Paying Attention to Details

The first step to writing about setting is to notice details. As you read, don't focus just on the action. Look around the characters to see where they are standing, what is in the background, and what objects they are holding as the action goes on around them. Your goal is to freeze the frame of the narrative and to compile lists of the surrounding details. As you develop your thoughts about setting, you must do something with that list. It is never enough just to list, but as you start to discuss a detail or two that you find particularly interesting, you will probably begin to see connections between that detail and other details of the setting. Ask yourself which details are most significant, explain why, and justify your rankings. Notice how these details have been presented, and think about how they contribute to the action that you were focused on before you began to focus closely on setting. When you write about setting, you will quickly discover that the setting is significant precisely because of the insight that it gives you about character or plot or some other element of the story. None of these elements exist in isolation, but the exercise of noticing setting helps a reader pay attention to details of all sorts.

---

## MODELING CRITICAL ANALYSIS: ROBERT BROWNING, MY LAST DUCHESS

Robert Browning's "My Last Duchess" (p. 76) is a **dramatic monologue**—that is, a poem in which a single speaker addresses an audience within a dramatic situation. We can start by thinking here of setting in specifically theatrical terms. To imagine in our mind's eye how Browning sets his stage, we need a chair that is positioned in front of the painting. And of course, we need the painting as well as the drawn curtain to the side of it. We also need some objects of art about the room to indicate the material grandeur of the place and a stairwell that suggests the two are in private quarters above the "company" on the main floor, who likely await news of the negotiation. This need not be a very elaborately set stage, but each item and its placement are important.

Once the scene is set, some interpretive possibilities become clearer. For example, it's possible we can learn something of the power relationship between the duke and the envoy by the position of the chair. Note that the duke seems to orchestrate things throughout. He moves the envoy in position in front of the painting and asks (directs?) him to sit and look carefully. The curtain is normally drawn, so it would seem the duke has a deliberate purpose in placing the envoy before his "last Duchess." Once seated, the duke recounts her story and her fate. She displeased him; she is dead. Once the duchess's story is told, the duke asks the envoy to rise from the chair. He makes his claim on a generous dowry from the prospective duchess's family. He is ready to return to the company. And as he invites (orders?) the envoy to go downstairs with him, he calls attention to a statue that depicts Neptune "Taming a sea-horse." Through that statue, Browning underscores the duke's obsession with control evident from the very start in the way he positioned the chair to direct the envoy's attention.

The specifically dramatic setting of "My Last Duchess" functions as part of the whole action, but it is not the only setting Browning employs. The duke's speech, in effect, also moves us offstage and conjures images of very different places. He recalls the duchess outdoors in an orchard relating to people other than the duke. We see her riding a mule around the terrace. The setting in which the meeting between the duke and envoy occurs grows still colder when contrasted to the vivacity of a life that was not bound by the walls of his house.

## Using Setting to Focus Writing and Discussion

- Collect the details that the author offers about the setting. In any constructed world, whether that world is on film or in text, every detail of setting has been created by the artist. Look at the details that we might think of as mundane or insignificant. How do these relate to the rest of the work?

- Where does the author describe the setting? Is it all in one place or dispersed throughout the text?

- Whose voice gives us this setting? In what ways is this fact significant?

- Which does the author describe first, the setting or the character? In what ways does the description of one influence the description of the other?

- To what extent does the setting determine how the characters act or think?
- To what extent is there some contrast, or even conflict, between the characters in the text and the setting that they occupy?
- If there are different settings within the work, how are these differences articulated, and how do the different settings play different roles in the text?
- In what way does the setting help establish a tone in this work?

# Rhythm, Pace, and Rhyme

## How Do Sounds Move?

Usually, when we think of rhythm, we think first of music. It's easy to understand why. We take in and express rhythms physically. We hear; we feel; we dance. Artists and critics together have created a rich technical language to analyze, describe, and appreciate the sensations that music inspires. We can speak of a bass line as what establishes something for all the other players to follow (clumsy dancers sometimes move to a song's melody or tune and disregard the deeper rhythms that melody is built upon). Rhythm is the pulse that undergirds everything; if the pulse grows faint, the entire composition can become vague or listless. If the pulse becomes irregular, the composition can become confusing, disturbing, challenging, annoying, or even comedic.

Many terms rooted in the study of music (*counterpoint/contrapuntal, amplification, cadence, measure, motif*, and so on) carry over easily to literary study—especially to the study of poetry. Poetry has always been music's close relative. And it is certainly true that poets attend strictly to lines (the way every word is sounded in every line and every line is arranged on every page) in a way that doesn't necessarily concern novelists, essayists, filmmakers, or most dramatists. But that said, it's also clear that poets aren't the only artists who care about rhythm. For the pulse that constitutes rhythm isn't something felt only in music and poetry—or experienced exclusively through sound. Even the word *pulse* tells us something: the beating of our hearts is the ultimate rhythmic touchstone. It shouldn't be surprising that a quality so basic to our very existence is accessed as well as expressed in a variety of ways; we hear, see, and feel rhythms.

In this chapter, we consider rhythm in the broadest—and most liberating—sense of the word. We think of rhythm along with related elements of sound, such as the speed or pace of delivery. We also consider distinct qualities of sound, such as rhyme in its various forms, and press further still to address visual and filmic rhythm. Such an approach suggests ways to open up the word *rhythm* and understand more fully how deeply rhythm infuses any kind of writing—not just poetry. This approach also encourages a flexible use of a technical, critical vocabulary without diminishing the precision of that vocabulary. Putting all of these elements in a larger context demonstrates how even the most highly specialized point of focus (for example, the metrical analysis of a poem) relates to vital critical concerns that cross familiar boundaries. We start by crossing a boundary that is often strongly marked: the one that separates sound from sight.

## FILMIC RHYTHM

Vladimir Nabokov has said that a good critic reads with his backbone. T. S. Eliot once noted that great art is felt before it is understood. Emily Dickinson was perhaps getting at the same thing when she said that she didn't know how to define "poetry" but knew a poem when she felt it take off the top of her head. These kinds of physical responses register a fine appreciation for rhythm. They also mark what for some people characterizes an essential dimension of the filmgoing experience. We take in the sensory impressions of film at an extraordinarily rapid pace—not too rapidly to process through our backbones but much too fast to immediately sort out intellectually. We know a film has an impact well before we appreciate exactly what that impact involves or how it was achieved. Accounting for the feeling, as noted previously, is the job of the critic. And this process of accounting through discussion and writing can send us back to the film (or other films) more receptive, more alert, and more alive to film's possibilities.

In a film, the illusion of movement is created by running a series of still frames rapidly by a viewer: movies are moving pictures. The component of film beyond the individual **frame** is the **shot**—a single length of film that communicates a continuous action on the screen. This length of film can, of course, be cut at any frame (that is, it can be a brief glimpse or a view that unfolds over many minutes). The joining/splicing (as well as the arranging, organizing) of shots is a function of **editing** (see a more complete discussion in Chapter 9). The relationship among shots (among varying lengths of film/varying lengths of time that pass from one shot to another) creates a rhythmic sense that can convey extraordinary depth of feeling.

It's important here to distinguish pace from rhythm. **Pace** indicates the relative speed of an unfolding action or the variety of actions that unfold within a defined length of time. We might speak of a story or film as fast or slow paced based upon the number of incidents that are packed into our reading or viewing experience. Whereas pace involves relatively simple standards of fast or slow narratives, **filmic rhythm** involves *patterns* of movement, composition, and sound. **Shot analysis** is a means to comprehend how a film (or section of film) communicates meaning and power. In shot analysis, one breaks a film down and assesses the relationship of shot to shot, the rhythms that are created, and the effects of the whole. Although such analysis ultimately involves more than simply measuring the length of each shot, that measurement is important in understanding filmic rhythm.

## Experiencing Film through Rhythm

If you've seen the popular film classic *Jaws* (1975), there is a good chance you remember the opening scene very well. That opening demonstrates Steven Spielberg's command of a film's rhythm.

Students off for summer vacations are partying at the beach after dark—and the party is at the sit-around-the-fire, drink-a-little-beer stage. Spielberg opens with a patient shot that slowly pans across the scene and pauses only to center us on one character—a young man who gazes across at a girl. A few brief shots move us back and forth between the boy and the girl who has

*Jaws* (1975)

caught his eye. Spielberg continues to cut fairly quickly, but in an evenly spaced way, between shots of the boy and of the girl as they break from the group and run along the beach, undressing as they run. The lines of dialogue, if read separately from the images, convey nothing beyond the most minimal exposition of character and action:

SCENE:  *Beach*
CASSIDY:  What's your name again?
CHRISSIE:  Chrissie!
CASSIDY:  Where are we going?
CHRISSIE:  Swimming!
CASSIDY:  Slow up, slow down! I'm not drunk! Slow down! Wait I'm com-
ing! I'm coming! I'm definitely coming! Wait, slow up! I can swim—
just can't walk or dress myself.
CHRISSIE:  Come on in the water!
CASSIDY:  Take it easy. Take it easy.
CHRISSIE:  Oh! God help me! God! Argh! God help!
CASSIDY:  I'm coming ... I'm coming.
CHRISSIE:  It hurts! It hurts! Oh my god! God help me! God please help!

This hardly seems inspired writing, but of course, words alone don't make up the movie. The whole *viewing* experience is terrifying. We see the unfortunate girl get to the water. The boy stumbles, falls on the sand, and goes to sleep. Spielberg again slows the exchange from shot to shot once the boy is out of the action; now the movement builds **tension** as Spielberg moves from a shot of the girl at the surface enjoying the water to a shot of equal length taken beneath from the perspective of the shark hunting for food, to a single brief shot of the boy asleep on the beach. Once the shark attacks, Spielberg holds the shot on the girl at the surface for what seems an excruciatingly long time. He wants to establish her (and our) helplessness in relation to this creature. He does so not by showing the creature itself but by showing what can happen to the people who enter its realm. After the girl is finally pulled under and quiet returns, Spielberg returns to a shot of the boy: silent, unknowing, oblivious to the world and all its dangers. The horror is established in context of the sleepy vacation town and the pleasures of beach life. The opposition finds expression largely through Spielberg's mastery of film's rhythmic possibilities.

## POETIC RHYTHM

Shot analysis in film involves closely observing and describing relationships among shots that function thematically and emotionally. It is useful to think of metrical analysis of poetry as in some fundamental way related to shot analysis (or the other way around). A filmmaker arranges and organizes a series of shots into a whole that expresses a pattern of movement— moments of stress and of relief. A poet arranges and organizes a pattern of sounds that reinforce or create meaning, that suggest feeling behind meaning.

In the analysis of poetry, **meter** refers to a regular (therefore discernible) rhythmic pattern of sounds that is charted line by line; in the analysis of film, a pattern of unfolding action is charted shot by shot. At some point, the analogy between analysis of film and the analysis of a poem's meter breaks down (as analogies usually do), but we can think of the poetic foot as the element that most closely corresponds to the frame (in that it is the smallest building block). A poetic **foot** is the combination of one stressed syllable with one or more unstressed syllables that constitutes the recurring rhythmic unit within the larger pattern of a poetic line or of any given stretch of text.

There are five standard units (feet) in English poetry:

- The **iambic** foot (the most common in English poetry) consists of two syllables, the first unstressed and the second stressed (toDAY, but WHY? inSPIRE). Any pattern that moves from unstressed to stressed syllables is sometimes called **rising meter**.

- The **trochaic** foot consists of two syllables, the first stressed and the second unstressed (TRAVel, STANdard). Any pattern that moves from stressed to unstressed syllables is sometimes called **falling meter**.

- The **anapestic** foot consists of three syllables, the first two unstressed and the third stressed (anyMORE).

- The **dactylic** foot consists of three syllables, the first stressed and the last two unstressed (FInally).

- The **spondee**, which consists of two consecutive stressed syllables (HOT DOG, OH MY!), and the **pyrrhic**, which consists of two consecutive unstressed syllables, are considered **variants** (or **substitutions**) of standard feet. That is, a spondee or a pyrrhic can break a prevailing pattern, but spondees and pyrrhics cannot make up a pattern (a line cannot be composed of all stressed syllables or all unstressed syllables, because one quality can be defined only in relation to the other).

A **metric line** of poetry is measured by the number of feet that it comprises. The most common lines are **trimeter** (three feet), **tetrameter** (four feet), **pentameter** (five feet), and **hexameter** (six feet).

If we extend our analogy to film a bit further here, we can think of a metric line of poetry as a shot; for example, a line of **iambic pentameter** (the prevailing rhythm of much English poetry—"oh, GENtle FAUstus, LEAVE this DAMnéd ART"—and a natural speech pattern) could be seen as analogous to a single length of film, a shot. Poetic lines may be organized in still larger patterns by rhyme schemes (arrangements of rhyming words), line length, or more complex metrical forms. These larger patterns are called **stanzas**—a verse paragraph. Lines make up stanzas much as shots in a film can be grouped as scenes. The following examples are common stanzaic forms:

- **couplet** (two lines)
  Early to bed and early to rise
  Makes a man healthy, wealthy, and wise.

- **tercet** (three lines)
  The winged seeds, where they lie cold and low,
  Each like a corpse within its grave, until
  Thine azure sister of the Spring shall blow.
                    —Percy Bysshe Shelley, from "Ode to the West Wind"

- **quatrain** (four lines)
  When the voices of children are heard on the green
  And laughing is heard on the hill,
  My heart is at rest within my breast
  And every thing else is still
                    —William Blake, from "Nurse's Song"

There are, of course, other stanzaic forms, most notably the **octave** (eight lines) and **sestet** (six lines). (See discussion of the sonnet in Chapter 8.)

## Experiencing Literature through Rhythm

Rhythm in much poetry in English must be charted by attention to both syllables and stresses. Such attention to the metrical shape of a poem is called **prosody**. To **scan** a line of poetry or any text is to define the rhythmic pattern. Such analysis, or **scansion**, must remain fairly rough (in this book, stressed syllables are shown in all uppercase letters, and unstressed syllables, in all lowercase letters). Syllables are, after all, pronounced with a wide and flexible range of emphases; marking every syllable either stressed (´) or unstressed (˘) cannot register that range with great precision. But judicious metrical analysis can help us describe what rhythms we hear and may deepen our appreciation of the writer's craft. Poets can achieve emphasis through meter; they can make us notice a key word or idea. And as the two following works make clear, a poet may even fuse meter and meaning.

Herman Melville (1819–1891)

# The Maldive Shark (1888)

About the Shark, phlegmatical one,
Pale sot of the Maldive sea,
The sleek little pilot-fish, azure and slim,
How alert in attendance be.
From his saw-pit of mouth, from his charnel of maw,                5
They have nothing of harm to dread,
But liquidly glide on his ghastly flank
Or before his Gorgonian head;
Or lurk in the port of serrated teeth
In white triple tiers of glittering gates,                        10
And there find a haven when peril's abroad,
An asylum in jaws of the Fates!
They are friends; and friendly they guide him to prey,
Yet never partake of the treat—
Eyes and brains to the dotard lethargic and dull,                 15
Pale ravener of horrible meat.

William Blake (1757–1827)

# Nurse's Song (1789)

When the voices of children are heard on the green
And laughing is heard on the hill,
My heart is at rest within my breast
And every thing else is still

Then come home my children, the sun is gone down           5
And the dews of the night arise
Come come leave off play, and let us away
Till the morning appears in the skies

No no let us play, for it is yet day
And we cannot go to sleep                                  10
Besides in the sky, the little birds fly
And the hills are all covered with sheep

"Well well go & play till the light fades away
And then go home to bed

The little ones leaped & shouted & laugh'd                                    15
And all the hills ecchoed

Read "The Maldive Shark" and "Nurse's Song" aloud several times, and
you'll begin to hear a lilting, rather fast meter. It is a rhythm like one you
have probably heard before in poems for children or in comic verse. The
strongly marked rhythm results from the repeated use of trisyllabic feet. In
the first line of "Nurse's Song" anapests prevail:

When the voices of children are heard on the green ...
(when the VOIces of CHILdren are HEARD on the GREEN)

In "The Maldive Shark," the opening line closes with an anapest, and
anapests and dactyls generally prevail throughout:

About the Shark, phlegmatical one ...
(aBOUT the SHARK, phlegMATical ONE)

In Blake's poem, the anapests seem clearly appropriate: "Nurse's Song" is (at
least on the surface) a song of innocence. The poem centers mainly on the
power of children's play and joy to transform the spirit of the speaker. But
note how Melville uses rhythms similar to Blake's to create a troubling
thematic undercurrent. The trisyllabic feet in "The Maldive Shark" do not
function to reinforce themes like innocence, childhood, and peace. The
lilting quality of Melville's meter starkly contrasts with images of death
and blunt power associated with the shark. The apparent split between
form and content suggests that things are not what they seem. A similar,
complex mixed signal is evident in the construction of the poem's first
sentence. The first *line* seems to announce the shark as subject of the poem
(this is a poem "about the shark"), but if we pay attention to the whole
sentence, which ends with line 4, we note the focus has shifted the shark isn't
even the grammatical subject. The poem actually centers on the "pilot-fish"
that swim "about the shark."

  The sleek, intelligent, quick, alert, attractive pilot-fish are set before us
in the rhythm of the poem; visual images of the heavy, dumb, slow, uncaring,
repellent shark move powerfully through this rhythm. The implication of
this contrast is that what we sometimes assume to be good or innocent often
operates together with what we see as evil or corrupt. In other words, what
seems not to go together goes together all too well. The pilot-fish lead the
shark to its prey so that they may be safe from its hunger. Melville's play with
meter challenges conventional and comfortable notions of morality and
order. His poem helps us understand that meter is not mere decoration.

  Melville and Blake make meter central to the meaning of these two
poems, but meter can be worth attending to even when it is not central to

the work. Note, for example, how Stephen Crane's opening sentences from his short story "A Bride Comes to Yellow Sky" rhythmically convey a sense of a train's relentless movement westward (and with the train's movement, the rolling influence of an entire culture):

The Great Pullman was whirling onward with such dignity of motion that a glance from the window seemed simply to prove that the plains of Texas were pouring eastward. Vast flats of green grass, dull-hued spaces of mesquite and cactus, little groups of frame houses, woods of light and tender trees, all were sweeping into the east, sweeping over the horizon, a precipice. ■

Interpretations of a line's rhythm are subject to debate—as is any kind of interpretation—but a good case could be made here for breaking the last sentence into poetic lines for the sake of directing an oral reading:

Vast flats of green grass,
Dull-hued spaces of mesquite and cactus,
Little groups of frame houses,
Woods of light and tender trees
All were sweeping into the east,
Sweeping over the horizon,
A precipice.

The opening line employs spondees; and trochees, not the more common iambs, prevail in the next three lines. It seems that Crane is both describing and embodying the train's movement along the tracks west. The fourth and fifth lines, though, break that pattern midline. But it's not just a shift to iambs in line 5; rather, in the middle of line 6 and the start of the final line, Crane substitutes pyrrhic feet (the two consecutive unstressed syllables) or perhaps anapests (two unaccented syllables followed by an accented syllable). The effect of the unaccented syllables run together is that his sentence gathers speed as it moves to the precipice. The old West, as we'll come to learn in the story, is falling over that precipice into a more "civilized" (more domesticated, tame) East.

Granted, these changes would fundamentally alter what Crane wrote. Crane didn't arrange his lines as we have. And his story could not reward from beginning to end the attention to rhythmic patterns we've devoted to this sentence. Still, it is worth remembering that Crane was a poet as well as a short story writer and journalist, and it's plain that in this passage he creates effects partly through his attention to both sound and sense. So the altering of the text is not an attempt to make it something it is not; rather, it is a way of revealing what we hear and feel, but imperfectly appreciate. From the perspective of a critical writer, attention to meter in a text may yield fresh insights about how that text achieves meaning and power.

## THE RHYTHM OF PAUSES

Scansion can reveal much of a writer's art, but obviously there are rhythmic effects that are not accounted for by marking poetic feet (just as shot analysis alone cannot account for all aspects of a film's rhythm). Artists in various mediums manage pauses of various weights to affect interpretation; much meaning or emotion can be conveyed by pauses (or by the lack of pause). An artist can hold an audience's/reader's attention on a word or image or make the audience/reader wait just a moment before delivering something profound.

Caesura is a pause *within* a line of poetry (sometimes called an **extra-metrical effect** and charted by a double slash [//] between words at the point of pause). A line that comes to a full stop at the end is **end-stopped**. A line that "strides over" into the next line without a pause is **enjambed** (the poet has employed **enjambment**). Although caesura, end stop, and enjambment are terms that apply specifically to the analysis of poetry (how pauses are managed within and between lines), many powerful effects in any piece of writing or film result from the careful management of pauses. A pause at the right time can anticipate a sudden turn; it can allow one to absorb an emotional effect; it can draw attention to what precedes or follows. It can accentuate a rhythmic quality of a text or make us keenly aware of rhythm by breaking the pattern (if something is too regular, we may hardly notice).

### Experiencing Literature through Rhythm

Samuel Johnson employs a carefully measured rhythm for thematic purpose. "On the Death of Dr. Robert Levet" is about a man who had a long and well-used life. Levet cut no great figure in terms of what the world values, but Johnson sees Levet's modest accomplishments as deserving real praise. In the context of the hard surrounding world (Johnson casts all humankind as workers in "Hope's delusive mine"), Levet toils faithfully in service to those who seek his help. Death, in Johnson's view, ends that difficult service and brings the aged Levet to his Maker.

**Samuel Johnson** (1709–1784)

# On the Death of Dr. Robert Levet (1783)

Condemn'd to Hope's delusive mine,
    As on we toil from day to day,
By sudden blasts, or slow decline,
    Our social comforts drop away.

Well tried through many a varying year,                          5
    See Levet to the grave descend;
Officious, innocent, sincere,
    Of every friendless name the friend.

Yet still he fills affection's eye,
    Obscurely wise and coarsely kind;                           10
Nor, letter'd Arrogance, deny
    Thy praise to merit unrefined.

When fainting nature called for aid,
    And hovering death prepared the blow,
His vigorous remedy display'd                                   15
    The power of art without the show.

In misery's darkest cavern known,
    His useful care was ever nigh,
Where hopeless Anguish pour'd his groan,
    And lonely want retired to die.                             20

No summons mock'd by chill delay,
    No petty gain disdained by pride,
The modest wants of every day
    The toil of every day supplied.

His virtues walked their narrow round,                          25
    Nor made a pause, nor left a void;
And sure the eternal Master found
    The single talent well employ'd.

The busy day, the peaceful night,
    Unfelt, uncounted, glided by;                               30

His frame was firm, his powers were bright,
  Though now his eightieth year was nigh.

Then with no throbbing fiery pain,
  No cold gradations of decay,
Death broke at once the vital chain,                                 35
  And freed his soul the nearest way.

The feeling in this poem is not narrowly for Levet's death. Indeed, Levet's sudden death is cast as a release. Whatever hardship one faces in this life, Johnson suggests, can be placed in a broader and well-ordered picture. The measured pauses within the lines enforce this sense of balance. Whatever our lot on earth, Johnson seems to say, God has structured a coherent master plan within which we can work. Note the clear midline pauses in lines 3 ("By sudden blasts, // or slow decline"), 10 ("Obscurely wise // and coarsely kind"), 26, 29, and 31. Many other lines convey a much less distinct, but still arguably evident, pause in the middle of the line. Consider, for example, lines 2 ("As on we toil // from day to day"), 14 ("And hovering death // prepared the blow") 16, 20, and 28. When caesuras do not so evenly divide a line in half, they still evenly divide the line, as in line 7 ("Officious, // innocent, // sincere") and 30 ("Unfelt, // uncounted, // glided by"). Johnson's phrasing suggests the steadiness he wishes to maintain in reflecting upon the life and death of his friend.

We could further note that Johnson maintains this steadiness through his management of the entire stanza. He gives us no metrical surprises, no pronounced breaks from the prevailing iambic tetrameter (a line of four iambic feet). He brings most lines to a full stop or end stop. Every quatrain (poetic paragraph of four lines) closes a complete thought and enforces a pronounced pause. The pace of the poem, the phrases so carefully balanced by caesuras, the structural clarity and consistency—all suggest a poet in command of his message and confident in his faith.

Ben Jonson feels no such emotional balance or spiritual assurance as he struggles to write about a very different sort of death. "On My First Son" expresses an intensely personal loss. Obviously, one's own seven-year-old child cannot serve as a point of reflection on a life well used and kindly ended—the kind of reflection that prevails in Samuel Johnson's tribute to his old friend Dr. Levet. The intense pain Ben Jonson feels cannot lead him to feel grateful that his son escaped pain by dying young. The grieving father is angry, confused, and hurt. Given such feelings, any measured, balanced, regular rhythm would seem strangely controlled. Not surprisingly, we do not get that steady rhythm.

**Ben Jonson** (1572–1637)

# On My First Son (1616)

Farewell, thou child of my right hand, and joy;
My sin was too much hope of thee, loved boy:
Seven years thou wert lent to me, and I thee pay,
Exacted by thy fate, on the just day.
O could I lose all father now! for why                                    5
Will man lament the state he should envy,
To have soon 'scaped world's and flesh's rage,
And, if no other misery, yet age?
Rest in soft peace, and asked, say, "Here doth lie
Ben Jonson his best piece of poetry."                                    10
For whose sake henceforth all his vows be such
As what he loves may never like too much.

Much of Jonson's unresolved emotional torment is conveyed by the sudden, irregularly placed caesuras (the pauses in this poem fall near the beginning or the end of several lines, but not in the middle). It is as if in the first four lines, the speaker makes a tentative, reluctant attempt to say good-bye. This attempt is broken by a rush of feeling that stalls just before the end of the fifth line. At that point, Jonson forces us to rush ahead without stop from the end of line 5 through line 6:

O could I lose all father now! // for why
Will man lament the state he should envy

The enjambment here suggests that emotions cannot be bound by the constraints of line. Again, rhythm relates to sense; it is part of the critic's job to help readers see that relationship.

---

## A Note to Student Writers: Commanding Attention

Clearly, pauses aren't the sole property of poets. Sentences, just like lines of poems, build and release tension in any number of ways. Good writers in any mode want to signal pace and emphasis for their readers. Readers need help sometimes in noticing what is really important. A carefully placed pause, a balanced series, an emphatic turn or break from a prevailing pattern—all can bring a point home. We suggest that you bring this insight into your own writing. You, like any writer, must find ways to make readers concentrate attention on the words that need or demand attention. One way of doing this (as mentioned before in other contexts) is to read your own work aloud periodically as you draft and revise. Reading aloud will help make you conscious of rhythmic effects in works of art and will lead you to appreciate how many of those effects play out in your own prose. We want you, in short, to be alert to how rhythmic effects are deeply part of almost any carefully constructed text—including the texts you construct.

## THE RHYTHM OF SOUNDS

The quality of sounds strongly influences the weight and stress we sense that fall on individual words. Sounds also influence the way we speak words in sequence—sounds of individual words influence the rhythm we feel arise from a group of words. And of course, sounds of individual words must be spoken and heard in relation to other words. People do not pronounce words in isolation (such tonelessness is for machines: consider the phonetic, word-by-word correctness of the mechanically generated voices you sometimes hear on phone message systems). We pronounce words in ways that mesh with how those words unfold in a line or a sentence as well as with how they balance, contrast with, or echo each other.

**Rhyme** serves as an especially powerful means of achieving such balance, contrast, or echo. **Full** or **perfect rhyme** consists of the similarity of sounds in accented vowels and any consonants that follow (*date, fate*). In a **masculine rhyme**, the stress is on the final syllable of the words (*clown, renown*). A **feminine rhyme** is one in which the final two syllables rhyme; the first rhyming syllable is stressed, and the final syllable is unstressed (*buckle, knuckle*). **Assonance** also consists of a similarity in vowel sounds, but the consonants that follow differ (*date, lake*). **Consonance** strikes a similarity in the sounds of the final stressed consonant; the preceding vowel differs (*date, rite*). Words that echo sounds in these ways are sometimes called **slant rhymes** or **off-rhymes**. **Alliteration** refers to the repetition of initial sounds in words (*date, dud*). All of these terms concern sounds, but rhyme generally refers to similar sounds that occur at corresponding places in a line of poetry. Assonance, consonance, and alliteration may be employed at various intervals throughout any given passage of poetry or prose. Rhymes in the middle of a line are called **internal rhymes**; those at the end of a line, **end rhymes**.

Rhyme is so strongly part of the way we voice a word that it sometimes overcomes other rhythmic signals and distorts the way we deliver a line. Think, for example, of the times you feel prompted to pause at the end of a rhymed line of poetry despite the syntactical demand to move forward. Small children will normally pause very heavily after every rhyme, and in a sense that tendency reflects a good impulse even if it is ultimately misguided. Of course, the sounds of words also have much to do with the rhythm and pace of a line. The running together of hard consonants will usually force readers to slow down; one simply can't perfectly pronounce passages full of *p* sounds without pausing and allowing each word to have some space. Other sounds glide together very easily and greatly speed rhythm. Alexander Pope's famous lines from his "Essay on Criticism" illustrate perfectly how slowness and speed can be suggested by sounds:

When Ajax strives some rock's vast weight to throw,
The line too labors, and the words move slow;
Not so when swift Camilla scours the plain,
Flies o'er the unbending corn, and skims along the main.

We also hear sounds differently depending on meaning and context. For example, one might think that the sibilants (*s* sounds) that dominate lines from Alfred, Lord Tennyson's "The Lotus Eaters" (1842) convey softness, easiness, sleepiness:

There is sweet music here that softer falls
Than petals from blown roses on the grass,
Or night-dews on still waters between walls
Of Shadowy granite, in a gleaming pass;
Music that gentlier on the spirit lies,
Than tired eyelids upon tired eyes;
Music that brings sweet sleep down from the blissful skies.

We can use the terms **euphony** (to describe pleasing, soothing sounds) and **cacophony** (to describe harsh, unpleasant sounds), but we do not hear the sounds as soothing purely because of the sounds themselves. There is nothing inherently soothing in the sound of the letter *s* (think of the hissing of a snake). Tennyson's meaning directs us to inflect these particular words with a particular languor. So this section ends with a warning: Avoid arguing a point from sound alone. Be sure that you are attentive to sound in relation to all the other evidence you gather to explain how a given work communicates.

### Making Connections

Sound and rhythm can have importance even when they have no apparent meaning. Consider, for example, how music functions in a film or a play. Even when you are absorbed by the action, the rhythmic unfolding of that action may be led by background music you don't consciously notice. Also, consider the way sounds and rhythms can serve as a kind of incantation—that is, sounds can weave a spell. Such atmospheric effects are (as discussed in Chapter 5) very important to gothic works.

## Experiencing Literature through Rhythm and Rhyme

As powerful as rhymes can be in the effect of the whole work, they may function in very subtle ways. In the following short poem, you probably will feel upon first reading the matter-of-fact finality of Randall Jarrell's closing line.


**Randall Jarrell** (1914–1965)

# The Death of the Ball Turret Gunner (1945)

From my mother's sleep I fell into the State,
And I hunched in its belly till my wet fur froze.
Six miles from earth, loosed from its dream of life,
I woke to black flak and the nightmare fighters.
When I died they washed me out of the turret with a hose.                    5


You might not notice, however, that the feeling is enforced by a rhyme: "hose" rhymes perfectly with "froze." Jarrell's poem does not have the metrical regularity that often leads us to anticipate a rhyme. Nor does the rhyme follow very closely: "froze" ends line 2; "hose" ends line 5. Yet this rather distant rhyme accounts in part for the sudden, forceful finish. The life of the gunner is absolutely over, and so is the poem; the rhyme accentuates the finish of both. It closes off this brief monologue.

Jarrell also employs internal rhymes (rhymes within the line instead of at the end of lines) and consonance to suggest the sensory assault of enemy gunfire that awakens the ball turret gunner to the nightmare of life: "woke to black flak." The sounds communicate experience as well as meaning; confusion and terror mark that experience. The hardness of the sounds in context of the meaning aggressively presses upon us as we read. The example here illustrates **onomatopoeia**—that is, the sounds of the words replicate the meaning they convey.

## Making Connections

Rhyme does more than accentuate rhythmic elements; rhyme can be a structuring device—a means to highlight a central meaning or problem (see the discussion of Millay's "I, Being Born a Woman and Distressed" [p. 150]). Robert Frost's "Fire and Ice" (p. 111) is tightly structured around three rhymes (A/B/A/A/B/C/B/C/B). The "A" rhymes set one side of an elemental opposition: fire and the emotion of desire. The "B" rhymes center around a feeling associated with "ice." The "C" rhymes identify that cold feeling: hate.

Frost's word choice (especially at the poem's finish) is also striking. *Suffice* hardly seems the word one would expect in wrapping up a thought about a power great enough to end the world. But the particular quality of hatred that Frost expresses needs to find expression in such a tightly limited, proper little word (for further discussion on word choice, see Chapter 11).

Robert Frost (1874–1963)

# Fire and Ice (1923)

Some say the world will end in fire,
Some say in ice.
From what I've tasted of desire
I hold with those who favor fire.
But if it had to perish twice,                                    5
I think I know enough of hate
To say that for destruction ice
Is also great
And would suffice.

## MODELING CRITICAL ANALYSIS: ROBERT BROWNING, MY LAST DUCHESS

Robert Browning's "My Last Duchess" (p. 76) reads very much like the one-way conversation Browning intends it to be. We hear a man, the duke, *speaking* to another man, the envoy. His delivery might be rather formal in places, but he is a duke after all—one with a "nine-hundred-years-old name." What most readers sense is the naturalness of his style.

Ralph Rader, a literary critic whose reading of this poem has influenced ours, suggests we should not be taken in by the duke's tone. Rader points to something very obvious that few people notice: this poem is written in rhymed couplets throughout. In fact, the rhymes are full or perfect end rhymes; the lines themselves are in iambic pentameter. Something must be amiss: How can we read as speech language that is so clearly crafted? How is it that anyone could read a poem and not notice that it is rhymed so regularly? Not notice that it is so carefully measured rhythmically?

One level of answers to such questions requires attention to Browning's technique. We don't pick up on the rhymes or the accentual/syllabic regularity of lines because Browning hides them. He employs caesuras at various points within the lines; he regularly enjambs lines; and he keeps the structure of his sentences (syntax) out of synch with the arrangement of his poetic lines. For example, notice that the full pause near the end of line 2 comes at the end of a sentence. The line, though, continues briefly after that pause and moves forward without a break into line 3, which then "strides over" into line 4. As a result, any good dramatic reading will not make us *hear* the end rhyme that is there if we *look* (*wall, call*).

So we are led to another question: Why should Browning bother to come up with perfect rhymes and then go to the trouble of making us *not* notice them? The answer, Rader suggests, is that Browning (the poet) wants readers to see how duplicitous the duke (the speaker) is. In other words, the duke only pretends to be casual and spontaneous. He only claims to be a man who has "no skill in speech." A careful reading of the poem—especially to rhythms and rhymes that are at once transparent and hidden—reveals a duke who knows exactly what message he wants to send to the envoy yet also knows not to send that message directly. To put it another way, Browning has built into the poem evidence of how crafty the duke is. And what is the duke's message? Rader argues that the duke wants to make it clear he expects the next wife to know exactly what is expected of her. He also wants everyone involved in the negotiation to know what the consequences of not meeting those expectations will be. Most readers see the duke as unintentionally revealing himself as cruel—indeed murderous. Rader looks to the rhythms and rhymes of Browning's poem to argue that the duke is in full, conscious control of his terrible message.

### Using Rhythm, Pace, and Rhyme to Focus Writing and Discussion

- To locate rhythms, we must look at individual words and at sentence structures within the text. What words or sounds are repeated within the text?
- What patterns govern these repetitions?
- What characteristics can we ascribe to the sounds of this text? Are they soothing? Harsh? How do these sounds correspond to the literal meaning of the text?
- Is there some contrast in rhythms? For instance, does the text set up a pattern and then break it? If so, what is the effect?
- What sentence patterns do we find in this work? Does the author use consistently short sentences? Long sentences? Any consistent variety?
- Are there different characters who speak with different rhythms in the text? How are these differences related to the role of the characters in the text?

# 7    Images

## How Do We Experience Sensations in a Written Text?

Whenever we set out to describe our experiences to others, we need to do more than recount actions. Life isn't bound merely by "what happens"; the distinct quality of sensory impressions lends substance, particularity, and emotion to events. Things we see, hear, feel, smell, or taste often serve as an index to our most important memories. Sometimes, a physical sensation *is* the memory. Yet it's also true that in the course of any given stretch of time, we can be unconscious of this most elemental truth. We move so quickly through a day that we sometimes don't pause to notice details. It's a common experience, for example, to drive for miles over familiar roads and then think, "Have we already passed Fairview?"

Artists work to make sure we don't pass through Fairview or any other place along the way without observing closely. They register sensory data in ways that make us alert to the physical substance of our experience. In many modest ways we're artists of our own lives. Our vacation pictures, for example, are fascinating to us because they help us pause over details of what we've seen. And they likely trigger memories of a special meal (a local fish caught fresh), a smell (crisp ocean air at daybreak), a sound (gulls squawking over breaking waves), or a touch (wet sand under bare feet). We edit our vacation pictures carefully so that we can more deeply absorb our experience and sensitize ourselves to possibilities that lie ahead in future trips. And we're likely to present our vacation pictures to others from a desire to help them share what we felt, not merely know what we did.

Our reading experience again is not so different from our life experience; the disciplined practice of paying attention to our senses yields much of value in life and art. The novelist Henry James advised that we all try to be someone "upon whom nothing is lost." James's standard may be too high, but all types of experience offer a richness of imagery that must be paused over, not merely "passed through." In this chapter, we'll consider how sensory images serve to intensify literary and, in turn, life experience.

## CREATING PICTURES WITH WORDS

It would be hard to overestimate the sheer volume of **visual images** in communication. Ironically, images of color and shape—of things seen—are so pervasive that they sometimes become almost invisible. A too common image may lose all force. A "red rose" or a "blue sky" can descend to the emptiness of advertising clichés like "golden brown french fries." Finding ways to make common descriptors convey an image vividly becomes a challenge that writers sometimes address consciously. Note how William Carlos Williams leads into the following poem by directly telling us that what we see—what we really see—counts for something, however mundane it may be.

**William Carlos Williams** (1883–1963)

# The Red Wheelbarrow (1923)

so much depends
upon

a red wheel
barrow

glazed with rain                                                5
water

beside the white
chickens.

We are drawn to see the red wheelbarrow here partly because we recognize in the simplicity of these images how much and how often we don't see what is plainly before us. Williams's opening line suggests that the physical act of seeing can become a worthy theme: "so much depends" upon what is before us in the immediate moment. Czeslaw Milosz also asks us to see, absorb, and reflect upon common sights. In "Watering Can" he suggests that images ground us in a concrete reality and help us hold tight against what can be threatening, debilitating abstractions.

## Czeslaw Milosz (1911–2004)

# Watering Can (Czeslaw Milosz and Robert Hass, trans; 1998)

Of a green color, standing in a shed alongside rakes and spades, it comes alive when it is filled with water from the pond, and an abundant shower pours from its nozzle, in an act, we feel it, of charity towards plants. It is not certain, however, that the watering can would have such a place in our memory, were it not for our training in noticing things. For, after all, we have been trained. Our painters do not often imitate the Dutch, who liked to paint still lifes, and yet photography contributes to our paying attention to detail and the cinema taught us that objects, once they appear on the screen, would participate in the actions of the characters and therefore should be noticed. There are also museums where canvases glorify not only human figures and landscapes but also a multitude of objects. The watering can has thus a good chance of occupying a sizable place in our imagination, and, who knows, perhaps precisely in this, in our clinging to distinctly delineated shapes, does our hope reside, of salvation from the turbulent waters of nothingness and chaos. ■

Milosz suggests that extremely close attention to the physical world that surrounds us is a responsibility no artist can afford to shirk. But what is involved in the powerful production and use of visual images? Why do some images work and others fail to convey anything vivid or substantial? Context is a partial answer to these questions. Artists find ways to frame images so that we focus our attention on them. "A red wheelbarrow" or a "watering can" doesn't automatically make for poetry. But Williams and Milosz make us pay attention. Williams structures his poem in a way that moves us patiently from image to image: "so much depends" not only on the red wheelbarrow but upon the linked clauses that constitute the poem's layered imagery. Milosz employs a common rhetorical strategy: after introducing his modest subject, he grants that it may not seem of much significance. But he quickly turns from that concession to place the watering can in relation to all physical things that we've been trained to notice by painters, filmmakers, photographers, and museum curators.

Milosz's point about attending to detail returns us to specific qualities of the individual image and leads to a yet fuller sense of how images work. It is worth thinking about how we see and communicate a sense of what we see. Digital photography has made us much more aware that a picture emerges from small units of shape and color, whether those units are specks of paint, pixels, or words. Those who sell us digital cameras have taught us that if we pay more to increase our camera's ability to record increasingly minute pixels, the clearer the resolution we can gain in larger and larger reproductions of our image. This paradox—the smaller the area where we are able to focus, the

These digital images illustrate the increasing clarity that comes with dense, numerous, and minute pixels.

Georges Seurat, Port-en-Bessin, *Entrance to the Harbor* (1888). Seurat was influenced by optical color theories that were current in the later nineteenth century. Upon very large canvases, he placed tiny brush strokes or points of color that would blend as they were seen from a distance.

more complete our view of a larger object—drives much of the literature that we read and should help us in our own writing.

Tiny details of shape, size, and color are the raw materials of powerfully realized experiences. In Alice Munro's short story "How I Met My Husband," the narrator remembers the simple pleasures of bathing in what is for her the grand home of her employers. Those pleasures are linked concretely to images of sight and touch.

The basin and the tub and the toilet were all pink, and there were glass doors with flamingoes painted on them, to shut off the tub. The light had a rosy cast and the mat sank under your feel like snow, except that it was warm. The mirror was three-way. With the mirror all steamed up and the air like a perfume cloud, from things I was allowed to use, I stood up on the side of the tub and admired myself naked, from three directions. ■

The intensity of the narrator's pleasure in her weekly bath is so great that she doesn't want to indulge it too often. An overload of such impressions might risk "making it less wonderful."

## Experiencing Literature through Imagery

We can, of course, question our dependence on visual images by considering how people may live intensely without them. In "Courtesy of the Blind," Wislawa Szymborska recognizes how difficult—even problematic—it may sometimes be to communicate what we see in words. Szymborska reflects on the visual images she is accustomed to use in order to connect with readers and to connect readers to the world. She displays a growing awareness of breakdowns between herself and others. In front of an audience of blind readers, she realizes how much of her work depends upon strategies that may often be naïve or misguided.

**Wislawa Szymborska** (1923– )

# The Courtesy of the Blind (Clare Cavanagh and Stanislaw Baranczak, trans; 2006)

A poet reads his lines to the blind.
He hadn't guessed that it would be so hard.
His voice trembles.
His hands shake.

He senses that every sentence 5
is put to the test of darkness.
He must muddle through alone,
without the colors or lights.

A treacherous endeavor
for his poems' stars, 10
dawn, rainbows, clouds, their neon lights, their moon,
for the fish so silvery thus far beneath the water,
and the hawk so high and quiet in the sky.

He reads—since it's too late to stop now—
about the boy in a yellow jacket on a green valley, 15
red roofs that can be counted in the valley,
the restless numbers on soccer players' shirts,
and the naked stranger standing in a half-shut door.

He would like to skip—although it can't be done—
all the saints on that cathedral ceiling, 20
the parting wave from a train,
the microscope lens, the ring casting a glow,
the movie screens, mirrors, the photo albums.

But great is the courtesy of the blind,
great is their forbearance, their largesse. 25

They listen, smile, and applaud.
One of them even comes up
with a book turned wrongside out
asking for an unseen autograph.

In this poem, Szymborska uses an image, such as "all those saints on the cathedral's ceiling," to show how this particular audience has challenged her entire method of communicating. She may have grown too sure that readers had seen something like this cathedral ceiling (or a "green meadow" or a "farewell wave"). Perhaps she feels she has become too dependent upon only one of her five senses. In any case, she suddenly doubts the power of all of the images that she has used as a poet. And yet, by invoking these images in this context, she encourages her sighted audience (like the audience for Williams's "The Red Wheelbarrow") to value the gift of sight—to *choose* to see what sometimes passes unnoticed.

# REGISTERING TASTE AND SMELL

It's generally understood that taste and smell powerfully connect us to memories and to specific feelings. In a famous passage from Marcel Proust's *Swann's Way*, the narrator catches a whiff of tea and madeleines (a type of French cookie) and with it reconnects to childhood. The smell acts as a trigger of sorts; it activates a part of the brain that holds not just a memory of past events but a feeling for their reality. Recent research in the physiology of the brain suggests that Proust was on to something. But capturing in words the sense of taste and smell is a difficult task. Certainly, much food and wine criticism struggles against the challenge. We simply don't have the well-tested vocabulary for smell and taste that we have for visual images. And although the senses of taste and smell recall memories vividly, we have a hard time evoking those senses through memory. But in the hands of a skilled writer, the lack of a standard vocabulary can become an opportunity (see the film still from *Sideways* for an example). If images grounded in the senses of taste and smell are less than plentiful, they can also be perhaps fresher.

Character Miles Raymond from *Sideways* describes the taste of his wine: "A little citrus. Maybe some strawberry. Mmm. Passion fruit, mmm, and, oh, there's just like the faintest soupçon of like, uh, asparagus, and, there's a, just a flutter of, like a, like a nutty Edam cheese."

## Experiencing Literature through Images

Salman Rushdie's account of his love for bread is a contemporary classic of sorts. As you read this reflection on the pleasures of eating and smelling bread, you won't need to think much of plot or character. Concentrate first on his descriptions—on the images he uses to convey his experience of bread. Rushdie was born in India and lives in England; much of his writing describes his native culture to those in the West. In this short essay, we experience the smells and tastes that help Rushdie describe what he sees as an essential difference between the cultures of the East and the West. As you read, pay attention to the different modes of representation Rushdie employs. At the start, Rushdie lists the varieties of unleavened bread that he grew up with in Bombay. Even if we are unfamiliar with these breads, his emphasis on the poetic quality of the names gives us some feeling for the quality of each of these breads that, of course, we cannot access literally through his prose. The "piping hot" phulka is followed by a series of breads that come to life as they are compared with one another in terms of their sweetness or luxury. As you move beyond the first paragraph, notice how comparison continues to function. *Luxury* may not be a term that we immediately associate with bread, but as soon as Rushdie relates "luxury" and bread, we work to make sense of it within the sensual realm. He describes an experience that most of his readers will not have had, so to present his particular situation, he compares his observations to things that might be more familiar to others. As you read, keep track of the way in which Rushdie uses sensory details (comments on texture, temperature, taste) to help us feel the cultural experience he recounts.

**Salman Rushdie** (1947– )

# On Leavened Bread (1996)

There was leavened bread in Bombay, but it was sorry fare: dry, crumbling, tasteless—unleavened bread's paler, unluckier relative. It wasn't "real." Real bread was the chapatti, or phulka, served piping hot; the tandoori nan, and its sweeter Frontier variant, the Peshawari nan; and, for luxury, the reshmi roti, the shirmal, the paratha. Compared with these aristocrats, the leavened white loaves of my childhood seemed to merit the description that Shaw's immortal dustman, Alfred Doolittle, dreamed up for people like himself: they were, in truth, "the undeserving poor."

My first inkling that there might be more to leavened bread than I knew came while I was visiting Karachi, Pakistan, where I learned that a hidden

Nun with bread

order of nuns, in a place known as the Monastery of the Angels, baked a mean loaf. To buy it, you had to get up at dawn—that is, a servant had to get up at dawn—and stand in line outside a small hatch in the monastery's wall. The nun's baking facilities were limited, the daily run was small, and this secret bakery's reputation was high. Only the early bird caught the loaf. The hatch would open, and a nun would hand the bread out to the waiting populace. Loaves were strictly rationed. No bulk buying was permitted. And the price, of course, was high. (All this I knew only by hearsay, for I never got up at such an unearthly hour to see for myself.)

The nun's bread—white, crusty, full of flavor—was a small revelation, but it was also, on account of its unusual provenance, eccentric. It came from beyond the frontiers of the everyday, a mystery trailing an anecdote behind it. It was almost—well, fictional. (Later, it became fictional, when I put the monastery in my novel "Midnight's Children.") Now, in the matter of bread such extraordinariness is not good. You want bread to be a part of daily life. You want it to be ordinary. You want it to be there. You don't want to get up in the middle of the night and wait by a hatch in a wall. So, while the Angels' bread was tasty, it felt like an aberration, a break in the natural order. It didn't really change my mind.

Then, aged thirteen-and-a-half, I flew to England. And suddenly there it was, in every shop window. The White Crusty, the Sliced and Unsliced. The Small Tin, the Large Tin, the Danish Bloomer. The abandoned, plentiful promiscuity of it. The soft pillowy mattressiness of it. The well-sprung boun- ciness of it between your teeth. Hard crust and soft centre: the sensuality of that perfect textural contrast. I was done for. In the whorehouses of the bakeries,

I was serially, gluttonously, irredeemably unfaithful to all those chapatis-next-door waiting for me back home. East was East, but yeast was West.

This, remember, was long before British bread counters were enlivened by the European invasion, long before ciabatta and brioche; this was 1961. But the love affair that began then has never lost its intensity; the new exotic breads have served only to renew the excitement.

I should add that there was a second discovery, almost as thrilling; that is, water. The water back home was dangerous and had to be thoroughly boiled. To be able to drink water from the tap was a privilege indeed. I have never forgotten that when I first arrived in these immeasurably wealthy and powerful lands I found the first proofs of my good fortune in loaf and glass. Since that time, a regime of bread and water has never sounded like a hardship to me. (*The New Yorker*, December 23 and 30, 1996) ■

By the time that Rushdie reaches the fourth paragraph and what he describes as his serial, gluttonous unfaithfulness to his native breads, the essay has built to a climax. It is memorable and often cited, perhaps because of the dense fabric of sensory details Rushdie weaves. This is the sort of text that enters into our real conversations, leading us to talk about our own favorite breads, Indian restaurants, and childhood food memories.

## INTERACTION OF THE SENSES

Our senses operate together. A good dinner isn't merely something tasted. It's well presented to the eye. If there is music playing in the background, it's the right music for the meal. Each bite will have a texture as well as a taste and an aroma. Literary works often build on the dense interaction of the senses to fully realize a scene. Think of, for example, how a nineteenth-century novelist describing a London street scene might register sounds and smells, as well as sights, in communicating a sense of busy urban life.

*Paradise Lost* is an epic poem in which John Milton reimagines the biblical story of Adam and Eve and their loss of Eden. In the brief excerpt that follows, Satan (here, variously called the "Serpent" and the "Evil-one") emerges from the horrors of Hell to encounter the beautiful Eve in the glorious setting of Eden. Milton wants us to appreciate the sensory experience of one who has been cut off from pleasures the unfallen world offers. We are to know Satan as a character largely through what he sees, hears, and feels as well as through our knowledge of what sights, sounds, and textures he has been denied.

In the first ten lines of this passage from *Paradise Lost*, Milton presents a **simile** (a comparison that links two things with *like* or *as*) so that the reader can appreciate what Satan might feel as he moves from Hell into Eden. An **epic simile** (such as the one in the passage) greatly elaborates one side of the comparison; note in the example that the initial "as" is followed by such a long description that we almost lose track of what comparison is being made. This particular epic simile starts off by describing a person who has come to the country from the city. Eventually we return to Satan; it is he who is *like* the stroller presented at such length. Milton uses the simile to humanize Satan; instead of making him unexplainable, Milton creates a Satan whose motivations seem familiarly human. The second section (lines 11–22) from *Paradise Lost* moves from the description of the city dweller who walks into the country for fresh air into the mind of Satan; this is how Milton imagines Satan viewing Eve; she embodies beauty in a beautiful world, and Satan's awe at this sight is intensified by its unfamiliarity. He has grown accustomed to the dismal surroundings of Hell. In the third section (lines 23–28), Satan overcomes his momentary lapse into stunned appreciation of beauty and resumes his usual wicked character. Track the sensory details in this passage to determine which are in the simile (after the initial "as") and which appear after the colon that ends the simile. Also note how Milton invokes multiple senses (sight, smell, touch, and sound).

**John Milton** (1608–1674)

## from Paradise Lost (1667)

As one who long in populous city pent,
Where houses thick and sewers annoy the air,
Forth issuing on a summer's morn, to breathe
Among the pleasant villages and farms
Adjoined, from each thing met conceives delight,     5
The smell of grain, or tedded grass, or kine,
Or dairy, each rural sight, each rural sound;
If chance, with nymph-like step fair virgin pass,
What pleasing seemed, for her now pleases more,
She most, and in her look sums all delight:     10
Such pleasure took the Serpent to behold
This flowery plat, the sweet recess of Eve
Thus early, thus alone: Her heavenly form
Angelic, but more soft and feminine,
Her graceful innocence, her every air     15
Of gesture or least action overawed
His malice, and with rapine sweet bereaved
His fierceness of the fierce intent it brought.

That space the Evil One abstracted stood
From his own evil, and for the time remained                    20
Stupidly good, of enmity disarmed,
Of guile, of hate, of envy, of revenge;
But the hot hell that always in him burns,
Though in mid Heaven, soon ended his delight,
And tortures him now more, the more he sees                     25
Of pleasure not for him ordained; then soon
Fierce hate he recollects, and all his thoughts
Of mischief, gratulating, thus excites.

In bringing this particular scene to life, Milton makes real the horror of Hell, the glory of Eden, the turpitude of Satan, and the beauty of Eve by calling up an image that is generally familiar, even mundane. In his simile, he borrows the common conceit that cities are like Hell—there are too many people, too much pollution, and bad sewers—and turns it around; in order to imagine Hell, we should imagine a city, because Hell is similar to a city. Satan emerging from Hell is like anyone leaving a city to visit the country and being delighted by everything simply because it is different and fresh. Instead of being some creature from a horror film, this Satan is so happy to be out of Hell that he is like a tourist sightseeing. This passage is filled with detail: "The smell of grain, or tedded grass, or kine [cattle], / Or dairy." In reading this passage, we must decide how to translate this scene into our picture of the Satan character who is about to seduce Eve (and, by extension, all of humanity) into disobeying the will of God. The naïve city person who Milton uses to represent Satan and who is delighted by sights, smells, and sounds of the country is a bit more sophisticated than he appears, and the sensory images in this passage help us understand this character as one shaken out of his usual sense of self and yet able to return quickly to that self. After all, how long are city folk generally excited by the smell of cattle?

Satan's visit to Eden raises a question of large importance for artists of all kinds: What happens when the demands on our senses exceed our ability to process, discriminate, and savor? A rush of sensory data can be exhilarating, as it is momentarily for Satan. When our senses, in effect, overload, we may be forced to take the world in differently and may feel, as a result, a sense of discovery or revelation. A rush of sights, sounds, textures, tastes, and smells can also prompt feelings of confusion and disorientation. The critic Pauline Kael maintained that film was an art form especially equipped to take advantage of the immediacy and multiplicity of sensory experience. In a dark theater, sitting before a giant screen, we're focused intently on complex, rapidly shifting sights and sounds. We don't have either the time or the opportunity to back off and think about what our senses take in at the very moment they are engaged so actively.

Although such qualities are often exploited to no purpose (do we need more explosions and car chases in "action films"?), Kael's observation helps us appreciate the sources of power that a good movie may access. Contrast, for example, Martin Scorsese's lavish re-creation of mid-nineteenth-century

*Gangs of New York* (2002)

*Lost in Translation* (2003)

urban life in *Gangs of New York* (2002) with Sophia Coppola's spare, precise, patient, and quietly rendered scenes of loneliness from the hotel bar in *Lost in Translation* (2003). These scenes convey sensory qualities of human life at a given moment: the mud, noise, and movement of the street; the soft and unconnected background noise in the near-empty bar late at night.

## Experiencing Literature through Images

Of course, movies have no exclusive right to sensory intensity. Nor do our senses necessarily disconnect from abstract thought or inevitably supplant thought. Richard Wilbur conveys a dense and moving fabric of sight and sound to convey the image of a fire truck careening along a street. The abrupt appearance of the noisy, red, large truck leaves those watching with the raw experience of the truck in the moment it passes but without an opportunity to think about the noise and the vehicle that has interrupted their routine activity. But in this poet's case, the overloading of the senses occasions a philosophical exploration of the relationship between objects, actions, and thoughts.

**Richard Wilbur** (1921– )

# A Fire-Truck (1961)

Right down the shocked street with a siren-blast
That sends all else skittering to the curb,
Redness, brass, ladders and hats hurl past,
   Blurring to sheer verb,

Shift at the corner into uproarious gear             5
And make it around the turn in a squall of traction,
The headlong bell maintaining sure and clear,
   *Thought is degraded action!*

Beautiful, heavy, unweary, loud, obvious thing!
I stand here purged of nuance, my mind a blank.         10
All I was brooding upon has taken wing,
   And I have you to thank.

As you howl beyond hearing I carry you into my mind,
Ladders and brass and all, there to admire
Your phoenix-red simplicity, enshrined         15
   In that not extinguished fire.

In the first two lines, Wilbur reproduces the impact of a fire truck by announcing its "siren-blast" but also by showing us the effect of this siren on the rest of the "shocked street" where everything is "skittering to the curb." Next, he gives four details that we are allowed to pick out of the blur of the passing truck: "Redness, brass, ladders and hats." Each of the details is something that we might associate with a fire truck, and each of us could easily fill in at least a half dozen other details of fire trucks, but these four words are enough to sketch the image that Wilbur calls up here. As soon as the image is distinct, Wilbur blurs it as it "hurl[s] past," and his narrator changes the concrete image into something else. The nouns that he has just listed blur "to sheer verb," and the fire truck itself, which begins as the representative noun, or the object that we are trying to see in this poem, becomes representative of action.

Wilbur starts with sensory impressions that obliterate intellectual abstractions; ultimately though, he asks that we reflect on the process of obliteration. Nouns describe objects; verbs describe action; and Wilbur uses the fire truck image to examine the problem of thinking itself. In his formulation, action happens; and thought, in an effort to make sense of that blurred fire truck, "*degrade[s] action*." A fire truck is a specific object, but our experience of fire trucks is greater than the things that we see as it rushes past. An integral aspect of our experience of the fire truck is its action: the speed as it roars by and the life-saving actions that it facilitates in emergencies. Therefore, as we think about this specific noun, "fire truck," we are also thinking about a series of verbs as well as the next list of adjectives: "Beautiful, heavy, unweary, loud, obvious." Each applies to the fire truck with its redness and hats, but by taking us into thought, Wilbur has left the realm of sensory experience. The adjectives that apply so well to a fire truck inspire a certain meditation that has very little to do with what the narrator has actually observed; we now begin to think about the nature of beauty, heaviness, weariness, obviousness, and the paradoxical "simplicity" of this fire truck that has inspired the narrator to set this scene and bring us along on the narrator's own inner journey.

### Making Connections

In Chapters 12 and 13, we consider how images may become **symbols**; that is, an image may come to represent something other than the specific object that the author names. One might argue that the fire truck in Wilbur's poem or the bread in Rushdie's essay signifies something else. In order to make such an argument, we must show how the author uses specific details in such a way to justify our interpretation. It is also important to remember that images don't need to mean something *else* in order to connect to powerful feelings.

# INTERACTION OF WORDS AND PICTURES

As they are used in literary works, images are the building blocks of experience. As words are used to build images, they also help interpret images or make those images achieve meaning or some particular emotional effect. Words contextualize images, just as the body of "A Fire-Truck" organizes and transforms the sensory experience of the fire truck rushing by into a philosophical musing. The further we examine this subject, the clearer it becomes that an image does not stand entirely alone. As Wilbur shows us in his poem, we process the sensory data that we take in. This process involves, among other things, a comparison of one image with others that are familiar to us or that come to us at the same time. Occasionally, it involves conflating senses that we normally take to be separate. Michael Ondaatje dramatizes such combinations in his poem "King Kong Meets Wallace Stevens." The unlikely pairing of the poet Stevens with the movie monster allows Ondaatje to consider his own reactions to the two images.

**Michael Ondaatje** (1943 – )

# King Kong Meets Wallace Stevens (1979)

Take two photographs—
Wallace Stevens and King Kong
(Is it significant that I eat bananas as I write this?)

Stevens is portly, benign, a white brush cut
striped tie. Businessman but                                              5
for the dark thick hands, the naked brain
the thought in him.

Kong is staggering
lost in New York streets again
a spawn of annoyed cars at his toes.                                     10
The mind is nowhere.
Fingers are plastic, electric under the skin.
He's at the call of Metro-Goldwyn-Mayer.

Meanwhile W. S. in his suit
is thinking chaos is thinking fences.                                    15
In his head the seeds of fresh pain
his exorcising,
the bellow of locked blood.

The hands drain from his jacket,
pose in the murder's shadow.                                    20

The last lines of Ondaatje's poem moves us beyond the mixture of senses or the interaction between sensations and words to what seems the conflation of all senses along with the intellect. How does "locked blood" find expression in a "bellow?" For that matter, how can blood be "locked?" And how can hands "drain" from one's jacket? What would those hands look like? These are difficult images to grasp securely, but if Ondaatje were after something that could be grasped securely, he might not bother to write a poem. As strikingly unusual as these images are, they play upon a fairly familiar notion: the most intense sensations and most subtle thoughts sometimes achieve a kind of fusion.

This conflation of senses is part of what made *American Beauty* (1999) such a moving film for many people. Early in the film, the main character, Lester Burnham (Kevin Spacey), inhabits a home and office environment stripped of any visual distinction. As Lester grows progressively rebellious, colors, textures, feelings, and sounds press upon him. Perhaps by the end of the film, just before his death, Lester could ask: "Have you ever felt a piece of music to be so beautiful that it hurt? Or perhaps even tasted that music?" This cross association—one kind of sensory experience evoking the experience of another kind—is called **synesthesia**. Until recently, synesthesia was

The poet Wallace Stevens

*King Kong* (1933)

considered a purely fanciful or "poetic" notion; whereas it may be telling to say a color is "loud," surely no one has ever really heard a color. In the past decade, however, advances in brain research have suggested that we can't be so confident in absolute distinctions. Neural activity controlling our sensory responses isn't always neatly compartmentalized in discrete parts of the brain. Some people—especially creative people—do see sounds or feel colors. Those of us not gifted in this way may still discover an inexplicable power or aptness in two senses registered in a single image.

## Experiencing Literature through Images

The Japanese **haiku** form of poetry foregrounds its attention to images. Often the poem itself seems to be nothing more than one or two specific images with no attempt to explain how that image is significant. In the following poetic sequence, the poet Yosa Buson offers a series of these short observational poems based upon the four seasons of the year. The third part of the poem, "Autumn," is one of the shorter sections. Buson begins by describing the experience of stepping on a comb—the comb of an absent (some translate "dead") wife. List the details in scenes that make up "Autumn."

What senses does Buson describe? How are the varied feelings connected to the immediate sensual experience of stepping on the comb? What details don't seem part of that immediate experience? How are all details important to Buson's experience of this moment? In the whole sequence, how are details interesting beyond the poet's experience of them?

**Yosa Buson** (1716–1784)

# from Hokku Poems in Four Seasons (Yuki Sawa and Edith M. Shiffert, trans; 1780)

SPRING

The year's first poem done,
with smug self confidence—
a haikai poet.

Daylight longer!
A pheasant has fluttered down                                                    5
onto the bridge.

*Yearning for the Past*

Lengthening days
Accumulate—farther off
the days of long ago!                                                                  10

Slowly passing days,
their echoings are heard
here in Kyoto.

The white elbow
of a priest who is dozing!                                                          15
Dusk in spring.

Into a nobleman
a fox has changed himself—
early evening of spring.

The light of a candle                                                                 20
is transferred to another candle—
spring twilight.

A short nap, then
awakening—the spring
day darkened.                                                    25


Who is it for,
the small bed pillow,
twilight in spring?


The big gateway's
massive doors—                                                  30
spring twilight.


Hazy moonlight!
Someone is standing
among the pear trees.


Flowers of the pear—                                            35
reading a letter by moon light,
a woman.


Springtime rain!
Almost dark, and yet
today still lingers                                             40


Springtime rain!
Little shells on a small beach,
enough to moisten them.



SUMMER

In the quietness
of a lull between visitors,                                     45
the peony flower!


A peony fallen—
on top of one another,
two petals, three petals.


Early summer rain—                                             50
facing toward the big river,
houses, two of them.

*At a Place Called Kaya in Tanba*

A summer river
being crossed, how pleasing!                                             55
Sandals in my hands.

The mountain stonecutter's
chisel is being cooled
in the clear water!

Rainfall on the grasses                                                 60
just after the festival cart
passed by.

To my eyes it is delightful—
the fan of my beloved,
completely white.                                                       65

Hototogisu
over the Heian castle town
flying aslant

In evening wind—
water is slapping against                                               70
legs of a blue heron.

An old well!
Jumping at a mosquito, a fish's
sound of darkness.

Young bamboo!                                                           75
At Hashimoto, the harlot,
is she still there or not?

After it has fallen
its image still stands—
the peony flower.                                                       80

*Ascending the Eastern Slope*

Flowering Thorn—
the pathway by my home village
is like this!

Feeling melancholy                                                      85
while climbing the hill,
flowering thorn.

## AUTUMN

It goes into me—
the comb of my long gone wife
to step on it in the bedroom.                    90

Compared to last year,
this has even more loneliness—
autumn evening.

Being alone
may also even be pleasant—                       95
autumn dusk.

Moon in the sky's center,
shabbiness on the village street—
just passing through.

While feeling sad                                100
a fishing line being blown
by the autumn wind.

## WINTER

I shall go to bed—
New Year's Day is a matter
for tomorrow.                                    105

Camphor tree roots
silently becoming wet
in a winter shower.

A handsaw
sounding like poverty                            110
at midnight in winter.

An old man's love.
while trying to forget it,
a winter rainfall.

In an old pond                                   115
a straw sandal half sunken—
wet snowfall!

Haiku poetry may be identified by its three-line stanza structure. Each three-line unit in Buson's poem can be read as an independent poem (the stanza that opens "Autumn" is often reprinted alone). In such short poems, there is often a concentrated attention upon a single image with little explanatory material; we access feeling through the quality and intensity of the image and the associations it provokes. Look back over Buson's poem, and notice how many of these three-line units are self-sufficient, yet consider how they work together (just as the seasonal sections work together) to amplify their individual ideas. In what ways does this collection of sensory images create, in the aggregate, a larger commentary? Why does the poet divide his images by seasons? Look, for instance, at the poet's comments about age within each separate season.

## A Note to Student Writers: Using Specific Detail

Your writing about literature and film will be most incisive and most immediate when you center your discussion on specific details and when you describe how these details lead you to the larger argumentative context that you provide in your analysis. It is important, though, *not* to get lost in details. Although in the early predraft writing stage you might want to make lengthy lists of various things you notice in a work (key words, recurring images, specific stylistic features, and so on), you'll certainly want to edit, order, and reduce that list as you write the paper. Good critical papers aren't defined by how many things they include; rather, they are characterized by how thoughtfully they select and explain what they include. It is the critic's job to convey some significant *aspect* of our experience of a text. You shouldn't try to "cover" everything so much as seek to register precisely and explain fully what is most relevant to your particular reading. Focus is important. A paper on imagery in Susan Glaspell's play *Trifles* will likely wander in several directions without every quite getting anywhere. A paper on images of unfinished work in *Trifles* might lead to real insight.

# MODELING CRITICAL ANALYSIS:
# T. S. ELIOT, THE LOVE SONG OF J. ALFRED PRUFROCK

T. S. Eliot's "The Love Song of J. Alfred Prufrock" echoes the conventions noted earlier that Milton employs to describe Satan's visit to Eden. The city is assumed or presented as a poisonous place of lonely, tired people. It's a place of grit and bad smells. Milton uses escape from the city to intensify Satan's rapt appreciation of the Edenic countryside. Eliot's poem keeps us confined almost entirely in the city. Prufrock never escapes. You'll note that

Eliot's imagery, like Milton's, is vivid and varied. At the start, he uses a simile: "When the evening is spread out against the sky / Like a patient etherized upon a table." He also employs **personification** (that is, he lends human/animal characteristics to an inanimate thing) to express a lingering, languidly moving, dirty quality of the "yellow fog" that hangs about the streets. His narrator's self-description (the bald spot, the clothes) as well as his descriptions of others ("arms that are braceleted and white and bare") offers precisely selected details that register a particular social class and the stifling qualities of that class. This complex and difficult poem has been so well and so widely appreciated largely because of Eliot's ability to make us see, feel, and taste details of place and person; his imagery lends a power to the poem even upon a first reading. Through striking images, Eliot helps us acquire a sense of place, character, and situation essential to our experience of the poem.

**T. S. Eliot** (1888–1965)

# The Love Song of J. Alfred Prufrock (1917)

*S'io credessi che mia risposta fosse*
*A persona che mai tornasse al mondo,*
*Questa fiamma staria senza più scosse.*
*Ma perciocchè giammai di questo fondo*
*Non tornó vivo alcun, s'i'odo il vero,*
*Senza tema d'infamia ti rispondo.*

Let us go then, you and I,
When the evening is spread out against the sky
Like a patient etherized upon a table;
Let us go, through certain half-deserted streets,
The muttering retreats                                                    5
Of restless nights in one-night cheap hotels
And sawdust restaurants with oyster-shells:
Streets that follow like a tedious argument
Of insidious intent
To lead you to an overwhelming question.... 10
Oh, do not ask, "What is it?"
Let us go and make our visit.

In the room the women come and go
Talking of Michelangelo.

The yellow fog that rubs its back upon the window-panes,                          15
The yellow smoke that rubs its muzzle on the window-panes
Licked its tongue into the corners of the evening,
Lingered upon the pools that stand in drains,
Let fall upon its back the soot that falls from chimneys,
Slipped by the terrace, made a sudden leap,                                       20
And seeing that it was a soft October night,
Curled once about the house, and fell asleep.

And indeed there will be time
For the yellow smoke that slides along the street,
Rubbing its back upon the window-panes;                                           25
There will be time, there will be time
To prepare a face to meet the faces that you meet;
There will be time to murder and create,
And time for all the works and days of hands
That lift and drop a question on your plate;                                      30
Time for you and time for me,
And time yet for a hundred indecisions,
And for a hundred visions and revisions,
Before the taking of a toast and tea.

In the room the women come and go                                                35
Talking of Michelangelo.

And indeed there will be time
To wonder, "Do I dare?" and, "Do I dare?"
Time to turn back and descend the stair,
With a bald spot in the middle of my hair—                                       40
(They will say: "How his hair is growing thin!")
My morning coat, my collar mounting firmly to the chin,
My necktie rich and modest, but asserted by a simple pin—
(They will say: "But how his arms and legs are thin!")
Do I dare                                                                         45
Disturb the universe?
In a minute there is time
For decisions and revisions which a minute will reverse.

For I have known them all already, known them all—
Have known the evenings, mornings, afternoons,                                    50
I have measured out my life with coffee spoons;
I know the voices dying with a dying fall

Beneath the music from a farther room.
　So how should I presume?

And I have known the eyes already, known them all—　　　　　55
The eyes that fix you in a formulated phrase,
And when I am formulated, sprawling on a pin,
When I am pinned and wriggling on the wall,
Then how should I begin
To spit out all the butt-ends of my days and ways?　　　　　60
　And how should I presume?

And I have known the arms already, known them all—
Arms that are braceleted and white and bare
(But in the lamplight, downed with light brown hair!)
Is it perfume from a dress　　　　　65
That makes me so digress?
Arms that lie along a table, or wrap about a shawl.
　And should I then presume?
　And how should I begin?

　　　　　*　*　*

Shall I say, I have gone at dusk through narrow streets　　　　　70
And watched the smoke that rises from the pipes
Of lonely men in shirt-sleeves, leaning out of windows?...

I should have been a pair of ragged claws
Scuttling across the floors of silent seas.

　　　　　*　*　*

And the afternoon, the evening, sleeps so peacefully!　　　　　75
Smoothed by long fingers,
Asleep...tired...or it malingers,
Stretched on the floor, here beside you and me.
Should I, after tea and cakes and ices,
Have the strength to force the moment to its crisis?　　　　　80
But though I have wept and fasted, wept and prayed,
Though I have seen my head (grown slightly bald) brought in upon a platter,
I am no prophet—and here's no great matter;
I have seen the moment of my greatness flicker,
And I have seen the eternal Footman hold my coat, and snicker,　　　　　85
And in short, I was afraid.

And would it have been worth it, after all,
After the cups, the marmalade, the tea,

Among the porcelain, among some talk of you and me,
Would it have been worth while,                                    90
To have bitten off the matter with a smile,
To have squeezed the universe into a ball
To roll it toward some overwhelming question,
To say: "I am Lazarus, come from the dead,
Come back to tell you all, I shall tell you all"—                  95
If one, settling a pillow by her head,
      Should say: "That is not what I meant at all.
      That is not it, at all."

And would it have been worth it, after all,
Would it have been worth while,                                    100
After the sunsets and the dooryards and the sprinkled streets,
After the novels, after the teacups, after the skirts that trail along the floor—
And this, and so much more?—
It is impossible to say just what I mean!
But as if a magic lantern threw the nerves in patterns on a screen:  105
Would it have been worth while
If one, settling a pillow or throwing off a shawl,
And turning toward the window, should say:
      "That is not it at all,
      That is not what I meant, at all."                           110

                    *    *    *

No! I am not Prince Hamlet, nor was meant to be;
Am an attendant lord, one that will do
To swell a progress, start a scene or two,
Advise the prince; no doubt, an easy tool,
Deferential, glad to be of use,                                    115
Politic, cautious, and meticulous;
Full of high sentence, but a bit obtuse;
At times, indeed, almost ridiculous—
Almost, at times, the Fool.

I grow old... I grow old...                                        120
I shall wear the bottoms of my trousers rolled.

Shall I part my hair behind? Do I dare to eat a peach?
I shall wear white flannel trousers, and walk upon the beach.
I have heard the mermaids singing, each to each.

I do not think that they will sing to me.                          125
I have seen them riding seaward on the waves,

Combing the white hair of the waves blown back
When the wind blows the water white and black.

We have lingered in the chambers of the sea
By sea-girls wreathed with seaweed red and brown        130
Till human voices wake us, and we drown.

## Using Images to Focus Writing and Discussion

- Locate significant images within this work. Is there any single image that seems to be especially significant? What details in the text signal this prominence?
- What sense (or senses) does the author use to convey these images?
- How does the author introduce images in this work? Do they come from a particular point of view? Do they come all at once?
- What is the significance of these images to specific characters within the text? How is this significance related to our experience of the text?
- Is there any pattern to the sorts of images that are prominent? For instance, are they generally associated with a single place or time in the text, or are they scattered throughout various places and times?
- How do the images relate to the ideas presented in the text?

# 8 Coherence

## Is There a Pattern Here?

## How Does This Fit Together?

In "real life," things are not neatly ordered. Anyone who has ever tried to organize a desk or a computer's desktop knows that maintaining order requires constant vigilance. Personal messages, advertisements, and interesting articles come to us in a random fashion. As receivers of these messages, we must develop some strategy to keep the avalanche of information from becoming incoherent noise that prevents us from doing the work that information is supposed to be facilitating. On desktops, we create folders to group similar items. Some people design very simple and transparent organizational plans. Others set up elaborate structures of networked folders that have an internal logic so complex that no one besides the organizer would ever recognize it. There must be method, though, in even the maddest systems.

In Nick Hornby's novel *High Fidelity* (1995), the main character, Rob Fleming, an avid thirty-something collector of vinyl records, deals with the emotional turmoil in his life by imposing order on something he can control. When his girlfriend leaves him, he turns to his record collection.

**Nick Hornby** (1957– )

## from **High Fidelity** (1995)

Tuesday night I reorganize my record collection; I often do this at periods of emotional stress. There are some people who would find this a pretty dull way

*High Fidelity* (2000). In the film adaptation of the novel, John Cusack plays Rob Fleming, who reorganizes his record collection as his life falls apart.

to spend an evening, but I'm not one of them. This is my life, and it's nice to be able to wade in, immerse your arms in it, touch it.

When Laura was here I had the records arranged alphabetically; before that I had them filed in chronological order, beginning with Robert Johnson, and ending with, I don't know, Wham!, or somebody African, or whatever else I was listening to when Laura and I met. Tonight, though, I fancy something different, so I try to remember the order I bought them in: that way I hope to write my own autobiography, without having to do anything like pick up a pen. I pull the records off the shelves, put them in piles all over the sitting room floor, look for *Revolver*, and go on from there; and when I've finished, I'm flushed with a sense of self, because this, after all, is who I am. I like being able to see how I got from Deep Purple to Howlin' Wolf in twenty-five moves; I am no longer pained by the memory of listening to "Sexual Healing" all the way through a period of enforced celibacy, or embarrassed by the reminder of forming a rock club at school, so that I and my fellow fifth-formers could get together and talk about Ziggy Stardust and *Tommy*.

But what I really like is the feeling of security I get from my new filing system; I have a couple of thousand records, and you have to be me—or, at the very least, a doctor of Flemingology—to know how to find any of them. If I want to play, say *Blue* by Joni Mitchell, I have to remember that I bought it for someone in the autumn of 1983, and thought better of giving it to her, for reasons I don't really want to go into. Well, you don't know any of that, so you're knackered, really aren't you? You'd have to ask me to dig it out for you, and for some reason I find this enormously comforting. ■

Fleming's love of—or need for—order shows itself at other important times in his life. Later, as he considers dating someone new, he muses over the proper arrangement of a mixed tape.

I spent hours putting that cassette together. To me, making a tape is like writing a letter—there's a lot of erasing and rethinking and starting again, and I wanted it to be a good one, because … to be honest, because I hadn't met anyone as promising as Laura since I'd started the DJ-ing, and meeting promising women was partly what the DJ-ing was supposed to be about. A good compilation tape, like breaking up, is hard to do. You've got to kick off with a corker, to hold that attention (I started with "Got to Get You off My Mind," but then realized that she might not get any further than track one, side one if I delivered what she wanted straightaway, so I buried it in the middle of side two), and then you've got to up it a notch, or cool it a notch, and you can't have white music and black music together, unless the white music sounds like black music, and you can't have two tracks by the same artist side by side, unless you've done the whole thing in pairs, and … oh, there are loads of rules. ■

Fleming's life is obviously less ordered than his record collection or his meticulously arranged song sets. Fleming is not alone in this novel in devising strategies to maintain order amid chaos; his friends also make lists that neatly arrange life. For our purposes, it's important to note that Hornby uses his characters' obsession with order as the structuring device in his novel; the list making and cataloguing connect the various parts of the story and become a subject of scrutiny within the story. Hornby weaves a dense fabric of systems people employ and prompts his reader to think of how—and how well—those systems function. Most chapters in his novel begin with a new list and some discussion of the standards used to generate that list: the best episode of *Cheers*, best A-side singles of all time, "my desert-island, all-time, top five most memorable split-ups, in chronological order." To the readers these lists are sometimes quite funny but also indicative of how hard it can be to assert control over the events of a life. They function to make the novel thematically coherent. They help us read and make sense of a lengthy narrative.

In this chapter, we'll examine a variety of strategies that writers/filmmakers employ to achieve a forceful, coherent work. We'll also call attention to ways that you, as a critical writer, can learn from these strategies.

## DESIGN AND SHAPE

Every literary work or film employs some strategy for how the various pieces fit together. Sometimes the strategy is obvious at a glance. For instance, there is a tradition of creating a poem in the physical shape of the poem's subject; in other words, the lines of the poem illustrate their own subject matter. This is often called **concrete poetry**. Perhaps the most famous of these concrete, or **shape poems**, is George Herbert's "Easter Wings," which actually looks like two pairs of wings.

**George Herbert** (1593–1633)

# Easter Wings (1633)

Lord, Who createdst man in wealth and store,
Though foolishly he lost the same,
Decaying more and more,
Till he became
Most poore:                                    5

With Thee
O let me rise,
As larks, harmoniously,
And sing this day Thy victories:
Then shall the fall further the flight in me.        10

My tender age in sorrow did beginne;
And still with sicknesses and shame
Thou didst so punish sinne,
That I became
Most thinne.                                  15

With Thee
Let me combine,
And feel this day Thy victorie;
For, if I imp my wing on Thine,
Affliction shall advance the flight in me.        20

Writing such a poem requires considerable craftsmanship. The poet must conceive of the poem's arrangement on the page as well as its theme and then find the words and the poetic structure necessary to carry out this plan. Herbert has managed to make the meaning of the lines themselves reflect the appearance of the poem. Where the lines reach their narrowest points, he describes a man who has constricted to become "Most poore" and "Most thinne." As the lines that follow expand, Herbert's idea of resurrection takes flight. Our awareness of the poem's shape helps us see the poem's ideas. It is no accident that the poem looks like wings, and as soon as we see these wings, we can look for corresponding winglike ideas in the poem.

Thomas Hardy's "The Convergence of the Twain" displays a similar correspondence between shape and theme. In each stanza his poem, written in response to the loss of the *Titanic*, suggests the shape of a ship and the shape of the iceberg. Hardy challenges us to meditate on the tragic bringing together of the two. Perhaps the poem's design also forcefully weights each stanza downward; the last line of each rests heavily at the bottom.

**Thomas Hardy** (1840–1928)

# The Convergence of the Twain (1912)

*Lines on the Loss of the Titanic*

1
In a solitude of the sea
Deep from human vanity,
And the Pride of Life that planned her, stilly couches she.

2
Steel chambers, late the pyres
Of her salamandrine fires,                                             5
Cold currents third, and turn to rhythmic tidal lyres.

3
Over the mirrors meant
To glass the opulent
The sea-worm crawls—grotesque, slimed, dumb, indifferent.

4
Jewels in joy designed                                                10
To ravish the sensuous mind
Lie lightless, all their sparkles bleared and black and blind.

5
Dim moon-eyed fishes near
Gaze at the gilded gear
And query: "What does this vaingloriousness down here?"                15

6
Well: while was fashioning
This creature of cleaving wing,
The Immanent Will that stirs and urges everything

7
Prepared a sinister mate
For her—so gaily great—                                          20
A Shape of Ice, for the time far and dissociate.


8
And as the smart ship grew
In stature, grace, and hue,
In shadowy silent distance grew the Iceberg too.


9
Alien they seemed to be:                                        25
No mortal eye could see
The intimate welding of their later history,


10
Or sign that they were bent
By paths coincident
On being anon twin halves of one august event,                  30


11
Till the Spinner of the Years
Said "Now!" And each one hears,
And consummation comes, and jars two hemispheres.

Such play with form and content provides an excellent exercise for a poet. For a reader, the design provides a concrete representation of an abstract idea. The shape provides a clear idea about what focus the poet feels is important. If we have trouble reading poems like "Easter Wings" or "The Convergence of the Twain," we can consult the shape to test interpretations we develop as we read.


## TRADITIONAL STRUCTURES

Just as our awareness of the shape of the previous poems helps us read those poems for complementary details and themes, an awareness of traditional literary structures will help us understand how works hold together.

Extended narratives may build upon large units that help readers pause over and process complex actions. For example, a chapter in a novel (often both numbered and titled) offers readers a chance to break from the story and reflect back on what has unfolded, as well as project ahead to what may occur.

Short story writers may insert more subtle graphic signals. In the short story "UFO in Kushiro," Haruki Murakami employs a simple and common visual cue: changes of scene (from home to workplace and so on) are marked by an extra space between lines. In the short story "A Rose for Emily," William Faulkner employs a more emphatic signal. His story is divided into five numbered parts. The division by five in this case underscores the development of the story from initial exposition (establishment of place and character) through steps in Emily's life that lead to the ultimate revelation and resolution.

Faulkner's five-part short story might remind us of the division of a full-length play into five acts. The acts in a play can serve multiple functions. They often serve to help an audience appreciate the building and release of tension, as noted in Chapter 1, but the acts also function to allow physical changes in the set. Murakami can move us from Komura's home to Komura's workplace instantly; the extra space is all he offers us in preparation for the shift. But a dramatist must think in terms of **staging** such movements—of how the actors and the stage properties will interact within the physical constraints of the stage, of what needs to be moved on or off the stage as well as how quickly the necessary changes can be made. Dramatists can choose, of course, to keep sets very plain and put trust in an audience's imagination, but that is a choice.

Very short works, particularly short poems, often build upon highly specific and elaborate traditions. The **sonnet** is a fourteen-line poetic structure that has been a proving ground for poets for centuries. Fourteen lines are enough to convey and explore a single coherent idea in some detail, but much discipline is required. Each line must have the same number of syllables (ten), and the final word in each line must follow a specific rhyme scheme that underscores a clearly marked **stanzaic structure;** that is, the rhyme scheme groups lines in regular, definable verse paragraphs. As arbitrary as these defining characteristics might sound, the structure lends itself to a particular kind of tightly logical development and allows for some variation ("defining characteristics" are not "rules"). The sonnet form has proven to be, in the hands of expert poets, dynamic and forceful.

But we should approach sonnets with the main organizational types in mind. A consciousness of basic structuring principles will help us read and understand. The **Italian** or **Petrarchan sonnet** is divided into two parts: the **octave** (eight lines) and the **sestet** (six lines). The pattern of rhyme (see Chapter 6 for more on rhyme) that distinguishes the octave defines two **quatrains** (stanzas of four lines each). The sestet may be marked by various rhyme schemes. The **English** or **Shakespearean sonnet** organizes itself quite differently. Instead of an octave/sestet (eight/six) division, the English sonnet breaks into three quatrains (each with a rhyme scheme of its own) and a **couplet** (a rhymed pair of lines); we have then a twelve (four, four, four)/two division.

The structural differences between these two principal sonnet forms should not obscure the rhetorical or argumentative logic they share—a logic that makes each form coherent. An Italian sonnet raises a problem, asks a question, or establishes a subject in the octave. An English sonnet does the

### Petrarchan or Italian Sonnet

| Line number | End sound | Form | |
|---|---|---|---|
| 1 | A | **Quatrain 1:** verse paragraph of 4 lines, followed by | This octave (lines 1–8) establishes complication (problem, issue or question). |
| 2 | B | | |
| 3 | B | | |
| 4 | A | | |
| 5 | A | **Quatrain 2:** verse paragraph of 4 lines | |
| 6 | B | | |
| 7 | B | | |
| 8 | A | | |

Turn away from/against complication established in octave occurs between lines 8 and 9.

| Line number | End sound | Form | |
|---|---|---|---|
| 9 | C | **Sestet:** final 6 lines | **Resolution:** responds to complication |
| 10 | D | | |
| 11 | E | | |
| 12 | C | | |
| 13 | D | | |
| 14 | E | | |

### Shakespearean Sonnet

| Line number | End sound | Form | |
|---|---|---|---|
| 1 | A | **Quatrain 1:** verse paragraph of 4 lines, followed by | Three quatrains establish the complication (problem, issue, or question). |
| 2 | B | | |
| 3 | A | | |
| 4 | B | | |
| 5 | C | **Quatrain 2:** verse paragraph of 4 lines, followed by | Each quatrain typically represents a variation upon or elaboration of the complication. |
| 6 | D | | |
| 7 | C | | |
| 8 | D | | |
| 9 | E | **Quatrain 3:** verse paragraph of 4 lines | These quatrains generally employ iambic pentameter and are sometimes called **heroic quatrains.** |
| 10 | F | | |
| 11 | E | | |
| 12 | F | | |

Turn away from/against complication established in quatrains occurs between lines 12 and 13.

| Line number | End sound | Form | |
|---|---|---|---|
| 13 | G | **Couplet:** 2 lines rhymed | **Resolution:** responds to complication |
| 14 | G | | |

*Sonnet charts*

same in the first twelve lines. The sonnet's opening section is often called the **complication**. In an Italian sonnet, the sestet responds to the problem, answers the question, or draws meaning from the subject established in the octave. The couplet in an English sonnet serves this same purpose. This second part of the sonnet's argumentative or rhetorical structure can be called the **resolution** (at least, if the particular poem allows for such a confident word). The brief transition space that gives us pause just between the complication and resolution is called the **turn**. Understanding an Italian sonnet or an English sonnet involves understanding the movement from the problem to the response. The following models represent the common stanzaic structures and signal the underlying argumentative logic of the sonnet (the letters along the left margin represent how the end rhymes are patterned).

Poets have melded aspects of the two main sonnet forms and experimented boldly with many different patterns of rhyme. The Italian sonnet and the English sonnet should not be understood as unbending or exclusive forms but as grids from which poets have worked. It's also useful to appreciate the different effects to which these principal forms lend themselves. Because the Italian sonnet allows space for a rather full response to the complication, it tends to achieve a meditative feel. The English sonnet, on the other hand, will often achieve in the compression of the couplet the effect of surprise, or even shock, as it turns suddenly on the complication. The couplet will also more easily allow a witty, playfully punning resolution.

## Experiencing Literature through Form

Although the sonnet has a well-defined form, close reading of some great sonnets quickly reveals that great variety can be realized within the fourteen lines. Knowing the basic forms can be very helpful, partly because variations on a fixed form often signal something meaningful. Sometimes an author can underscore or redefine a message simply by breaking an established pattern. If a poem, for instance, has a steady rhyming pattern, we notice when the author breaks that pattern. Structural variations as well as structural consistency are part of a writer's resources. As you read the following three sonnets, identify patterns of rhyme and trace the argumentative logic those patterns imply. Also consider how the sonnet form in each case becomes part of the poem's meaning. In "Nuns Fret Not," William Wordsworth examines the constrictions of tradition and finds constriction liberating. In "I, Being Born a Woman and Distressed," Edna St. Vincent Millay uses the sonnet to critique gender assumptions that sonnets by males have long perpetuated (see, for example, the selection of love sonnets by William Shakespeare, p. 202). Note in particular in the octave how the words grouped as A rhymes differ significantly from those of the B rhymes. That difference clarifies the problem or conflict Millay wants to establish. Finally, Robert Frost in "Design" uses the scale and tightness of his sonnet's construction to raise profound questions of scale and design in the universe.

**William Wordsworth** (1770–1850)

# Nuns Fret Not (1807)

Nuns fret not at their convent's narrow room;
And hermits are contented with their cells;
And students with their pensive citadels;
Maids at the wheel, the weaver at his loom,
Sit blithe and happy; bees that soar for bloom,                               5
High as the highest Peak of Furness-fells,
Will murmur by the hour in foxglove bells:
In truth the prison, unto which we doom
Ourselves, no prison is: and hence for me,
In sundry moods, 'twas pastime to be bound                                   10
Within the Sonnet's scanty plot of ground;
Pleased if some Souls (for such there needs must be)
Who have felt the weight of too much liberty,
Should find brief solace there, as I have found.

**Edna St. Vincent Millay** (1892–1950)

# I, Being Born a Woman and Distressed (1932)

I, being born a woman and distressed
By all the needs and notions of my kind,
Am urged by your propinquity to find
Your person fair, and feel a certain zest
To feel your body's weight upon my breast:                                   5
So subtly is the fume of life designed,
To clarify the pulse and cloud the mind,
And leave me once again undone, possessed.
Think not for this, however, the poor treason
Of my stout blood against my staggering brain,                               10
I shall remember you with love, or season
My scorn with pity,—let me make it plain:

I find this frenzy insufficient reason
For conversation when we meet again.

**Robert Frost** (1874–1963)

# Design (1936)

I found a dimpled spider, fat and white,
On a white heal-all, holding up a moth
Like a white piece of rigid satin cloth—
Assorted characters of death and blight
Mixed ready to begin the morning right,        5
Like the ingredients of a witches' broth—
A snow-drop spider, a flower like a froth,
And dead wings carried like a paper kite.

What had that flower to do with being white,
The wayside blue and innocent heal-all?        10
What brought the kindred spider to that height,
Then steered the white moth thither in the night?
What but design of darkness to appall?—
If design govern in a thing so small.

Wordsworth explores the paradox of all structure. Does a confining structure have to be a prison? he asks. Is there some relief in "escaping" from the stress of living (and writing) in a world where one has "too much liberty"? Wordsworth suggests that there is. The sonnet form offers some comfort to the reader as well. We expect to hear rhymes at the end of each line, and they are there. This regularity helps us read. Because we are not "surprised" by the form, we can direct our attention to the content of a sonnet. We know something of the convention that this particular poem is joining, so we can pay closer attention to the use of words and to the poet's skill at placing these words within a predetermined form. We can also compare this particular example of the form to other sonnets that we might have read.

### Making Connections

Robert Pinsky's "Lines in Any Order" (p. 4) is a perplexing poem that adopts the form of the sonnet. Explain how thinking of this poem in terms of the sonnet's essential structure helps you make sense of the seeming randomness of the lines. Could you argue that there is a turn before the final two lines? That the final two lines reflect back on the chaos of the first twelve lines?

The sonnet is the poetic form with perhaps the richest history, especially in the English language, but it is hardly the only form. In French verse, the **sestina**, for example, consists of six sestets (six-line stanzas) and three final lines. In this form, the final words in each line of the first sestet are repeated as the final words of each line in each of the next five sestets, but the order changes in each sestet according to a specific pattern. As you can see just from this one obscure example, lists of rules regarding poetic forms as well as the names of the forms can quickly feel intimidating; sometimes, the best approach is to simply attend closely to what a specific poem actually does. Look at each line of the poem. Look for rhyming patterns among the lines. Sometimes, a poem will be written in **blank verse**, a verse form without rhymes but with consistent rhythms, generally iambic pentameter, in each of its lines. Look for structural patterns within the poem. For example, the **villanelle** is certainly a complicated poetic structure. It's unlikely you will read enough villanelles to make memorizing defining characteristics of much value. So rather than review a list of the characteristics of the structure, read the most famous example of the type, "Do Not Go Gentle into That Good Night" by Dylan Thomas. As you look for the pattern here, pay attention to rhyming words, to repetitions, and to the number and groupings of lines.

Dylan Thomas (1914–1953)

# Do Not Go Gentle into That Good Night (1952)

Do not go gentle into that good night,
Old age should burn and rave at close of day;
Rage, rage against the dying of the light.

Though wise men at their end know dark is right,
Because their words had forked no lightning they                    5
Do not go gentle into that good night,

Good men, the last wave by, crying how bright
Their frail deeds might have danced in a green bay,
Rage, rage against the dying of the light.

Wild men who caught and sang the sun in flight,                    10
And learn, too late, they grieved it on its way,
Do not go gentle into that good night,

Grave men, near death, who see with blinding sight
Blind eyes could blaze like meteors and be gay,
Rage, rage against the dying of the light.     15

And you, my father, there on the sad height,
Curse, bless, me now with your fierce tears, I pray.
Do not go gentle into that good night,
Rage, rage against the dying of the light.

If you are interested in writing poetry, this form provides an excellent challenge. The rigorous form requires thirteen words with the first rhyming sound (A) and six words with the second rhyming sound (B). The poet must work quite dexterously with words to convey any idea within such a constricted form. A less than expert poet will expend all creative energy on merely fitting words into the scheme; a less than expert reader will simply identify the scheme. A really accomplished poet will discover in the structure a form that accommodates a particular expression; a really accomplished reader will appreciate that melding of form and content. Thomas has chosen to use a strategy of repetition to fit the structure, but this strategy does more than that. He alternates the line "Rage, rage against the dying of the light" with the line "Do not go gentle into that good night" as the repeated **refrain** at the end of each stanza. Each time we see the same line again, it has acquired new meaning so that the repetition amplifies the original meaning. For instance, the third repetition of the "rage, rage" line takes on an added power because the other two lines speak of blindness. This loss of *sight* (the word that will rhyme with *light*) is an added incentive to "rage."

## A Note to Student Writers: Complicating a Thesis

The argumentative logic that we've seen operating at the core of a sonnet is a highly compacted form of a common rhetorical ploy that critical writers often use. At the start of an essay, critical writers may establish an issue, a problem, a question. Then they turn to some striking assertion—a thesis—that responds to the issue/problem/question. The complication/turn/resolution that underlies sonnets is similar to the movement that characterizes introductory paragraphs in many critical essays. Consider the following paragraph from a student paper. Note how the writer quickly establishes a problem (action films are getting tiresome) and turns against the complication (however) in order to respond to the issue raised (action in this case is made meaningful):

In many action films, action overwhelms everything else. Lost amid the crashes, explosions, and shootings is any sense of character, coherence, or even purpose. Do we need movies to show us ever more buildings collapsing, cars colliding, trains overturning? Why do we need to see such extravagant destruction? Do we care anymore? It seems that as special effects get more special, movies get more ordinary. Steven Spielberg's *War of the Worlds* reminds us, however, that the dismal state of big-budget action films can't be blamed altogether on an excess of technical wizardry. Spielberg manages to make the action of his film integral to real and pressing fears. Violent action in this film echoes and comments upon the paranoia that has arisen in our post–9/11 world. ■

   The poems that you have just read may provide still other valuable lessons for writers of analytical prose. Critical writers may learn from poets to make their essays coherent by carefully woven patterns of key words or phrases. In essays, transitions from one paragraph to another often serve to explicitly point back to the end of the previous paragraph as they move forward to a new point. Critical writers don't merely want to list insights; they want to show how insights connect and build one upon another. Look back over the section that you have just read in this book. Pay particular attention to the ends and beginnings of paragraphs. Note that the beginning of paragraphs often refers back to some important idea or word expressed in the paragraph just ended. The goal is to help the reader understand how everything fits together.

---

## COHERENCE WITHOUT TRADITIONAL OR FIXED STRUCTURE

Achieving coherence is not merely a matter of poetic shape or form. There is nothing traditional in the form of the following poem by Philip Levine, yet there is clearly some sense of structure—some way the whole poem holds together and achieves force.

**Philip Levine** (1928– )

# The Simple Truth (1995)

I bought a dollar and a half's worth of small red potatoes,
took them home, boiled them in their jackets
and ate them for dinner with a little butter and salt.
Then I walked through the dried fields

on the edge of town. In middle June the light                    5
hung on in the dark furrows at my feet,
and in the mountain oaks overhead the birds
were gathering for the night, the jays and mockers
squawking back and forth, the finches still darting
into the dusty light. The woman who sold me                     10
the potatoes was from Poland; she was someone
out of my childhood in a pink spangled sweater and sunglasses
praising the perfection of all her fruits and vegetables
at the road-side stand and urging me to taste
even the pale, raw sweet corn trucked all the way,              15
she swore, from New Jersey. "Eat, eat" she said,
"Even if you don't I'll say you did."
                              Some things
you know all your life. They are so simple and true
they must be said without elegance, meter and rhyme,
they must be laid on the table beside the salt shaker,          20
the glass of water, the absence of light gathering
in the shadows of picture frames, they must be
naked and alone, they must stand for themselves.
My friend Henri and I arrived at this together in 1965
before I went away, before he began to kill himself,           25
and the two of us to betray our love. Can you taste
what I'm saying? It is onions or potatoes, a pinch
of simple salt, the wealth of melting butter, it is obvious,
it stays in the back of your throat like a truth
you never uttered because the time was always wrong,           30
it stays there for the rest of your life, unspoken,
made of that dirt we call earth, the metal we call salt,
in a form we have no words for, and you live on it.

This poem is held together by the image of the potatoes. That image begins the poem, and the poet's ruminations about the potatoes take him home, back to the woman who sold them to him, and onto the idea that one might "taste" what he is saying. Notice that the potatoes begin the poem as actual objects that the poet boils, butters, and eats. By the end, the potatoes, with their butter and salt, become an image for an idea that "we have no words for," simple enough to stand, Levine says, outside meter and rhyme. Levine gives us a first stanza full of specific, concrete detail and a second in which those details help him express the more abstract feelings that remain largely unspoken. This progress, in which some specific object inspires a more general observation, is a common structuring device. Levine re-creates the seemingly random thought process that a person goes through, and as we think about the poem this way, we begin to realize how much structure Levine has added in order to render this otherwise anarchic process as a poem, simple in its profundity. Levine's poem reminds us that a simple truth about **free verse** is that "free" doesn't mean artless. The term merely indicates that the poem employs no regular meter or rhyme scheme.

What Levine does in "The Simple Truth" suggests one of the principal ways in which not only poems but stories, novels, plays, and films achieve coherence. Carefully managed **repetition** of a key element, image, or phrase can be extraordinarily valuable. The word **motif** is used sometimes to refer to a recurring element in literature or film. In this sense of the word, a play or novel that opens with a fresh-faced young country boy's decision to move to the city employs a motif; the audience may expect a story of innocence lost because so many stories have opened with just this scene. The word, however, is not used only for something that recurs *across* numerous texts; motif may be applied to an image, word, or action that is repeated *within* a single text. A motif provides structure; it may signal a theme or sustain a mood. This chapter opened with a discussion of how Nick Hornby employs notions of cataloguing as a cohering motif in his novel *High Fidelity*. In any lengthy work, there is a danger that the various parts will become disconnected. Novelists must certainly deal with that danger.°

Even the longest and most complex works may be grounded in a key image or phrase. For example, whiteness (as a blank, as a mystery, as both a kind of innocence and a kind of terrifying emptiness) dominates Herman Melville's *Moby-Dick*. In *Macbeth*, Shakespeare employs the motif of ill-fitting clothes; Macbeth murders the king to become king, but he finds that his new robes are too big for him. The repeated play upon ill-fitting clothes helps us pull together the whole of the action thematically: a person cannot become something greater than he or she is. In Francis Ford Coppola's *Godfather* films, the offhand invocation of business

### Making Connections

We can think back to Christopher Nolan's *Memento* in context of this discussion of coherence. We discussed that film in Chapter 1, to clarify how artists may ask us to reflect upon the meaning of plot as plot. But without a deliberate "playback" to a scene that just unfolded, without heavy repetition, an audience could easily become as confused as the main character. The main character's life is fragmented by his inability to remember from moment to moment, but our grasp of the film's meaning is strong. Nolan has figured out a way to help us understand a film that is largely about misunderstanding.

---

° And so, too, must critical writers attend to the dangers of disconnection. By referring back to Hornby here, we're trying to underscore our concern for coherence, but we're also trying to build the chapter as a coherent whole. In this case, we're circling back in order to tie together.

("just business"; "we're all businessmen here"; "smart business") in the context of the most brutal actions keeps readers alert to the suffering linked to our culture's competitive ethic of material success.

## MODELING CRITICAL ANALYSIS: T. S. ELIOT, THE LOVE SONG OF J. ALFRED PRUFROCK

Especially difficult works of art may seem on the surface to be formless—to defy a reader's search for coherence. It's often true, however, that these difficult works employ a variety of devices to help the audience through. Consider again T. S. Eliot's "The Love Song of J. Alfred Prufrock," first introduced in our discussion of images (p. 136). Many readers find this poem, upon first reading, to be very confusing. Basic questions such as, "Where are we?" "What is happening?" "Who is involved?" become hard to answer. But if we stay alert, we'll find Eliot gives us considerable help.

We are guided through "The Love Song of J. Alfred Prufrock" by a single speaker, one who invites us on a walk through dingy streets and allows us in on thoughts concerning aging, death, failure, cowardice, and so on. We are first centered on a collection of images that make us feel the city's inhospitable environment. It is soon clear that Prufrock is very much a part of the whole environment—of the evening spread against the sky "Like a Patient etherized upon a table," of the lonely city of narrow "half-deserted streets." In fact, Eliot echoes the clinical simile of the city midway through the poem when Prufrock thinks of himself as a mere specimen of others' study: "And when I am formulated, sprawling on a pin, / When I am pinned and, wriggling on the wall." It's clear that the speaker is alien to the world he so timidly encounters. He is even disassociated from his own life.

Repetition functions powerfully to help us grasp the whole of a poem that seems to scorn transitions. We get a series of questions that aren't answered but that collectively make us feel the speaker's inability to take charge or to take risks ("Do I dare?"; "So how should I presume?"; "And how should I begin"; "Shall I part my hair behind?"). We also become aware of Prufrock's painfully self-conscious manner; the line "They will say: 'How his hair is growing thin!'" prepares us for the fear he explicitly registers in line 85, as well as the fear he has that the grandest assertions may meet flat dismissal: "That is not what I meant at all." And consider the following stanza:

> In the room the women come and go
> Talking of Michelangelo.

This stanza appears twice. Although these lines seem to come from nowhere, the repetition cues us in on their place in the whole. Prufrock is a man who hasn't found substance in life. He doesn't find relief from a cold and dreary city in social chat. His disconnection comes through profoundly in relation to women—women whose emptiness makes him intensely aware of his own hollow self. The airy nothingness of the repeated stanza plays out in other clearly painful sexual encounters. The women are mere "eyes" that "fix" him coolly in place or disembodied "arms" that do not caress. It can be of no surprise to us that he thinks it would have been better to be altogether removed from such an empty social life and from the burden of his own humanity: "I should have been a pair of ragged claws / Scuttling across the floors of silent seas."

## Using Coherence to Focus Writing and Discussion

- What structuring devices appear in this work?
- How does the physical layout on the page signal this structure? Look first for line-level divisions. In poetry, see how long each line is. Is there some consistent pattern?
- Next, look for sectional divisions. What defines each of the sections? Are all sections of equal length?
- Can you label this structuring device with any of the terms that we have discussed?
- How does this structure help shape the impact of the work?

# 9 Interruption

## Where Did That Come From?

## Why Is This Here?

The previous chapter details literary structures and conventions that create a sense of coherence within a crafted text. One of the great attractions of ... Cut the transition. Let's move on to the subject of this chapter: interruption.

Although we do as much as we can to separate our lives into distinct, coherent units (and books into tidy chapters), those divisions inevitably disintegrate. Perhaps the most ubiquitous interruptions in our current culture are the cell phone ring tones that blast out of someone else's purse or pocket during class or at some quiet moment in the middle of a movie. These interruptions break the trance that the undisturbed moment held. But in some respects they are more normal than the perfect silence they violate: How much time in any given week do we spend quietly sitting in a lecture hall or movie theater? Interruptions compel us to be aware of how unusual settled composure is. In this respect, interruption and coherence are closely related. Without order, an interruption is insignificant. Without interruption, we'd hardly appreciate order. In this chapter, we'll look at specific interruptions and interruptive techniques that writers use to create an impact or suggest a theme.

## INTERRUPTING THE FICTIONAL FRAME

The technique of interruption sometimes allows an author to signal a self-conscious attitude toward narrative. The popular children's film *The Princess*

*Bride* (1987) begins with a grandfather (Peter Falk) reading a story to his grandson. As the story (in the book) begins, the movie leaves the child's bedroom and follows the "fictional" story. At points, the grandfather's voice interrupts the narrative of the fantasy "book" world, and the film returns to the child's bedroom until we plunge again into the world of the book. The abrupt shifts remind us of the fragile nature of the imaginary world we are entering. The grandson resists entering the book world at the outset of the film, but as the story goes on, he doesn't want anything to interrupt the story. By watching this child, we see something of our own role as an audience. We choose to embrace the fiction of this story just as the skeptical grandson does. The gap between reading a story and being in the story allows the director to play more than usual with the conventions of the fantasy world. There is a sense that the film is allowed to laugh at these conventions even as it employs them. Calling dangerous and fearful creatures "Rodents of Unusual Size," for instance, has a certain literariness; it is a bookish name that might not sound right without the interrupting frame that shows us that this is a story coming out of a book.

There is a long and distinguished history of strategic breaks in fictional narratives. In *Oedipus the King*, Sophocles employs a **chorus** to interrupt, interpret, and even take part in the play's action. This group of voices begins

*The Princess Bride* (1987). Fred Savage and Peter Falk in the "real world," where Falk reads the fairy tale to his grandson.

*The Princess Bride* (1987). Mel Smith, André the Giant, and Mandy Patinkin in the fantasy world of the fairy tale.

and ends scenes in the play. They analyze Oedipus's actions. They act like a community in response to this king. They ask him questions; they announce the arrival of characters onstage; they react to the developments within the play. We can think of the chorus as the first audience for what occurs onstage; in that capacity, they help shape our (the second audience's) reactions. If the chorus were removed, we would be without an important interpretive guide. If the choral lines were given to specific characters (or even new characters) within the play, we would be forced to assess different questions of perspective. How did she know that? Why did he tell us that? Of course, some choral lines might seem simply inappropriate coming from the mouth of an actual character. The chorus provides an interruption that guides our response without undermining our investment in the reality of the main action. *The Princess Bride* lets us see two worlds simultaneously; how does the use of the chorus in *Oedipus the King* achieve a similar effect?

## Experiencing Literature through Interruption

In dramatic presentations, characters may actually intrude into the action and change our consciousness of the action. In texts that we read, another common form of interruption is the footnote. Traditionally reserved for academic works, a footnote indicates a piece of information that helps support the text but is not quite important enough to include in that text. The simplest use of a footnote is to document a source of a statement, but footnotes become much more compelling when they present pieces of information that are too interesting to be excluded but not quite relevant enough to fit into the main text. These are the extra facts that the scholar has discovered and can't bear to leave out entirely. They give a certain personality to the larger work. Some fiction writers pick up on this effect and use it for their creative purposes.

In *The Hitchhiker's Guide to the Galaxy*, Douglas Adams constructs a wildly inventive novel in the form of a travelogue. Adams uses footnotes to offer "factual" background on the unfolding fictional story. In this case, the facts are meant to be entries from the fictional handbook of this comic novel. This guide supposedly contains entries on all significant facts within the galaxy, and the pride of the novel is that a writer is doing research to help update the guide. The novel makes a distinction between the casual style of the guide and the more formal entries that are contained in an imaginary reference work that exists only in the world of the novel, the *Encyclopedia Galactica*. Adams's novel might be classified as a sort of science fiction, comic, social commentary. The plot is rather episodic. The characters are wacky aliens who exhibit familiar social types. Here is an excerpt from Chapter 4 introducing the character of Zaphod Beeblebrox, along with its accompanying footnote.

**Douglas Adams**  (1952– 2001)

# from The Hitchhiker's Guide to the Galaxy (1980)

But it was not in any way a coincidence that today, the day of culmination of the project, the great day of unveiling, the day that the Heart of Gold was finally to be introduced to a marveling Galaxy, was also a great day of culmination for Zaphod Beeblebrox. It was for the sake of this day that he had first decided to run for the presidency, a decision that had sent shock waves of astonishment throughout the Imperial Galaxy. Zaphod Beeblebrox? *President?* Not *the* Zaphod Beeblebrox? Not *the* President? Many had seen it as clinching proof that the whole of known creation had finally gone bananas.

Zaphod grinned and gave the boat an extra kick of speed.

Zaphod Beeblebrox, adventurer, ex-hippie, good-timer (crook? quite possibly), manic self-publicist, terribly bad at personal relationships, often thought to be completely out to lunch.

President?

No one had gone bananas, not in that way at least.

Only six people in the entire Galaxy understood the principle on which the Galaxy was governed, and they knew that once Zaphod Beeblebrox had announced his intention to run as President it was more or less a fait accompli: he was ideal presidency fodder.*

What they completely failed to understand was why Zaphod was doing it.

---

*President: full title President of the Imperial Galactic Government.

The term *Imperial* is kept though it is now an anachronism. The hereditary Emperor is nearly dead and has been for many centuries. In the last moments of his dying coma he was locked in a stasis field which keeps him in a state of perpetual unchangingness. All his heirs are now long dead, and this means that without any drastic political upheaval, power has simply and effectively moved a rung or two down the ladder, and is now seen to be vested in a body that used to act simply as advisers to the Emperor—an elected governmental assembly headed by a President elected by that assembly. In fact it vests in no such place.

The President in particular is very much a figurehead—he wields no real power whatsoever. He is apparently chosen by the government, but the qualities he is required to display are not those of leadership but those of finely judged outrage. For this reason the President is always a controversial choice, always an infuriating but fascinating character. His job is not to wield power but to draw attention away from it. On those criteria Zaphod Beeblebrox is one of the most successful Presidents the Galaxy has ever had—he has already spent two of his ten presidential years in prison for fraud. Very very few people realize that the President and the Government have virtually no power at all, and of these few people only six know whence ultimate political power is wielded. Most of the others secretly believe that the ultimate decision-making process is handled by a computer. They couldn't be more wrong. ■

---

Note that this footnote gives a feeling of authority to the fictional world of the text. It creates the illusion that this world has layers of experience from which the book is drawing. This footnote, added to the casual narration of the story itself, suggests a history that has passed since the narrative was written. It also suggests that there are different narratives available about this single story; the footnoted narrative is a bit more academic, perhaps even a bit more "objective," than the version in the main body of the text. This particular interruption gives the illusion that a different consciousness is available to understand the events being narrated, that there is a strand of thought and conversation about these events other than the single strand recounted in the main narrative.

### Making Connections

Interruptions like the ones we've just discussed raise questions of perspective—specifically, of reliability or the lack of reliability. The interruption of a footnote gives us a presence from outside the story that can comment upon, judge, or add to the main action. But do we necessarily trust the footnote more than the story? And if we do, why should we? Do you think the footnote (with its academic or scholarly associations) seems a stronger, surer guide than a chorus? Or do you find it easier to trust the chorus? What do you look for to indicate how much you should trust the "outside" voice? What might indicate that the footnote is no more the author's voice than any other part of the text?

## STRUCTURAL INTERRUPTIONS

In the previous examples, a primary effect of the interruption was to enhance the audience's awareness of its own role within the action. The chorus, for example, models an audience that is more involved in the action than any actual audience. Interruption, though, can do more than create audience awareness. It can draw our attention to important moments. For example, look at the following poem by William Butler Yeats.

**William Butler Yeats** (1865–1939)

# The Folly of Being Comforted (1902)

One that is ever kind said yesterday:
"Your well-belovèd's hair has threads of grey,
And little shadows come about her eyes;
Time can but make it easier to be wise
Though now it seems impossible, and so                              5
All that you need is patience."
                              Heart cries, "No,
I have not a crumb of comfort, not a grain.
Time can but make her beauty over again:
Because of that great nobleness of hers                             10
The fire that stirs about her, when she stirs,
Burns but more clearly. O she had not these ways
When all the wild Summer was in her gaze."
O heart! O heart! if she'd but turn her head,
You'd know the folly of being comforted.                           15

You don't even need to read the words to notice that line 7 looks different from the rest of the poem; it is markedly shorter than any of the others. When we look closely at the poetic structure of the poem, we see that this line should be part of line 6; "No" rhymes with "so," and the poem is made up of a series of rhyming couplets. But this break reflects a real break within the action the poem recounts. The first part of the poem is an offer of comfort, but at line 7, the poet rejects that comfort. The comforting thought is interrupted, just as the line is interrupted, with Heart's cry. There is a certain passionate violence to this interruption. The broken line shows us that Heart has lost patience listening to the kind words. The break in the pattern of the poem illustrates the passion of the heart that refuses all rational words of comfort.

Look for a similar division within Mary Oliver's "Bone Poem." The poem begins with a focus on the "litter" from owl meals as it "Sinks into the wet leaves" (line 4). At line 5, the poem begins to change as "time sits with her slow spoon." Within the next three lines (5–8), we move forward through "light years" so that the poet speaks of a singular "*we*"; from this distance, distinct beings are reduced to the primal substances that make up all living things.

**Mary Oliver** (1935– )

# Bone Poem (1979)

The litter under the tree
Where the owl eats—shrapnel

Of rat bones, gull debris—
Sinks into the wet leaves

Where time sits with her slow spoon,                                     5
Where *we* becomes singular, and a quickening

From light-years away
Saves and maintains. O holy

Protein, o hallowed lime,
O precious clay!                                                         10

Tossed under the tree
The cracked bones

Of the owl's most recent feast
Lean like shipwreck, starting

The long fall back to the center—                                       15
The seepage, the flowing,

The equity: sooner or later
In the shimmering leaves

The rat will learn to fly, the owl
Will be devoured.                                                       20

The interruption occurs in the middle of line 8. One sentence ends, and suddenly, "O holy" crowds into the line. The exclamation continues for two more lines (9–10) ("O holy Protein, o hallowed lime, / O precious clay!"), proclaiming the substances that are the essence of this more distant point of view. After this outburst, the poem returns to the specific debris from "the owl's most recent feast" as these bones start their "long fall back to the center" (line 15) and to their elemental nature. Here the interruption is a central outburst, almost a big bang after which the poem returns to the form, subject, and philosophical musings that it had before the interruption.

## Experiencing Film through Interruption

Interruptions often cause us, as the audience of the work, to reexamine our relation to the work that we are viewing. Think about the following example.

Many performing arts venues want to quiet the electronic noises that often interrupt performances. One strategy has been to create a loud ring tone just as the show is about to get under way. This fake interruption (followed by an announcement about turning off all phones) makes people in the audience uncomfortable. First, we are ready to glare at the offender. Then, we realize that we have been drawn into a fiction. This ring tone is not real, but our own real phone has the potential to be just as disruptive. As audience members, we participate in the performance, even if our part in the performance is simply our silence. In fact, this created "interruption" illustrates an aspect of the complex relation that we have to fiction itself. Although people tend to ignore an announcement they have heard many times before (such as the emergency information that flight attendants recite before a plane takes off), they react to this fictional interruption differently. They are prompted to think about the way they relate to the fiction.

Film has been particularly adept at playing with the relations between the fictional world on the screen and the world outside that screen—between reel life and real life. Which of these worlds is the interruption? Are we challenged to question what we take as real by such films as Woody Allen's *The Purple Rose of Cairo*? In the 1984 film, a movie hero steps out of the screen and into the life of a lonely woman watching the picture. That break leads us (like the woman, we are moviegoers) to reflect on our desire to stay in the fictional world that is on the screen. Gary Ross's *Pleasantville* (1998) reverses the ploy; two contemporary characters are thrust into a 1950s black-and-white TV world. This abrupt interruption of a contemporary suburban family drama eventually leads us to rethink our problems as well as our nostalgia for a "better time" that we like to believe really existed. Films can also break our narrative expectations and thereby make us more sensitive to those expectations. The multiple plots of *Pulp Fiction* (1994) and their seemingly random order disrupt our sense of how a film should tell a story, but the apparent disorder actually evolves into its own coherence. When we see

*Pulp Fiction* (1994). This film still shows Vega, played by John Travolta, in the closing scene of the film. The audience sees him alive and happy *after* seeing him killed.

Vincent Vega (John Travolta) strolling casually offscreen at the end of the film in his UC Santa Cruz Banana Slugs T-shirt, we feel a kind of lightness even though we know Vincent is soon to die humiliatingly while sitting on the toilet. Or perhaps it's more accurate to say we know he has already died in an earlier scene in the movie. The action that unfolds on the screen doesn't mesh with our sense of normal time or linear development of a story. Is director Quentin Tarantino teasing us about our needs for a happy ending or for the artifice of the many happy endings we've seen in movies? Or is he demonstrating that movies have the power to transcend real pain; maybe that, for Tarantino, is their special gift. The sort of disruption that operates so effectively in *Pulp Fiction*, and in a film such as *Run Lola Run* (1999), challenges our notions of what filmed stories can be.

## JUXTAPOSITION

**Juxtaposition** is the rhetorical technique of putting two (or more) things next to each other; the resulting contrast or similarity makes us see both objects differently than we saw them when each stood by itself. A simple exercise in juxtaposition uses two colored fabrics. When two colors are placed next to each other, the juxtaposition will bring out qualities in both colors that are not evident when the colors sit separately. For instance, it might be difficult to determine whether a particular fabric is black or navy blue. By setting the fabric in question next to a fabric that you know to be black, it becomes easier to judge. Neither color has changed, but slight differences become apparent with the comparison. In works of art, juxtapositions are often more strongly marked; radical contrasts break or interrupt our customary ways of interpreting the world. The pairing of objects that initially appear unrelated forces us to search for connections amid obvious differences.

Juxtaposition is especially effective in photography. Margaret Bourke-White's photograph of a bread line of real people (African Americans) standing in front of a fictional white family in the propaganda poster delivers a clear message. The contrast between the real and the imaginary here is stark. The seriousness of the people standing in line makes a mockery of the claim on the billboard. The jubilant white family enjoying a comfortable life above seems to bear no real relation to the American lives being led by the people in line below. "There's no way like the American Way" takes on a different meaning from the billboard's intent because of Bourke-White's juxtaposition. In the photograph, we see an irony of race and class in American society. The sign insists that the country has the "World's Highest Standard of Living," but the real people in this scene have no access to the material goods that the family in the poster behind them are celebrating.

Margaret Bourke-White, *At the Time of the Louisville Flood* (1937)

As we use this photograph to illustrate the idea of juxtaposition, it is important to acknowledge that there is no necessary relation between the particular people standing in line and the billboard that happens to be behind them. As soon as we look at Bourke-White's composition, the convergence of real people and propaganda takes on meaning. **Synchronicity** refers to events that coincide in time and appear to be related but have no discoverable causal connection. In this instance, the people and the poster illustrate tensions within American society more clearly than any extended exploration of race and class in our culture. This moment that Bourke-White has captured symbolizes larger social problems. We should notice the sophistication necessary to read the ironic juxtaposition that appears here. Unless we are aware of the discrepancy between white and black culture and unless we can read the markers of wealth and poverty, we cannot appreciate the synchronicity that Bourke-White has captured. When we compared two fabrics to discover which one was blue, we had a particular standard that we were trying to test; the comparison was useful because we knew what we were looking for. When we come to this photograph, we bring a set of cultural standards that help us see the meanings that Bourke-White presents.

## Making Connections

**Irony** can be considered a strategy of interruption because it works by introducing the unexpected. In general, irony arises from a gap between expectation and actuality, intention and realization, appearance and truth. Because irony depends upon suggestion rather than explicit statement, it requires that a viewer or reader be alert to small signals. It is by nature complex and subject to subtle shading and **ambiguity** (uncertainty or multiplicity of meaning, suggestive qualities of expression, contradictory implications). Critics often specify distinct types of irony. **Dramatic irony** refers to a gap between what a character knows and what an audience understands; a character who doesn't appreciate the significance of the words he or she speaks conveys a dramatic irony. The audience is, in effect, alerted to meanings that the author wants to communicate from outside the character's consciousness. A character who deliberately plays upon the difference between words and meaning expresses **verbal irony**; such a character might deliberately understate a problem to emphasize its gravity or overstate a problem to highlight its triviality. Bourke-White's photograph illustrates what is often called **contextual** or **situational irony** — an irony that arises from coincidence or circumstances.

## Experiencing Literature through Juxtaposition

In "Tattoo," Ted Kooser uses juxtaposition to examine the tattoo that he sees on the arm of a man at a yard sale. But instead of describing just the tattoo, Kooser describes the context in which he sees the mark. He reads the tattoo as a signal of an identity that seems out of place in the mundane domestic world of a yard sale.

**Ted Kooser** (1939– )

# Tattoo (2005)

What once was meant to be a statement—
a dripping dagger held in the fist
of a shuddering heart—is now just a bruise
on a bony old shoulder, the spot
where vanity once punched him hard                           5
 and the ache lingered on. He looks like
someone you had to reckon with,
strong as a stallion, fast and ornery,
but on this chilly morning, as he walks
between the tables at a yard sale                            10
 with the sleeves of his tight black T-shirt
rolled up to show us who he was,
he is only another old man, picking up
broken tools and putting them back,
his heart gone soft and blue with stories.                  15

Compare the scene that Kooser presents here with Bourke-White's photograph. In the photograph, we see a scene that captures disturbing inequities within American culture. What does Kooser capture in the tattoo that he sees at this yard sale? Think, too, about the process of conveying this juxtaposition. Bourke-White presents only the image. What commentary does Kooser add to the image that he sees? Look at the specific words and phrases he uses so that we will see the juxtaposition as he sees it.

## MONTAGE

In elementary school, you may have been asked to do a montage—that is, to paste a collection of images onto a single sheet of paper. The images might at first glance seem altogether random, but randomness wasn't the point of the assignment. The idea was to create an effect or underscore a theme through juxtaposed images. **Montage** (echoing a French verb meaning "to assemble") is a useful word in the study of both film and literature.

In film criticism, montage refers to a style of editing that uses sudden juxtapositions of images, surprising cuts, and radical shifts in perspective. This technique differs greatly from what has been called the "classic Hollywood" or "invisible" style of editing—a style that seeks to achieve naturalistic effects. The montage style is essentially interruptive; it shakes viewers from a settled attention to narrative and character and forces them to experience film as film. It deliberately breaks the illusion we often seek in films of observing actions as they actually happen.

Literary critics have borrowed the word *montage* to describe dramatic juxtapositions of images or scenes or even narrative voices. A novelist might, for example, break a narrative by inserting actual advertising jingles, headlines, even news stories from the historical time of the narrative to contextualize the fictional action. A fictional or dramatic montage might also be constructed from a collection of short stories/skits or character sketches— almost snapshots of life. Sandra Cisneros's *The House on Mango Street* does just that. A poet might give us a series of images, as does Wallace Stevens in "Thirteen Ways of Looking at a Blackbird," and not require us to connect the images thematically. Stevens wrote, for example, that his famous poem aimed at communicating a series of "sensations."

## Experiencing Film through Juxtaposition

Filmmaker Michael Moore is a master of juxtaposition, a gift that has earned him both an Oscar and harsh criticism. In his first film, the documentary *Roger and Me* (1989), Moore argues that corporations have a responsibility to the communities in which they work, not just to their shareholders.

This film traces the actions of General Motors in Flint, Michigan, where the company had recently shut down manufacturing plants and moved production to countries where labor was cheaper. Films and dramatic productions can, of course, add sound as yet another element in the mix: what we see clashes with what we hear. In the devastating final scene, Moore shows General Motors chairman Roger Smith, the "Roger" of the film's title, delivering a banal Christmas address to GM workers, talking about compassion, and quoting Charles Dickens, as "an expert on Christmas" while a choir sings in the background. Moore cuts away from the film footage of the speech to show a laid-off GM worker and her family in Flint being evicted from their home on Christmas Eve. On the sound track, Smith continues to drone on about caring for others while we watch the eviction officer setting the family's Christmas tree and presents out by the curb. As Moore has edited this scene, Smith's words seem empty, self-serving, and hypocritical. By juxtaposing the bland unreality of Smith's speech and the harsh suffering of the evicted family, Moore uses the scene as the culmination of the

A publicity shot for *Roger and Me* dramatizes director Michael Moore's techniques in the film. Moore dresses as a common man who identifies with the hard times suffered in Flint, Michigan, when General Motors closed production facilities there.

Moore juxtaposes news photos, such as this shot of General Motors chairman Roger Smith meeting with President Ronald Reagan, with Smith's on-camera refusal to meet with Moore to talk about laid-off workers in Flint.

argument he is making in his film that Smith, who serves as a symbol of corporate America, is responsible for both the content of this speech and for the corporate actions that impact American workers. The images and words set in such marked contrast make Moore's argument.

In this context, the juxtaposition echoes the work of Bourke-White. Because editing is so apparent in Moore's work, some critics argue that his "documentary" distorts the truth. His editorial techniques, they claim, create a fictional version of reality that suits his political purpose. Try to use the same critique to challenge Bourke-White's image. This photograph suggests that the people standing in line have some actual relation to the poster. Are they deliberately contradicting its image? Is the poster there to mock them? Is the single image more or less manipulative than film? However we respond to such questions, it is clear that we are responding to a crafted work of art.

## A Note to Student Writers: Making Comparisons Relevant

Observing juxtaposition as an effective strategy in these crafted texts can help us in our own writing. A common writing assignment will ask students to "compare and contrast" two subjects (books, characters, settings, poems, films, and so on). This technique casts a wide net in the hope that students might find something of value in the comparisons. By juxtaposing, we gain a clearer sense of the issues/elements under analysis. The technique, however, brings with it potential problems.

All writers must be careful to measure and evaluate the demands any form of interruption makes on a reader. In Ted Kooser's "Tattoo," juxtaposition is used to imply or suggest a thought or feeling. Kooser never tells us that the man at the yard sale was foolish to get a tattoo in his earlier life or that the man has now settled down into some sort of domesticity or that his former ferociousness has faded. It is up to us to draw conclusions from the juxtaposition of the yard sale scene and the tattoo's image. The suggestive power of the poem is part of its beauty. An analytical paper that stays at the level of suggestion and implication won't likely be read so favorably. Critical papers usually need to be more explicit about the purpose and the point of the comparison. In a similar way, an abrupt turn in a poem, story, play, or movie might serve as an effective interruption. It might jar us into paying attention or shake us out of our standard way of seeing things. But a strong interruption in a critical essay might be taken as incoherence, or just plain sloppiness. Writers must understand that readers don't come to every text with the same set of expectations and demands.

Compare/contrast assignments are challenging largely because they require you to bring together what might seem dissimilar things. The very nature of the task carries a risk of confusing the reader (what does A have to do with B?; does a discussion of B merely interrupt the discussion of A?). In writing a compare/contrast paper, you are required to bring together ideas whether or not an author has already done that for you. In this sort of paper, the comparison is entirely yours. You must, therefore, justify your approach. It's not enough in a compare/contrast paper to simply note similarities and differences and trust the reader to make sense of how everything adds up. You need to think about how the process of setting two texts alongside each other allows you to see something you might otherwise miss.

As a writer, it is helpful to imagine a nagging voice at your ear, constantly asking, "So what?" about everything that you write down. Your answer to that question is the beginning of your analysis. That answer will structure your paper. Until you answer that question, you have only made observations about the materials you are studying. And after you answer that question the first time, you should continue to ask it of every point of comparison or contrast. The more insistent you can be in challenging your own material, the more effective your analysis will be.

There is yet another lesson about compare/contrast papers to be learned from Michael Moore's film: an organizational lesson. Moore keeps the policies of Roger Smith parallel to the poverty in Flint, Michigan. His attempts to talk with Roger Smith are part of the discussions that he carries on with the unemployed people of Flint. When he talks with the managers at GM, he talks about the responsibility of the corporation to the workers it employs and to the surrounding community. He does not devote half the film to poverty and then switch to a discussion of GM policies. The two strands of the discussion are consistently integrated. By the time we reach the climactic final scenes in the film, Moore has prepared us as viewers to see the connections between Smith's words and the evicted family. Whether or not we agree with Moore's argument, we can see that it is a powerful rhetorical strategy and one that you can adopt for your own purposes.

---

# MODELING CRITICAL ANALYSIS:
# T. S. ELIOT, THE LOVE SONG OF J. ALFRED PRUFROCK

As we return to Eliot's "Prufrock" (p. 136), we see how much this poem is marked by interruptions of various sorts. The stanzas are irregular. There are rhymed couplets that might be described as a chorus ("In the room the women come and go / Talking of Michelangelo"). Stanzas are divided sometimes with simply a blank line (see for instance, the division between lines 12 and 13); other times there are sectional markers dividing them (between lines 69 and 70, 74 and 75, 110 and 111). Within the stanzas, ellipses, or three successive dots (lines 10, 72, 77, and 120); dashes (lines 83, 95, 102, and 103); and parentheses (lines 41, 44, and 64) interrupt the narrative. Often, it seems the speaker is interrupted before he can complete an idea. In this poem the sheer volume of the interruption is staggering. It is useful to go through and mark each interruption, but in our analysis, we will concentrate on just a few and explain why we find those particular interruptions significant to our growing understanding of this complex poem.

The poem begins with a command, "Let us go," and throughout the first stanza, we see that command three times (lines 1, 4, and 12). The narrator describes the scenes where he means to be going, but by line 10, we feel the tension between that impulse to move forward and the voice that signals inertia. The interruption at line 10 is a series of three dots. The poem's first sentence has finally ended, and the three dots indicate a pause. At the end of this sentence, the narrator compares the streets he describes to a form of intellectual inquiry ("like a tedious argument / Of insidious intent / To lead you to an overwhelming question"). As the speaker interrupts his rambling simile about "half-deserted streets," we begin to see the irony within this voice: in spite of the "Let us go" that begins the sentence, this tendency to lapse into intense scrutiny is precisely what keeps the speaker from going anywhere. We hear that conflict in line 11, a line that interrupts the abstraction of the "overwhelming question" by getting back to the desire to go: "Oh, do not ask, 'What is it? / Let us go and make our visit.'" Suddenly, we have two sentences in two lines. There are no images to wade through here. This rhymed couplet reacts against the wandering construction of the first ten lines of the poem. This interruption sounds like a different voice from the one that offers elaborate descriptions, not of any destination, but of the circuitous route that they must take as they go. So, the interruption here moves us out of the first stanza as it shows us that there are opposing impulses leading us through the poem.

Lines 13 and 14 offer another interruption: "In the room the women come and go / Talking of Michelangelo." We are suddenly off the street. These women and their room appear out of nowhere. What can we do with these two lines? As noted in the discussion of coherence in the previous chapter, it's helpful to note that they are repeated in lines 35 and 36. When a song has a chorus, a soloist might sing the verse and invite the audience to join in at the chorus. The chorus is usually short and simple enough that everyone can join in at the appropriate moment. In a song it functions to anchor us rhythmically, emotionally, and thematically. But what does Michelangelo have to do with Prufrock's visit? This chorus suggests that the talk about Michelangelo may be rather empty even though it is intimidating to someone who is not part of the women's social circle. The women belong to a place where Prufrock might like to be, but a place he cannot quite bring himself to go. The lines function to interrupt and disconcert Prufrock—the confident chorus in contrast to his tentative indecision. At the same time, they lend some coherence to the poetic form. The repeated interruption offers something familiar within a poem that appears at first to be nothing but interruptions. And as mentioned at the start of the chapter, if there were no structure, there would be nothing to interrupt.

## Using Interruption to Focus Writing and Discussion

■ An interruption suggests that there should be some established order to interrupt. What is that order? How is it established in this particular work?

- Is there some interruption of the stasis within the text? For instance, is action interrupted by inaction; inaction interrupted by action; action interrupted by another action; a thought interrupted by action; a thought interrupted by another thought? Is there some interruption of the movement of the text itself? Does a poem suddenly stop rhyming, or is the rhythm thrown off; does a narrator become incoherent; does the style of the section change? Is there something that is simply surprising and difficult to account for? What is the interruption?

- Identify the moment that the interruption occurs in the text. Try to isolate the moment as specifically as possible. Is there a single sentence, phrase, or word that embodies the interruption?

- How is this word (or series of words) somehow different from the words around it? What makes it stand out? Is there some graphic method of representing the difference? What does the author do to announce this interruption? What makes you notice this interruption?

- What are we supposed to do with the interruption? Does the author give us any clues? Does the author offer any analysis of the moment? If so, describe how the author tells us this interruption is important.

- Is there a return to the original order that was interrupted? Or is there some new order? Has all order been lost? Has the text simply gone on to something else? Is there some pattern of interruptions?

- Why is this interruption interesting? Looking at an increasing number of different interruptions, you may begin to see patterns in their significance. How does this specific interruption fit into the patterns of interruptions that we have studied within this chapter?

- What is the purpose of the interruptions? What happens in the text that could not happen without the interruption?

- Locate specific juxtapositions that the interruptions in the text make available to us.

  - What images, ideas, characters, or situations have been paired in this particular text?
  - How is it that the audience gains access to each image?
  - How does one add meaning to the other?
  - In what ways do the two images work differently?
  - How does the author compel the audience to look at the two together?

- How does the comparison of the world of the text before and after the interruption offer insight into the routine that has been interrupted? How much of this insight is available to characters within the text, and how much is available to those who are reading the text?

# 10 Tone

## Did I Hear That Right?

A tone is simply a sound—a sound that by duration, pitch, or volume achieves a certain quality. The tones we notice most contrast sharply with what we usually hear: "When my mother uses that tone, all trouble stops" or "Don't use that tone with me, young man." When we discuss tone, we refer to the way that a person delivers a message rather than just the message itself. This delivery includes the quality of voice and the choice of words; it tells us about the deliverer's attitude toward the message, and it has an impact upon how we hear the message.

The visual arts also use the quality of tone to describe the impact that an artist creates. The blinking light on the photocopy machine tells us that the machine is low on toner, the pigment used to create the range of black and gray that makes up the images on our page. In black-and-white photography, the photographer might replace the black with the rich brown of sepia to give the print an older appearance. Attention to such toning elements does not change the document that we are photocopying or the scene in the photograph, but it has a marked impact upon the printed images that we see. The photocopy made without enough toner will look quite light, whereas the original sepia photograph, although new, looks as if it came from another time. The tone determines how we receive these visual images just as a tone of voice influences our understanding of the words that we hear.

# HEARING RIGHT

Hearing right can make all the difference. The same words delivered with a different tone of voice can have very different meanings. Consider the following poem:

**Margaret Atwood** (1939– )

# you fit into me (1971)

> You fit into me
> like a hook into an eye
> A fish hook
> An open eye

The first words, "you fit into me," make us think that the poem is a love poem. Working through the simile, we imagine the hook and eye that are used as clothing fasteners, but the last two lines shock us out of this reading with the violent image of a fishhook piercing an eyeball. That change in the final lines suggests a severe bitterness about the relation between the narrator and the "you" in the poem. It is no mistake that we read the first lines as almost loving, yet we must abruptly rethink that immediate response. We realize in the final lines that what we read as a shift in tone is really a shift in our understanding of that tone. The narrator has been bitter throughout the poem; we simply do not realize it until we get to the third line.

We usually pick up on conversational signals instantly, but when words are written down, it is sometimes difficult to "hear" clearly. How can you tell that someone is being reverent rather than ironic? One clue is our knowledge of that person. The same sort of knowledge is useful when we read, though more challenging to attain. We learn about certain authors, so we know what to expect from them. This knowledge often makes us better readers. As you get to know authors, your ability to hear their tone improves. But in the Atwood poem, the poet might be taking advantage of what a reader doesn't know about her attitudes toward the difficult complexity of relationships. **Irony** requires us to hold up two possible meanings simultaneously—the narrator could be expressing a great love or could be expressing great revulsion—and to pick one of those readings. Setting up the first interpretation by playing to our investment in the idea of romantic love makes the second (real) interpretation so much more stinging and darkly humorous. Atwood presses toward **sarcasm**—an extreme and aggressive form of **verbal irony** in which the thing *said* and the thing *meant* stand in stark opposition. When we discuss tone in a text, we generally refer to complex forms of expression that do not announce their intentions clearly. A **sincere** tone, for instance, may accurately describe a particular work but would rarely generate much discussion. Sincerity may be taken as the other extreme of sarcasm, for a sincere expression matches word and meaning. When we discuss tone, we usually refer to the distortions that influence how we hear words and how we learn to interpret those words.

What if you have never read the works of a particular author? How can you hear the tone of someone whose work is new to you? Remember that even in conversation, you are aware of the context in which something has been said. A commonplace saying like "Have a nice day" could be either sarcastic or sincere, but in most cases it is unlikely we would have trouble hearing the difference. When someone says that this is the best time he or she has ever had, you have clues surrounding you about whether or not that person seems to be having a good time. Is the person enthusiastic? Do things really appear to be going well? Those clues help you figure out what meaning to take from the words.

## Experiencing Literature through Tone

Dorothy Parker, whom you should never trust to deliver a toneless poem, uses the conventions of love poetry to talk about the "perfect rose" that she has received.

**Dorothy Parker** (1893–1967)

# One Perfect Rose (1926)

A single flower he sent me, since we met.
  All tenderly his messenger he chose;
Deep-hearted, pure, with scented dew still wet—
  One perfect rose.

I knew the language of the floweret;                                    5
  "My fragile leaves," it said, "his heart enclose."
Love long has taken for his amulet
  One perfect rose.

Why is it no one ever sent me yet
  One perfect limousine, do you suppose?                               10
Ah no, it's always just my luck to get
  One perfect rose.

Look closely at her word choice that shows how she suggests the tone of conventional love poetry in her first two stanzas. Which word changes the tone of this entire poem? How does this shift change the meaning of all of the lines that have come before it? By the end of the poem, we're ready to go back and read everything differently. Like Atwood, Parker turns against the conventions of romantic love. But her turn doesn't communicate quite the same painful edginess.

Next, look at another of Parker's poems. What common ideas do you associate with the title "Thought for a Sunshiny Morning"?

**Dorothy Parker** (1893–1967)

# Thought for a Sunshiny Morning (1936)

It costs me never a stab nor squirm
To tread by chance upon a worm.
"Aha, my little dear," I say,
"Your clan will pay me back one day."

Notice that having read another poem by Parker does not spoil this second poem. In fact, our experience with the two poems helps us form a preliminary feeling for Parker's distinctive voice. We do have some idea of the sort of thing that we might expect, but here the tone begins with a title that contrasts sharply with the subject of death. The simple rhyme scheme and rhythmic pattern also contribute to the almost cheerful fatalism of Parker's poetic voice. With these two examples, how might you begin to define Parker's tone?

The tone in John Donne's poem "The Flea" is altogether different, but understanding the tone remains an essential key to unlocking the poem. Donne also holds up multiple meanings; he dismisses serious issues of virtue by asking whether a flea has stolen his lover's virginity by sucking first his blood and then hers. Even as Donne delights in turning the metaphor inside out, he hardly seems to be mocking virtue or his beloved. We might say he maintains a playfully sincere tone in this poem.

**John Donne** (1572–1631)

# The Flea (1633)

Mark but this flea, and mark in this,
How little that which thou deniest me is;
It suck'd me first, and now sucks thee,

And in this flea our two bloods mingled be.
Thou know'st that this cannot be said                                5
A sin, nor shame, nor loss of maidenhead;
　Yet this enjoys before it woo,
　And pamper'd swells with one blood made of two;
　And this, alas! is more than we would do.

O stay, three lives in one flea spare,                              10
Where we almost, yea, more than married are.
This flea is you and I, and this
Our marriage bed, and marriage temple is.
Though parents grudge, and you, we're met,
And cloister'd in these living walls of jet.                        15
　Though use make you apt to kill me,
　Let not to that self-murder added be,
　And sacrilege, three sins in killing three.

Cruel and sudden, hast thou since
Purpled thy nail in blood of innocence?                             20
Wherein could this flea guilty be,
Except in that drop which it suck'd from thee?
Yet thou triumph'st, and say'st that thou
Find'st not thyself nor me the weaker now.
　'Tis true; then learn how false fears be;                         25
　Just so much honour, when thou yield'st to me,
　Will waste, as this flea's death took life from thee.

As we make our way through this poem, Donne's language of virtue constantly must compete with the fact that his subject is really the flea that she
kills. Her nail "Purpled" in the "blood of innocence" gives the event an
inappropriately lofty language. Until we realize that his single goal here is to
break down her virtue, this language may make the poem itself appear much
more lofty than it is. Donne wants the flea, now dead even though it had
swallowed her blood, to symbolize the meaninglessness of conventions that
enforce virginity.

# MIXING AND BALANCING OPPOSING TONES

Ted Kooser writes a poem in which he captures the idiosyncratic tone of a
person who might be anyone's "Aunt Belle" remarking on a terrible tragedy.

The name of the person gives us a sense of the chattiness and random connections that often accompany such relations where there are shared memories and understandings that help maintain a sense of family. As you read this "letter," note how the tone shifts abruptly as a core story haltingly unfolds. In what ways is this uneven tone appropriate? What details from Aunt Belle's correspondence define this tone for you? Is this poem ultimately about a tragic event or about a character? Perhaps it is about a specific character's response to tragedy.

**Ted Kooser** (1939– )

# A Letter from Aunt Belle (2004)

You couldn't have heard about it there—
I'll send the clippings later on.

The afternoon that the neighbors' stove exploded—
how it reminded me of … Sarah's garden wedding!
Do you remember? It was beautiful.                                           5

As I was watering those slips
I promised you—the violets—
there was an awful thud, and Samson's wall
puffed up and blew the windows out.
It turned some pictures in the living room,                                   10
and that lovely vase you children gave to me
Christmas of '56 fell down, but I can glue it.

That Franklin boy you knew in school—
the one who got that girl in trouble—
ran in the Samson's house, but she was dead;                                  15
the blast collapsed her lungs, poor thing.
She always made me think of you,
but on the stretcher with her hair pinned up
and one old sandal off, she looked as old
as poor old me.                                                              20
               I have to go—
I've baked a little coffee cake
for Mr. Samson and the boys.

The violet slips are ready—
                    Write.

Identify the clues that help you recognize the tone of this letter: the questions, the promises of future correspondence, the references to an old neighbor, the assumption of authority over the reader, the neighborliness, the chattiness, the gossipy delivery of the tragic news. All of these details teach us to know the character who is writing and help us interpret her words. Notice how this tone nearly hides the most significant news the letter has to communicate. Buried inside the offer of violet slips and memories of Sarah's garden wedding is the death of a wife and mother. But the chatty delivery of this news doesn't lessen the poem's impact. It actually deepens our sense of the speaker; it helps us know her better than she knows herself. Aunt Belle may revert to conversational niceties, but she is struck by this death: "she looked as old / as poor old me." And she does what she can to alleviate the grief of "Mr. Samson and the boys." The poem offers a full account of her old-fashioned neighborliness: she gossips, but she also feels a responsibility to those who live around her.

## Experiencing Literature through Tone

Like all considerations of tone, humor requires some understanding of the context in which the performance occurs. Much humor involves an upsetting of traditional, recognizable, and well-understood structures. To recognize that a structure has been upset, one must be fairly familiar with the original. In order to appreciate irreverence, one needs some experience with reverence. In some ways, irreverence may be the more complex attitude, at least in terms of interpretation. In the following passage from *Mules and Men*, Zora Neale Hurston sets us down in the middle of a conversation about the nature of religious controversy in a small town. The main character, Charlie, creates a story that conflates several familiar stories from the New Testament. In order to appreciate Charlie's story (and to laugh with the others around this particular table), one has to know the originals. The religious teachings of Jesus sometimes depend upon a clear literalness; other times they are metaphors. When Jesus says, "Upon this rock, I will build my church," it is generally understood that he is playing with the derivation of Peter's name—he will build a church upon the bedrock, the faith that Peter (*petra*, "rock") has professed. In other biblical incidents, the Christian tradition emphasizes the literalness of Jesus' miraculous work—he was able to feed thousands of people with only five loaves of bread, and he turned water into wine. This particular story finds its humor by having Charlie take everything literally.

**Zora Neale Hurston** (1891–1960)

## from **Mules and Men** (1935)

As the prayer ended the bell of Macedonia, the Baptist church, began to ring.

"Prayer meetin 'night at Macedony," George Thomas said.

"It's too bad that it must be two churches in Eatonville," I commented. "De town's too little. Everybody ought to go to one."

"It's too bad, Zora, and you know better. Fack is, de Christian churches nowhere don't stick together," this from Charlie.

Everybody agreed that this was true. So Charlie went on. "Look at all de kind of denominations we got. But de people can't help dat cause de church wasn't built on no solid foundation to start wid."

"Oh yes, it twas!" Johnnie Mae disputed him. "It was built on solid rock. Didn't Jesus say 'On dis rock Ah build my church?'"

"Yeah," chimed in Antie Hoyt. "And de song says 'On Christ solid rock I stand' and 'Rock of Ages.'"

Charlie was calm and patient. "Yeah, he built it on a rock, but it wasn't solid. It was a pieced-up rock and that's how come de church split up now. Here's de very way it was:

Christ was walkin' long one day wid all his disciples and he said, 'We're goin' for a walk today. Everybody pick up a rock and come along.' So everybody got their selves a nice big rock 'ceptin' Peter. He was lazy so he picked up a li'l bit of a pebble and dropped it in his side pocket and come along.

Well, they walked all day long and de other 'leven disciples changed them rocks from one arm to de other but they kept on totin' 'em. Long towards sundown they come 'long by de Sea of Galilee and Jesus tole 'em, 'Well, le's fish awhile. Cast in yo' nets right here.' They done like he tole ,em and caught a great big mess of fish. Then they cooked 'em and Christ said, 'Now, all y'all bring up yo' rocks.' So they all brought they rocks and Christ turned 'em into bread and they all had a plenty to eat wid they fish exceptin' Peter. He couldn't hardly make a moufful offa de li'l bread he had and he didn't like dat a bit.

Two or three days after dat Christ went out doors and looked up at de sky and says, 'Well, we're goin' for an other walk today. Everybody git yo'self a rock and come along.'

They all picked up a rock apiece and was ready to go. All but Peter. He went and tore down half a mountain. It was so big he couldn't move it wid his hands. He had to take a pinch-bar to move it. All day long Christ walked and talked to his disciples and Peter sweated and strained wid dat rock of his'n.

Way long in de evenin' Christ went up under a great big ole tree and set down and called all of his disciples around 'im and said, 'Now everybody bring up yo' rocks.'

So everybody brought theirs but Peter. Peter was about mile down de road punchin' dat half a mountain he was bringin'. So Christ waited till he got dere. He looked at de rocks dat de other 'leven disciples had, den he seen dis great big mountain dat Peter had and so he got up and walked over to it and put one foot up on it and said, "Why Peter, dis is a fine rock you got here! It's a noble rock! And Peter, on dis rock Ab'm gointer build my church.'

Peter says, 'Naw you ain't neither. You won't build no church house on dis rock. You gointer turn dis rock into bread.'

Christ knowed dat Peter meant dat thing so he turnt de hillside into bread and dat mountain is de bread he fed de 5,000 wid. Den he took dem 'leven other rocks and glued 'em together and built his church on it.

And that's how come de Christian churches is split up into so many different kinds cause it's built on pieced-up rock." ∎

### Making Connections

Consider how the tonal clash between different kinds of language and representation function in other works you've read or films you've seen. Shakespeare, for example, is known for mixing the formal and the informal, the "high" and the "low." Suzan-Lori Parks, a prizewinning contemporary playwright, mixes conventionally high and low to great effect in *Topdog/Underdog*. In that play, one character enacts in a cheap boardwalk show a major event in U.S. history that has been recounted solemnly in standard textbooks. Perhaps Parks sets the tone of the boardwalk show against that of the history books in order to comment on the attitude we usually take toward the national tragedy of President Lincoln's assassination. In effect, she challenges us to rethink the kind of importance we usually grant the event.

The humorous tone of Hurston's story is also created out of the informal retelling of what are taken as sacred texts. Such mixing of **colloquial** (spoken) with consciously literary (written) styles is a common way to refresh or challenge language that has grown distant in its formality. Charlie may not have a strong command of the King James Bible (an early seventeenth-century translation that has been called "the noblest monument of English prose"), but he cannot be accused of being a passive reader. We might ask, How does Hurston want us to see Charlie? Do we come away from this comic dialogue with a sense of his foolishness or an appreciation for his wit?

## IRONY AND INTROSPECTION

There is something appealing about the fact that opposites can coexist. Peter and his disjointed united church present an explanation of one such coexistence. In the following poem, Margaret Atwood builds upon the legend of the Sirens, the beautiful bird-women whose songs are so alluring that they cause sailors to crash upon the rocks. In this poem, Atwood chooses to imagine that beautiful music from the singer's perspective. That shift again leads to a dramatically different tone.

**Margaret Atwood** (1939– )

# Siren Song (1976)

This is the one song everyone
would like to learn: the song
that is irresistible:
the song that forces men
to leap overboard in squadrons                                5
even though they see the beached skulls
the song nobody knows
because anyone who has heard it
is dead, and the others can't remember
Shall I tell you the secret                                  10
and if I do, will you get me
out of this bird suit?
I don't enjoy it here
squatting on this island
looking picturesque and mythical                             15
with these two feathery maniacs,
I don't enjoy singing
this trio, fatal and valuable.
I will tell the secret to you,
to you, only to you.                                         20
Come closer. This song
is a cry for help: Help me!
Only you, only you can,
you are unique

At last. Alas                                                25
it is a boring song
but it works every time.

Atwood's poem requires that we know something of another work. If we have no knowledge of Homer's *Odyssey*, we will not fully appreciate the dramatic range of tones her poem encompasses. In Chapter 15, we address the art of allusion—that is, enriching a work of art by reference to other works of art. The strategy is a common one and is not limited to references to "high" culture. The deliberate mixing of very different types of materials often contributes to a comic or satiric tone. Think, for example, of almost any episode of *The Simpsons*. Within thirty minutes, an alert viewer is likely to note allusions to other cartoons, films, classic literature, television commercials, and so on.

The song that the sailor considers worth risking his life for is "boring" to the woman who is singing it. This irony is based on perceptions, on the different points of view; the two individuals represented in the story perceive the details in the story completely differently. Suddenly, what we may have heard as beautiful (an appeal to strength and uniqueness)sounds disturbing and illusive.

Often tonal shifts signal ironic gaps between the passionate beliefs of a character and the quite different judgments of the narrator or author. In Chinua Achebe's "Dead Men's Path," for instance, Michael Obi's conviction that the old needs to be replaced by the modern must be assessed in light of the quiet assurance of the narrative (and of the village priest) that old ways must be respected. As you read, note how the story sets up Obi, and note the specific instances in the narrative where Obi's confident convictions seem foolish rather than insightful.

**Chinua Achebe** (1930– )

# Dead Men's Path (1972)

Michael Obi's hopes were fulfilled much earlier than he had expected. He was appointed headmaster of Ndume Central School in January 1949. It had always been an unprogressive school, so the Mission authorities decided to send a young and energetic man to run it. Obi accepted this responsibility with enthusiasm. He had many wonderful ideas and this was an opportunity to put them into practice. He had had sound secondary school education which designated him a "pivotal teacher" in the official records and set him apart from the other headmasters in the mission field. He was outspoken in his condemnation of the narrow views of these older and often less-educated ones.

"We shall make a good job of it, shan't we?" he asked his young wife when they first heard the joyful news of his promotion.

"We shall do our best," she replied. "We shall have such beautiful gardens and everything will be just *modern* and delightful ..." In their two years of married life she had become completely infected by his passion for "modern methods" and his denigration of "these old and superannuated people in the teaching field who would be better employed as traders in the Onitsha market." She began to see herself already as the admired wife of the young headmaster, the queen of the school.

The wives of the other teachers would envy her position. She would set the fashion in everything ... Then, suddenly, it occurred to her that there might not be other wives. Wavering between hope and fear, she asked her husband, looking anxiously at him.

"All our colleagues are young and unmarried," he said with enthusiasm  5
which for once she did not share. "Which is a good thing," he continued.

"Why?"

"Why? They will give all their time and energy to the school."

Nancy was downcast. For a few minutes she became skeptical about the new school; but it was only for a few minutes. Her little personal misfortune could not blind her to her husband's happy prospects. She looked at him as he sat folded up in a chair. He was stoop-shouldered and looked frail. But he sometimes surprised people with sudden bursts of physical energy. In his present posture, however, all his bodily strength seemed to have retired behind his deep-set eyes, giving them an extraordinary power of penetration. He was only twenty-six, but looked thirty or more. On the whole, he was not unhandsome.

"A penny for your thoughts, Mike," said Nancy after a while, imitating the woman's magazine she read.

"I was thinking what a grand opportunity we've got at last to show these  10
people how a school should be run." Ndume School was backward in every sense of the word. Mr. Obi put his whole life into the work, and his wife hers too. He had two aims. A high standard of teaching was insisted upon, and the school compound was to be turned into a place of beauty. Nancy's dream-gardens came to life with the coming of the rains, and blossomed. Beautiful hibiscus and allamanda hedges in brilliant red and yellow marked out the carefully tended school compound from the rank neighborhood bushes.

One evening as Obi was admiring his work he was scandalized to see an old woman from the village hobble right across the compound, through a marigold flower-bed and the hedges. On going up there he found faint signs of an almost disused path from the village across the school compound to the bush on the other side.

"It amazes me," said Obi to one of his teachers who had been three years in the school, "that you people allowed the villagers to make use of this footpath. It is simply incredible." He shook his head.

"The path," said the teacher apologetically, "appears to be very important to them. Although it is hardly used, it connects the village shrine with their place of burial."

"And what has that got to do with the school"? asked the headmaster.

"Well, I don't know," replied the other with a shrug of the shoulders. 15
"But I remember there was a big row some time ago when we attempted to
close it."

"That was some time ago. But it will not be used now," said Obi as he
walked away. "What will the Government Education Officer think of this
when he comes to inspect the school next week? The villagers might, for all I
know, decide to use the schoolroom for a pagan ritual during the inspection."

Heavy sticks were planted closely across the path at the two places where
it entered and left the school premises. These were further strengthened with
barbed wire.

Three days later the village priest of Ani called on the headmaster. He was an
old man and walked with a slight stoop. He carried a stout walking-stick
which he usually tapped on the floor, by way of emphasis, each time he made a
new point in his argument.

"I have heard," he said after the usual exchange of cordialities, "that our
ancestral footpath has recently been closed ..."

"Yes," replied Mr. Obi. "We cannot allow people to make a highway of 20
our school compound."

"Look here, my son," said the priest bringing down his walking-stick,
"this path was here before you were born and before your father was born. The
whole life of this village depends on it. Our dead relatives depart by it and our
ancestors visit us by it. But most important, it is the path of children coming
in to be born ..."

Mr. Obi listened with a satisfied smile on his face.

"The whole purpose of our school," he said finally, "is to eradicate just
such beliefs as that. Dead men do not require footpaths. The whole idea is just
fantastic. Our duty is to teach your children to laugh at such ideas."

"What you say may be true," replied the priest, "but we follow the practices of our fathers. If you re-open the path we shall have nothing to quarrel
about. What I always say is: let the hawk perch and let the eagle perch." He
rose to go.

"I am sorry," said the young headmaster. "But the school compound 25
cannot be a thoroughfare. It is against our regulations. I would suggest your
constructing another path, skirting our premises. We can even get our boys to
help in building it. I don't suppose the ancestors will find the little detour too
burdensome."

"I have no more words to say," said the old priest, already outside.

Two days later a young woman in the village died in childbed. A diviner
was immediately consulted and he prescribed heavy sacrifices to propitiate
ancestors insulted by the fence.

Obi woke up next morning among the ruins of his work. The beautiful
hedges were torn up not just near the path but right round the school, the

flowers trampled to death and one of the school buildings pulled down ...
That day, the white Supervisor came to inspect the school and wrote a nasty
report on the state of the premises but more seriously about the "tribal-war
situation developing between the school and the village, arising in part from
the misguided zeal of the new headmaster." ■

Authors often want us to understand more about a situation than their
characters can grasp. In this sense, we sometimes need to hear things
differently, pick up different tones, than do key characters. This gap between a character's understanding and our own is called **dramatic irony**.
When Achebe's narrator speaks of Obi, for example, the narrator and the
reader see the irony, but Obi does not. Atwood's Siren's wisdom is something that no sailor will be able to appreciate, for the sailor is lured to
destruction before wisdom can be appreciated. When Hurston presents the
story of Peter's rock, the critique is of a church in which the speakers
participate. The same technique, though, applies well to **introspection**—a
personal willingness to take in and reflect upon ideas that may seem to
conflict but at some level make sense together. A **paradox** exists when some
truth is embodied in what on the surface seems a contradiction. Czeslaw
Milosz's poem "If There Is No God" contemplates the responsibilities that
come with a godless universe. How would such a "fact" change the nature of
existence?

**Czeslaw Milosz** (1911–2004)

# If There Is No God (Translated from the Polish by the author and Robert Haas, 2004)

If there is no God,
Not everything is permitted to man.
He is still his brother's keeper
And he is not permitted to sadden his brother
By saying there is no God.                                                    5

Milosz suggests that the religious responsibilities of the atheist would actually increase "If there is no God." Recognizing paradox often seems to result
from introspection and to result in an introspective tone. How is Milosz's
tone here different from the religious inquiry in Hurston's story or the
tender affection that Kooser offers in his poem? Do you feel that Milosz
speaks more directly through his speaker? Is the effect more sincere and less
ironic?

*A Note to Student Writers: Signaling Your Own Understanding of Tonal Shifts*

When you write critically about a literary text or film, it's important that you be very clear about signaling your own understanding of tonal shifts or of ironic gaps between author and character. Your reader, of course, will understand that a character, a speaker, and an author may possess distinct voices, but if you do not keep the distinctions clear, your *own* understanding may be called into question. Therefore, build into your text explicit explanations. For example, there is an enormous difference between the following two summary remarks regarding the eleventh paragraph in "Dead Men's Path":

1. Mr. Obi is assigned to work in a school stuck in a primitive past. He brings a very high educational standard as well as a love of beauty to the backward village.

2. Mr. Obi can only view the school as backward and in great need of rigorous teaching. He also wants to transform the school compound into a place that meets his preconceived idea of beauty.

The first summary registers Mr. Obi's thoughts without suggesting that any other thoughts might be important in the story. It doesn't suggest a coming transition to any other perspective. In short, it fails to catch anything distinctive about the tone of the paragraph from Achebe's story.

The second makes it clear that judgmental words such as *backward, rigorous, transform*, and *beautiful* all belong to a particular character. It will allow the writer to move easily to distinctly different perspectives (those of the narrator and the village chief). It prepares us to "hear" a different tone than Obi himself can appreciate.

# MODELING CRITICAL ANALYSIS: JOEL COEN AND ETHAN COEN, O BROTHER, WHERE ART THOU?

On its surface, O *Brother, Where Art Thou?* (2000) might appear to offer an accurate re-creation of Depression-era Mississippi. Every image from the film, especially the tin of Dapper Dan pomade, looks as though it came directly out of that era, and the sound track transformed obscure folk music from the time and region into a popular album. This movie serves as a useful example in the discussion of tone because, in spite of the film's careful re-creation of historical detail, the audience does not judge the film as it might judge a historical epic. If a film purports to present a true story, we expect it to be faithful to that story; we will challenge such a film when it chooses to depart into fiction. But the opening sequence in O *Brother, Where Art Thou?* sets a tone that frees us from a narrow demand for historical accuracy. A chain gang in striped prison garb opens the film, singing and keeping time with their picks and hammers. The film next shifts to three prisoners, chained together, escaping from the gang. Hampered by their chains, they trip over one another as a traditional version of the folk classic "Big Rock Candy Mountain" tells of a hobo heading toward an imaginary land with cigarette trees and lemonade springs. The music and the carefully choreographed movement of the characters tilt the film more toward the comic than historic mode.

The episodic story stars George Clooney as Ulysses Everett McGill, a hero with a powerful "gift of gab" and an extraordinary attention to his slicked-back hair through all of his adventures. His convoluted language, with its slight grammatical slips, period idioms ("You two are just dumber than a bag of hammers"), and foolishly pretentious vocabulary are hardly what we expect to hear in an argument between escaped prisoners:

> Pete, the personal rancor reflected in that remark I don't intend to dignify with comment. But I would like to address your general attitude of hopeless negativism. Consider the lilies of the goddamn field or ... hell! Take at look at Delmar here as your paradigm of hope.

McGill's tireless analytical bent displays a limited self-consciousness that straddles the past in the historical character he inhabits and our

Margaret Bourke-White, *Guard with a shotgun over his shoulder overseeing men working in a ditch while on chain gang, Hood's Chapel, Georgia* (1937)

*O Brother, Where Art Thou?* (2000)

present. For instance, he claims that he deserves to be the leader of the group because, unlike his fellow travelers, he has a "capacity for abstract thought." He is a walking encyclopedia of information completely useless to someone in his particular circumstances. In answer to a question about the physical description of the devil, he answers, "Well, there are all manner of lesser imps and demons, Pete, but the great Satan hisself is red and scaly with a bifurcated tail, and he carries a hay fork." This out-of-place encyclopedic knowledge can help us hear a tone in a film that announces in the credits that it is "based upon *The Odyssey* by Homer."

Like McGill, the film itself offers choice tidbits of knowledge that seem randomly delivered. Some links to the *Odyssey* are clear enough: John Goodman plays a one-eyed Bible salesman who resembles a Cyclops; three women Sirens doing laundry and singing a lullaby lure the travelers from their journey. Other connections to Homer's epic are far more obscure. But the often-wild mixture of parts is what constitutes the tone of the whole. There is something serious about this comedy. *O Brother, Where Art Thou?* juxtaposes shots that borrow images from the socially conscious photography of Walker Evans, Dorothea Lange, and Margaret Bourke-White with slapstick comedy. In what ways does the scene from *O Brother, Where Art Thou?* differ from the historical photo? What details help you identify the tone in the film still?

The film offers a rather subtle reading of the *Odyssey*, but in their publicity for the movie, the Coen brothers claimed that they never read the original. This self-deprecation makes them seem like students who write book reports for class without doing the reading; it also disguises, through the disarmingly dim characters of McGill and his companions, a thorough knowledge of the epic as well as a detailed rendering of American history, American cinema, and American music. O *Brother, Where Art Thou?* ultimately comments on weighty matters of race, class, progress, and religion. From the early scenes, the Coen brothers establish a tone that guides us to insights none of their characters could ever realize. That is, we hear what the characters say but understand that Ethan and Joel Coen want to say a good deal more to us.

## Using Tone to Focus Writing and Discussion

- How does the author set the tone? Is there some lens that teaches us, as readers, how to read what follows? Remember that tone can come out of many of the other literary elements that we have discussed, including setting, character, point of view, and rhythm.

- Does the author reveal the tone immediately? Or does the piece depend upon our discovery of that tone later in the work?

- What is the prevailing effect in this work? Is the tone light or dark? Earnest or mocking? Straightforward or sarcastic? Outraged or enraptured? These are only a few possibilities, but they offer a good starting point for our definition of the tone that we find within any specific work.

- Is there a specific character who speaks or a specific occasion that might give us some clue about the mood of this particular work?

- What role does the tone play in this particular work? Is the tone transparent—is it something that we don't really notice as we read—or is the tone visible? Is it integral to the story?

- Does the tone change over the course of the text? For instance, there might be two different characters who approach a scene differently. The contrast between their tones might be an important barometer into meaning within the work.

- How can a discussion of tone benefit our analysis of this particular work? For instance, contrasts in tone can serve as a topic of discussion, and it may also be fruitful to discuss works that share particular tonal elements.

# 11 Word Choice

## Why This Word and Not Another?

If you have ever stood in front of a display of Valentine's Day greeting cards, you have faced the difficulty of translating true sentiment into language. When you walk into that card shop, you are motivated by the desire to express a real emotion to a person you care about. But as you look through all of the cards for sale, you discover that you are standing with other customers who are all buying the same cards to express the same emotions to their own significant others. You might feel frustrated at this point because as clever as any single card might be, it fails to capture a sincere, powerful, individual emotion. If you sit down and try to write your own poetry, you may feel a similar futility: all the variations of "Roses are red, violets are blue" have already been written by someone else, and original and inspiring verses of your own are elusive.

In this chapter, we ask you, as a reader, to consider how authors make words count, how they communicate distinct emotions and ideas with words that may seem in other contexts common. Remember that every word you read is the result of a choice. The author has decided to use a specific word instead of any other that has a similar meaning. By following authors through some of their choices (and the context within which the choices are made), we can see how attention to language can lead us to the sort of critical analysis that we have been describing throughout this book. We will also look at two important language resources—dictionaries and thesauruses—and suggest ways in which these tools can deepen our conversations about the literature we read.

# PRECISION AND PLAYFULNESS

Desiderius Erasmus, a sixteenth-century humanist whose many interests included developing methods for instruction in language and writing, recommended that writers have at their disposal a plentiful supply of words. In his colloquy on copiousness (abundance), *De Duplici Copia Verborum et Rerum* (1512), he encourages writers to invent different ways of saying the same thing. Such an exercise stimulates a writer's creativity; also, as his examples show, each variation creates a slightly different meaning. Erasmus chose to begin with the banal sentence "Your letter pleased me very much"; he then wrote 150 variations. Before you read any further, try this exercise yourself. Generate at least five variations of Erasmus's core sentence. Then, having begun, examine this selection of Erasmus's variations, translated from his original Latin. The first examples are largely technical:

**Using synonyms.**
Your epistle gladdened me wonderfully.
**Variations of sentence construction.**
It is impossible to say how gladdened I was by your writing.
**Changing verbs.**
I got incredible pleasure from your letter.
Your writing brought me no mean joy.
Your writing filled me with joy.
Your letter moved me with singular pleasure.
**Using the verb "to be."**
Your letter was in many ways most pleasing to me.
Your letter was as pleasurable as could be.
Your letter was an unspeakable pleasure to us.
Your letter was an incredible happiness.
**Change to the negative.**
Nothing in my life more pleasing than your letter has befallen me.
I never took so much pleasure in anything as in your very lovely letter.
**Put into the form of a question.**
What in life could have been more pleasing than your letter?

If we stay in the simple mode of reading for meaning, Erasmus's sentences quickly grow monotonous. But if we read to appreciate subtle differences in tone, we can appreciate Erasmus's artistry. It is especially useful to read aloud to capture the glorious absurdity of the exercise, especially as Erasmus moves on to literary **tropes** (see Chapter 13) and his mundane phrase begins to take on literary airs and resemble the very worst poetry:

The banquet of your writing refreshed us with most delightful dishes.
Your kind epistle far surpassed all carob and Attic honey and sugar, nectar, and ambrosia of the gods.
As long as the boar loves the mountain ridges, as long as fish the stream, I will recall the sweetness of your letter.
What clover is to bees, what willow boughs are to goats, what honey is to the bear, your letter is to me.
No luxuries titillate the palate more agreeably than what you wrote titillates my mind.

These effusions are but a sampling of the examples that Erasmus offers, but they are enough to show that even though these sentences reproduce the initial thought, the later sentences are certainly not the same as the first. The basic idea may be the same, but the specific method of expression greatly changes the nature of that expression. In these final examples, Erasmus is writing poetically about a situation that simply does not deserve the poetic treatment that he gives it. No sober writer would use any of these expressions to thank a correspondent for a letter, but the exercise demonstrates the author's facility with words as well as his judgment about which words are most appropriate for a given situation.

In fact, Erasmus wrote about this systematic approach to invention in order to instruct schoolchildren to develop their writing skills. The technique was widely used in English schools in the sixteenth century, so it is likely that Shakespeare, for instance, would have encountered this sort of school exercise in his youth. The fundamental aim of Erasmus's exercise is to make writers conscious of word choice, or **diction**. It raises an interesting question for writers of literature: Does a work of art require special diction, **poetic diction**? In the eighteenth century some poets, perhaps too well trained by exercises like the one above, maintained that the language of poetry was *necessarily not* the language of common life. At its most extreme, this led to what seem now some comic choices: a school of fish, for example, could become a "finny tribe"; or a flock of sheep, a "fleecy tribe." William Wordsworth, Samuel Taylor Coleridge, and other poets of the early nineteenth century insisted that absolute distinctions between poetic language and everyday language were unnecessary. Although we now allow literary artists a wide range of words to choose from, no one will ever settle on a simple standard for appropriate diction. Writers must always contend with questions of what is the best word for a particular situation: the best word may or may not be a common one.

A consciousness of levels of formality is certainly essential. A **colloquial expression** may register a speaker's everyday conversation and help us relate to that speaker. But a deliberate move to literary language might be necessary to emphasize an emotional or thematic shift. The quality of specific choices can never be divorced from context. For example, a **euphemism** (a deliberately indirect mode of expression) could be comic ("afflicted by vapors" instead of "suffering from gas"); dignified (a "lasting sleep" instead of a "death"); or morally problematic ("collateral damage" instead of "civilians killed").

## Experiencing Film and Literature through Diction

The film *Moulin Rouge* (2001) explores the problem of living in a world where various forms of cultural production have already anticipated all emotions any of us could ever feel. As is true of most works we discuss, this film could fit in just about any section of this book. The story is set in a stylized version of late nineteenth-century Paris and borrows many narrative elements from popular opera, even from ancient mythology. The sets create a fictional version of the cityscape that is indebted to a tradition of artistic representations of Paris at least as much as it is inspired by actual Parisian settings. The rich texture of the entire film, especially the gaudy colors and elaborate sets, alludes to an entire history of movie musicals, perhaps the least realistic of film types, as characters express their emotions with staged outbursts of song. The film particularly salutes India's Bollywood films, world cinema's most vibrant musicals.

But the problems raised by word choice itself are especially prominent in *Moulin Rouge*'s musical numbers; characters sing familiar late twentieth-century pop music with all the familiar words in nineteenth-century settings. For instance, the "original" song "Elephant Love Medley" weaves a musical conversation out of pop hits from the last half-century. The young poet Christian (Ewan McGregor) believes that his emotions are truly original, and he seeks to find a language to voice these emotions. But whenever he bursts into song, we hear words that we already know. To tell the kind-hearted prostitute Satine (Nicole Kidman) that he loves her, he begins with a sentence that has become clichéd through decades of abuse as, among other things, a song title and a movie title "Love is a many splendored thing." Then he begins his potpourri of musical quotations with Joe Cocker and Jennifer Warnes's "Love lifts us up where we belong." He quotes the Beatles, "All you need is love." Throughout the medley, Satine counters his quotation from idealist love songs with her own from more cynical songs about the same subject.

This medley and the film as a whole undercut Christian's youthful enthusiasm by showing us that his "unique" artistic output, as well as his personal emotion, falls into a long tradition. He might feel something that is new to him, but when he tries to express that new feeling, he has to depend on words that have been used repeatedly by others before him—words or expressions that are used lazily or imprecisely and that often become **clichés**. But buried in the cliché may well be a sincere desire to communicate something fresh and (for the speaker) new. The director/writer Baz Luhrman manages to have us both share in Christian's enthusiasm for his love and reflect upon the language all of us use to register and communicate love.

CHRISTIAN:  Love is a many splendored thing
    Love lifts us up where we belong
    All you need is love
SATINE:  Please don't start that again
CHRISTIAN:  All you need is love
SATINE:  A girl has got to eat
CHRISTIAN:  All you need is love
SATINE:  She'll end up on the street
CHRISTIAN:  All you need is love
SATINE:  Love is just a game

*Moulin Rouge* (2001)

CHRISTIAN: I was made for loving you baby
    You were made for loving me
SATINE: The only way of loving me baby
    Is to pay a lovely fee
CHRISTIAN: Just one night
    Give me just one night
SATINE: There's no way
    'Cause you can't pay
CHRISTIAN: In the name of love
    One night in the name of love
SATINE: You crazy fool
    I won't give in to you
CHRISTIAN: Don't leave me this way
    I can't survive without your sweet love
    Oh baby don't leave me this way
SATINE: You think that people would have enough of silly love songs
CHRISTIAN: I look around me and I see it isn't so, oh no
SATINE: Some people wanna fill the world with silly love songs
CHRISTIAN: Well what's wrong with that
    I'd like to know
    Cause here I go again
CHRISTIAN: Love lifts us up where we belong
    Where the eagles fly
    On a mountain high
SATINE: Love makes us act like we are fools
    Throw our lives away
    For one happy day
CHRISTIAN: We can be heroes
    Just for one day
SATINE: You, you will be mean
CHRISTIAN: No I won't
SATINE: And I, I'll drink all the time
CHRISTIAN: We should be lovers
SATINE: We can't do that
CHRISTIAN: We should be lovers
    And that's a fact
SATINE: No nothing would keep us together
CHRISTIAN: We could steal time
CHRISTIAN & SATINE: Just for one day
    We can be heroes
    Forever and ever

We can be heroes
Forever and ever
We can be heroes
CHRISTIAN: Just because I, and I will always love you
SATINE: I only can't help
CHRISTIAN & SATINE: Loving You
SATINE: How wonderful life is now
CHRISTIAN & SATINE: You're in the world

Luhrman has done something remarkable in this patched-together song. Although all of his word choices are culled from familiar sources, they feel altogether original in this rousing musical number. The words aren't original if we think of them only as words, but in the setting Luhrman has created, we hear them as fresh and alive. We're convinced that Christian does indeed love Satine, even though we know his passion (from a larger perspective) is hardly as unique as he thinks it is.

### Making Connections

The Making Connections features in this book act as interruptions of the main text. But at some level, the intent is to connect (connect to ideas in other chapters, to experiences you may have beyond the classroom, to the writing process). Here, we interrupt to suggest that before you read these poems, you should recall the specific elements of the **sonnet** form that we discussed in Chapter 8. Take note of structural features, track the rhyme, and sum up the argument (the complication and the resolution). Notice that Shakespeare sets up a general principle in the first four lines (quatrain). The next two quatrains apply this general principle to the specific instance that he is describing. And the final couplet offers a conclusion and a way for the young man addressed in the sonnet to rectify the "problem" that the poem has just described.

## BEYOND SUMMARY

Variation upon a common theme—the challenge of making distinctive and individual feelings that are universal—is also a central concern in Shakespeare's sonnet sequence. In the brief selection that follows, you'll note considerable thematic overlap from poem to poem. But the sequence doesn't stall; each poem offers a distinct experience for the reader.

**William Shakespeare** (1564–1616)

# Sonnet 1 (1609)

From fairest creatures we desire increase,
That thereby beauty's rose might never die,
But as the riper should by time decease,
His tender heir might bear his memory:
But thou, contracted to thine own bright eyes,                              5
Feed'st thy light's flame with self-substantial fuel,
Making a famine where abundance lies,
Thyself thy foe, to thy sweet self too cruel.
Thou that art now the world's fresh ornament
And only herald to the gaudy spring,                                        10
Within thine own bud buriest thy content
And, tender churl, makest waste in niggarding.
   Pity the world, or else this glutton be,
   To eat the world's due, by the grave and thee.

The poet admires the beauty he sees in the young man he addresses and argues that this youth has a responsibility to procreate. But this simple message is less interesting than the strategies that the poet uses to make his argument; Shakespeare surprises us with the word choices that he makes. In the first quatrain (lines 1–4), the poet speaks of a general desire for immortality, yet he never uses that word. We desire the "fairest creatures," he says, to "increase" (1). Notably, he avoids any of the words that we might think to use in summarizing this poem: *reproduction, procreation, fatherhood, children,* or any other simple variation of that idea. Instead, he talks about a "tender heir" (4) of "beauty's rose" (2) that "might bear his memory" (4), implying that when we see beauty (in something like a rose), we wish that that beauty might endure. In the second quatrain (lines 5–8), the poet shifts to a condemnation of the youth: "thou, contracted to thine own bright eyes" (5). Instead of sharing his beauty, this subject is self-absorbed, and the poet claims that this inward tendency defies the natural order and creates "a famine where abundance lies" (7). What is this famine? It seems a lack of beauty in the world, worsened by the knowledge that, without an heir, the young man's beauty will vanish. And the final lines of the poem emphasize this waste. The youth should be "herald to the gaudy spring" (10). He should be father to a whole field but instead remains a solitary flower. The poet tells him that as a flower, "[thou] buriest thy content" within "thine own bud" (11) instead of sharing with the passing wildlife, thereby preventing the propagation of other flowers. The act of propagation, as depicted in these lines, appears quite passive. By the end of the third quatrain (lines 9–12), the young man is denigrated as a "churl" who paradoxically "makest waste in niggarding" (12). How can saving (or hoarding) be a wasteful activity? In the final couplet (lines 13–14), "beauty's rose" has become a "glutton" (13) consuming "the world's due" (14), killing off potential fields of flowers through his selfishness and knowing that he must eventually die. As is often the case in the sonnet form, the final couplet affects our reading of the previous twelve lines. The **hyperbole** in these final lines (that is, the deliberate exaggeration or overstatement) marks a stark contrast to the apparent restraint at the beginning. Through the poet's choice of words and images, feelings escalate through the sonnet as the narrator becomes more aggressive in pursuit of connections to the flower image.

Let's go back to our initial summary of the poem: "The poet admires the beauty he sees in the young man he addresses and argues that this youth has a responsibility to procreate." Although this summary may accurately recount the general subject of the poem, it fails to capture the poem's impact because the poem is not a generalization but a series of precise words. Yes, the poem is a plea for this young man to sow his seed, but until we look closely at the words that the poet uses to make this plea, we cannot see the images, the twists of meaning, the logical games that the poet plays; in short, we have not begun any analysis. Of course, this process should go beyond what we present here. What can we say about the tone of this particular narrative? As we look at more sonnets, do we develop some sense of a consistent character narrating these individual units? How do differences between similar sonnets alter our readings?

Now, compare your findings from the first sonnet to the second sonnet in Shakespeare's sequence. How different is your summary of this sonnet from that of the first? Does Shakespeare use the same pattern here? Where are the differences? Does his use of clothing as an image (instead of harvests) change the nature of the case that he makes? How directly are the elements of clothing related to his demand? How does this image develop throughout the sonnet?

# Sonnet 2 (1609)

When forty winters shall beseige thy brow,
And dig deep trenches in thy beauty's field,
Thy youth's proud livery, so gazed on now,
Will be a tatter'd weed, of small worth held:
Then being ask'd where all thy beauty lies,           5
Where all the treasure of thy lusty days,
To say, within thine own deep-sunken eyes,
Were an all-eating shame and thriftless praise.

How much more praise deserved thy beauty's use,
If thou couldst answer "This fair child of mine          10
Shall sum my count and make my old excuse,"
Proving his beauty by succession thine!
   This were to be new made when thou art old,
   And see thy blood warm when thou feel'st it cold.

As you move through the following sonnets, you will find that reading for a simple summary is no longer necessary. Shakespeare's first twenty sonnets form a sequence that is rather similar to the Erasmian exercise. Instead of reading for their general meaning—as they all convey essentially the same message—you should be reading for the specific words Shakespeare uses to conjure ideas and images about love. Look for any words or combinations of words that are repeated among the sonnets. Look for the juxtaposition of words that might not seem to fit together—for instance, can "Nature" really have such attributes as "thriftiness"?

# Sonnet 3 (1609)

Look in thy glass, and tell the face thou viewest
Now is the time that face should form another;
Whose fresh repair if now thou not renewest,
Thou dost beguile the world, unbless some mother.
For where is she so fair whose unear'd womb          5
Disdains the tillage of thy husbandry?
Or who is he so fond will be the tomb
Of his self-love, to stop posterity?
Thou art thy mother's glass, and she in thee
Calls back the lovely April of her prime:          10
So thou through windows of thine age shall see
Despite of wrinkles this thy golden time.
   But if thou live, remember'd not to be,
   Die single, and thine image dies with thee.

# Sonnet 9 (1609)

Is it for fear to wet a widow's eye
That thou consum'st thyself in single life?
Ah! if thou issueless shalt hap to die,
The world will wail thee, like a makeless wife;
The world will be thy widow and still weep          5

That thou no form of thee hast left behind,
When every private widow well may keep
By children's eyes her husband's shape in mind.
Look, what an unthrift in the world doth spend
Shifts but his place, for still the world enjoys it;                    10
But beauty's waste hath in the world an end,
And kept unus'd, the user so destroys it.
  No love toward others in that bosom sits
  That on himself such murd'rous shame commits.

# Sonnet 18 (1609)

Shall I compare thee to a summer's day?
Thou art more lovely and more temperate:
Rough winds do shake the darling buds of May,
And summer's lease hath all too short a date:
Sometime too hot the eye of heaven shines,                    5
And often is his gold complexion dimm'd;
And every fair from fair sometime declines,
By chance or nature's changing course untrimm'd;
But thy eternal summer shall not fade
Nor lose possession of that fair thou owest;                    10
Nor shall Death brag thou wander'st in his shade,
When in eternal lines to time thou growest:
  So long as men can breathe or eyes can see,
  So long lives this and this gives life to thee.

As you read these sonnets in sequence, you may recognize sonnets that you
have read before. Sonnet 18, for example, is often the first of Shakespeare's
sonnets that students read. How does reading a familiar sonnet in the context
of the other sonnets lend it additional meaning? Does the sonnet itself seem
different when it appears with the others?

## A Note to Student Writers: On the Paraphrase

To summarize is to convey in your own words an essential idea from a source. To paraphrase is to *restate* the original source in a fairly detailed way. Anytime we paraphrase,
we are making choices about the words that we use. However closely we attend to the
piece we paraphrase, we inevitably change it in our restatement. As we saw previously in
Erasmus's exercise, subtle changes emerge with each variation we choose. Often, the

difference is not immediately apparent, but if we paraphrase our own paraphrase, we will begin to see how specific words in different combinations create different meanings. Look back at one of Shakespeare's sonnets, and write three distinct paraphrases of it. By generating multiple paraphrases of the poem, you should begin to clarify your own understanding of that poem. At the same time, you will realize that a poem cannot be reduced to a paraphrase.

## DEFINITION AND USAGE

Shakespeare's talent for variation shouldn't lead you to think that variation in and of itself is a virtue. To grant yourself a wider vocabulary, you can turn to a thesaurus, but the choices it offers aren't necessarily helpful. As you begin to look through the entries under *love*, for instance, you will find a list similar to this one:

> fondness, liking, inclination, desire, regard, admiration, affection, tenderness, heart, attachment, yearning, gallantry, passion, flame, devotion, infatuation, adoration, idolatry, benevolence

None of these words precisely replaces the word *love*. Some of them won't do at all for expressing the particular kind of love you want to communicate. But to an inexpert user, a thesaurus might give the false impression that it is appropriate to substitute any one of these words for another. The results of such a misunderstanding can be amusing or bewildering. A bad choice makes it instantly clear: subtleties matter. The poet Billy Collins suggests that we find unnatural groupings in a thesaurus. As you read, follow the images Collins creates to describe the project of clustering synonyms.

**Billy Collins** (1941– )

# Thesaurus (1995)

It could be the name of a prehistoric beast
that roamed the Paleozoic earth, rising up
on its hind legs to show off its large vocabulary,
or some lover in a myth who is metamorphosed into a book.

It means treasury, but it is just a place                                5
where words congregate with their relatives,
a big park where hundreds of family reunions
are always being held,

*house, home, abode, dwelling, lodgings,* and *digs,*
all sharing the same picnic basket and thermos;                    10
*hairy, hirsute, woolly, furry, fleecy,* and *shaggy*
all running a sack race or throwing horseshoes,
*inert, static, motionless, fixed* and *immobile*
standing and kneeling in rows for a group photograph.

Here father is next to sire and brother close                      15
to sibling, separated only by fine shades of meaning.
And every group has its odd cousin, the one
who traveled the farthest to be here:
*astereognosis, polydipsia,* or some eleven
syllable, unpronounceable substitute for the word *tool.*          20
Even their own relatives have to squint at their name tags.

I can see my own copy up on a high shelf.
I rarely open it, because I know there is no
such thing as a synonym and because I get nervous
around people who always assemble with their own kind,             25
forming clubs and nailing signs to closed front doors
while others huddle alone in the dark streets.

I would rather see words out on their own, away
from their families and the warehouse of Roget,
wandering the world where they sometimes fall                      30
in love with a completely different word.
Surely, you have seen pairs of them standing forever
next to each other on the same line inside a poem,
a small chapel where weddings like these,
between perfect strangers, can take place.                         35

Collins appreciates the "warehouse" that Roget has created in the thesaurus, but it is a tool that he keeps high on a shelf, he tells us. Collins learns more when he finds words that appear in unexpected and perhaps unusual pairings. As Collins demonstrates, a synonym never really means the *same* thing as another word. Each word has its own meaning; as similar as it may be to another, it is not identical.

A thesaurus tries to generalize; it gives us groupings of words that have approximately the same meaning. A dictionary, on the other hand, makes distinctions among words. Although a dictionary's definitions generally begin with synonyms, the best dictionaries then clarify and justify these definitions with examples or elaboration. The *Oxford English Dictionary* (*OED*), for example, will list a series of quotations using the specified word and show how that word has been used differently at different times. Such a project shows that deriving a precise definition for an abstract term can be a difficult process. Here are only a few excerpts from the OED definitions of *love* that begin to show that words can never be pinned down:

1. That disposition or state of feeling with regard to a person which (arising from recognition of attractive qualities, from instincts of natural relationship, or from sympathy) manifests itself in solicitude for the welfare of the object, and usually also in delight in his or her presence and desire for his or her approval; warm affection, attachment. Const. *of, for, to, towards*.

2. In religious use, applied in an eminent sense to the paternal benevolence and affection of God towards His children, to the affectionate devotion due to God from His creatures, and to the affection of one created being to another so far as it is prompted by the sense of their common relationship to God. (Cf. CHARITY 1.) Theologians distinguish the *love of complacency*, which implies approval of qualities in the object, and the *love of benevolence*, which is bestowed irrespective of the character of the object.

3. Strong predilection, liking or fondness *for*, or devotion *to* (something). Const. *of, for, to* (arch.), *unto. to give, bear love to*: to be devoted or addicted to.

4. a. That feeling of attachment which is based upon difference of sex; the affection which subsists between lover and sweetheart and is the normal basis of marriage. *for love* (*in love*): by reason of love (often placed in opposition to pecuniary considerations); also in weakened sense; *love at first sight*: the action or state of falling in love with someone whom one has never previously seen; *love's young dream*: the relationship of young lovers; the object of someone's love, a man regarded as the perfect lover.

Perusing the entries for a specific word, comparing the entries in different dictionaries, and thinking about the relation between definitions and specific uses of a word can serve as the subject of extended discussions. The complete entry on *love* from the OED is a record of a scholarly conversation about the meaning of this very familiar word; the editors assemble a collection of specific instances in which the word *love* has been used in order to show how definitions evolve over time.

The entry on *love* from the OED aims to register far more than the literal meaning of the word, or its **denotation**. Such a definition would be impossibly narrow. Note how much of what is quoted from the OED concerns a wide range of associations suggested by the word. A grasp of a word's **connotations** (what it suggests beyond the most literal level) is essential to our understanding. Oftentimes, it's useful to use a dictionary to look up a word that you already know, for a dictionary may help you catch shadings that could easily be missed. In the same way, a thesaurus is not just a tool to find a different word but a means to reflect upon a widened range of possible associations.

## Experiencing Literature through Word Choice

Our understanding of words, our own use of language comes not from our knowledge of words in isolation but from our familiarity with their use. In the following poem, Robert Sward enacts a frustration to express what he feels as true in the face of an overbearing tradition of words and the conventions of poetry. His wife in this poem complains that the words that he writes are a different enterprise than "attending to me." To some extent, she is right. The need to choose the precise words turns attention from her to, as the title notes, the dictionary. Yet, although the impersonal definitions in the dictionary make the words that the poet uses mechanical, his own acknowledgment of this challenge helps reclaim those words. He admits to his words' shortcomings but embraces them as his best and only tools. As he plays with words at the end of the poem, he makes them his own and makes them (one would imagine) meaningful to Gloria.

**Robert Sward** (1933– )

# For Gloria on Her 60th Birthday, or Looking for Love in Merriam-Webster (1991)

"Beautiful, splendid, magnificent,
delightful, charming, appealing,"
    says the dictionary.
And that's how I start... But I hear her say,
"Make it less glorious and more Gloria."          5

Imperious, composed, skeptical, serene,
lustrous, irreverent,
she's marked by glory, she attracts glory
"Glory," I say, "Glory, Glory."

"Is there a hallelujah in there?"                                                    10
she asks, when I read her lines one and two.
"Not yet," I say, looking up from my books.
She protests, "Writing a poem isn't the same

"As *really* attending to me." "But it's for
your birthday," I say. Pouting,                                                      15
playfully cross, "That's the price you pay
when your love's a poet."

She has chestnut-colored hair,
old fashioned Clara Bow lips,
moist brown eyes...                                                                  20
                    arms outstretched, head thrown back
she glides toward me and into her seventh decade.

Her name means "to adore,"
"to rejoice, to be jubilant,
to magnify and honor as in worship, to give or ascribe glory—"
      my love, O Gloria, I do, I do.                                                 25

The literate self-consciousness that we see in this poem differs from the more
common *Moulin Rouge* dilemma of borrowing the words of others to express
our own feelings. We pick out the words that we believe have come closest to
what we think; perhaps these words even shape our thoughts.

## CRITICALLY REFLECTING ON WORDS

Writers sometimes refine their sense of "right words" by noting what makes for
imprecise or ineffective choices. Choosing words deliberately for their wrongness makes for a satiric game. In the annual Bulwer-Lytton contest, writers
take a perverse pleasure in competing to compose the worst opening line for
an imaginary novel. The contest often favors entries that rely upon overly
melodramatic diction. But before we present samples of those entries, we'll
insert a brief observation on bad writing from *The Turkey City Lexicon*. These
phrases come from a science fiction writers' workshop in which writers gather
and read one another's work, seeking to improve their own writing through
mutually constructive criticism. What follows are common problems identified so that they can be avoided.

Lewis Shiner (1950– )

# from The Turkey City Lexicon: A Primer for Science Fiction Workshops (1990)

**Gingerbread:** Useless ornament in prose, such as fancy sesquipedalian Latinate words where short clear English ones will do. Novice authors sometimes use "gingerbread" in the hope of disguising faults and conveying an air of refinement. (Attr. Damon Knight)

**Not Simultaneous:** The mis-use of the present participle is a common structural sentence-fault for beginning writers. "Putting his key in the door, he leapt up the stairs and got his revolver out of the bureau." Alas, our hero couldn't do this even if his arms were forty feet long. This fault shades into "Ing Disease," the tendency to pepper sentences with words ending in "-ing," a grammatical construction which tends to confuse the proper sequence of events. (Attr. Damon Knight)

**Pushbutton Words:** Words used to evoke a cheap emotional response without engaging the intellect or the critical faculties. Commonly found in story titles, they include such bits of bogus lyricism as "star," "dance," "dream," "song," "tears" and "poet," clichés calculated to render the SF audience misty-eyed and tender-hearted.

**Roget's Disease:** The ludicrous overuse of far-fetched adjectives, piled into a festering, fungal, tenebrous, troglodytic, ichorous, leprous, synonymic heap. (Attr. John W. Campbell)

With descriptions from the lexicon in mind, look at the following prize-winning examples of overwrought, hyperventilated prose (often called "purple prose") from the Bulwer-Lytton contest. Explain why judges might deem each entry worthy a prize for badness. Which insights from the *Turkey City Lexicon* best apply to each?

## Bulwer-Lytton Contest Winners

On reflection, Angela perceived that her relationship with Tom had always been rocky, not quite a roller-coaster ride but more like when the toilet-paper roll gets a little squashed so it hangs crooked and every time you pull some off you can hear the rest going bumpity-bumpity in its holder until you go nuts and push it back into shape, a degree of annoyance that Angela had now almost attained.

— Rephah Berg, Oakland CA (2002)

Sultry it was and humid, but no whisper of air caused the plump, laden spears of golden grain to nod their burdened heads as they unheedingly awaited the cyclic rape of their gleaming treasure, while overhead the burning orb of luminescence ascended its ever-upward path toward a sweltering celestial apex, for although it is not in Kansas that our story takes place, it looks godawful like it.

— Judy Frazier, Lathrop, Missouri (1991)

The bone-chilling scream split the warm summer night in two, the first half being before the scream when it was fairly balmy and calm and pleasant for those who hadn't heard the scream at all, but not calm or balmy or even very nice for those who did hear the scream, discounting the little period of time during the actual scream itself when your ears might have been hearing it but your brain wasn't reacting yet to let you know.

— Patricia E. Presutti, Lewiston, New York (1986)

Dolores breezed along the surface of her life like a flat stone forever skipping across smooth water, rippling reality sporadically but oblivious to it consistently, until she finally lost momentum, sank, and due to an overdose of fluoride as a child which caused her to lie forever on the floor of her life as useless as an appendix and as lonely as a five-hundred-pound barbell in a steroid-free fitness center.

— Linda Vernon, Newark, California (1990)

Now at the penultimate point of the current chapter in the tome that you, dear reader, currently peruse, it's time to turn attention to a film that has much to add to our discussion of diction.

## MODELING CRITICAL ANALYSIS: JOEL COEN AND ETHAN COEN, O BROTHER, WHERE ART THOU?

The film *O Brother, Where Art Thou?* is a loose retelling of the *Odyssey* set in the Depression era. In Homer's epic, Athena, the goddess of wisdom, protects Odysseus; whenever he gets into trouble, he is able to come up with some quick turn of phrase that puts him at the advantage over his adversaries. In this film, Ulysses Everett McGill fills the Odysseus role. He is full of big words, but these words are never quite as wise as he thinks they are, and more often than not, they get him into deeper trouble. For example, when McGill finally first sees his "Penelope"—the wife Penny (Holly Hunter) he has sought to return to—the meeting hardly begins well. Penny has told her seven children (all girls) that their father was run over by a train, a more respectable end she thinks than the reality (McGill is a convicted con artist and petty thief who was serving hard time on the chain gang before his escape). Penny has grown tired of waiting for McGill and has agreed to marry Vernon T. Waldrip (Ray McKinnon); indeed, the marriage is set for the next day. The Coen brothers set up the romantic struggle in broadly comic terms. Vernon T. Waldrip, as the name might suggest, is hardly a dashing adventurer. He is, however, a man with "prospects"; indeed, he is (as we hear from Penny and the older children) "bona fide." These descriptors aptly capture the whole of Vernon's limited attractions. There is no romance in the relationship between Penny and Vernon, but Vernon offers stability and a kind of social legitimacy that McGill has failed to provide.

The initial contest between the men is contained by words of law and possession, not the sorts of words that suggest caring or passion. McGill says that as the "paterfamilias" he is "put in a difficult position vis-à-vis my progeny." *Paterfamilias* is a Latin word for "father" or "master of the house." In Roman society, the term had specific legal meaning: it designated an independent man in charge of a family's holdings. McGill's use of "vis-à-vis" (literally, "face-to-face," but suggesting here "in relation to") continues the dispute in comically legalistic terms. In this context, the words "husband," "wife," and "fiancé" are about social arrangements. Even the word "Daddy" gets swallowed up in matters of legal status: McGill might be "Daddy" today, but "Uncle Vernon" will be "Daddy" tomorrow if the marriage comes off as planned. McGill will then no longer be a "husband" but "just a drifter, a no good drifter."

But there are real emotions barely covered by the silly, Latinate, and inappropriate language of law and property. The Coen brothers make sure we know that Ulysses Everett McGill feels passionately for his Penny. That passion shows partly in the desperate way he attacks her: "you lying, unconstant succubus." The "unconstant" may be less than correct ("inconstant" is the word he wants), and "succubus" is typical of his verbal overreaching. But the words do suggest anger and the hurt that generates anger. More significantly, in the middle of all the foolish talk (and silly diction), Ulysses speaks a line that lends real dignity to his quest: "I've traveled many a weary mile to be back with my wife." The plainness of this statement and apt fit between the character's education, his situation, and his dreams remind us that something is at stake in this comic odyssey. Here, the simple language stands out because so much of the surrounding language is not simple. The Coen brothers shift the level of their hero's diction to help us hear what really lies behind all the fancy expressions. Such moves from a high to a low register (or the other way around) are often used to lend power to words that might, in other contexts, be overlooked.

**Using Word Choice to Focus Writing and Discussion** _____

- To examine a selection's word choice, begin by summarizing. As you put the ideas into your own words, which of the author's words seem unusual or are words that you would not have chosen?

- Are there any cases in which the author uses a word in a way different from the conventional definition of the word? When you think about word choice, it is useful to keep a dictionary at hand. There are often multiple definitions of words. Check to see whether an author is using an older or less common definition of a word.

- If there are different characters in the text, do they choose their words differently? Point to specific examples of such differences. Can you tell from their words which characters are speaking?

- How do specific words in the passage convey a tone or attitude about the subject matter? Often, attention to words will help us make our arguments about other elements in the text.

- How are words placed next to one another? Find specific instances where the combination of words makes us notice the words.

- Does the author break grammatical conventions? If so, what is the impact of this break?

# 12 Allegory

## Is This Supposed to Mean Something Else, Too?

Consider for a moment the concept of "duty." You could look the word up in a dictionary, although you probably don't feel the need. Duty seems a familiar if rather dry notion. We tend to think politely of duty as a good thing. Duty compels us to act in ways we're "supposed" to act. It's what guides us to make tough choices or prompts us to serve others, even when such service is inconvenient or dangerous. But if we think long enough, our simplest responses may begin to seem inadequate. Duty can't be touched, weighed, or counted; it can only be held in our minds. Duty is an abstraction that may call forth a wide range of associations. What distinguishes "duty" in a positive sense from other abstractions that register overlapping and disturbing qualities (narrow devotion, slavish obligation, external compulsion, societal demand)? Even assuming we are able to stay clear of such ambiguity, how can we write about duty in a way that is positive, educational, and interesting? How can we foreground the idea of duty and make that idea clear without resorting to a straightforward (and most likely ineffective and/or reductive) lecture or sermon? How can we make something so vague and intangible come alive?

**Allegory** is a means to convey meaning. In allegory, abstract notions are embodied and given life by concrete characters and actions. Usually, there is a lesson set out for us to grasp. For example, imagine a story in which a violent character named "Anger" attacks a gentle character named "Love." Anger soon expends every ounce of energy and crashes down exhausted and alone, whereas Love (nursed by two friends, Patience and Duty) recovers quickly from the assault. We know there is a lesson being taught, and we are not likely to mistake the main points: Love (the character and the quality) is stronger than Anger (the character and the quality). Duty and Patience serve Love but cannot help Anger.

Although this type of story is premised in the belief that lessons can be taught in compelling and entertaining ways, we have all suffered through a television special, an earnest song, or a textbook reading exercise (like the one just given) whose good intentions far surpass its aesthetic qualities. Contrived lessons about caring for the environment and being kind to others who are different from us tend to be the greatest offenders in our current culture; such themes are important, but importance alone doesn't make for a great poem, film, or play. Fortunately, on occasion an artist is able to break through with a remarkable image or with a story that achieves a working (and often dynamic) balance between the moral and the action. This sort of achievement is one that we can easily appreciate, perhaps because we have so much experience with less successful examples.

## LEARNING THROUGH LIKENESS

We sometimes forget that the literary experience can be socially and morally instructive. Works driven by an explicit teaching purpose are called **didactic works**. One of the clearest examples of a transparently didactic allegorical tale is Gertrude Crampton's *Tootle* (1945), a children's picture book that remains in print and tells the story of a little train who must learn that it is wrong to go off the tracks. When Tootle wanders out into a delightful meadow, his teacher conspires with the inhabitants of Lower Trainswitch to make him think that life off the established track is filled with red flags. Crampton describes Tootle's submission to discipline.

> There were red flags waving from the buttercups, in the daisies, under the trees, near the bluebirds' nest, and even one behind the rain barrel. And, of course, Tootle had to stop for each one, for a locomotive must always Stop for a Red Flag Waving.
>
> "Red flags," muttered Tootle, "This meadow is full of red flags. How can I have any fun?
>
> "Whenever I start, I have to stop. Why did I think this meadow was such a fine place? Why don't I ever see a green flag?"
>
> Just as the tears were ready to slide out of his boiler, Tootle happened to look back over his coal car. On the tracks stood Bill, and in his hand was a big green flag. "Oh!" said Tootle.
>
> He puffed up to Bill and stopped.
>
> "This is the place for me," said Tootle. "There is nothing but red flags for locomotives that get off their tracks."

Gertrude Crampton, *Tootle* (1945)

"Hurray!" shouted the people of Lower Trainswitch, and jumped from their hiding places. "Hurray for Tootle the Flyer!" ■

Through characters like Tootle's teacher, Bill, and the jubilant townspeople, the story insists that only by following social regulations can a train—or, in other words, an unruly child—feel truly free. But the coercive nature of Tootle's training and the narrator's voice give this lesson book a somewhat hollow ring. As mature readers, we tend to be unruly, like the young Tootle. We don't want the message to be spelled out in too heavy a fashion. We might ask if it really was all right for Bill and the townspeople to trick Tootle. Wouldn't Tootle have enjoyed the meadow if they had not placed all the red flags about? Doesn't it seem a little small-minded of them to hide and watch him suffer and then shout happily when Tootle "learns his lesson"? But Gertrude Crampton tries to discourage such questions. She wants us to stay on the tracks and learn what she teaches.

Allegories constructed to force us down a single track can quickly grow tiresome. Fortunately, allegories need not be so controlling. In some ways, we can think of an allegory as an extended or elaborate **simile**. A simile explicitly associates (through the words *like* or *as*) an abstraction with a concrete image: for example, love is like a red rose. Such comparisons are directive, of course, but similes can provoke complex responses to likeness and difference. Love, like a red rose, is beautiful in bloom—full, richly layered, deeply fragrant. But rosebushes do have thorns. Red roses in particular wither quickly. The simile initiates not just a simple thought but a range of thoughts.

If we strip away all the directional signals from Tootle, we are left with a core simile such as the following: social conventions are like railroad tracks. Left at that elemental level, we're encouraged to play more freely with the comparison than Crampton might wish. Social customs and rules may, like tracks, keep us moving toward something. These tracks (when we stay on them properly) help us avoid collisions with others. Tracks allow us to move faster. But we can also be "stuck" on the tracks. We can be "railroaded." We may complain of someone who has a "one-track mind." And tracks are fixed, whereas customs and rules are varied, changeable, and open. Tracks are something we are either on or off. People may engage with customs and rules actively—even playfully. A simile such as "social conventions are like railroad tracks" might lead us to think from many different perspectives. An allegory could well be built on such a simile that would extend or complicate the possibilities—not just shut them down.

Some critics prefer to think of allegory as an extended **metaphor**. In a metaphor, the explicit connection (*like* or *as*) is dropped. Love is not merely like a red rose, it *is* a red rose. Social conventions *are* tracks we are all placed on. The qualities of one thing are fused (not merely paralleled) with the other. Simile invites comparison; it calls attention to sometimes surprising likenesses and asks that we test out or seek the meaning of the aligned parts. Metaphor presses boldly toward some elemental correspondence. It is perhaps more suggestive (less directive) than simile. For this reason, we'll have more to say about metaphor in Chapter 13. Here it's sufficient to say that allegory involves an extended parallel between concrete characters, things, and actions on one side and abstract meanings on the other.

## A Note to Student Writers: Using Analogies in Arguments

A simile involves a comparison between what might seem unlike things; a simile leaves it to the reader to tease out the meaning or effect. An **analogy** also involves a comparison. But in an analogy, the comparison depends upon likeness and is intended to serve a point—to build a logically forceful argument. Students are often warned not to build arguments from perceived similarities: "Don't argue from analogy" or "That's a false analogy." Although it is certainly true that you're not likely to successfully sustain an argument based on likeness through an entire paper, it is possible to illustrate a point or develop part of an argument through a carefully thought out analogy. For instance, Oliver Wendell Holmes, while Chief Justice of the Supreme Court, argued that the right to free speech must be limited when the speech in question is like someone shouting "Fire!" in a crowded theater.

Because many writers have, along with Holmes, used analogy effectively in analytical and argumentative essays, it seems plain wrong to require students to avoid analogies altogether. But it's not wrong to warn students to construct (or evaluate) an analogy with care. When you use (or read) an analogy, consider the following: First, are the two things that are put together really similar? Second, is the similarity *relevant* to the point made? Third, is there some difference between the two things that undermines the point? Use these questions to test a specific application of Holmes's analogy.

---

## Experiencing Literature through Allegory

Crampton's train is part of a tradition of stories in which the actors are not human; Tootle is a **personification** of an unruly child. This train acts exactly like a child, but the story and the pictures are engaging precisely because a train is *not* a child: we see a familiar world altered. Even children who don't want to accept Crampton's lesson might smile at the thought of a train sitting in a schoolroom. In this sort of story, anthropomorphic animals often present models of appropriate and inappropriate human behavior. The most famous may be the many ingenious animals that Aesop created to personify human dilemmas.

**Aesop** (620 BC–564 BC)

# The Crow and the Pitcher (ca. 300 BC)

A Thirsty Crow found a Pitcher with some water in it, but so little was there that, try as she might, she could not reach it with her beak, and it seemed as though she would die of thirst within sight of the remedy. At last she hit upon a clever plan. She began dropping pebbles into the Pitcher, and with each pebble the water rose a little higher until at last it reached the brim, and the knowing bird was enabled to quench her thirst.

Moral: *Necessity is the mother of invention.* ∎

In Aesop's **fable**, the crow is hardly developed as a character. It is important that she be a crow primarily so that she cannot have hands to pick up the pitcher. Her only attributes in this short paragraph are her ingenuity and her thirst. In illustrations of this tale, the crow looks like a crow. Unlike the story of Tootle, the fable of the crow and the pitcher seems like it could be true. The pithy moral conjoined to the image of the crow using pebbles to quench her thirst has a remarkable staying power.

Part of that power arises from the fit between concrete images and intangible qualities. Aesop helps us picture necessity, invention, and resourcefulness (all qualities difficult to describe). The thirsty crow stands for all forms of necessity; the pebble trick signifies all forms of invention. Readers take it from there. We're not bound by the moral to limit "necessity" to thirst. As soon as we understand the situation of the crow, we see how this instance could be illustrated by many other similar situations (even though few seem to be able to do it as economically as Aesop's tale). His fable is very clear, yet it's not restrictive.

Perhaps still less restrictive is the miniature allegory of Eden that Emily Dickinson offers us about the everyday beauties of life we may miss through inattention.

Walter Crane, *Illustration for Aesop's "The Crow and the Pitcher"*

**Emily Dickinson** (1830–1886)

# [Eden is that old-fashioned House] (ca. 1861)

Eden is that old-fashioned House
We dwell in every day

Without suspecting our abode
Until we drive away.

How fair on looking back, the Day                                          5
We sauntered from the Door—
Unconscious our returning,
But discover it no more.

Eden is established at the outset as our familiar home—a place we live in yet
do not recognize. Only in losing home, it seems, do we appreciate it. Yet
with the insight is loss, for the insight cannot bring us back to the original
state of perfection. As you read this poem, ask yourself: Why are "House,"
"Day," and "Door" capitalized? How closely allegorical is Dickinson's logic?
That is, does the parallel between Eden and the House hold through the
whole poem?

# EMBODYING TIMELESS QUALITIES

Most of us recognize the blindfolded figure of Justice holding a set of scales in
one hand and a sword in the other. We have learned that the blindfold helps

Engraving of Statue of Justice holding the scales

Dosso Dossi, *Allegory of Fortune* (ca. 1530)

her be impartial so that she will weigh the two sides in a dispute evenhand-
edly, without bias, and her sword will render that verdict. When she makes
her decision, the figure suggests, her verdict will be fair and will help
contribute to the civility of our society. We are familiar with the image
largely because it is repeated in various forms at courthouses throughout the
country.

The allegorical figure of Fortune may be a bit less familiar, but the
explanation of the objects in the image is clear enough. The female Fortune
holds a cornucopia representing the bounty that she offers, but she sits upon a
bubble (easily burst) to indicate the fleeting nature of her gifts. The man with
her is Chance, whose lottery tickets offer little more than the dream of owning
that cornucopia.

These images deal with qualities we often consider universal or timeless.
Justice is not thought of as a construction of a particular culture; we typically assume it's a transcendent value that all must seek. Chance is a condition that operates far above any individual level. If we doubt the eternal
quality of such notions, the figures of Justice and Fortune may start to look
a bit tacky and outdated. The poet Billy Collins observes that the contemporary literary scene is largely devoid of allegorical figures. As he introduces
each figure, he calls up familiar images from a tradition in which these
figures played much more prominent roles. He then observes that it is
only the plainest things—bare of any explicit meaning—that we choose to
invoke.

Billy Collins (1941– )

# The Death of Allegory (1999)

I am wondering what become of all those tall abstractions
that used to pose, robed and statuesque, in paintings
and parade about on the pages of the Renaissance
displaying their capital letters like license plates.

Truth cantering on a powerful horse,     5
Chastity, eyes downcast, fluttering with veils.
Each one was marble come to life, a thought in a coat,
Courtesy bowing with one hand always extended,

Villainy sharpening an instrument behind a wall,
Reason with her crown and Constancy alert behind a helm,     10
They are all retired now, consigned to a Florida for tropes.
Justice is there standing by an open refrigerator.

Valor lies in bed listening to the rain.
Even Death has nothing to do but mend his cloak and hood,
and all their props are locked away in a warehouse,     15
hourglasses, globes, blindfolds and shackles.

Even if you called them back, there are no places left
for them to go, no Garden of Mirth or Bower of Bliss.
The Valley of Forgiveness is lined with condominiums
and chainsaws are howling in the Forest of Despair.     20

Here on the table near the window is a vase of peonies
and next to it black binoculars and a money clip,
exactly the kind of thing we now prefer,
objects that sit quietly on a line in lower case,

themselves and nothing more, a wheelbarrow,     25
an empty mailbox, a razor blade resting in a glass ashtray.
As for the others, the great ideas on horseback
and the long-haired virtues in embroidered gowns,

it looks as though they have traveled down
that road you see on the final page of storybooks,     30
the one that winds up a green hillside and disappears
into an unseen valley where everyone must be fast asleep.

Collins speaks longingly of a time when artists engaged with big ideas and compares that to a current time when allegorical figures are much less meaningful, when artists concentrate on the details of everyday life. The ideas that have replaced such "tall abstractions" as Truth and Chastity are the "lowercase objects" that populate this poem. Although it seems true that contemporary artists resist grand generalities and abstractions, Collins's observation says much about allegory in any age. Much of the inclination to use allegory, even in the older times that Collins celebrates, begins with the sense that big ideas are a thing of the past. The statue that adorns the Department of Justice was not a product of ancient Greece or Rome but was made deliberately to invoke those times. Its form suggests the links between the modern courthouse and classical civilization. The statue depicts an ancient ideal of justice and gives us more faith in the system than we might gain from a statue of a modern lawyer. Allegory has long exploited this sense of an idealized past. When Edmund Spenser wrote the *Faerie Queene* in 1596, he constructed a deliberately artificial and antique language in which to present his allegories. Just as the statue of Justice hearkens to an earlier iconography, Spenser, like many of the artists in the Renaissance, gave his own work an appearance of being older than it really was to lend seriousness to his project. So even in the sixteenth century, Spenser's allegory seemed like a literary style from the past.

> **Making Connections**
>
> Reread Czeslaw Milosz's "Watering Can" (p. 115) and William Carlos Williams's "The Red Wheelbarrow" (p. 114) in light of Billy Collins's remarks on the decline of allegory. Explore the differences among the ideas presented by these three poets. How does Collins's lament about the decline of allegory relate to Milosz and Williams and their insistence on "things"? How would you defend Milosz and Williams against a charge that they diminish poetry's grand potential?

## READING ALLEGORY

Static allegorical figures like the ones pictured on pages 221–222 and like the ones Collins refers to strike some people as rather cold. They are, after all, forever frozen in a moment that captures a specific meaning. For example, in Dosso Dossi's painting, Fortune sits perpetually on her bubble. The idea is that the bubble is always on the verge of breaking, yet in the image itself the bubble will never burst. As soon as we make a story out of the image that is presented in the painting, the balance may be broken. The bubble could burst. And if it did, we'd have a particular, dynamic situation—not simply a fixed universal message.

Plato uses the image of a dark cave as an instructional device so that the students of Socrates (the primary speaker in Plato's dialogues) can understand his distinction between the physical, observable world and some greater reality unavailable to ordinary human perception. This allegorical world contains some slight action as figures pass in front of the light and cast shadows and as a figure moves from the cave to the sunlight and back again; but for the most part, Plato's world can be viewed much as one views the allegorical paintings. Plato is after a general and stable truth. All of the details of the allegory are there to help us understand an idea, not as the setting for a story. We use the constructed cave world to see Plato's abstract point. We can keep coming back to Plato's allegory to grasp the larger reality of those imprisoned in any cave of ignorance.

**Plato** (428 BC–348 BC)

# The Allegory of the Cave (from Book VII of The Republic)
(ca. 360 BC)

[SOCRATES is speaking with GLAUCON.]

SOCRATES: And now, I said, let me show in a figure how far our nature is enlightened or unenlightened: —Behold! human beings living in a underground den, which has a mouth open towards the light and reaching all along the den; here they have been from their childhood, and have their legs and necks chained so that they cannot move, and can only see before them, being prevented by the chains from turning round their heads. Above and behind them a fire is blazing at a distance, and between the fire and the prisoners there is a raised way; and you will see, if you look, a low wall built along the way, like the screen which marionette players have in front of them, over which they show the puppets.

GLAUCON: I see.

SOCRATES: And do you see, I said, men passing along the wall carrying all sorts of vessels, and statues and figures of animals made of wood and stone and various materials, which appear over the wall? Some of them are talking, others silent.

GLAUCON: You have shown me a strange image, and they are strange prisoners.

SOCRATES: Like ourselves, I replied; and they see only their own shadows, or    5
the shadows of one another, which the fire throws on the opposite wall of the cave?

GLAUCON: True, he said; how could they see anything but the shadows if they were never allowed to move their heads?

SOCRATES: And of the objects which are being carried in like manner they would only see the shadows?

GLAUCON: Yes, he said.

SOCRATES: And if they were able to converse with one another, would they not suppose that they were naming what was actually before them?

GLAUCON: Very true.                                                                                   10

SOCRATES: And suppose further that the prison had an echo which came from the other side, would they not be sure to fancy when one of the passers-by spoke that the voice which they heard came from the passing shadow?

GLAUCON: No question, he replied.

SOCRATES: To them, I said, the truth would be literally nothing but the shadows of the images.

GLAUCON: That is certain.

SOCRATES: And now look again, and see what will naturally follow if the      15
prisoners are released and disabused of their error. At first, when any of them is liberated and compelled suddenly to stand up and turn his neck round and walk and look towards the light, he will suffer sharp pains; the glare will distress him, and he will be unable to see the realities of which in his former state he had seen the shadows; and then conceive some one saying to him, that what he saw before was an illusion, but that now, when he is approaching nearer to being and his eye is turned towards more real existence, he has a clearer vision, —what will be his reply? And you may further imagine that his in-structor is pointing to the objects as they pass and requiring him to name them, —will he not be perplexed? Will he not fancy that the shadows which he formerly saw are truer than the objects which are now shown to him?

GLAUCON: Far truer.

SOCRATES: And if he is compelled to look straight at the light, will he not have a pain in his eyes which will make him turn away to take refuge in the objects of vision which he can see, and which he will conceive to be in reality clearer than the things which are now being shown to him?

GLAUCON: True, he said.

SOCRATES: And suppose once more, that he is reluctantly dragged up a steep and rugged ascent, and held fast until he's forced into the pres-ence of the sun himself, is he not likely to be pained and irritated? When he approaches the light his eyes will be dazzled, and he will not be able to see anything at all of what are now called realities.

GLAUCON: Not all in a moment, he said.                                                         20

SOCRATES: He will require to grow accustomed to the sight of the upper world. And first he will see the shadows best, next the reflections of men and other objects in the water, and then the objects themselves; then he will gaze upon the light of the moon and the stars and the spangled heaven; and he will see the sky and the stars by night better than the sun or the light of the sun by day?

GLAUCON: Certainly.

SOCRATES: Last of all he will be able to see the sun, and not mere reflections of him in the water, but he will see him in his own proper place, and not in another; and he will contemplate him as he is.

GLAUCON: Certainly.

SOCRATES: He will then proceed to argue that this is he who gives the sea-   25
son and the years, and is the guardian of all that is in the visible world, and in a certain way the cause of all things which he and his fellows have been accustomed to behold?

GLAUCON: Clearly, he said, he would first see the sun and then reason about him.

SOCRATES: And when he remembered his old habitation, and the wisdom of the den and his fellow-prisoners, do you not suppose that he would felicitate himself on the change, and pity them?

GLAUCON: Certainly, he would.

SOCRATES: And if they were in the habit of conferring honours among themselves on those who were quickest to observe the passing shadows and to remark which of them went before, and which followed after, and which were together; and who were therefore best able to draw conclusions as to the future, do you think that he would care for such honours and glories, or envy the possessors of them? Would he not say with Homer, "Better to be the poor servant of a poor master, and to endure anything, rather than think as they do and live after their manner?"

GLAUCON: Yes, he said, I think that he would rather suffer anything than   30
entertain these false notions and live in this miserable manner.

SOCRATES: Imagine once more, I said, such a one coming suddenly out of the sun to be replaced in his old situation; would he not be certain to have his eyes full of darkness?

GLAUCON: To be sure, he said.

SOCRATES: And if there were a contest, and he had to compete in measuring the shadows with the prisoners who had never moved out of the den, while his sight was still weak, and before his eyes had become steady (and the time which would be needed to acquire this new habit of sight might be very considerable), would he not be ridiculous? Men would say of him that up he went and down he came without his eyes; and that it was better not even to think of ascending; and if any one tried to loose another and lead him up to the light, let them only catch the offender, and they would put him to death.

GLAUCON: No question, he said.

SOCRATES: This entire allegory, I said, you may now append, dear Glaucon, 35
to the previous argument; the prison-house is the world of sight, the
light of the fire is the sun, and you will not misapprehend me if you interpret the journey upwards to be the ascent of the soul into the intellectual world according to my poor belief, which, at your desire, I have
expressed whether rightly or wrongly God knows. But, whether true or
false, my opinion is that in the world of knowledge the idea of good
appears last of all, and is seen only with an effort; and, when seen, is
also inferred to be the universal author of all things beautiful and right,
parent of light and of the lord of light in this visible world, and the immediate source of reason and truth in the intellectual; and that this is
the power upon which he who would act rationally, either in public or
private life, must have his eye fixed.

You'll note that in this dialogue, Socrates does most of the talking; he controls
the responses of Glaucon, his student. Plato presents all so that Glaucon (and
the readers of the dialogue) will arrive at the desired insight. But it's rare that a
narrative can keep such a tight control over materials so complex.

## Experiencing Film through Allegory

In the film The Matrix (1999), Andy and Larry Wachowski create a film
version of Plato's allegory. By turning the allegory into action, the Wachowskis must test the limits of the scenario that Plato has created. An advantage
of pushing beyond the static quality of Plato's allegorical world is that further
development reveals problems that Glaucon had not noted. In moving from
Plato's largely descriptive "story" into the plot of a mainstream movie, the
tension that emerges occurs between the nearly invisible characters who
control the puppets in Plato's cave and those who have seen the light. Plato
describes the difficulty of convincing prisoners with such limited life experience that there was anything that they might want to escape. The screen-
writers, though, begin to ask questions that the original allegory does not
attempt to answer. For instance, Why are these people being held prisoner?
What sort of evil force would be responsible for such cruelty? How could
anyone ever escape from this enslavement? Would escape be desirable given
the paucity of the real world that remains?

The Matrix's plot concerns the difficulty of conveying the message of the
light to the prisoners. Neo (Keanu Reeves) must battle against these prison
keepers as well as against his own perception of which world is reality. The
life that he has experienced before his awakening is, like the cave, merely a
shadow that has been presented to him by the machines in order to keep him

*The Matrix* (1999)

in captivity. In opening up Plato's allegory, the Wachowskis also stumble upon ironies they seem unable to solve (or perhaps do not even recognize). For example, it is often not noticed amid all the expertly choreographed action that Neo kills the sorts of people he is supposed to be liberating. The guards and police gunned down in the final scene are shadows projected by the prison keepers, but these shadows are connected to the mental activity of real people wired into the matrix by the masters. Their death in the projected world leads to their physical death in the world not seen. So, are these unconscious victims mere collateral damage? Are we to assume that some shadows are more equal than others? Does Neo (or anyone else in his group) stop to think of the difference between the puppets/ humans and the puppet masters/ machines? It seems that the

### Making Connections

The language of war often makes use of the allegory. War posters have traditionally pictured figures such as Liberty, Truth, or Justice (almost always female) in order to represent the cause for which soldiers are fighting. The opponent is typically presented as some sort of animal or menacing threat. Examine contemporary military recruiting ads (posters and print ads, but also short narratives played in movie theaters before the trailers or during televised sports events), and analyze how allegories are used today. Explain how the allegory is designed to address a particular context.

highly controlled sorts of meaning that Crampton had sought through allegory aren't achieved by many provocative works. Sometimes, allegory becomes most interesting when it breaks down and allows the reader/viewer to participate strongly in the creation of meaning.

## MODELING CRITICAL ANALYSIS:
## JOÃO GUIMARÃES ROSA,
## THE THIRD BANK OF THE RIVER

"The Third Bank of River" by João Guimarães Rosa defies easy interpretation. If we think of it as a realistic story, it becomes confusing. The general tone seems fairly straightforward, and there is nothing startling in the first few paragraphs, but the story's action quickly grows impossible. This father leaves his family and lives silently for many years on a little boat just beyond the old home. How could he survive? The narrator tells us that he has been taking food to the father, but that hardly seems a satisfactory answer. No one could live on such a boat subject to the elements in complete silence and survive for so long. We can't answer many other simple questions about this story: Why doesn't someone go bring the father in? Why doesn't the father ever seem delirious? How is it that the family grows accustomed to such a strange situation? The fact that we cannot easily respond to these questions suggests that they are the wrong kinds of questions. Guimarães Rosa may well be writing about something very real, but this is not a realistic story.

**João Guimarães Rosa** (1908–1967)

# The Third Bank of the River (Willian L. Grossman, trans; 1967)

My father was a dutiful, orderly, straightforward man. And according to several reliable people of whom I inquired, he had had these qualities since adolescence or even childhood. By my own recollection, he was neither jollier nor more melancholy than the other men we knew. Maybe a little quieter. It was Mother, not Father, who ruled the house. She scolded us daily—my sister, my brother, and me. But it happened one day that Father ordered a boat.

He was very serious about it. It was to be made specially for him, of mimosa wood. It was to be sturdy enough to last twenty or thirty years and just large enough for one person. Mother carried on plenty about it. Was her husband going to become a fisherman all of a sudden? Or a hunter? Father said nothing. Our house was less than a mile from the river, which around there was deep, quiet, and so wide you couldn't see across it.

I can never forget the day the rowboat was delivered. Father showed no joy or other emotion. He just put on his hat as he always did and said good-by to us. He took along no food or bundle of any sort. We expected Mother to rant and rave, but she didn't. She looked very pale and bit her lip, but all she said was: "If you go away, stay away. Don't ever come back!"

Father made no reply. He looked gently at me and motioned me to walk along with him. I feared Mother's wrath, yet I eagerly obeyed. We headed toward the river together. I felt bold and exhilarated, so much so that I said: "Father, will you take me with you in your boat?"

He just looked at me, gave me his blessing, and by a gesture, told me to    5
go back. I made as if to do so but, when his back was turned, I ducked behind some bushes to watch him. Father got into the boat and rowed away. Its shadow slid across the water like a crocodile, long and quiet.

Father did not come back. Nor did he go anywhere, really. He just rowed and floated across and around, out there in the river. Everyone was appalled. What had never happened, what could not possibly happen, was happening. Our relatives, neighbors, and friends came over to discuss the phenomenon.

Mother was ashamed. She said little and conducted herself with great composure. As a consequence, almost everyone thought (though no one said it) that Father had gone insane. A few, however, suggested that Father might be fulfilling a promise he had made to God or to a saint, or that he might have some horrible disease, maybe leprosy, and that he left for the sake of the family, at the same time wishing to remain fairly near them.

Travelers along the river and people living near the bank on one side or the other reported that Father never put foot on land, by day or night. He just moved about on the river, solitary, aimless, like a derelict. Mother and our relatives agreed that the food which he had doubtless hidden in the boat would soon give out and that then he would either leave the river and travel off somewhere (which would be at least a little more respectable) or he would repent and come home.

How far from the truth they were! Father had a secret source of provisions: me. Every day I stole food and brought it to him. The first night after he left, we all lit fires on the shore and prayed and called to him. I was deeply distressed and felt a need to do something more. The following day I went down to the river with a loaf of corn bread, a bunch of bananas, and some bricks of raw brown sugar. I waited impatiently a long, long hour. Then I saw the boat, far off, alone, gliding almost imperceptibly on the smoothness of the river. Father was sitting in the bottom of the boat. He saw me but he did not row toward me or make any gesture. I showed him the food and then I placed it in a hollow rock on the river bank; it was safe there from animals, rain, and dew. I did this day after day, on and on and on. Later I learned, to my surprise, that Mother knew what I was doing and left food around where I could easily steal it. She had a lot of feelings she didn't show.

Mother sent for her brother to come and help on the farm and in business matters. She had the schoolteacher come and tutor us children at home because of the time we had lost. One day, at her request, the priest put on his vestments, went down to the shore, and tried to exorcise the devils that had got into my father. He shouted that Father had a duty to cease his unholy obstinacy. Another day she arranged to have two soldiers come and try to frighten him. All to no avail. My father went by in the distance, sometimes so far away he could barely be seen. He never replied to anyone and no one ever got close to him. When some newspapermen came in a launch to take his picture, Father headed his boat to the other side of the river and into the marshes, which he knew like the palm of his hand but in which other people quickly got lost. There in his private maze, which extended for miles, with heavy foliage overhead and rushes on all sides, he was safe.

We had to get accustomed to the idea of Father's being out on the river. We had to but we couldn't, we never could. I think I was the only one who understood to some degree what our father wanted and what he did not want. The thing I could not understand at all was how he stood the hardship. Day and night, in sun and rain, in heat and in the terrible midyear cold spells, with his old hat on his head and very little other clothing, week after week, month after month, year after year, unheedful of the waste and emptiness in which his life was slipping by. He never set foot on earth or grass, on isle or mainland shore. No doubt he sometimes tied up the boat at a secret place, perhaps at the tip of some island, to get a little sleep. He never lit a fire or even struck a match and he had no flashlight. He took only a small part of the food that I left in the hollow rock—not enough, it seemed to me, for survival. What could his state of health have been? How about the continual drain on his energy, pulling and pushing the oars to control the boat? And how did he survive the annual floods, when the river rose and swept along with it all sorts of dangerous objects—branches of trees, dead bodies of animals—that might suddenly crash against his little boat?

He never talked to a living soul. And we never talked about him. We just thought. No, we could never put our father out of mind. If for a short time we seemed to, it was just a lull from which we would be sharply awakened by the realization of his frightening situation.

My sister got married, but Mother didn't want a wedding party. It would have been a sad affair, for we thought of him every time we ate some

10

especially tasty food. Just as we thought of him in our cozy beds on a cold, stormy night—out there, alone and unprotected, trying to bail out the boat with only his hands and a gourd. Now and then someone would say that I was getting to look more and more like my father. But I knew that by then his hair and beard must have been shaggy and his nails long. I pictured him thin and sickly, black with hair and sunburn, and almost naked despite the articles of clothing I occasionally left for him.

He didn't seem to care about us at all. But I felt affection and respect for him, and, whenever they praised me because I had done something good, I said: "My father taught me to act that way."

It wasn't exactly accurate but it was a truthful sort of lie. As I said, Father didn't seem to care about us. But then why did he stay around there? Why didn't he go up the river or down the river, beyond the possibility of seeing us or being seen by us? He alone knew the answer.

My sister had a baby boy. She insisted on showing Father his grandson. One beautiful day we all went down to the riverbank, my sister in her white wedding dress, and she lifted the baby high. Her husband held a parasol above them. We shouted to Father and waited. He did not appear. My sister cried; we all cried in each other's arms.

My sister and her husband moved far away. My brother went to live in a city. Times changed, with their usual imperceptible rapidity. Mother finally moved too; she was old and went to live with her daughter. I remained behind, a leftover. I could never think of marrying. I just stayed there with the impedimenta of my life. Father, wandering alone and forlorn on the river, needed me. I knew he needed me, although he never even told me why he was doing it. When I put the question to people bluntly and insistently, all they told me was that they heard that Father had explained it to the man who made the boat. But now this man was dead and nobody knew or remembered anything. There was just some foolish talk, when the rains were especially severe and persistent, that my father was wise like Noah and had the boat built in anticipation of a new flood; I dimly remember people saying this. In any case, I would not condemn my father for what he was doing. My hair was beginning to turn gray.

I have only sad things to say. What bad had I done, what was my great guilt? My father always away and his absence always with me. And the river, always the river, perpetually renewing itself. The river, always. I was beginning to suffer from old age, in which life is just a sort of lingering. I had attacks of illness and of anxiety. I had a nagging rheumatism. And he? Why, why was he doing it? He must have been suffering terribly. He was so old. One day, in his failing strength, he might let the boat capsize; or he might let the current carry it downstream, on and on, until it plunged over the waterfall to the boiling turmoil below. It pressed upon my heart. He was out there and I was forever robbed of my peace. I am guilty of I know not what, and my pain is an open wound inside me. Perhaps I would know—if things were different. I began to guess what was wrong.

Out with it! Had I gone crazy? No, in our house that word was never spoken, never through all the years. No one called anybody crazy, for nobody is crazy. Or maybe everybody. All I did was go there and wave a handkerchief so he would be more likely to see me. I was in complete command of myself. I waited. Finally he appeared in the distance, there, then over there, a vague shape sitting in the back of the boat. I called to him several times. And I said what I was so eager to say, to state formally and under oath. I said it as loud as I could:

"Father, you have been out there long enough. You are old.... Come     20
back, you don't have to do it anymore.... Come back and I'll go instead. Right now, if you want. Any time. I'll get into the boat. I'll take your place."

And when I had said this my heart beat more firmly.

He heard me. He stood up. He maneuvered with his oars and headed the boat toward me. He had accepted my offer. And suddenly I trembled, down deep. For he had raised his arm and waved—the first time in so many, so many years. And I couldn't... In terror, my hair on end, I ran, I fled madly. For he seemed to come from another world. And I'm begging forgiveness, begging, begging.

I experienced the dreadful sense of cold that comes from deadly fear, and I became ill. Nobody ever saw or heard about him again. Am I a man, after such a failure? I am what never should have been. I am what must be silent. I know it is too late. I must stay in the deserts and unmarked plains of my life, and I fear I shall shorten it. But when death comes I want them to take me and put me in a little boat in this perpetual water between the long shores; and I, down the river, lost in the river, inside the river... the river... ■

What happens if we try to read this story as an allegory? It's worth noticing that the father is "very serious" about the boat. It is made to carry one person and one person only. When it is delivered, the father shows no emotion. He simply says "good-by" to the family and heads off to the river. The son wants to go with him, but the father sends him back and moves off silently, alone. Is it possible that Guimarães Rosa's story allegorizes death and the process of grief? If we think in such terms, we may be prepared to answer new questions: How is it that the father doesn't "come back" or "go anywhere"? How can he be so present and so absent? The boat carries only one because only one dies; others left behind must deal with the death. The father is no longer a physical presence in the life of his family, but his death has not ended a relationship that transcends the physical. The son, in particular, struggles with his own identity in the father's absence. He works hard to keep the father alive in memory.

Such a reading begins to open possibilities, but it doesn't suddenly snap everything into place. It seems that Guimarães Rosa's story has allegorical elements but never sustains a clear and consistent parallel between the concrete and the abstract. We're invited to consider alternative readings. Perhaps rather than death, Guimarães Rosa's allegory concerns more generally disconnection and loneliness in families. Or perhaps the emphasis needs to shift to the narrator, to the son. How do we read this story if we think of it as the struggles of a young man to grow up? Is separation from the father a crucial part of that maturation? Has the narrator been unable to accept the distance his father has established in their relationship? Understanding how allegory works helps us enter the world of this story and respond to it powerfully.

## Using Allegory to Focus Writing and Discussion

- What makes you think that it is appropriate to read this work allegorically? Find specific signals that the author gives to allow you to explore allegorical interpretations.

- Describe the tone of the work. How does the tone of the surface narrative lead us to allegorical interpretations?

- If we can offer sufficient proof that there is some justification in the text for an allegorical interpretation, we can go on to the next questions.

- Set up an interpretive table to explain the significance of specific characters within the work. To develop this chart, identify the character by name, the idea that this character represents, and your justification (from the text itself) that allows you to make this connection.

- What is the advantage of reading the text allegorically? How does this interpretation offer insight that is not available by reading the surface narrative "straight"?

- Why is it useful for the author to approach this particular subject indirectly?

# 13 Symbolism

## How Do I Know When an Event or an Image Is Supposed to Stand for Something Else?

One of the easiest questions to ever appear in an exam for a driver's license is the following:

When you come to a stop sign at an intersection, you should

A. slow down and proceed with caution

B. continue only if the intersection is clear

C. pass stopped cars on the left

D. stop

We'll assume that all of you (whether you drive or not) would answer "D." A stop sign means stop, a meaning we can all agree upon. But how exactly do a few marks (letters), a shape (an octagon), and a color (red) so uniformly make the point? The answer is pretty simple (even if the implications of that answer are more complicated): We have collectively agreed within our time and place to use these marks, this shape, and that color to signal "stop." The choice was not "natural" in the sense that only these marks, this shape, and that color would do. But we as members of a particular society made the choice and live with it so easily that it seems natural. A stop sign is not ambiguous or unknown to us. A local traffic court judge wouldn't accept alternative interpretations from a ticketed driver.

Literature and film also employ some easy-to-read signs. In monster movies from the 1950s and early 1960s, the monster would die in the final scene, the closing credits would announce "The End," and then a question mark would emerge from the darkened screen. Every person in the theater knew that the terrifying creature that had lurked beneath the dark waters of the lake didn't actually die, even though the characters in the film thought so. All in the audience realized that "The End...?" meant "sort of the end": leave the theater, but take your scary feelings home with you because the monster is still "out there." Although this sign prompts a bit more open interpretation than a stop sign does, it still severely limits likely responses. In both literature and life, we are trained to read and interpret the most common signs in particular ways by experience. The simplest signs express a remarkably narrow range of meanings.

What happens, though, when one thing suggests possible meanings without being specific about any particular single meaning? How can we read and interpret a sign when we are not taught by established custom exactly how to read it? Or when the function of the sign is *not* to communicate a specific, limited meaning (a prohibition, an order, a direction)? What happens when a sign provokes conflicting responses? The backslash across the hand signaling stop shown here builds in a contradiction that forces us to read, interpret, and argue by giving us something we are not accustomed to see.

The slash could be read to cancel out the hand signal. It suggests "don't stop," but it's not clear what it is exactly that we're not supposed to stop. We might consider many possibilities: If we see this sign carried by a protester in

front of a police station, we might think it means "don't listen to authority" or "don't stop defying rules"; if we see the same sign inside a nightclub, we might think it means "don't stop dancing" or "don't stop having fun." In any case, we'll need to consider this sign and consciously interpret it rather than just accept it.

At some point we need a new word. The stop sign that speaks so clearly at the corner of an intersection becomes a bit less clear when the extra graphics are added, and it begins to move from sign to **symbol**. In the broadest sense, all words are symbols, or words that stand in for something else. But it's useful to define symbol as something (an object, a word, an image) that is used to suggest a range of associations or feelings. Symbols prompt reflection and inquiry; they don't (like signs) point us to a highly defined action or message. Symbols are oftentimes highly personal—not controlled by an established public understanding. Symbols force us to grapple with meanings that are suggestive, resonant, and subtly nuanced. This can lead to uncomfortable territory for some readers. One of the most frustrating experiences many people have with complex literary works and films arises from the sense that one thing means something else, yet that "something else" can hardly be identified, captured, or named. To a person who wants things clear-cut, a discussion of symbols can seem like an imposition: a "reading into" a text rather than a "reading of" a text.

But we cannot dismiss the power of symbols because we sometimes find them hard to read. And we need not be helpless before them. Writers don't want symbols to obscure meaning. They want to use symbols to reach new meaning. If we trust the signals writers provide and don't expect only highly defined messages, we'll find that symbols don't present any special problems. Our efforts to understand and articulate how symbols emerge and take on meaning can be profoundly rewarding. In this chapter, we'll consider how we can be released from explicit and easily identified directions and still develop grounded, persuasive readings.

## FIGURATIVE LANGUAGE

**Figurative language** is, broadly defined, any language that is used in ways that deviate from standard significance, order, or meaning. Such language may lend freshness or strength to expression. It may also extend or complicate the meaning of a word or expression. Figurative language, then, moves us from signs to symbols.

Figurative language is often divided into two types. A **rhetorical figure** uses a word or words in an unusual context or sequence but does not radically change the customary meaning of the word or words. For example, an **apostrophe** refers to the speaker's direct address to an absent person or to some abstract idea or spirit; although we don't usually speak to someone or something that is not physically present, the words themselves may be familiar.

Of greater importance for our purposes is the second type of figurative language. A **trope** (sometimes called a **figure of thought**) differs from a rhetorical figure in that it moves us to a changed or significantly extended meaning of a word or words. **Personification** is an example of a trope; to personify is to cast an abstract concept or inanimate material as a living thing endowed with human qualities. When the wrestler-turned-movie star "The Rock" chose his stage name, he used a trope—he sought to personify qualities of strength, indestructibility, hardness. The name may come to take on broader meanings depending on the roles he plays (indicating solidity, steadiness, and so on). **Similes** and **metaphors** are also tropes. As we noted in Chapter 12, such figures of thought move us into the realm of allegory and symbol.

The roots of the word *trope* are from Greek: "to turn" or "a turning." Tropes use words to *turn* someone from conventional understanding; they test the elasticity of language. A writer might help us see that "stop" does not need to be fixed in meaning by the function of an octagonal red sign. This "turning" though is different from arbitrarily redefining a word. If we were all to invent our own definitions for words, our language would fail. We depend upon some common understanding in order to communicate. An effectively employed trope will bring new meaning from old. The old or the familiar will give us, along with our understanding of the surrounding situation, an interpretive lead. We know, for example, that the red sign usually means "stop your car." We know that the backslash cancels the primary message. When we see the backslash laid over the stop sign, we look for clues that might help us understand what it is we need to go forward with, what it is we should not stop.

What we're suggesting is that readers not "hunt" for symbols as an archeologist hunts for evidence of a buried civilization. Symbols arise out of the suggestive turns an artist employs (whether consciously or not). An effective "turn" moves *from* something familiar (established, conventional) *to* something fresh. Such turns are part of what brings symbols to the surface for us to see, feel, and reflect upon. So, to find symbols, don't dig for what is covered. Start by paying close attention to the signals a text provides.

## Experiencing Literature through Symbols

Words, things, and images do not become symbols in isolation. Symbols
are defined by and emerge from what surrounds them. In her poem "Home
Movies," Mary Jo Salter reviews the images in her family's home movies to
find scenes that have meaning to her now. She rejects the most common
scenes and signs: "Christmases" and "birthday candles." The same holiday
rituals repeated year after year have lost meaning to her over the years.
Her father's attempt to create richer symbolism through photography also
fails to achieve any lasting effect. It is finally "the stoneware mixing bowl"
that the speaker still has in her own kitchen that emerges with symbolic
force. The bowl moves her because it connects her current life to a rare
moment of childhood happiness with her mother. In this poem, the
ordinary object takes on meaning that it did not have before the poet
reviewed the home movies. As she says, this object has meaning only for
her in this particular context. And the poem shares that private symbol
with us. The mixing bowl is symbolic of any ordinary object that might
have meaning to us because of its connection to our peculiar interactions
with it.

**Mary Jo Salter** (1954– )

# Home Movies: A Sort of Ode (1999)

Because it hadn't seemed enough,
after a while, to catalogue
more Christmases, the three-layer cakes
ablaze with birthday candles, the blizzard
Billy took a shovel to,                                          5
Phil's lawnmower tour of the yard,
the tree forts, the shoot-'em-ups
between the boys in new string ties
and cowboy hats and holsters,
or Mother sticking a bow as big                                 10
as Mouseketeer ears in my hair,

my father sometimes turned the gaze
of his camera to subjects more
artistic or universal:
long closeups of a rose's face;                                 15
a real-time sunset (nearly an hour);

what surely were some brilliant autumn
leaves before their colors faded
to dry beige on the aging film;
a great deal of pacing, at the zoo,                                    20
by polar bears and tigers caged,
he seemed to say, like him.

What happened between him and her
is another story. And just as well
we have no movie of it, only                                          25
some unforgiving scowls she gave
through terrifying, ticking silence
when he must have asked her (no
sound track) for a smile.
Still, what I keep yearning for                                       30
isn't those generic cherry
blossoms at their peak, or the brave
daffodil after a snowfall,

it's the re-run surprise
of the unshuttered, prefab blanks                                     35
of windows at the back of the house,
and how the lines of aluminum
siding are scribbled on with meaning
only for us who lived there;
it's the pair of elephant bookends                                    40
I'd forgotten, with the upraised trunks
like handles, and the books they meant
to carry in one block to a future
that scattered all of us.

And look: it's the stoneware mixing bowl                              45
figured with hand-holding dancers
handed down so many years
ago to my own kitchen, still
valueless, unbroken. Here
she's happy, teaching us to dye                                       50
the Easter eggs in it, a Grecian
urn of sorts near which—a foster
child of silence and slow time
myself—I smile because she does
and patiently await my turn.                                          55

### Making Connections

The symbolic importance of Salter's mixing bowl is signaled by how she calls attention to it at the start of the final stanza and how, in that stanza, she elevates this "valueless" object by referring to another well-known poem, John Keats's "Ode on a Grecian Urn." Keats addresses the urn as a "foster-child of silence and slow time." For Keats, the urn captures in its design something eternal—a feeling of a moment that is fleeting in life but maintained forever in art. By asking us to think of Keats's poem, Salter encourages us to consider how Keats's symbolic use of the urn relates to her mixing bowl. For further attention to the effect of such references, see Chapter 15.

There isn't, of course, anything inherently symbolic about a mixing bowl. Salter looks for an object that can capture something essential about her relationship with her mother. She tells us that what she is "yearning for" isn't the "generic cherry / blossoms." It's something captured in a few assorted things; then, in the last stanza, she lights upon the mixing bowl. The speaker's moment of recognition ("And look: it's the stoneware mixing bowl") becomes our moment of recognition. We're alerted to see this object as full of significance.

## RECOGNIZING SYMBOLS

As we noted previously, an object is not a symbol until it is used as a symbol. Salter treats a mixing bowl in a way that makes us think of memory, mothers and daughters, family tensions. Her treatment is so persuasive that we may now look at a mixing bowl and think of Salter's mother, Easter eggs, and even other literary texts. We need to always consider how the surrounding words support a symbolic (rather than a literal) reading. The following pages contain images with apples in various symbol contexts. Consider how the apple's use in each image supports a different symbolic reading of the apple.

Now, think for a moment of an orange, a fruit whose symbolic use is rather less common than the apple's. What comes to mind? First responses are likely to be to the thing itself: color, weight, shape, smell, and taste. We think in terms of concrete images. We don't necessarily go beyond those images. As we pointed out in Chapter 7, we don't always need or want to go beyond those images. You'll note that Gary Soto's "Oranges" registers physical characteristics of the fruit. You will also be encouraged to think of the oranges as symbols. How does Soto persuade us to move from one kind of understanding to another? Compare his first mention of a cold twelve-year-old, "weighted down / With two oranges" (lines 3–4), with his glorious "I peeled my orange" (line 51) near the end of the poem. He only mentions "orange" three times,

# What does an apple symbolize?

Churchman's Cigarettes

Gravity

# What does an apple symbolize?

yet our sense of how we interpret oranges changes considerably. What has happened to give the orange symbolic meaning?

**Gary Soto** (1952– )

# Oranges (1995)

The first time I walked
With a girl, I was twelve,
Cold, and weighted down
With two oranges in my jacket.
December. Frost cracking                                    5
Beneath my steps, my breath
Before me, then gone,
As I walked toward
Her house, the one whose
Porch light burned yellow                                  10
Night and day, in any weather.
A dog barked at me, until
She came out pulling
At her gloves, face bright
With rouge. I smiled,                                      15
Touched her shoulder, and led
Her down the street, across
A used car lot and a line
Of newly planted trees,
Until we were breathing                                    20
Before a drugstore. We
Entered, the tiny bell
Bringing a saleslady
Down a narrow aisle of goods.
I turned to the candies                                    25
Tiered like bleachers,
And asked what she wanted—
Light in her eyes, a smile
Starting at the corners
Of her mouth. I fingered                                   30
A nickel in my pocket,
And when she lifted a chocolate
That cost a dime,
I didn't say anything.
I took the nickel from                                     35

My pocket, then an orange,
And set them quietly on
The counter. When I looked up,
The lady's eyes met mine,
And held them, knowing                                    40
Very well what it was all
About.

Outside,
A few cars hissing past,
Fog hanging like old                                     45
Coats between the trees.
I took my girl's hand
In mine for two blocks,
Then released it to let
Her unwrap the chocolate.                                 50
I peeled my orange
That was so bright against
The gray of December
That, from some distance,
Someone might have thought                               55
I was making a fire in my hands.

By the time Soto gives us his most precise physical description of the orange (near the end of the poem), the orange has grown symbolically rich. His desire to impress this girl is so intense that he has persuaded the woman behind the counter in the drugstore to enter into his world. She has accepted his orange as sufficient payment for the candy bar that the girl wants; the saleslady understands that he has only half as much money as he needs to buy this candy bar and that to admit his poverty here will destroy him. He persuades the saleslady to abandon the conventional sign—one candy bar is equivalent to one dime—and to accept his substitution of an orange for the missing nickel. This story describes the triumph of the poet's act of symbolism. He presents his symbol powerfully enough that someone outside his consciousness agrees to accept that symbol. In the final scene, he revels in his triumph, consuming an orange that means so much more than it meant at the beginning of the poem.

## ALLEGORY AND SYMBOL

Allegory, as discussed in Chapter 12, develops a parallel between the concrete and the abstract that is generally sustained throughout a narrative. In allegory, we observe two levels of meaning that play out in a fairly consistent manner as actions unfold. The elements of a straightforward allegory can be likened to signs—signs that most readers interpret in similar ways. Just as driving experience teaches us to respond to a variety of road signs confidently and coherently, literary experience teaches us to sort out and read the many signs that make up an allegory.

Of course, no literary text is as reductive as a stop sign. And some texts are more reductive than others. But it's fair to say that symbols ask us to move between the concrete and the abstract rather more flexibly than allegory does. Because a symbol is not conditioned by parallels sustained and consistently reinforced over the course of an entire narrative, we have more room to speculate.

- Allegory *tends* to direct readers to a level of meaning that is *relatively* defined, uniform, and instructional (didactic).

- Symbols *generally encourage* readers to reflect upon meaning that is *relatively* luminous, multiple, and abstract.

You might note we've left these distinctions a little blurry ("allegory *tends*," "symbols *generally encourage*," and "*relatively*"). Some interpretive challenges as well as interpretive pleasures occur in the gray areas.

## Experiencing Literature through Symbolism

We mentioned in Chapter 12 that even though Nathaniel Hawthorne's "Young Goodman Brown" can be considered an allegory, it can't be easily reduced to any single lesson. In fact, some critics have insisted that Hawthorne is essentially a symbolist, for there is no consistent parallel carried throughout the story that clarifies every element and guides us through to a moral. These critics point out that although Goodman Brown himself seems to read things with great certainty, we have little reason to accept his interpretation. Did he lose "his faith" or cruelly reject a loving wife? Did he encounter and ultimately recoil from pure evil, or did he fail to contend with moral complexity? Did he grow bitter because he could not accept wickedness or because he could not tolerate truth? Was he innocent before his journey or merely naïve? Is he experienced after the journey, or is he still naïve?

Hawthorne himself said he worked in the shadowy areas of the human spirit. And we can get some sense of the shadow land we will enter in the first few paragraphs of his story. The very first begins to signal the symbolic undercurrent of the whole:

> Young Goodman Brown came forth at sunset into the street at Salem village; but put his head back, after crossing the threshold, to exchange a

parting kiss with his young wife. And Faith, as the wife was aptly named, thrust her own pretty head into the street, letting the wind play with the pink ribbons of her cap while she called to Goodman Brown.

Note that the wife is not only named "Faith" but that Hawthorne calls attention to the name for us. And in the introductory paragraphs to follow, we find "my love and my Faith," "dear Faith," and "poor little Faith." The pink ribbons may not seem important immediately but are soon noted twice more. Note how subtly Hawthorne moves from something as tangible as a doorway to multiple abstractions suggested by the doorway. When Goodman Brown steps out the door, he crosses a "threshold." Faith stays in the house. But note how they kiss: Goodman Brown moves back near the door, and Faith moves her head forward across the threshold into the street. As the story develops, we sense the importance of these two spaces: one kind of space (the home with Faith) is protected, enclosed, small, known, safe; the other (the street and beyond into the forest) is wild, open, large, mysterious, dangerous.

If we are to insist on allegory, we might maintain that the protected space inside the door is pure. We might argue that Hawthorne has a lesson to teach and uses the doorway as one piece of an allegory: don't cross the threshold (that is, don't seek knowledge you are not supposed to have). But as the story develops, it seems there are other, more open possibilities. Perhaps this purity is only an illusion. Perhaps reality, not wild wickedness, lies across the threshold. However we interpret it, the doorway/threshold seems to suggest a critical point that once passed cannot be regained. The threshold may be a psychological one, or a moral one, and/or an experiential one.

Note that when we think of a doorway/threshold as a symbol, we don't give it some random meaning nor do we identify a single meaning. Although our response to a symbol isn't as conditioned as our response to a stop sign, interpretation still depends upon linguistic, cultural, interpretive cues. We have many here to work with. We can start with plain meanings. A doorway, after all, does mark boundaries; it leads from one place to another. We commonly speak both literally and figuratively of "walking out," "coming in," or "crossing over." Within the story, Hawthorne **foregrounds** (calls attention to) the doorway by word choice (*threshold*), by the doorway's place in the narrative (the crossing marks the start of a journey), and by Faith's appeals at the threshold (don't leave this house tonight). Given what happens after Goodman Brown steps out, we are encouraged to consider what doorways/thresholds we all must cross in life. We could argue that crossing the threshold doesn't set up a lesson for us; rather, it leads to a revelation about Brown's character: Young Goodman Brown cannot handle truth or complexity. The doorway symbolizes a passage from the comfortable innocence of youth. We all must cross thresholds—real and symbolic. We need to think about how we process the experience of crossing thresholds.

As mentioned previously, critical writers offer *a contribution* to an ongoing conversation about a text; a contribution isn't a "solution," a "proof," or a "last word." But we cannot contribute to a discussion without engaging others who are involved in the discussion. Solid contributions depend upon attention to textual evidence and to relevant scholarship. Writing about a symbol is ultimately no different from writing about any element. We must always think about evidence, about how we account for/explain an interpretation, and about how we draw out the significance of an interpretation. Analysis involves "taking apart" in order to see how parts "fit together."

An attraction of reading for symbols is thinking that there is a reason for the otherwise inexplicable. Once we begin to find symbols in literary works, it is easy to jump to symbolic interpretations. We like to think that an author is exercising a higher power and that every object must be there for some symbolic reason. But power, beauty, and significance don't depend upon cleverly making one thing seem to be something else. A "deep reading" is not necessarily a reading that centers on symbols. So don't abandon all of the other literary elements for the sake of symbols. Remember that it is not enough to assert that an object symbolizes something; such a claim is an argument that we must back up by providing evidence in the literature and by showing how such symbolism helps us understand/experience the whole text. It may be useful to hold yourself to a higher standard whenever you claim to see symbols. Keep some basic questions in mind:

- What in the work encourages you to think beyond the concrete?

- Why is it important to appreciate a particular image as symbolic?

- How are words or images used in ways that "turn" us from straightforward meanings?

# MODELING CRITICAL ANALYSIS: JOÃO GUIMARÃES ROSA, THE THIRD BANK OF THE RIVER

In Chapter 12, we present an allegorical reading of João Guimarães Rosa's "The Third Bank of the River." Guimarães Rosa's narrative teases us to consider how each part along the way means something about a process, perhaps a process of grieving or of separation. The son may stand in for all children who lose parents or, even more broadly, all children who need to grow into their own selves, separate from parents. The father's "going out" on the river may be an abandonment that is both essential and inevitable. Perhaps we're to consider how a son registers the death of a father, how he contends with the loss or tries to deny the full meaning of the loss.

But our testing out did not and perhaps could not confidently identify a parallel sustained throughout the narrative between the concrete and the abstract. By loosening us from the control exercised by the kind of point-to-point correspondences we find in a work such as *The Faerie Queene*, Guimarães Rosa casts us into the realm of symbol. We're encouraged to play out multiple possibilities. And we're not forced to consider those possibilities as a set of "either-or" propositions. In other words, the river in Guimarães Rosa's story can suggest a widely resonant and textured set of meanings. We may think of how the experience of death unfolds for those left behind and may reflect more generally upon themes of abandonment. We may also consider how Guimarães Rosa projects feelings of loneliness (as a feeling, as a necessary fact of human existence?). It's not that Guimarães Rosa's tale can mean anything we want it to mean but that elements in it are laid out in ways that prompt a disciplined, yet open-ended meditation upon profound abstractions.

## Using Symbolism to Focus Writing and Discussion

- What makes you think that this object is a symbol?
- What clues does the author give us that we should look at this object symbolically?
- How can we justify the meaning that we ascribe to this symbol?
- What alternative meanings might this symbol have? Does it make sense to entertain these alternative meanings simultaneously? Why might it be appropriate to abandon these alternative meanings?
- What nuances does this particular symbol give to the meaning that we identify here? What does the author gain by using a symbol rather than stating the idea directly?
- For whom does this symbol have meaning? Is it necessary to be part of some particular group or to have some specific experience in order for this symbol to have significance?
- How does our attention to this detail as a symbol enhance our understanding of the text?

# 14 Context

## What Outside Information Do We Really Need to Know to Understand the Text?

It's often claimed that great art transcends the specific context within which it is produced: great works are timeless. That common assertion seems credible enough when we think of Greek drama, or *Othello*, or *Don Quixote*. But as durable as such masterpieces have proven to be, it seems far too simple to cite abstract "universals" like *anger, love, jealousy*, and *idealism* as the source of our continued appreciation. It's more accurate to say that great art prompts fresh, varied, powerful, new, and concrete experiences of fundamental human concerns. A play like *Othello* (with its themes of jealousy and envy as well as its racial subtext) hasn't so much transcended our time as it has *absorbed* our time and remained powerful. Issues of race, for example, can't ultimately mean the same thing for twenty-first-century Americans that they meant for the Elizabethan audience. When our literary experiences bridge the cultural gap between then and now, the literature enables us to enlarge our sense of who we are and of the world that surrounds us.

Good reading involves sustaining a healthy tension. On the one hand, we don't want to disregard a text's origins. We want to understand the history and culture of the author. On the other hand, we cannot—and should not—avoid experiencing art in terms of who we are now. We cannot avoid bringing new knowledge to old texts. In this chapter, we'll consider how our contemporary situation affects our experience of art as well as how knowledge of a work's historical context can deepen that experience.

## HOW DOES NEW KNOWLEDGE INFLUENCE OUR EXPERIENCE OF OLD TEXTS?

In writing about the action that takes place in a literary text, it's customary to use the present tense. Shakespeare wrote *Othello* early in the seventeenth century, but Othello kills Desdemona every time we read the play. This is a small stylistic convention, but it's a convention that suggests something important. *A literary text comes alive as we experience it; the action is always present.* Othello the play and Othello the character aren't frozen in place by the words on the page. If we keep this in mind, we can understand how it is that our *Othello* isn't necessarily the same *Othello* that someone in Victorian England might have experienced. And of course, texts that Victorians produced aren't necessarily read today as they were when they first appeared.

Over a century and a half ago, Alfred, Lord Tennyson read a newspaper account of a confused and disastrous cavalry charge of British soldiers in the Crimean War. He was inspired to commemorate that event. Tennyson's poetic intent was to valorize his country's military men. They served, followed orders, and died valiantly in a cause. Tennyson's key themes were loyalty, courage, discipline, patriotism. He wrote from a conviction of his country's goodness and the legitimacy of its imperialistic endeavors. The poem was a great success in some ways, exactly the sort of poem a poet laureate (the official poet of the state) was expected to produce. Since its appearance, many a schoolchild both in Great Britain and the United States has stood before a class and dutifully recited "The Charge of the Light Brigade." Despite the poem's popularity, there has always been a ripple of uneasiness among some readers about the tone of unqualified military zeal it endorses. The light brigade, after all, charged forward to death on botched orders in service of an uncertain cause. That ripple grew to waves in England after World War I and in the United States during the Vietnam War. Tennyson's poem today hardly works as a lofty tribute; we're more likely to respond to themes of waste, futility, and patriotic vanity—themes that Tennyson himself didn't intend to strike. The words of the poem haven't changed, but the surrounding cultural/historical **context** has changed.

**Alfred, Lord Tennyson** (1809–1892)

# The Charge of the Light Brigade (1854)

### 1
Half a league, half a league,
Half a league onward,

All in the valley of Death
  Rode the six hundred.
"Forward the Light Brigade!                        5
Charge for the guns!" he said.
Into the valley of Death
  Rode the six hundred.

               2
"Forward, the Light Brigade!"
Was there a man dismayed?                      10
Not though the soldier knew
  Someone had blundered.
Theirs not to make reply,
Theirs not to reason why,
Theirs but to do and die.                     15
Into the valley of Death
  Rode the six hundred.

               3
Cannon to right of them,
Cannon to left of them,
Cannon in front of them                    20
  Volleyed and thundered;
Stormed at with shot and shell,
Boldly they rode and well,
Into the jaws of Death,
Into the mouth of hell                    25
  Rode the six hundred.

               4
Flashed all their sabers bare,
Flashed as they turned in air
Sab'ring the gunners there,
Charging an army, while                    30
  All the world wondered.
Plunged in the battery smoke
Right through the line they broke;
Cossack and Russian
Reeled from the saber stroke               35
  Shattered and sundered.
Then they rode back, but not,
  Not the six hundred.

5

Cannon to right of them,
Cannon to left of them, 40
Cannon behind them
  Volleyed and thundered;
Stormed at with shot and shell,
While horse and hero fell.
They that had fought so well 45
Came through the jaws of Death,
Back from the mouth of hell,
All that was left of them,
  Left of six hundred.


6

When can their glory fade? 50
O the wild charge they made!
  All the world wondered.
Honor the charge they made!
Honor the Light Brigade,
  Noble six hundred! 55

Tennyson invokes a number of abstractions he could expect to be taken as "universals": nobility, bravery, self-sacrifice, and honor. He writes with a confident assumption that those abstractions will long endure: "All the world" is caught in rapt admiration of the brigade's martial virtues. The closing stanza asks the question, "When can their glory fade?" which implies an answer: not for a long, long time, not for as long as we honor courage and steadfast loyalty to a cause.

Of course, Tennyson could not envision the human costs of World War I. Nor could he be expected to imagine wars in Vietnam or Iraq from the perspective of a U.S. citizen. But these wars are part of our political, moral, and historical identity. Lines like "Theirs not to reason why, / Theirs but to do and die" strike most of us as disturbing and even dangerous. It's worth noting that we commonly misquote these lines in a way that diminishes the discomfort they have come to produce. One may hear the phrase repeated as "theirs but to do *or* die." It may seem a small matter, but *or* serves to soften Tennyson's point and perhaps helps sustain his romantic notions of war. If we charge forward boldly enough, we may die but we may instead accomplish something and still live (do and *not* die). Tennyson writing in 1856 seemed so secure in his ideals of duty that a perfect willingness to "do *and* die" only underscored for him the nobility of the act.

Perhaps the quickest way to imagine a modern counterpoint to Tennyson's vision is to recall any one of several notable American films about the war in Vietnam. For example, Francis Ford Coppola's *Apocalypse Now* (1979) depicts commitment to the cause as a kind of insanity, or perhaps even more accurately Coppola depicts zealous military commitment as a cause of insanity. *Apocalypse Now* is based on Joseph Conrad's novel *Heart of Darkness*, which chronicles the effects of imperialism in the Congo at the end of the nineteenth century. Both *Heart of Darkness* and *Apocalypse Now* strip away the sorts of abstract notions that Tennyson calls on for inspiration. Coppola uses the grand sweep of the film screen to suggest the enormity of destruction, cruelty, and death. He undercuts rather than invokes patriotic themes.

### Making Connections

Varied elements of any work of art will work together to achieve an effect. How does the rhythm and pace of "The Charge of the Light Brigade" complement the theme? How do the rhymes work to mark Tennyson's perspective on the event? Does Tennyson's technical command make the poem compelling, or does it merely exaggerate themes many modern readers find problematic (see Chapters 3 and 6)?

*Apocalypse Now* (1979)

# HOW IS KNOWLEDGE "OUTSIDE" THE TEXT HELPFUL?

Some poems, of course, manage to generalize on matters of the human condition in ways that hold up, or promise to hold up, very well. As much as we warn you against easy notions of "universals," we don't want to dismiss what has long been a motivating belief in the enduring power of art. Czeslaw Milosz in "A Song on the End of the World" relies upon simple images to invoke a sense of the universal. In Milosz's poem, nature provides a constant: bees approach the flower, porpoises jump, sparrows play. Human activity runs a familiar course: fishermen mend nets, women walk in fields, a "drunkard grows sleepy." Although Milosz employs concrete images of nature and everyday life, he has in the body of the poem deliberately avoided the sorts of specifics that allow us to "locate" the action in any narrow way; we are not tied to any particular time and place.

**Czeslaw Milosz** (1911–2004)

# A Song on the End of the World (1944)

On the day the world ends
A bee circles a clover,
A fisherman mends a glimmering net.
Happy porpoises jump in the sea,
By the rainspout young sparrows are playing                    5
And the snake is gold-skinned as it should always be.

On the day the world ends
Women walk through the fields under the umbrellas,
A drunkard grows sleepy at the edge of a lawn,
Vegetable peddlers shout in the street                         10
And a yellow-sailed boat comes nearer the island,
The voice of a violin lasts in the air
And leads into a starry night.

And those who expected lightning and thunder
Are disappointed.                                              15
And those who expected signs and archangels' trumps
Do not believe it is happening now.
As long as the sun and the moon are above,
As long as the bumblebee visits a rose,
As long as rosy infants are born                               20
No one believes it is happening now.

Only a white-haired old man, who would be a prophet
Yet is not a prophet, for he's much too busy,
Repeats while he binds his tomatoes:
There will be no other end of the world,                                    25
There will be no other end of the world.

*Warsaw, 1944*

Now ask yourself, what is the last line of this poem? One answer seems obvious: "There will be no other end of the world." But another possible answer lies just below that line: "*Warsaw, 1944.*" Milosz included that identifying place and date in the text of the poem as it appears in his collected poems. If taken as part of the poem, it stands as a resonant and dramatic close that influences how we absorb the lines that precede it. Poland was sacrificed to the Germans by the rest of the world in hopes that Hitler's ambitions would find a limit. Those ambitions, of course, knew no limits, and the cost to Poland, particularly Polish Jews, was staggering. By 1944, the disaster had unfolded for all to see who were willing to look and not flinch. Only the most deliberately resistant could refuse to acknowledge the end of the world that was "happening."

Milosz has achieved in this poem a balanced tension that he seeks in so many of his poems: The desire to find something real and eternal is set against a recognition of the most profound dishonesty or disconnection; the need to identify what it means to be human is placed in the context of a brutal, inhuman history. He wants us to engage the **universal** and the **particular**, the **abstract** and the **concrete**. If we don't know anything of Milosz's life, of the history he has experienced—if we erase "*Warsaw, 1944*" from the end of his poem, we still have a beautiful poem. But with that historical marker, we're prompted to think not only of Poland's tragic history but also of how the poem applies to the various large-scale traumas that have unfolded within our own history. We can add new particulars to give the abstractions life. The best readers will respond with curiosity about Milosz's closing signal and a willingness to follow it by learning more of the author, his poetry, and the history he grapples with. Those readers will also consider how Milosz speaks from this rich context to our condition now.

## Experiencing Literature in Context

The following biographical sketch of Milosz touches only lightly on major events of a long and full life, but even the barest knowledge of such events will influence responses to Milosz's poetry.

CZESLAW MILOSZ BIOGRAPHY

Czeslaw Milosz (1911–2004) was born in Wilno, Lithuania, which was then controlled by czarist Russia. At the outbreak of World War I, his father was drafted as an engineer by the czar's army, and the family spent the war years traveling throughout Russia and Siberia. After the Russian Revolution in 1917, the family returned to the village of his birth. Milosz published his first poems in 1930, the year after he graduated from high school.

In 1935, he began to work for Polish Radio. During the first days of World War II, he was sent to the front as a radio operator. In January 1940, he returned to Wilno and was caught there when Soviet tanks entered the city. In July, he escaped across Soviet lines into Poland and spent most of the war working for underground presses in Nazi-occupied Warsaw.

After the war, Milosz came to the United States as a diplomat for the new government of the People's Republic of Poland. In 1950, he was transferred to Paris, where he requested and was granted asylum the following year. He spent the next decade writing in Paris. Among the most famous of his works during this period is *The Captive Mind* (1953), in which Milosz writes about "the vulnerability of the twentieth-century mind to seduction by sociopolitical doctrines and its readiness to accept totalitarian terror for the sake of a hypothetical future." In 1960, he accepted a post at the University of California, Berkeley. He was awarded the Nobel Prize in literature in 1981. That year, he returned to Poland for the first time since his exile in 1951 and met with solidarity leader Lech Walesa. Shortly thereafter, Polish presses published Milosz's poetry, making it possible for Poles to read their celebrated national poet for the first time. Milosz's wife, Janka, died in 1986 after a ten-year battle with Alzheimer's disease. His second wife, Carol, died in 2002.

Now as you read the next Milosz poem, you are prepared in subtle yet profound ways to experience more in the act of reading. His reflection in "Christopher Robin" on much-loved characters from a famous children's book, for example, can hardly be seen as mere playfulness once we know something of what Milosz had lived through.

Czeslaw Milosz (1911–2004)

# Christopher Robin (1998)

*In April of 1996 the international press carried the news of the death, at age seventy-five, of Christopher Robin Milne, immortalized in a book by his father, A.A. Milne, Winnie-the-Pooh, as Christopher Robin.*

I must think suddenly of matters too difficult for a bear of little brain. I have never asked myself what lies beyond the place where we live, I and Rabbit, Piglet and Eeyore, with our friend Christopher Robin. That is, we continued to live here, and nothing changed, and I just ate my little something. Only Christopher Robin left for a moment.

Owl says that immediately beyond our garden Time begins, and that it is an awfully deep well. If you fall in it, you go down and down, very quickly, and no one knows what happens to you next. I was a bit worried about Christopher Robin falling in, but he came back and then I asked him about the well. "Old Bear," he answered. "I was in it and I was falling and I wore trousers down to the ground, I had a gray beard, then I died. It was probably just a dream, it was quite unreal. The only real thing was you, old bear, and our shared fun. Now I won't go anywhere, even if I'm called for an afternoon snack." ■

What do you make of Christopher Robin's remark to Pooh that falling into "Time" is "quite unreal"? Is Milosz suggesting that "real" life is full of delusions? Could he be commenting instead (or in addition) on how strenuously some people escape living actively and responsibly? Do you think the world of "Time" is real for Milosz?

# DO WE NEED TO KNOW *EVERYTHING* IN ORDER TO UNDERSTAND?

Poems like "The Charge of the Light Brigade," "A Song on the End of the World," and "Christopher Robin" help us consider questions about what knowledge we need to bring to texts as well as what knowledge we unavoidably bring to texts. These poems also help us respond to a problem some people have with reading serious literature or seeing ambitious plays and films: serious work (the complaint goes) demands "too much" knowledge. We believe that it's a rare text that asks "too much" of a reader. The charge of "too much" builds on a mistaken and unrealistic notion of "understanding." Understanding or not understanding is rarely an either-or proposition. In reading or viewing a challenging text, we commonly gain some understanding as we read and seek more as we write, re-read, and re-see. It's also normal to *not* understand some things at the same time we respond powerfully to others. Dismissing the task as too hard from the outset presumes that reading is something we do in a straight line and that when we get to the end of the

line, our reading is over; once the pages are turned, we're done. This misleading notion of reading presumes that the only good reading is a "complete"
reading. But denying the centrality of process cuts us off from the chance to
discover what the text may offer. It forces us to think of one final understanding that we must get in order to validate our effort. It dismisses the renewed
and deepened pleasure we can experience in successive readings. It also
prevents us from acquiring the "knowledge" that we sometimes complain
we don't possess. So, what we don't know about European history shouldn't
stop us from reading Milosz and coming to a valuable understanding of his
work; and reading Milosz will help us learn a great deal about European
history.

It might seem odd to move from Milosz's poem to a one-liner in a
Woody Allen story, but jokes illustrate nicely how we can sometimes
"understand" quite a bit without "knowing" much. In "Mr. Big," a comic
detective piece, Allen presents a scene in which a glamorous woman clings
to a tough, "hard-boiled" detective named Kaiser Lupowitz and pleads, "Just
don't get ontological, not now. I couldn't bear it if you were ontological
with me." Even with the minimal context we've supplied, it's possible you

"Just don't get ontological, not now. I couldn't bear it if you were ontological with me."

find the line funny. We can use it as a caption to the photograph from *The Maltese Falcon* (1941) to mimic the joke's working dynamic.

If the photograph has absolutely no resonance for you (you've *never* seen Humphrey Bogart play a detective, *never* read Raymond Chandler or Dashiell Hammett, *never* read or seen other works of this type), the line will fall flat. Although some slight knowledge is absolutely necessary, extensive knowledge really isn't required to "get" the joke. You need to know only enough to sense, for example, that most tough guys in detective stories aren't named "Kaiser Lupowitz." More important, you need to know enough to recognize that the word *ontological* doesn't fit the character type of the speaker. You don't even need to know what *ontological* means as long as you recognize that it doesn't sound tough, sexy, or colloquial. So we can have one kind of **understanding** (the word *sounds* funny) without another kind of understanding (the definition of the word). In this case, the former kind of understanding is far more important than the latter. *Ontological* pertains to a philosophical theory of reality that presumes universal and essential characteristics of all existence. Knowing that, we think, doesn't make the joke much funnier.

We're not suggesting that knowing things isn't important, but we do make the following claims:

■ We often *do* know more than we realize.

■ We don't need to know *everything* in order to *understand many things* very well.

■ We acquire new knowledge by encountering things we don't know.

## Experiencing Art in Context

Look carefully at the painting *Young Man at His Window*. The painting evokes in most people a sense of loneliness. The young man, back turned to us, stands by himself in a room and looks out on almost empty streets. Everything darkens from the window inward; the young man seems boxed in. The railing and the window frame separate the young man from the world outside. That outside world also seems contained. The large buildings across from his room close in the street on all sides. Only a small bit of sky shows at the top of the picture. The city is all around. And yet people are almost entirely absent. Only one woman is visible on the streets below the young man's window, and she is a distant figure. The young man seems tired, disconnected, and alone.

This interpretation may be argued from the painting itself. What is within the frame can inspire a thoughtful response—a valuable level of understanding. But we don't need to stop at that level. Caillebotte was not only a painter but also a collector and a scholar. He knew Caspar David Friedrich's *Wanderer above the Sea of Fog* (p. 60) very well. Friedrich's painting spoke to the Byronic spirit of his day. That is, it captured a feeling for the powerful man depicted by the Romantic poet Byron, who sought to move beyond the limits set by society. It placed a grand figure on a mountaintop aggressively confronting the vastness of nature itself. One could argue that Caillebotte echoes Friedrich's painting. He has his figure stand—like the wanderer—with his back to us as he looks over the world before him. But Caillebotte's figure strikes a less confident pose. A visible shrug seems much different than the posture of the one who just strode to the top of a mountain. The city, not nature, spreads out in front of Caillebotte's young man. In fact, nature has nearly been squeezed out of the picture. If we see Caillebotte's painting as a conscious revision of (and commentary on) Friedrich's well-known work, our response to *Young Man at His Window* will become more richly textured although not necessarily more correct or even necessarily different in the main points. The theme of "loneliness" now might

### Making Connections

Artists who choose to deal with historically distant subjects may find ways to build the necessary context into their work. In the poem "Shelley," for example, the contemporary poet Galway Kinnell provides information that allows readers who may know nothing of the title subject to understand the essential point he wants to make. The poem is for the most part a brief and wrenching summary of key events in Shelley's domestic life (suicides of lovers, deaths of children) framed by two different perspectives: one of youthful idolatry and the other of painful disengagement. Kinnell includes a great deal in relatively few lines that allows readers to understand his poem without having read previously about Shelley's life.

Gustave Caillebotte, *Young Man at His Window* (1875)

be seen more sharply as a condition of urban life. Caillebotte may well be commenting on a broad-scale cultural change: As an earlier generation "conquered" nature, the new generation has become progressively disconnected from life as it deals with the consequences of that conquering. There's no space for Caillebotte's young man to move, no opportunities for a heroic gesture.

# WHAT IF SUBSTANTIAL OUTSIDE KNOWLEDGE IS ESSENTIAL?

What happens to a literary text that gets heavily caught up in historical particulars? Can an audience's shifting interests and changed knowledge base make a great work into an irrelevant or hopelessly opaque work? These are questions that we need to consider even if we can't finally answer them. Some texts do require us to work, and it's reasonable that we ask if the effort is worth it. Herman Melville's "The House-Top," like "A Song on the End of the World," makes a date important to the reading of the poem. Melville provides the date up front with a subheading that fleshes out the setting (on a "house-top" at night). But for most readers, the date marks nothing specific that easily comes to mind. And the setting hardly helps upon first reading. Our guess is that you'll find it impossible to get a grip on the following poem without some background that lies outside most readers' knowledge base. Still, we'll present the poem here without preparation. Read it to the end, even though you'll likely feel lost. Then return to the poem once you've read the background information following the poem.

**Herman Melville** (1819–1891)

# The House-Top (1866)

A Night Piece.
(July, 1863)

No sleep. The sultriness pervades the air
And binds the brain—a dense oppression,
As tawny tigers feel in matter shades,

Vexing their blood and making apt for ravage.
Beneath the stars the roofy desert spreads 5
Vacant as Libya. All is hushed near by.
Yet fitfully from the far breaks a mixed surf
Of muffled sound, the Atheist roar of riot.
Yonder, where parching Sirius set in drought,
Balefully glares red Arson—there—and there. 10
The Town is taken by its rats—ship-rats
And rats of the wharves. All civil charms
And priestly spells which late held hearts in awe—
Fear-bound, subjected to a better sway
Than sway of self; these like a dream dissolve, 15
And man rebounds whole aeons back in nature.
Hail to the low dull rumble, dull and dead,
And ponderous drag that shakes the wall.
Wise Draco comes, deep in the midnight roll
Of black artillery; he comes, though late; 20
In code corroborating Calvin's creed
And cynic tyrannies of honest kings;
He comes, nor parlies; and the Town, redeemed,
Gives thanks devout; nor, being thankful, heeds
The grimy slur on the Republic's faith implied, 25
Which holds that Man is naturally good,
And—more—is Nature's Roman, never to be scourged.

In "The House-Top," Melville is casting a very specific event in broad
philosophical and theological terms. He's placing a contemporary situation
in relation to distant historical periods in order to universalize the poem;
he raises fundamental questions about law, power, and human nature. The
problem is that almost all readers today are at a loss concerning either the
specific or the general as it plays out in this poem. Melville was a voracious
reader, and the knowledge he draws on can be baffling—even off-putting. To
make things more difficult, the event that inspired him to write is not one that
gets much space in most general history textbooks. Is this poem, then, dead as
a piece of literature? If not, what must we do to rescue it or, as a scholar might
say, preserve it as literature?

The questions we've asked are the sorts of questions you'll ultimately
have to answer for yourself, but we think that "The House-Top" is absolutely worth the demands it makes, that even the slightest historical gloss
makes the poem not only accessible but urgently alive. July 1863 is the date
of the draft riots that occurred in New York City. Hundreds of young men
(mostly poor young men because the wealthy could choose to buy their way

out of the draft) rebelled at the prospect of forced service in the Union cause. The city's blacks were blamed for these men's situation. If it were not for the North's abhorrence of slavery, there would be no Civil War. At least that was the feeling of the moment. The angry crowds moved through the city at night and turned much of their frenzied energy on those they blamed. They burned a black church and a black orphanage: people suffered, people died. Melville, who lived in New York, was appalled. For him, the fact of slavery made the Civil War a moral necessity for the North. That citizens would attack helpless people in defiance of that cause was a profound mark of human depravity. The rioters, then, are the "rats" that have taken the town. The personified "red Arson" glares from flames seen, and the "Atheist roar" can be heard from the house-top. The town is overtaken by an evil that is no longer controlled by "civil charms" (laws) or "priestly spells" (religious beliefs) that had earlier worked effectively through the power of fear.

This endorsement of fear as a means to control helps us understand the darkness of Melville's vision and the depth of his anger. Laws and beliefs at least forced people to obey something outside their own selfish nature (the "sway of self"). Draco, the harsh lawgiver, marches to reassert order, but Melville's Draco is not the severe and cruel figure of common understanding; he is "wise," for he understands Calvin's insight: Humans are by nature bad. The town's citizens are "redeemed," but that word must be seen as loaded with irony. They are thankful for being saved from themselves, yet they do not acknowledge the underlying (and unpleasant) message (the "grimy slur") about their foolish belief in the natural goodness of humankind. A Roman citizen was not subject to the punishment of whipping; Americans, Melville suggests, like to think of themselves as Nature's Roman citizen. But in fact, they deserved, needed, and received a whipping from authorities who came to reclaim the city.

If the previous summary serves to replace the poem, then the poem is indeed dead. But we'd suggest you take the information we have supplied and read the poem over several times. Melville's images, his word choice, his allusions, his close engagement with a powerful moment in his own history and his willingness to imagine what that moment means in larger terms operate together to create a powerful and unsettling vision of society and law. Our summary informs but doesn't encourage the kind of experience available in a work of art. And though the context we've supplied may seem substantial, it is not hard to acquire. Professional scholars will often provide useful glosses that accompany modern editions of older works. And standard reference books along with useful websites allow us to quickly access information about names we don't recognize, events we hadn't learned in class, ideas we hadn't encountered in our earlier reading.

The birth of the World Wide Web has changed strategies for doing background research, but it's important to understand the limits of the Web. Although you can find much useful information online, an enormous amount of irrelevant, erroneous, and distracting information also waits there. A Google search of "Draco" yields more than thirty-four thousand entries; far more of those address Draco Malfoy, a villain in the Harry Potter series, than the Roman man of law in Melville's allusion. "Wise Draco" gets us quickly to the poem itself, but that is no help. "Cynic" yields more than a million hits. "Calvin's creed" leads to discussions of Calvinism (a promising start), but a closer look reveals that the first discussion in the list of possibilities comes from a very specific political interest group. Of course, by the time you are reading this book, any search you undertake will differ. But you'll face the same sorts of traps and bad leads we found. Wikipedia has become a favorite online source for many college students; it's a site that offers an alternative to traditional methods of prioritizing and disseminating information. All readers of Wikipedia are allowed to participate as editors. This openness enables the site to draw upon the knowledge of millions of people, but it also creates a much larger pool for errors to creep into the database. The problems shouldn't keep you from the Web but should remind you that reference *books* still have value.

One source a student of literature should know is the *Oxford English Dictionary* (commonly referred to as the *OED*). As discussed in Chapter 11, the *OED* provides not just definitions but histories of words. At the simplest level, it helps us through the confusion over words that may arise with change: "berries" can be "rude" in Milton's work because *rude* in the seventeenth century could mean "unripe." But the *OED* can provoke us to explore fundamental interpretive matters. Hamlet's charge to Ophelia, "Get thee to a nunnery!" seems straightforward enough, but the *OED* tells us that *nunnery* in Shakespeare's day could also refer to a house of prostitution. Does Shakespeare want us to set the two meanings in opposition? Does he want us to understand Hamlet's command as cruelly sarcastic? What might we learn from the *OED* about Melville's use of the "cynic" to modify the "tyrannies" that are expressed by "honest kings"?

As you might imagine, the *OED* is a huge, multivolume work. Your library, however, may have the *OED* in electronic form. This makes it possible to quickly cross-reference words. It also allows you to search the *OED* for quotations (every entry has examples of a word's use over time). Obviously, if you are concerned only with the contemporary meaning and usage of a word, consult one of the many current desk dictionaries now available.

Specialized handbooks, encyclopedias, dictionaries, and "companions" provide brief, informative discussions of plots, authors, characters, critical terms, and aesthetic movements. One widely used series that offers much biographical, textual, and historical background is published by the Oxford University Press: *The Oxford Companion to English Literature, The Oxford Companion to American Literature, The Oxford Companion to the Theatre, The Oxford Companion to Film* (*to Art, to the Bible*, and so on) are particularly useful to students of literature and film. Although the book you are reading offers much information on critical terms, other reference works are still worth noting: *The Princeton Encyclopedia of Poetry and Poetics*; M. H. Abrams's *A Glossary of Literary Terms*; Ira Konigsberg's *The Complete Film Dictionary*. There are also substantial, sophisticated works that provide much information helpful to critical writers who desire a broad grasp of intellectual context: *The Encyclopedia of Philosophy* and *A Dictionary of the History of Ideas* are both likely to be part of your college's reference library.

The range, variety, and accessibility of such works make even poems as densely packed as Melville's "The House-Top" quite approachable. So we hope that you read ambitiously and without fear of what you don't know; we also hope that you'll read with confidence about what you do know and what you can learn.

# MODELING CRITICAL ANALYSIS: JOÃO GUIMARÃES ROSA, THE THIRD BANK OF THE RIVER

In Chapters 12 and 13, we considered how João Guimarães Rosa's "The Third Bank of the River" provokes allegorical or symbolic readings. The title itself demands that we move beyond the limits of a realistic story. What would a "third bank of a river" be, after all? We might try to imagine a sharp bend in a river that makes from some perspectives a sort of third bank, but such a literal approach would surely seem strained. Given the story we read, it seems clear Guimarães Rosa asks us to consider some new dimension to what we ordinarily consider the real. So far, we have taken on the challenge without addressing any matters of Guimarães Rosa's life or language.

It's likely that you haven't read Guimarães Rosa before. He is greatly admired and the author of a novel many critics consider to be one of the great works of the twentieth century, *Grande Sertão: Veredes (The Devil to Pay in the Backlands)*. But Guimarães Rosa writes in Portuguese, not a language as widely translated for English readers as, say, Spanish or French. Some of his books are also quite demanding—even for those who are native speakers of Portuguese. Fortunately, "The Third Bank of the River" doesn't require any special context for a deeply rewarding reading in English. But that hardly means that context is irrelevant. Consider how any of the following background might help you return to "The Third Bank of the River" with an openness to new interpretive possibilities.

Guimarães Rosa has been considered by some a regional writer; to the extent this is true, his region is Minas Gerais—a state in Brazil's interior notable for its mining and its agriculture. He was trained and practiced as a medical doctor in Minas Gerais. Some of his stories catch the flavor of local idioms and legends he may have heard from patients. But *regionalist* is far too narrow a word to describe his ambition or achievement. Guimarães Rosa possessed a lifelong fascination with languages; he spoke six well and read several other languages. He was a diplomat (stationed for some years in Colombia). And he was an avid reader of world literatures. His stories are not tied to regional traditions either in subject matter or in technique.

In 1958, at the age of fifty, Guimarães Rosa suffered a life-threatening heart attack. The collection in which "The Third Bank of the River" appeared, *Primeiros Estórias*, was published four years later. These were not "first stories" in the usual sense, but they were the first stories Guimarães Rosa wrote and published after the heart attack. The stories in this collection, according to one critic, involve a profound change that "implies the crossing of a threshold." In this respect, "The Third Bank of the River" seems typical—even central. In fact, the English translation of *Primeiros Estórias* is *The Third Bank of the River and Other Stories*. In an index to the first edition of the stories, Guimarães Rosa signaled themes of change, transition, and transcendence in what we might call a set of hieroglyphics for every story. The hieroglyphic line for "The Third Bank of the River" ends with a symbol of infinity. The entire line appears as follows:

Does knowledge of Guimarães Rosa's medical training, his heart attack, the general themes of the stories in the collection that followed that heart attack, the title of the collection in which the story first appeared, and the hieroglyph pictured contribute to your understanding of "The Third Bank of the River"? Does any of this contextual material enrich or change your reading? Does it merely reinforce an original impression? How is this knowledge relevant or irrelevant to your reading experience?

## Using Context to Focus Writing and Discussion

- What outside knowledge do you have in addition to the knowledge the text itself offers? How is any piece of this information relevant to the text that you are reading? For instance, we might know when the author lived. If the author wrote a work of fiction set in some historical event that the author experienced, how would that knowledge influence our reading of the fictional text? If the author wrote a work of fiction set in a different time, how would our knowledge of the author's life help us read this work of fiction?

- What specific connections can you draw between the literary work and its context? Why are these connections interesting? (Just finding connections isn't enough to make them interesting.)

- How does your understanding of the text change as you learn historical or biographical facts that relate to its production?

- How influential is the context in guiding your reading of the text? For instance, were you aware of or asking questions about the author's life and times as you were reading the text?

- How does the work change as you read it in different contexts? For instance, how do you read a poem that was written to raise spirits about a war that is long over?

- Make a list of abstract words that appear in more than one text in this anthology (such as *courage, hero, great*). Explain how these words take on different meanings depending upon the context the writer supplies or assumes.

- How are readers encouraged to—or discouraged from—generalizing the meaning of a particular work? In other words, how closely are we tied to the specific war or battle that is the subject of the work? Is there any work in which the specific historical circumstances are unimportant?

- Which works demand the most contextual knowledge? Are any unreadable without substantial background information? What kinds of information do you need to achieve understanding? Conversely, what kinds of information seem nonessential to your understanding?

# 15 Allusions

## In Order to Understand This Text, Is There Something Else I Am Supposed to Have Read?

In personal conversations, we speak in passing about some event or person with only a reference to a name or a quick description of some part of the event. "Remember the story about your uncle Art, who went out to the desert to look for silver and came back with a pile of worthless rocks?" This brief reference works upon the assumption that those participating in the conversation are familiar with the events in question and interpret them similarly. We might shorten the reference considerably. For instance, as a warning to someone about to set off on some ill-conceived adventure: "Remember Uncle Art." Instead of retelling the story, we refer to a story that we have told (probably many times) before. The longer people are together and the more experiences they share, the less they need to engage in the complexities of linguistic exchange. They develop a shorthand of brief phrases—code words, if you will—looks and signs that convey meanings available only to those who have shared the same experiences. And these words and phrases need not be reductive. The smallest remark can trigger layered memories that convey emotions, beliefs, and values. Writers develop their own shorthand to thicken the texture of their works. They know their readers come to any new piece with some previous literary experience. They may invoke that experience through a brief reference to a passage or scene from another work—through an **allusion**.

# CREATING COMMUNITY

An old joke tells of prisoners who had been together in the same cell block for many years. A new convict assigned to the cell block found their conversation bewildering. "Fifty-three!" called a large bald fellow, and the rest burst into riotous laughter. An ancient sailor with a blurred blue anchor tattooed on his arm hollered, "One hundred twenty-six!" Again the rest of the block dissolved in laughs. When he had a chance, the newcomer spoke privately with a white-haired old-timer. The old man explained that they had one joke book in the cell block. No one remembered where it came from, but the jokes in it never failed. The men in this cell had been telling them to one another for decades, yet each joke still struck all of them as much as it had the first time they had heard it. Over the years, they came to know the book so well that they didn't have to deliver the entire joke anymore. A guy would read the first line, and everyone would start laughing; no one needed to make it to the punch line. Now, they had reached the point that they just read out page numbers as their evening's entertainment. Emboldened, the new convict studied the ragged book. After about a week of listening evening after evening to the numbers called and the laughter in response, the new guy hollered, "Twenty-seven!" All the laughter stopped. The old-timer turned to him, "Some guys can just tell them better than others."

Within this joke, we see two important aspects of allusion. First, an allusion is brief. Instead of retelling an entire story, the speaker relies on the common knowledge of the audience in order to convey a complex idea that otherwise would have taken a long narrative or full explanation. Second, an allusion may depend on, create, or limit a sense of community. Within the cell block, a long-established community defines its membership by a person's knowledge and command of a special language. Access to this community isn't easy. The new convict, for example, lacks the common experience that allows him to join. He studies the book but perhaps needs to observe and internalize the small gestures that will allow him both to hear and tell "jokes" in the cell block. Or perhaps he must be a recognized figure in the community to use their private language.

This power of allusion to exclude as well as include might make us wary of highly allusive works. Allusions do sometimes seem to be a way for authors to show off, especially to any of us who feel left outside the conversation that is going on. We might ask why an author needs to display knowledge, especially if the story can do without it. But mere display is rarely the point or the purpose of an allusion. When an author alludes to another work, that author is invoking some quality of the work to enrich the new text. The allusion isn't something merely to recognize; it is something to absorb and appreciate as an integral part of a whole.

Consider, for example, the famous opening sentence of J. D. Salinger's *The Catcher in the Rye*: "If you really want to hear about it, the first thing you'll probably want to know is where I was born, and what my lousy childhood was like, and how my parents were occupied and all before they had me, and all that David Copperfield kind of crap, but I don't feel like going into it, if you want to know the truth." The allusion here is to Charles Dickens's massive autobiographical novel; the first chapter is titled "I am Born." By having Holden Caulfield refer so dismissively to this classic, Salinger achieves a good deal. We know immediately that the narrator doesn't accept conventional judgments. He's not interested in what other people consider "classic." He has his own opinions to register. We also understand that Holden's story will be a focused one. He's not working on a broad canvas, as Dickens did. And if he is not to start where Dickens started, it's likely he won't end where Dickens ended (happily for David—with marriage, children, and professional success). The allusion catches a kind of attitude or tone that helps establish Holden's character.

As we read further in *The Catcher in the Rye*, the allusion to *David Copperfield* makes still more sense. We learn that Holden has been kicked out of Pencey Prep, his elite boarding school. He is failing four of his five courses, mostly because he finds those courses boring and irrelevant. For Holden, Pencey Prep is all about a sterile process of socialization. It's about attitude and gesture with no substance. Pencey people read Dickens because they are supposed to read Dickens; any real engagement with novels (or with history, or with any subject) won't happen in Pencey Prep courses. We can also imagine that the success David Copperfield wins in Dickens's novel would bother Holden because he sees success as built on dishonesty. When his history teacher, Mr. Spencer, echoes a common bit of wisdom about life as a game, Holden thinks to himself: "Game, my ass. Some game. If you get on the side where all the hot-shots are, then it's a game, all right—I'll admit that. But if you get on the other side, where there

### Making Connections

Salinger's allusion to *David Copperfield* also works because of the place that novel had in the curriculum of college and college prep classes at the time that *The Catcher in the Rye* was set and written (the late 1940s and early 1950s). Salinger needed to invoke a book that was often assigned (not the same as often read) in a certain sort of class at a certain sort of school. He is alluding to the book not only for its content but for its status as a cultural commodity. If you were to recast Salinger's novel in the context of a current college prep course, it's likely you'd pick a different book—a book you feel is assigned today out of habit. As we note in Chapter 17, standards of quality or relevance do change over time. What might be a good substitute for *David Copperfield* if you were to revise that first sentence for a reader today?

aren't any hot-shots, then what's a game about it? Nothing. No game."
The kind of Victorian earnestness that Dickens affirms in *David Copperfield*
has become for Holden a thoroughgoing "phoniness" that he cannot
tolerate. Salinger's allusion defines a community of outsiders who will
follow Holden through the narrative.

## Experiencing Literature through Allusions

In "My Weariness of Epic Proportions," the poet Charles Simic's first sentence assumes that his reader is familiar with Achilles. Classical mythology
has been included in Western education for centuries; authors frequently use
allusions to the most famous, widely read works of a given culture (such as
those by Homer, Shakespeare, Dante, and Cervantes) without any explanation. But Simic's opening allusion doesn't assume we must all accept the
classics for what they have often been taken to represent. Homer celebrates
the exploits of Achilles and sets up most of the warriors who died in the
Trojan War as remarkable individuals worthy of heroic status. So Simic's
allusive opening is rather jarring.

### Charles Simic (1938– )

# My Weariness of Epic Proportions (1982)

I like it when
Achilles
Gets killed
And even his buddy Patroclus—
And that hothead Hector—                                5
And the whole Greek and Trojan
*Jeunesse dorée*
Are more or less
Expertly slaughtered
So there's finally                                      10
Peace and quiet
(The gods having momentarily
Shut up)
One can hear
A bird sing                                             15
And a daughter ask her mother

Whether she can go to the well
And of course she can
By that lovely little path
That winds through                                                                    20
The olive orchard

We don't normally like it when the heroes of a story are "Expertly slaugh-tered." Simic's poem puts itself in opposition to our usual reading experience from the very start: his speaker likes it when Achilles, Patroclus, Hector, and the whole mass of Greek and Trojan soldiers die in battle. Anyone who has read *The Iliad* can quickly grasp Simic's perspective: peace and quiet are indeed refreshing after widespread carnage—however heroic we might have taken that violence to be. Simic conveys through allusion at the start of the first stanza the overwhelming exhaustion that comes from reading *The Iliad*—an epic poem full of descriptions of relentless destruction. Simic's second stanza turns to very different matters: descriptions of simple, peaceful, ordi-nary events that don't belong to the world of *The Iliad*. Yet even as Simic claims to be weary of "epic proportions," the proportions and scale of the epic help reaffirm the value of the everyday, peaceful existence he cham-pions. He intensifies our sense of the latter qualities by setting them against the action of Homer's epic.

## REVISITING AND RENEWAL

The previous example clarifies another aspect of allusion. The allusion not only can work to enrich a new piece but can encourage us to rethink a past literary experience. Simic's poem challenges us to consider what it means to read Homer in ways that many people have read Homer. He may make us more sensitive to suffering and less enamored of heroic deeds when we return to *The Iliad*. In this way, allusions can be critical and generative of new readings.

In "Up Home Where I Come From," the poet Dick Barnes presents an account of a hawk that a trapper caught accidentally. The first nineteen lines describe the hawk and its wild dignity. At line 19, Barnes offers an allusion. The allusion affects the meaning of Barnes's poem profoundly. It changes our understanding of what comes before and after it. This allusion also challenges us to think freshly about the source text. In other words, the allusion doesn't just use an older story; it challenges our conventional understanding of the older story.

**Dick Barnes** (1933–2000)

# Up Home Where I Come From (2005)

Roy Smith ran traps for furs
but a hawk got caught in one of them

spreading its wings, there in the trap
turning its sharp beak toward him

as he came to get it out, its glaring eyes so deep          5
they seemed to open onto another world in there

and steady: thus the hawk in time past
came to be an image of aristocracy.

One leg hung by a tendon; with his sharp pocketknife
Roy cut it off and left it lay          10

but brought the hawk home
to feed it til it got well.

There in his basement, in a hutch built for rabbits,
it glared at us with its unfathomable eyes,

accepted the dead meat he brought it, even hamburger,          15
unquenched. That wildness

is what we can know of dignity.
We aspire to it ourselves but seldom—

seldom. Nailed to the tree
Jesus must have been as still as that,          20

as wild. And I'd say
that was the right way to be, there.

Later it got well and he let it go,
our hearts leapt up when we saw it

living somehow in the wild with its one leg:          25
in its life we felt forgiven.

Probably it learned to pin its prey to the ground
and eat there, running that risk.

Risen, that was one thing Jesus did too:
showed he was alive and could still eat.                                                30


Barnes expects his reader to have at least an elementary knowledge of the
Christian story that tells of Jesus being nailed to a cross, dying, and being
resurrected to continue his ministry. In this poem, though, the allusion is
something of a surprise. The poet concentrates on the wildness of the hawk
and its dignity even in captivity. Comparing that wounded hawk to Jesus
creates a particular poetic experience in which the familiar story changes.
The poet asks us to use the image of Jesus on a cross and to make his dignity
akin to the wildness that we see in this injured hawk. With this allusion, we
ask how that dignified, wounded hawk compares to the crucified figure of
Jesus on a cross that adorns so many Christian churches. The hawk is so
powerfully established in particular detail that the allusion midway through
the poem challenges any comfortable interpretation of the religious story.
What happens when we place the Jesus commonly depicted eating in
Leonardo da Vinci's *The Last Supper* against the one-legged hawk that has

Leonardo da Vinci, *The Last Supper* (1496–1498)

learned to pin its prey to the ground? Barnes's allusion develops a complex image of both figures. When the poet ends by saying that Jesus "showed he was alive and could still eat," the comparison might seem to reduce the religious narrative to a story of simple survival. But the hawk's resilience in the face of the accidental trapping, its ability to reclaim its life and to adjust to the unwanted changes offers a powerful natural lesson to the poet that echoes the story of Jesus. It is not the same story, but the poet shows us how the incident gives him insight into the more familiar religious narrative.

Barnes includes one more subtle allusion toward the end of the poem when the trapper lets the hawk go: "our hearts leapt up when we saw it." This seems to recall William Wordsworth's "My Heart Leaps Up."

**William Wordsworth** (1770–1850)

# My Heart Leaps Up (1807)

My heart leaps up when I behold
    A rainbow in the sky:
So was it when my life began;
So is it now I am a man;
So be it when I shall grow old,                    5
    Or let me die!
The Child is father of the Man;
And I could wish my days to be
Bound each to each by natural piety.

The natural piety that Wordsworth seeks here is a deep responsiveness to the power of natural things. Life for him isn't life without the intensity gained through that responsiveness. Is Barnes using Wordsworth to help us interpret the quality of "forgiveness" that he refers to in line 26? How does this forgiveness relate to the New Testament story to which Barnes alludes?

## Experiencing Film through Allusions

Legend has it that Quentin Tarantino trained to be a film director by working as a clerk in a video store where he immersed himself in countless old films. It is a plausible legend. As a director, Tarantino has created a fresh new film style that builds heavily upon allusions to old films and yet refuses to use the structures of the films to which he alludes. His films make so many references to other movies that each of his films has inspired hundreds of web pages that document what goes on in every frame. But it's not just film geeks who are interested in Tarantino's work. *Pulp Fiction* (1994) in particular stands as a powerfully innovative and influential film. Understanding that film requires more than close attention to how many allusions Tarantino employs (a mere accounting of allusions)—it requires careful thought about how allusions may function. Consider, for example, the scene in which Mia insists that her escort, Vincent, join her in a dance contest. If John Travolta were not cast as Vincent, this scene might simply function to define the sort of playfully charged relationship that seems to be unfolding. But because John Travolta *is* cast as Vincent, viewers over the age of thirty will almost surely recognize an allusion and respond to the whole scene with that allusion in mind.

In the early 1990s, before *Pulp Fiction* was released, John Travolta was best known for having been a movie star in the 1970s. When he, as Vincent

John Travolta and Karen Lynn Gorney in
*Saturday Night Fever* (1977)

John Travolta and Uma Thurman in *Pulp Fiction*
(1994)

Vega in *Pulp Fiction*, comes out on the dance floor with Mia Wallace (Uma Thurman), much of the original audience could not help remembering a younger, skinnier Travolta dancing in *Saturday Night Fever*—a tremendous hit in 1977. The reference does not necessarily change the meaning of the scene itself, but it deepens our reaction. We see the character in *Pulp Fiction* about to begin dancing, but we also see a familiar actor regaining his status as a movie star and commenting upon his past and potential within a notoriously fickle industry. These allusions to the old film and to the characters he used to play create a tension within us as we ask whether this older Travolta can go out and dance the way he used to. Which character are we responding to in this movie? The conflicted thoughts that we have about John Travolta, a public figure who has a life in our own experiences outside this particular film, bring us into an active engagement with the story.

There is clearly a way in which such allusions remind us of the fictionality of the entire enterprise; in this case, art refers us back to art, not to life. Is *Pulp Fiction* really about two hit men in Los Angeles? Or is it about the pleasure we've experienced watching movies about all sorts of things that would be very unpleasant in real life? *Pulp Fiction* is violent—brutally violent—profane and oftentimes deliberately over the top, but viewers generally respond to all with a sense of exuberance. Tarantino's playful self-consciousness (his sense that in a movie anything can happen) comes through in the way he fractures the sequence of events so that Vincent Vega can stroll away coolly in the final scene after an earlier scene of his dismal death. The tendency to make transparent through allusion the unreality of art is characteristic of works we've come to label "postmodern." The implications of **postmodernism** aren't necessarily light or purely comic; they are more characteristic of the **absurd** (that is, characteristic of a vision that sees meaning drained from life). Postmodernism blurs distinctions between the real and imagined. It suggests that in our commodified world—a world where everything becomes a product for sale and consumption—the reality of most people is a reality created by popular fictions (television, advertising, personality magazines, and so on). Perhaps allusions in works like *Pulp Fiction* center so heavily on pop culture because some people have come to feel that pop culture is what dominates our experience of the world.

# IDENTIFYING AND RESPONDING TO ALLUSIONS

An allusion works only if we catch it, so we've attended mainly to fairly clear examples in this chapter. But once we know about allusions, we might become anxious as readers. Are we passing over important things because we don't share the author's aesthetic experience? Although most allusions are hardly hidden, they sometimes do restrict access to a text. The uninitiated, those who don't have particular experiences, like the new convict (p. 271), are not allowed to share in the communal experience. The problem is compounded by the fact that many highly allusive texts arose out of societies that are far more homogeneous than any that exist today. John Milton could take it for granted that anyone who read his *Paradise Lost* in seventeenth-century England had a thorough knowledge of the Bible and could appreciate some subtleties of religious controversy. But far more people are exposed to *Paradise Lost* today than the narrow group of the educated elite that first appreciated its significance. And today's readers are hardly in the know about the theological concerns that occupy Milton. There are many such examples. James Joyce wrote as though his readers knew the details of the Catholic liturgy, the streets of Dublin, Irish music, and Irish politics. These texts are challenging for anyone, but readers who are not Irish might find portions particularly obscure.

These problems lead us to a practical reflection. It is important to remember that literary texts and films are rich works of art. Allusions may be *one* element in a complex system of meaning; in other words, you don't necessarily fail to read a work well because you've missed some allusions. And even when allusion is a main element, you need not catch every allusion (nor are you likely to catch every allusion) in any single reading/viewing. One simple bit of advice is to read confidently and take the time to appreciate what you do catch (as opposed to anxious concerns over what you don't). Patience, in this case, is a virtue. The more you read, the more receptive you'll be to allusion. And although that may sound discouraging in the short term, it really should not be. The literary experience can be a lifelong experience. A sense of new discovery is part of what keeps the experience alive over time. So read and view boldly. Trust that you'll find much that is rewarding and will keep finding more as you experience more.

There are, however, some shortcuts you should be aware of and use. In many cases, modern editions of older works point out important allusions for us. These, as well as printed guides and web sources, can help lead us through the thickest of allusive texts. For example, more than one modern paperback edition of Dickens's *Great Expectations* identifies the following allusion for us. Pip, the narrator, is reflecting on the startling news that the person who "made him a gentleman" is himself no gentleman. The criminal Magwitch, now returned illegally to England, has set up Pip's expectations. Pip remarks on the feeling of being chased down: "The imaginary student pursued by the misshapen creature he had impiously made, was not more wretched than I, pursued by the creature who had made me, and recoiling from him with a stronger repulsion, the more he admired me and the fonder he was of me." In this line, we're told in notes of varying length that Pip compares himself to Victor Frankenstein pursued by the monster he has created.

Those who know Mary Shelley's novel might notice that Pip revises the roles between Victor and his monster. Pip doesn't claim the role of creator: he is himself the product of the creature and is pursued not out of a desire for revenge but from admiration, even love. This variation on the Frankenstein/monster theme adds layers of complexity to Pip's character and situation. Pip seems still morally confused at this point. He hasn't quite realized that he is the monster, nor has he fully appreciated the admiration and fondness Magwitch has for him—however inconvenient those feelings may be. Yet Pip's self-confessed repulsion does anticipate the mature and responsible insight he ultimately must attain.

Our example of allusion and its explanation are meant to suggest, first, that you do not need to resign yourself to missing allusions: help is available. But we also suggest that identifying allusions isn't ultimately the most important aspect of reading. This chapter has not concentrated on finding allusions (identifying, listing, and so on); our efforts are to show how allusions work and what purposes they serve. We have explored ways to approach, analyze, and understand allusions. Responding to an allusion is a far more substantial matter than merely finding or identifying one. Our poor convict from the joke early in this chapter did not understand the difference.

### A Note to Student Writers: Reference versus Allusion

Allusions are generally thought of as a tool for the creative writer to use and for the critical writer to avoid. That is not altogether bad advice. Allusions are suggestive more than directive. They invite the reader to draw upon experience from other texts but don't spell out fully what the reader should do with that experience. Dickens teases us into thinking about how the *Frankenstein* allusion works. He doesn't explain. Critical writers are, though, expected to explain. A brief allusion in an analytical essay to another critic or to a work of literature might well be seen as inappropriately showing off. Rather than richly suggestive, such an allusion might seem superficial. It's usually important to thoroughly integrate references—to lead into them and to follow them out. Never "plug in" a source or simply "drop" a reference in order to meet a quota. Critical writers need to show why a reference appears in the text; readers need to grasp where that reference comes from and how it applies. An overly allusive style in a critic can quickly become mannered and exclusive. That is, such a critic implies there is a little club of experienced readers who will understand and a larger group of outsiders who need not bother.

Although the previous information stands as good advice and useful commentary, nothing about writing is ever simple or absolute. As mentioned before, critical writing takes place in the context of an ongoing conversation. Critical writers seek to contribute to the conversation. On occasion, you may feel the conversation is so well established for your audience that you can refer very briefly to a key critic or to an important line or scene in a well-known literary text. Just be sure that any quick reference you make has a clear function in the context of your larger discussion and that it draws from something your audience will recognize and apply easily. Also be sure that you do not assume a very brief reference will carry more weight than it can sustain; a well-placed allusion might highlight a point or signal your place in a community of writers, but it won't make an argument. Ultimately, to allude or not to allude is not the question; it is better to ask whether and how an allusion will work for a particular audience at a specific point in an essay.

## MODELING CRITICAL ANALYSIS: TOM STOPPARD, THE FIFTEEN MINUTE HAMLET

We normally think of allusions as short elements existing within texts; we don't think of them as constituting a whole text, as they do in Tom Stoppard's *The Fifteen Minute Hamlet*. In the play, we get nothing but allusions—in this case, exact words lifted from Shakespeare and strung together to make what seems a brief highlight film of famous moments from this most famous of plays. Beginning with the title, Stoppard assumes we are familiar with William Shakespeare's *Hamlet*—so familiar that we'll enjoy the radical cutting and splicing that he has done. But also beginning with the title, we might ask how much we have to know about the real *Hamlet* to appreciate the fifteen-minute version.

**Tom Stoppard** (1937– )

# The Fifteen Minute Hamlet (1976)

### CHARACTERS

MARCELLUS, BERNARDO, LAERTES, HORATIO (*Scenes 1, 3, and encore*)
FRANCISCO, OSRIC, FORTINBRAS, GRAVEDIGGER, GHOST, HORATIO (*Scene 1*)
OPHELIA
GERTRUDE
HAMLET
SHAKESPEARE, CLAUDIUS, POLONIUS

TIME AND SCENE: *The action takes place at a shortened version of Elsinore Castle.*

**Scene 1**

*A castle battlement. Thunder and wind. Two guards,* BERNARDO/MARCELLUS *and* FRANCISCO/HORATIO, *enter.*
BERNARDO/MARCELLUS:  Who's there?
FRANCISCO/HORATIO:  Nay, answer me.

BERNARDO/MARCELLUS: Long live the King. Get thee to bed.

FRANCISCO/HORATIO: For this relief, much thanks.

BERNARDO/MARCELLUS: What, has this thing appeared again tonight?  5

FRANCISCO/HORATIO: Peace, break thee off: look where it comes again. *(He points off left.)*

BERNARDO/MARCELLUS: Looks it not like the King?

FRANCISCO/HORATIO: By heaven, I charge thee, speak!

BERNARDO/MARCELLUS *(He points and looks left.):* 'Tis here.

FRANCISCO/HORATIO *(He points and looks centre.):* 'Tis there.  10

BERNARDO/MARCELLUS *(He looks right.):* 'Tis gone.

FRANCISCO/HORATIO: But look, the morn in russet mantle clad
  Walks o'er the dew of yon high eastern hill.

BERNARDO/MARCELLUS: Let us impart what we have seen tonight
  Unto young Hamlet.  15

*(They exit.)*


## Scene 2

*A room of state within the castle. A flourish of trumpets as* CLAUDIUS *and* GER-
TRUDE *enter.*

CLAUDIUS: Though yet of Hamlet our dear brother's death
  The memory be green

*(HAMLET enters.)*
  our sometime sister, now our Queen,
  Have we taken to wife.
  But now, my cousin Hamlet, and my son—  5

HAMLET: A little more than kin, and less than kind.
  *(CLAUDIUS and GERTRUDE exit.)*
  O that this too too solid flesh would melt!
  That it should come to this—but two months dead!
  So loving to my mother: Frailty, thy name is woman!
  Married with mine uncle, my father's brother.  10
  The funeral baked meats did coldly furnish forth
  The marriage tables.

*(HORATIO rushes on.)*

HORATIO: My lord, I think I saw him yesternight—
  The King, your father—upon the platform where we watched.

HAMLET: 'Tis very strange.  15

HORATIO: Armed, my lord—
  A countenance more in sorrow than in anger.

HAMLET: My father's spirit in arms? All is not well.
  Would the night were come!

*(HAMLET and HORATIO exit to the parapet.)*

## Scene 3

*The castle battlements at night. There is the noise of carousing, cannon, fire-*
*works.* HORATIO *and* HAMLET *appear on the parapet.*

HAMLET: The King doth wake tonight and takes his rouse.
    Though I am native here and to the manner born,
    It is a custom more honoured in the breach
    Than in the observance.
    *(There is the sound of wind.)*

HORATIO: Look, my lord, it comes. *(He points.)*     5
*(The* GHOST *enters.)*

HAMLET: Angels and ministers of grace defend us!
    Something is rotten in the state of Denmark!
    Alas, poor ghost.

GHOST: I am thy father's spirit.
    Revenge his foul and most unnatural murder.     10

HAMLET: Murder?

GHOST: The serpent that did sting thy father's life
    Now wears his crown.

HAMLET: O my prophetic soul! Mine uncle?
*(The* GHOST *exits.)*
*(To* HORATIO.*)* There are more things in heaven and earth     15
    Than are dreamt of in your philosophy.
*(*HORATIO *exits.)*
    Hereafer I shall think meet
    To put an antic disposition on.
    The time is out of joint. O cursed spite
    That ever I was born to set it right!     20
*(*HAMLET *exits.)*

## Scene 4

*A room within the castle. There is a flourish of trumpets, leading into flute and*
*harpsichord music.* POLONIUS *enters and immediately* OPHELIA *rushes on.*

POLONIUS: How now, Ophelia, what's the matter?

OPHELIA: My lord, as I was sewing in my chamber, Lord Hamlet with his
    doublet all unbraced, no hat upon his head, pale as his shirt, his
    knees knocking each other, and with a look so piteous, he comes be-
    fore me.     5

POLONIUS: Mad for thy love?
    I have found the very cause of Hamlet's lunacy.
    *(*HAMLET *enters as* OPHELIA *exits.)*
    Look where sadly the poor wretch comes reading.
    What do you read, my lord?

HAMLET:  Words, words, words.                                                    10
POLONIUS:  Though this be madness, yet there is method in it.
HAMLET:  I am but mad north northwest: when the wind is southerly! I
   know a hawk from a handsaw.
POLONIUS:  The actors are come hither, my lord. *(He goes.)*
HAMLET:  We'll hear a play tomorrow.                                             15
   I have heard that guilty creatures sitting at a play
   Have by the very cunning of the scene
   Been struck so to the soul that presently
   They have proclaimed their malefactions.
   I'll have these players play something                                       20
   Like the murder of my father before mine uncle.
   If he but blench, I know my course,
   The play's the thing
   Wherein I'll catch the conscience of the King.
   *(Pause.)*
   To be, or not to be *(He puts a dagger to his heart.)*                       25
   *(*CLAUDIUS *and* OPHELIA *enter.)*
   that is the question.
OPHELIA:  My lord—
HAMLET:  Get thee to a nunnery!
*(*OPHELIA *and* HAMLET *exit.)*
CLAUDIUS:  Love? His affections do not that way tend
   There's something in his soul                                                30
   O'er which his melancholy sits on brood.
   He shall with speed to England.
*(*CLAUDIUS *exits.)*


### Scene 5

*A hall within the castle. A flourish of trumpets heralds the entrance of* HAMLET
*and* OPHELIA, MARCELLUS *and* HORATIO *who are joking together,* CLAUDIUS *and*
GERTRUDE.

HAMLET *(to imaginary players.):* Speak the speech, I pray you, as I pro-
   nounced it to you; tripplingly on the tongue. Hold, as t'were, the mirror
   up to nature.
*(Everyone sits to watch imaginary play. Masque music is heard.)*
   *(to* GERTRUDE.*)* Madam, how like you the play?
GERTRUDE:  The lady doth protest too much, methinks.                             5
HAMLET:  He poisons him in the garden for his estate. You shall see
   anon how the murderer gets the love of Gonzago's wife.
   *(*CLAUDIUS *rises.)*
   The King rises!

(*Music stops, hubbub noise starts.*)
What, frighted with false fire?
(CLAUDIUS *exits; re-enters at side as* POLONIUS.)
ALL:  Give o'er the play.                                                                      10
HAMLET:  Lights! Lights! Lights! I'll take the ghost's word for a thousand
     pounds!
(*Exeunt all except* POLONIUS.)
POLONIUS (*standing at side.*):  He's going to his mother's closet. Behind the
     arras I'll convey myself to hear the process.

### Scene 6

*The* QUEEN's *apartment.* POLONIUS *slips behind the arras as it is raised. Lute
music is heard.* HAMLET *and* GERTRUDE *enter.*
HAMLET:  Now, Mother, what's the matter?
GERTRUDE:  Hamlet, thou hast thy father much offended.
HAMLET:  Mother, you have my father much offended. (*He holds her.*)
GERTRUDE:  What wilt thou do? Thou wilt not murder me? Help! Help! Ho!
POLONIUS (*behind arras.*):  Help!                                                              5
HAMLET:  How now? A rat? (*He stabs* POLONIUS.) Dead for a ducat, dead!
GERTRUDE:  O me, what has thou done?
HAMLET:  Nay, I know not.
GERTRUDE:  Alas, he's mad.
HAMLET:  I must be cruel only to be kind. Good night, Mother.                                   10
(HAMLET *exits dragging* POLONIUS. GERTRUDE *exits, sobbing. The arras is dropped.*)

### Scene 7

*Another room in the castle. Flourish of trumpets as* CLAUDIUS *and* HAMLET
*enter.*
CLAUDIUS:  Now, Hamlet, where's Polonius?
HAMLET:  At supper.
CLAUDIUS:  Hamlet, this deed must send thee hence.
     Therefore prepare thyself,
     Everything is bent for England.                                                           5
     (HAMLET *exits.*)
     And England, if my love thou holds't at aught,
     Thou mayst not coldly set our sov'reign process,
     The present death of Hamlet. Do it, England!
(CLAUDIUS *exits.*)

### Interlude

*At sea. Sea music.* HAMLET *enters on parapet, swaying as if on a ship's bridge.
Sea music ends.* HAMLET *exits.*

## Scene 8

*Yet another room in the castle. Flourish of trumpets as* CLAUDIUS *and* LAERTES *enter.*

LAERTES:  Where is my father?

CLAUDIUS:  Dead.

(OPHELIA *enters in mad trance, singing. Lute music is heard.*)

OPHELIA:  They bore him barefaced on the bier,
  Hey nonny nonny, hey nonny.
  And on his grave rained many a tear . . .                                5

LAERTES:  O heat dry up my brains—O kind Sister,

(OPHELIA *falls to ground.*)

  Had'st thou thy wits, and did'st persuade revenge
  It could not move thus.

CLAUDIUS:  And where the offence is, let the great axe fall.

(CLAUDIUS *and* LAERTES *exit. Gravestone rises to hide* OPHELIA. *Bell tolls four times.*)


## Scene 9

*A churchyard. A* GRAVEDIGGER *and* HAMLET *enter.*

HAMLET:  Ere we were two days old at sea, a pirate of very warlike appoint-
  ment gave us chase. In the grapple I boarded them. On the instant they
  got clear of our ship; so I alone became their prisoner. They have dealt
  with me like thieves of mercy.

GRAVEDIGGER:  What is he that builds stronger than either the mason, the     5
  shipwright or the carpenter?

HAMLET:  A gravemaker. The houses he makes will last till Doomsday.

(GRAVEDIGGER *gives skull to* HAMLET.)

  Whose was it?

GRAVEDIGGER:  This same skull, Sir, was Yorick's skull, the King's jester.

HAMLET:  Alas, poor Yorick. (*He returns skull to* GRAVEDIGGER.)                10

  But soft—that is Laertes. (*He withdraws to side.*)

(LAERTES *enters.*)

LAERTES:  What ceremony else?
  Lay her in the earth,
  And from her fair and unpolluted flesh
  May violets spring. I tell thee, churlish priest,                        15

(CLAUDIUS *and* GERTRUDE *enter.*)

  A ministering angel shall my sister be
  When thou liest howling.

HAMLET (*offstage.*):  What, the fair Ophelia?

LAERTES:  O treble woe. Hold off the earth awhile,
  Till I have caught her once more in my arms.                             20

HAMLET (*re-entering acting area.*):
  What is he whose grief bears such an emphasis?
  This is I, Hamlet the Dane!
LAERTES: The devil take thy soul.
(*They grapple.*)
HAMLET: Away thy hand!
(CLAUDIUS *and* GERTRUDE *pull them apart.*)
CLAUDIUS AND GERTRUDE: Hamlet! Hamlet! (*speaking together.*)          25
HAMLET: I loved Ophelia. What wilt thou do for her?
GERTRUDE: O he is mad, Laertes!
(CLAUDIUS, GERTRUDE *and* LAERTES *exit.*)
HAMLET: The cat will mew, and dog will have his day!
(*He exits. Gravestone is dropped.*)

**Scene 10**

*A Hall in the castle. A flourish of trumpets as* HAMLET *enters.*
HAMLET: There's a divinity that shapes our ends, rough hew them how
  we will. But thou would'st not think how ill all's here about my
  heart. But 'tis no matter. We defy augury. There is a special provi-
  dence in the fall of a sparrow. If it be now, 'tis not to come; If it be
  not to come, it will be now; it if be not now yet it will come. The          5
  readiness is all.
  (LAERTES *enters with* OSRIC *bearing swords followed by* CLAUDIUS *and*
  GERTRUDE *with goblets.*)
  Come on, Sir!
LAERTES: Come, my lord.
(*Fanfare of trumpets.* LAERTES *and* HAMLET *draw swords and duel.*)
HAMLET: One.
LAERTES: No.          10
HAMLET: Judgement?
OSRIC: A hit, a very palpable hit.
CLAUDIUS: Stay, give me a drink.
  Hamlet, this pearl is thine, here's to thy health.
(*He drops pearl in goblet.*) Give him the cup.          15
GERTRUDE: The Queen carouses to thy fortune, Hamlet.
(GERTRUDE *takes the cup.*)
CLAUDIUS: Gertrude, do not drink!
GERTRUDE: I will, my lord. (*She drinks.*)
LAERTES: My lord, I'll hit him now.
  Have at you, now!          20
(HAMLET *and* LAERTES *grapple and fight.*)
CLAUDIUS: Part them, they are incensed.
  They bleed on both sides.
(OSRIC *and* CLAUDIUS *part them.* OSRIC *exits.*)

LAERTES:  I am justly killed by my own treachery. *(He falls.)*
GERTRUDE:  The drink, the drink! I am poisoned! *(She dies.)*
HAMLET:  Treachery! Seek it out.                                    25
*(*FORTINBRAS *enters.)*
LAERTES:  It is here, Hamlet. Hamlet thou art slain.
   Lo, here I lie, never to rise again.
   The King, the King's to blame.
HAMLET:  The point envenomed too?
   Then venom to thy work. *(He kills* CLAUDIUS.*)*            30
LAERTES:  Exchange forgiveness with me, noble Ha … m … *(He dies.)*
HAMLET:  I follow thee.
   I cannot live to hear the news from England.
   The rest is silence. *(He dies.)*
FORTINBRAS:  Goodnight sweet prince,                               35
   And flights of angels sing thee to thy rest.
   *(He turns to face away from audience.)*
   Go, bid the soldiers shoot.
   *(Four shots heard from off stage. All stand, bow once and exit.)*

END

**The Encore**

*A stagehand enters with a placard bearing the legend "Encore." He parades across the stage and exits. A flourish of trumpets.* CLAUDIUS *and* GERTRUDE *enter.*
CLAUDIUS:  Our sometime sister, now our Queen,
   *(*HAMLET *enters.)*
   have we taken to wife.
HAMLET:  That it should come to this!
*(*CLAUDIUS *and* GERTRUDE *exit. Sound of wind.* HORATIO *enters.)*
HORATIO:  My lord. I saw him yesternight—
   The King, your father.                                       5
HAMLET:  Angels and ministers of grace defend us! *(He exits, running,*
   *through rest of speech.)* Something is rotten in the state of Denmark.
*(*GHOST *enters above.)*
GHOST:  I am thy father's spirit.
   The serpent that did sting thy father's life.
*(*HAMLET *enters above.)*
   Now wears his crown.                                          10
HAMLET:  O my prophetic soul!
   Hereafter I shall think meet
   To put an antic disposition on.
*(They exit. Short flourish of trumpets. Enter* POLONIUS *below, running.)*
POLONIUS:  Look where sadly the poor wretch comes.
*(*POLONIUS *exits, running.* HAMLET *enters.)*

HAMLET: I have heard that guilty creatures sitting at a play    15
    Have by the very cunning of the scene been struck.
    (*Enter* CLAUDIUS, GERTRUDE, OPHELIA, MARCELLUS *and* HORATIO *joking.*
    *All sit to watch imaginary play.*)
    If he but blench, I know my course.
    (*Masque music.* CLAUDIUS *rises.*)
    The King rises!
ALL: Give o'er the play!
(*Exeunt* ALL *except* GERTRUDE *and* HAMLET.)
HAMLET: I'll take the ghost's word for a thousand pounds.    20
    (POLONIUS *enters, goes behind arras. Short flourish of trumpets.*)
    Mother, you have my father much offended.
GERTRUDE: Help!
POLONIUS: Help, Ho!
HAMLET (*He stabs* POLONIUS.): Dead for a ducat, dead!
    (POLONIUS *falls dead off stage.* GERTRUDE *and* HAMLET *exit. Short flourish*
    *of trumpets.* CLAUDIUS *enters followed by* HAMLET.)
CLAUDIUS: Hamlet, this deed must send thee hence.    25
    (HAMLET *exits.*)
    Do it, England.
(CLAUDIUS *exits.* OPHELIA *enters and falls to the ground. Gravestone rises to hide*
    *her. Bell tolls twice.* GRAVEDIGGER *and* HAMLET *enter.*)
HAMLET: A pirate gave us chase. I alone became their prisoner. (*He takes*
    *skull from* GRAVEDIGGER.) Alas poor Yorick—but soft (*He returns skull to*
    GRAVEDIGGER.)—This is I, Hamlet the Dane!
(GRAVEDIGGER *exits.* LAERTES *enters.*)
LAERTES: The devil take thy soul!    30
(*They grapple, then break. Enter* OSRIC *between them with swords. They draw.*
    *Enter* CLAUDIUS *and* GERTRUDE *with goblets.*)
HAMLET: Come on, Sir!
(LAERTES *and* HAMLET *fight.*
*Pause.*)
OSRIC: A hit, a very palpable hit
CLAUDIUS: Give him the cup. Gertrude, do not drink!
GERTRUDE: I am poisoned? (*She dies.*)
LAERTES: Hamlet, thou art slain? (*He dies.*)    35
HAMLET: Then venom to thy work! (*He kills* CLAUDIUS.)
    The rest is silence. (*He dies.*)
(*Two shots off stage.*)

## END

    Shakespeare's play is longer than fifteen minutes—about four hours longer! It is, in fact, the longest of Shakespeare's works. Efforts to trim the play into a manageable stage production or movie always ignite controversy among the Shakespearean purists. How could anyone be so brazen as to trim anything from this masterpiece? Yet trimming is what has happened routinely in productions of the last few centuries. Stoppard takes the task of trimming to a whole new level. He boldly reduces every aspect of the play but still maintains the basic elements of the tragic plot. What are we to make of what is left? We have a series of familiar quotes strung together. It's almost as if Stoppard has lifted the yellowed-over lines from his old class text and made those lines his play.

One thing that is clearly lost is any sense of character development. Hamlet's most famous soliloquy becomes simply "To be, or not to be / that is the question" before he is interrupted by Ophelia. His speech has been replaced by its first line. The rhetorical term **synecdoche** describes a situation in which the whole is represented by just a part. For instance, when a ship's captain orders, "All hands on deck," he does not want just the hands; he wants the entire sailor even though it may be primarily the hands that will do the work. Similarly, in this version of the play, the opening line stands in for the entire soliloquy; the wide familiarity with the whole makes this work—sort of. Obviously, mere recognition of the speech doesn't equal the impact of the whole in a conventional production. Just as the audience gears up for the famous speech, the speech is over, and Hamlet has moved on to his next famous line, "Get thee to a nunnery!" The tragic plot remains true to the original, but by the elimination of any attempt to develop character or motive in the play, the impact becomes comic. We laugh at this Hamlet, who doesn't bother to ponder about anything, not because he says or does anything that is funny but because the juxtaposition of what little he says here and what we know he should really have said is so jarring.

There may be a more subtle allusion to something not directly expressed in Stoppard's play. A longstanding critical argument concerns Hamlet's hesitation: Why does he delay in acting upon the command of his father's ghost? Stoppard may be teasing those who obsess too much about this matter. If things move quickly, after all, we have an altogether different main character and an altogether different play. Hamlet is meditative, conflicted, a sensitive man in an insensitive world. When we rocket through the main points toward the general destruction at the end, we no longer have Hamlet, play or character, even though the lines are all taken directly from the original.

## Using Allusions to Focus Discussion and Writing

- A particular challenge with allusions is figuring out whether or not there is any reason to research them. Can we tell whether a name within a work, for instance, is just an author's arbitrary invention or whether it refers to some other character in another work? Don't overdo your attention to allusions. When you see them, or when your professor or your footnotes point them out to you, try to establish how your attention to this allusion can help you engage with your analysis of this text.

- What is the specific reference?
- How can we tell that this is a reference to another text, to a historical event, or to some existence outside the text?
- How does the author introduce the allusion? How is it incorporated within this text? For instance, is the allusion something that the fictional characters in the story are conscious of, or is it introduced by a third-person narrator?
- How does the author interpret the allusion? How does the text ask us to read this outside event?
- How does the allusion impact our understanding of or engagement in the present text? For instance, does it shape the text itself?

# 16 Genre

## How Do Our Expectations Impact Our Literary Experience?

## How Are Those Expectations Formed?

If you've grown up in the United States, it's likely you think of an avocado as a salad vegetable or salad fruit. If you've grown up in Brazil, it's likely you think of the avocado as a dessert fruit. Neither way of classifying arises from what an avocado "really" is; nor are categories like "appetizers," "salads," "main courses," "desserts"—even "fruits" and "vegetables"—universally fixed. Custom and use guide our understanding. In the United States, we see avocados sliced over lettuce and added to sandwiches with onions and tomatoes; avocados are served before or with the main meal. We don't think of ordering an avocado milk shake for a snack or enjoying a frothy avocado mousse after dinner. But in Brazil, an avocado is customarily prepared as a sweet, as a dessert; avocados come after the meal or altogether separate from it.

Of course, there is nothing wrong with either way of looking at the avocado—that is, as long as the way of looking allows you to enjoy avocados. If you've grown to love them in a salad, try them with arugula or watercress. If you've grown accustomed to thinking of them as dessert, feel free to make an avocado cake. But in either case, it's good to know that the avocado doesn't have to be one type of food or the other; if you are locked into a single way of using an avocado, you'll probably find variations distasteful or strange. If you are an adventurous diner, you might want to try both American and Brazilian ways of preparing an avocado, or you might thoroughly rethink the categories or even discard categories altogether in order to consider the avocado purely as an avocado.

A work of art, like an avocado, can be put into a category according to custom and use. A work of art, also like an avocado, can be moved from one group to another. And the groups themselves may be redefined or discarded. Determinations of kind or type along with decisions about what individual items belong to those types are variable; they are not absolute, not unchanging. With literature and film, we often find ourselves adjusting the basis upon which distinctions of kind are made. This ever-shifting way of defining a category and of what belongs in a category is what makes the concept of genre such a tricky subject.

## WHAT IS GENRE?

**Genre** is defined most broadly as a literary/artistic type or kind; it suggests the grouping of individual works into larger categories. That grouping can be made in various ways. Genres are commonly defined by reference to fairly basic **expectations** an audience brings to a work. Some of the most basic expectations have long been observed: a **tragedy** ends in death; a **comedy** ends in marriage. To expand upon that distinction slightly, we expect tragedies to concern grand failures—a powerful sense of lost promise is crucial. We expect comedies to offer some sense of fulfillment, albeit oftentimes of a small sort. Characters in comedies overcome misunderstandings and limitations to achieve their fair share of happiness.

There are, of course, different kinds of comedies and tragedies. There are additional terms that register more specific expectations. A **farce** (a form of **low comedy**) sustains no tension that arises from complexities of character. Consequently, a farce builds upon silly actions that require only superficial resolution (there may be situational complexities in farce, but not emotional ones). The pleasure of watching *Seinfeld* depends largely on how cleverly episode after episode adds up to nothing. In contrast to such light entertainments, **high comedy** delivers the emotional substance of complex people. For example, the lovers in Shakespeare's *Much Ado about Nothing* face great obstacles created by ill will, anger, pride, and jealousy. They also suffer for the mistakes they make. And partly because of this capacity to suffer, they can appreciate the happiness they finally achieve.

Although it is important to know the key terms commonly used to identify elements of a genre, it is more important to understand how identifying those elements helps us appreciate an individual text. A good critic must do more than merely name genres or provide information *about* genres.

Shakespeare's foolish busybody Polonius from *Hamlet* takes the naming approach, and it leads him to a long and ultimately pointless list: "tragedy, comedy, history, pastoral, pastoral-comical, historical pastoral, tragical-historical, tragical-comical-historical-pastoral." Polonius does not understand that a genre is something to explore and test, not merely to label and list. The study of genre demands that we reflect upon categories we identify and name. We must consider what we have been taught to expect from a particular kind of work and ask ourselves what those expectations signify. We must understand the following aspects of genre:

- Creative works of art precede the critical discussion of those works as representative of a type or kind. Aristotle wouldn't have written about tragedy as a genre if he had not viewed many plays that he felt shared essential characteristics. (We wouldn't consider an avocado a salad fruit if we had not grown up eating avocados in salads.)

- Defining a genre does not fix the characteristics of a genre permanently in place. Aristotle was a brilliant critic, but his description of tragedy should not be taken as a set of rules all tragedies must follow. (Even if you think of avocados only as a salad fruit, there remain many inventive ways to use avocados in a great variety of salads.)

- If it doesn't help you to think of a particular work existing within a particular genre, don't hesitate to move that work into another genre, redefine the genre, or dismiss the notion of genre. (If you are tired of avocados in salads, try an avocado dessert, make an avocado main dish, or just eat the avocado plain.)

# CONVENTIONS

Elements that have become familiar through our reading/viewing experience are called **conventions** (**formula** is a related although somewhat stricter word). Without conventions, there can be no genre. Our recognition of conventions becomes the basis upon which we construct a sense of genre. Often conventions emerge in elements of plot. In teen horror films (like *Halloween* or *Nightmare on Elm Street*), our viewing experience leads us to expect a crazed killer to attack the young couple who have sneaked off to make out. In courtroom dramas (like *A Few Good Men*), we learn to expect an explosive confrontation between a defense lawyer and a difficult witness that will reveal the truth that has been hidden. In romantic comedies (like *My Best Friend's Wedding* or *Pride and Prejudice*), we learn to expect the leading male and female characters to stumble over a series of misunderstandings before they discover that they are meant for each other. We often take satisfaction in such familiar genre stories because they at some level provide reassurance. They confirm unspoken beliefs or underscore common wisdom: young couples shouldn't sneak around to make out, false accusations will not be sustained in our courts, or true love always finds a way.

Conventions, of course, don't take shape only in elements of a story line. Anything our reading/viewing experience has taught us to expect as essential to a type can trigger our identification of a genre. A dark and stormy night serves as a conventional setting for certain types of gothic fiction. A character sporting a straggly mustache and a black hat instantly signals a threat in the world of the western. A pairing of unlike personalities in a shared endeavor becomes the basis for dozens of buddy films. And the mood or tone of reflective sadness over the death of a promising youth marks the conventional tone and subject of the elegy. We begin to respond to many individual works in context of a body of expectations we have acquired in our past reading and viewing.

## Experiencing Literature through Genre

Ghost stories often begin by establishing a tension between rational skepticism and unexplained, disturbing occurrences. The initial tension acknowledges our resistance to tales of the supernatural in order to lure us in. Readers are, in effect, moved from their mundane lives into fictional worlds where anything can happen. Consider how quickly Mrs. J. H. Riddell (a nineteenth-century writer of supernatural tales) invokes basic generic conventions in the opening paragraphs of one of her many ghost stories. We are introduced to a no-nonsense narrator and his more vulnerable family. As you read, think of how this opening relates to familiar elements in ghost stories you may have heard or of horror films you have seen.

**Mrs. J. H. Riddell** (1832–1906)

## from Nut Bush Farm (1882)

When I entered upon the tenancy of Nut Bush Farm almost the first piece of news which met me, in the shape of a whispered rumour, was that "something" had been seen in the "long field."

Pressed closely as to what he meant, my informant reluctantly stated that the "something" took the "form of a man," and that the wood and the path leading thereto from Whittleby were supposed to be haunted.

Now, all this annoyed me exceedingly. I do not know when I was more put out than by this intelligence. It is unnecessary to say I did not believe in ghosts or anything of that kind, but my wife being a very nervous, impressionable woman, and our only child a delicate weakling, in the habit of crying himself into fits if left alone at night without a candle, I really felt at my wits' end to imagine what I should do if a story of this sort reached their ears. ∎

This narrator represents a kind of commonsense approach to the world, but he does not seem at the outset a very sympathetic figure. We're hardly surprised or disappointed to see this narrator shaken progressively from his confident faith in the material reality of everyday life. We expect and want ghost stories to shake up the most hardheaded skeptics. That is what ghost stories do. Significantly, by the end of this tale, we have the same tension we had at the start. But now it is the narrator who is shaken and the people who surround him who are the skeptics. We're now able to align ourselves with the narrator against all those sensible fools who refuse to accept a reality that lies outside the ordinary. Note how the essential dynamic has been repeated and yet revised in the closing lines from "Nut Bush Farm."

My brother took Nut Bush Farm off my hands. He says the place never was haunted—that I never saw Mr. Hascot except in my own imagination—that the whole thing originated in a poor state of health and a too credulous disposition!

I leave the reader to judge between us. ∎

We may well finish our reading of "Nut Bush Farm" still thinking of ghosts as existing only in stories, but the generic elements evident in the passage are clearly intended to help us accept *in the reading of the story* an alternative belief.

# DISRUPTIONS

Genres depend upon our recognition of familiar features. But it would be a mistake to assume a genre piece never veers from the expected. Genres aren't absolutely fixed or altogether predictable. A deviation from an established convention—a surprise that results from breaking an expectation—is called a **disruption**. The familiar element is revised or even reversed. A disruption can be thought of as a specific kind of interruption (see Chapter 9)—one that serves to challenge thematic implications of a genre. Disruptions in a genre piece may call into question the beliefs that lie behind the conventions. If the sexually eager young couple we think is doomed in a horror movie turn out to have a good (and safe) time together, maybe we shouldn't worry so much about young couples sneaking off; if the defense lawyer in a courtroom drama can't break through what we see as a tissue of lies, maybe our legal system doesn't work as well as we like to think; if the "right couple" in what appeared to be a conventional romantic comedy turns out to be very wrong together, maybe our notions of "true love" need to be rethought. While conventions reassure, disruptions challenge and upset. Mixing familiar conventions that do not normally appear together is a common mode of disruption.

## Experiencing Literature through Genre

A famous example of generic mixing occurs in Shakespeare's *Macbeth*. Just after the king has been assassinated, just as Macbeth and Lady Macbeth begin to feel the terrible weight of what they have done, a foulmouthed, drunken Porter arrives at the castle and seeks entrance. He knocks at the gate. He speaks (to himself, Macduff, the audience, and anyone who will listen from within the castle walls) about subjects that hardly seem fitting in context of the grand tragedy that has begun to unfold. He punctuates his rambling, bawdy soliloquy with continued knocking at the gate. As you read the following dialogue, keep in mind that it is placed just after the murder of the king and just before the general discovery of the murder. Some of the grandest and most intense lines in the play bracket the lowly dialogue we've reprinted here. For example, just before the entrance of the Porter, Macbeth reflects upon his act.

To know my deed, 'twere best not know myself.
(*Knock*)
Wake Duncan with thy knocking! I would thou couldst.

And shortly after the Porter's final line, we have Macduff's announcement upon finding the King slain:

Confusion now hath made his masterpiece:
Most sacrilegious murder hath broke ope
The Lord's anointed temple and stole thence
The life of th' building!

In the middle of such lines the Porter's speech might seem out of place.

William Shakespeare  (1564–1616)

from **Macbeth** (1607)

## ACT II

Scene 3
*The court within the castle.*
*(Enter a* PORTER.*)*
*(Knocking within.)*
PORTER:  Here's a knocking, indeed! If a man were Porter of Hell Gate, he
should have old turning the key. *(Knocking.)*  Knock, knock, knock.
Who's there, i'th'name of Belzebub?—Here's a farmer, that hang'd himself on th'expectation of plenty: come in, time-pleaser; have napkins
enow about you; here you'll sweat for't. *(Knocking.)*  Knock, knock.
Who's there, i'th'other devil's name?—Faith, here's an equivocator,
that could swear in both the scales against either scale; who committed
treason enough for God's sake, yet could not equivocate to heaven: O!
come in, equivocator. *(Knocking.)*  Knock, knock, knock. Who's
there?—Faith, here's an English tailor come hither for stealing out of a
French hose: come in, tailor; here you may roast your goose.
*(Knocking.)*  Knock, knock. Never at quiet! What are you?—But this
place is too cold for Hell. I'll devil-porter it no further: I had thought to
have let in some of all professions, that go the primrose way to
th'everlasting bonfire. *(Knocking.)*  Anon, anon: I pray you, remember
the Porter.
*(Opens the gate.)*
*(Enter* MACDUFF *and* LENOX.*)*
MACD.:  Was it so late, friend, ere you went to bed,
That you do lie so late?
PORT.:  Faith, Sir, we were carousing till the second cock;
and drink, Sir, is a great provoker of three things.
MACD.:  What three things does drink especially provoke?
PORT.:  Marry, Sir, nose-painting, sleep, and urine. Lechery, Sir, it provokes, and unprovokes: it provokes the desire, but it takes away the
performance. Therefore, much drink may be said to be an equivocator
with lechery: it makes him, and it mars him; it sets him on, and it
takes him off; it persuades him, and disheartens him; makes him stand
to, and not stand to: in conclusion, equivocates him in a sleep, and,
giving him the lie, leaves him.
MACD.:  I believe, drink gave thee the lie last night.

The Porter alludes in his speech to serious matters (the Jesuits tried for political conspiracies against the crown were considered by Protestants to be "equivocators") but immediately turns such serious matters to bawdy jokes on how drink makes him both sexually aroused and sexually incapable. The low comic tone clashes greatly with the tragic weight and dignity of the surrounding text.

Some critics call this kind of mixing **comic relief**, but that term hardly fits this instance. In this case, Shakespeare is clarifying and intensifying— not undercutting—the tragedy of *Macbeth*. The knocking-at-the-gate scene provokes at most uncomfortable laughter; the wrongness of the deed has thrown everything out of synch. The Porter's incessant pounding at the gate intensifies the horror of what has occurred within the gates. Macbeth's treasonous and brutal act has undermined the stability and integrity of his world. The breakdown of generic categories through the mixing of the high and the low complements the moral breakdown that results from the murder.

## DISPLACEMENT AND PARODY

A **displacement** of one genre for another or a complete **blending** of genres extends mixing to its furthest limit. Joss Whedon's television series *Buffy the Vampire Slayer* places conventional high school coming-of-age stories in context of the horror genre. Comedy blends with terror; the mundane ("does this boy/girl like me?") blends with the cosmic ("the end of the

The demon here (in the lower left corner of the publicity poster) is dressed and posed very much like a conventional song-and-dance man, but he has a demon's face and does pose a threat that seems out of place amid the stars and clouds of this musical package.

world is upon us"). We come to understand that the comic is at times horrific or that the mundane can feel cosmic (a breakup in a serious relationship may indeed seem like the end of the world). Once Whedon establishes the ongoing generic blend, he can overlay still more generic elements as he wishes in individual episodes. A particularly striking instance is the musical episode "Once More, with Feeling" (2001). In that episode, a particularly inventive singing demon gains power over residents of Sunnydale (the town's name, of course, is part of the generic fusion). People burst into song and dance, very much in the fashion of standard Broadway musicals. The catch is that they must sing the feelings that best remain private. Eventually, they burst not just into song but into flames. The lightness of a conventional musical takes a bitter and genuinely dangerous edge. The various genres merge as something new and provocative.

Perhaps the most radical disruption involves mockery; the very elements that had been established as meaningful in a genre become the subject of ridicule. Such sustained comic imitation of a serious work is called **parody**. Although parody is sometimes thought to mark the death of a genre, it's perhaps more accurate and useful to consider it a form of revision. If the genre were really dead, the parody wouldn't be funny and wouldn't serve any purpose. Why laugh at something that no one cares about? Occasionally, critics will use the term **self-parody**. Whereas a parody is a controlled work of satire, a purposeful diminishment of a work or works taken by some as serious, a self-parody is an unintentional revelation of empty and tired formulas. Self-parody results from a genre writer/director who fails to infuse conventions with meaning or life; the result of such a failure is often that we laugh at the conventions rather than respond to them in ways that we are "supposed" to respond. Think of a spy film, for example, that tries very hard to be sexy and suspenseful but turns out to be so clichéd that it becomes funny. Or a horror movie that guarantees everyone scares and frights but delivers its "shockers" so lamely that the audience responds only with laughter.

### Making Connections

An allusion calls to mind ideas or associations that a reader has acquired from previous reading experience (see Chapter 15). A writer's purposeful use of genre also demands prior experience from the reader. It might seem, then, that a heavily allusive text is essentially the same as a genre work. Although there may be overlap, it is useful to make a distinction. An allusion casts the reader back to a particular text or type of texts at a particular place in a text. There may be many allusions in a single work, and those allusions might be drawn from various texts. Each allusion demands particular consideration in the context of its specific occurrence. Genre works ask us to think in more general terms of patterns, types, or kinds. That is, we're asked to think of how shared features work similarly in different texts.

Mark Twain's "Ode to Stephen Dowling Bots, Dec'd" shows that it is possible to parody a type of work that has already diminished itself by numerous uninspired formulaic pieces. Twain is motivated not so much by the badness of a kind of work but by the widespread acceptance of that bad work. He suggests that our culture produces and praises a ponderous and polite literature that needs to be seen for what it is—fake, empty, cliché ridden, and dishonest. It's worth noting that the conventions of an **ode** have in the last century become less conventions of form and more conventions of mood and subject. That is, odes were once structured in three parts that reflected their origins as public poems, performed by a chorus that moved in one direction as it delivered the first part (the **strophe**), the opposite direction as it voiced the second part (the **antistrophe**), and stood still as it came to the final section (the **epode**). Now we may think of odes as substantial poems of a meditative cast. They normally sustain a tone of dignity, high seriousness, and calm dispassion in dealing with a public matter. These conventions, although broadly defined, may be considered a basis for thinking of the ode in terms of genre. But Twain wants to explode what he sees as stifling conventions of propriety that keep people distant from real feelings. In his parody, he calls attention to our low expectations by meeting them only too well.

**Mark Twain** (1835–1910)

# Ode to Stephen Dowling Bots, Dec'd

(from *Adventures of Huckleberry Finn*, 1884)

And did young Stephen sicken,
   And did young Stephen die?
And did the sad hearts thicken,
   And did the mourners cry?

No; such was not the fate of               5
   Young Stephen Dowling Bots;
Though sad hearts round him thickened,
   'Twas not from sickness' shots.

No whooping-cough did rack his frame,
   Nor measles drear, with spots;            10
Not these impaired the sacred name
   Of Stephen Dowling Bots.

Despised love struck not with woe
   That head of curly knots,
Not stomach troubles laid him low;                      15
   Young Stephen Dowling Bots.

O no. Then list with tearful eye,
   Whilst I his fate do tell.
His soul did from this cold world fly,
   By falling down a well.                                   20

They got him out and emptied him;
   Alas it was too late;
His spirit was gone for to sport aloft
   In the realms of the good and the great.

After reading Twain's parody, we're likely to be very careful about the ways we speak or write about death in formal or public occasions. The last thing we'll want to do is trust too much in the most common of generic expressions. In this case, the conventions have been so overused that the poem loses any authentic relationship to the individual supposedly being honored.

# GENRE AND POPULAR CULTURE

When we think hard about genre, we learn about the culture that produces the genre. Conventions embody values, wishes, and fears. For example, until the late 1960s the western was among the most clearly established film genres and a popular genre of fiction as well. Many children growing up in the United States of the 1950s had thoroughly internalized the western's conventions. Television stories, dime novels, Saturday matinees had laid down the guidelines. Boys especially learned to recognize and employ all the necessary elements.

    American children of this generation had no difficulty recognizing a western. Although they had no critical consciousness of genre, their expectations were easily put into play. When they saw the quiet stranger ride into town, they knew much of what was to follow. The stranger would befriend a weak person. He would stand tall against a threatening bad guy (usually a braggart). He would resist "gunplay," but after many provocations he would enter and win a shoot-out. Then a grateful town would watch him ride off into the sunset. In various forms, all had seen that story many times. Good and bad were black and white. Good guys didn't want to fight, yet they always won the fights they entered—at least the fight that really counted, the decisive shoot-out at the climax. Civilization, peace, and stability were at stake at the

Very young boys who grew up in the 1950s learned to mimic the gestures of their western heroes.

Note that the conventional signs of the western are placed amid more generalized military symbols.

opening of the film and were accomplished facts by the end. Of course, the real world of the 1950s was not so simple. No period of history is ever simple. But the highly conventionalized westerns of that time may have signaled a desire for clarity or perhaps a denial of complexity.

## Experiencing Film through Genre

Popular movies provide especially clear illustrations of how genres take shape and change to reflect the mood of the times. Film and television are, after all, the most widely shared forms of artistic expression in our culture. We sit with others to watch a movie; we see and hear how others respond as we respond. We come to build a shared knowledge of scenes, characters, images, and plots that we bring to and add to each movie we see. We can all readily identify a wealth of types: screwball comedies, combat films, horror films, musicals, gangster movies, buddy movies, and so on. Thinking about three western movies from three different periods can help us see how—and to what end—conventions take shape and are disrupted as social and political attitudes shift.

*Shane* (1953) has been called the "perfect" western, and to the extent that it embodies key elements of the classic western, it may well be. Based on a 1949 novel of the same title by Jack Schaefer, *Shane* evokes a myth of growth and opportunity that had a powerful hold on the United States just after World War II. The country had come out of the Depression and a war. Men were coming back to start careers. Women were sometimes forced to leave careers to make room for those men. Tract homes were laid down; marriages made; children born; schools built. It's this cultural context that gives rise to *Shane*. The main action of *Shane* deals with the threat to the Starrett family and resolves itself in the defense of that family. Joe (Van Heflin), Marian (Jean Arthur), and their son (Brandon De Wilde) are the idealized ancestors of people going to the movies in 1953. Those moviegoers appreciated the conventions that both tested and rewarded the Starretts' hard work, honesty, determination, and decency. They felt that they had inherited the world that Shane and the Starretts had labored and fought to secure.

By the mid- to late 1960s, the western's myth of progress seemed too accepting of conventional roles and rules and too optimistic about what violence could achieve. *Shane* had been one of the most popular films of its day, but by 1970 straightforward westerns had nearly disappeared. In fact, one of the biggest box-office hits of 1974 was *Blazing Saddles*—a western made to ridicule westerns. In this film, director Mel Brooks shrewdly plays a fairly common strategy: when a genre becomes overworked or out of touch, it

*Shane* (1953)

is ripe for satire. The values that once gave it force become subject to dismissal. In *Blazing Saddles*, the western's conventions are wildly disrupted. The main result is a kind of low humor: cowboys noisily fart around the campfire after eating beans; the barmaid (Madeline Kahn) enjoys decidedly phallic sausages at dinner with the new sheriff (Cleavon Little). In the more serious parts of the general fun, Brooks pokes holes in racial and gender assumptions built into conventional westerns: a crooked politician (Harvey Korman) appoints an African American man sheriff because he knows that the racist townspeople won't accept the rule of law from a man they consider inferior. By mocking most everything that was presented seriously in *Shane*, *Blazing Saddles* signaled a new perspective on earlier notions of social progress. A popular genre, along with the beliefs that the genre supported, seemed almost laughed out of existence.

The western, however, was too much a part of the general culture to die out completely. Even if people could no longer accept conventions of the western uncritically, they could still be trusted to recognize those conventions and the values they once encoded. In *Unforgiven* (1992), director Clint Eastwood found ways to use the audience's knowledge of genre in serious and unsettling ways. Working from a screenplay by David Webb Peoples, Eastwood creates a film that subtly disrupts the conventional western point by point. *Unforgiven* makes us reflect upon the significance of the

*Unforgiven* (1992)

expectations shaped by classic westerns like *Shane*. William Munny (played by Eastwood)—a man of notorious temper and character—has been "reformed" by the love of a woman. This seems to begin where Shane wanted to end, but *Unforgiven* opens with Munny digging his wife's grave. Although Munny had become a hardworking family man, he finds the farm and the children offer little satisfaction. To make matters worse, Munny's pigs have "the fever." As he labors to separate those infected from the few that remain healthy, Munny is literally dragged through the mud and excrement. Conventionalized scenes of work in *Shane* had idealized the healthiness and productivity of hard work.

Munny soon receives an offer to join in the contract killing of two cowboys who "cut up a woman." So, like Shane, he finds himself returning to his violent past; unlike Shane, however, Munny returns to type at the beginning, not the end, of the story. Even though Munny at first says the cowboys "deserve" killing, it quickly becomes clear that "deserve has nothing to do with it" (a point made explicit at the end).

## A Note to Student Writers: Moving beyond Formulaic Writing

Genres aren't identifiable only in stories, poems, films, and plays. Academic essays also develop generic characteristics. Although it is important to understand that conventions of form, tone, argument, and presentation do operate in critical essays of various types, far too often academic genres are reduced to one overly simple and severely limited formula: "five-paragraph essay." This formula is sometimes presented (or understood) as a fixed model. Students are taught that they *must* introduce a topic and assert a thesis in the first paragraph, follow the thesis with three supporting points (a paragraph for each point), and conclude in a final paragraph. More generous, but still cramped, lessons allow for a slight expansion of the same basic model (that is, students are allowed an additional paragraph or two in the body for more supporting points). If we understand the teaching of such models as intended to communicate very basic ideas about structure (that papers should have a beginning, middle, and end), there is little harm done. But it is very important to realize that not all "good writing" about any subject can be neatly contained by an inflexible organizational formula.

Perhaps the biggest problem with working from any set model is that such a practice makes the formula the primary point. In other words, the structure doesn't allow for ideas to grow. It imposes limits upon any complex thoughts we may discover or hope to explore. A careful reading of almost any good essay will reveal that one point need not be contained by one paragraph, that there is no "right" number of paragraphs. Writers don't "fill in" a preset number of paragraphs; they develop paragraphs as their ideas unfold and as the argument demands. We suggest that you remember that academic genres, like literary genres, are multiple and are subject to change. Most important, remember that genres function to shape and express meaning, not to box meaning in.

# MODELING CRITICAL ANALYSIS:
# TOM STOPPARD, THE FIFTEEN MINUTE HAMLET

Tom Stoppard's *The Fifteen Minute Hamlet* (p. 282) presents much of the action of the original play: the ghost of Hamlet's father comes and asks for revenge; Hamlet rebukes his mother; Hamlet kills Polonius; Claudius sends him away; Ophelia goes mad, dies, and is buried; Laertes mourns. Laertes strikes Hamlet with a poison-tipped foil; Hamlet cuts Laertes with the same; Gertrude drinks unknowingly from a poisoned cup; Hamlet stabs Claudius. All die. Fortinbras arrives and acknowledges Hamlet's nobility. Surely all that death adds up to tragedy—or surely not. Stoppard's radical cutting disrupts any sense of tragedy. Aristotle defined tragedy as an imitation of a profound action that an audience could identify with and through that identification achieve a kind of release, what Aristotle termed **catharsis**. Stoppard keeps a distance from reality; he imitates only a play. We're conscious from the start of gaps in character development as his version of *Hamlet* rockets forward. Because we're not given any reason to care about the characters, we cannot react emotionally to their fates. In fact, we have no reason to think of these characters as having any existence off the stage. The artifice of it all is made especially apparent by the fact that in this fifteen-minute version, everyone dies twice—once in the main body of the play and once in the still more radically abbreviated encore.

By racing through Shakespeare's *Hamlet* and grabbing tiny bits of memorable lines and key scenes, Stoppard asks us to consider what constitutes the play and the genre. We know this is not *Hamlet*, yet we recognize much of *Hamlet* in it. Whatever made that play a tragedy gets left out. What is left in moves us to a very different genre. Imagine how this play would be performed. The speed would lend it many of the characteristics of a slapstick comedy or farce (a physical comedy): characters in *The Fifteen Minute Hamlet* charge about, rush onstage and offstage, deliver lines without context, fall down dead, get up, and fall down dead again before getting up once more to welcome the cheers of the audience. The audience at a well-produced staging of *The Fifteen Minute Hamlet* will be laughing throughout.

Stoppard may also be asking us to reflect back seriously on Shakespeare's play and on the way we may diminish tragedies. It's possible his reduction serves as a comment on a common resistance to really experiencing literature. Do we engage great works of art directly or look for shortcuts (study guides, for example) that allow us to display knowledge (on tests or in social situations) about great works? Do we too often substitute secondhand representations of literature in place of literature itself? Do we learn "about" literature, or do we read and respond? Stoppard reminds us that a plot summary cannot communicate the experience that we have when we watch or read *Hamlet*; the work is a complex organism that deserves study because of the careful balance that it achieves among all literary elements. And if we've read it only for what happens, we've written our own fifteen-minute version without knowing it. If that were the case, the laugh would be on us.

## Using Genre to Focus Writing and Discussion

To write about any genre, we must establish the characteristics that define it. Remember that in most cases, the label of type of genre comes after the creation of the text. The generic label is a critical tool that we can use to group similar works together, and it is quite appropriate to consider a single work in multiple generic categories.

- To define the genre, first consider which specific works we have grouped together. What common elements do these works share? What is the rationale for this particular grouping?

- How important are these particular elements to understanding each work?

- How do we understand each of the works better because we have grouped them in this manner?

- To what extent is our definition of this genre something that the works themselves are conscious of? How can you demonstrate this consciousness? For instance, are there allusions to other works within the genre or discussions of conventions within the work itself or disruptions of the generic conventions within the work?

- What aspects of the work does our attention to genre keep us from considering?

- What other genres might we use to group any of the works that we have gathered here?

- Considerations of genre are often fairly clear in the field of film. Think of a recent film that you think belongs to a well-established genre. What would you call the genre? What elements are repeated? What expectations are invoked? Does this film disrupt any conventions? How would you describe the disruption? What is the effect of both the conventions and the disruptions?

# 17 The Production and Reproduction of Texts

## How Does Retelling and Revising Impact My Experience of a Text?

## How Can Literary Theory Clarify What Constitutes That Experience?

Whatever historical or social changes surround a work of art and however those changes influence our perception of the work, we tend to trust in the stable reality of a physical text. After all, words move from left to right across a page; pages are bound to turn in a fixed order. Film winds from one spool to another; the images pass across the projecting light in a set sequence. Given the arguments and ambiguities that are part of any serious reading, it's nice to think we have in hand a text—a single object—that grounds our study and gives us a common starting point for critical discussion.

But maybe that object isn't as stable as we usually assume. Given the labor William Blake put in to meld word and image onto an elaborately designed page, is it adequate to read just the poems themselves as they are presented in books like the one you are reading now? Charles Dickens first published all of his novels in weekly or monthly serial forms. What happens when the experience of those novels is no longer extended in small parts on a regular basis over a long period of time? Francis Ford Coppola ambitiously re-edited *Apocalypse Now* years after its original release. Which version should command our critical attention now? And is the experience of the film altered by its transmission to DVD and, consequently, from the theater to our living room?

Academic critics and scholars tend to be a fussy group. Some are especially devoted to the presentation of the truest text. But the most sophisticated textual critics understand that the notion of a single "best" text or "pure" text is problematic. Literature isn't merely an *object* of academic study. It's a human activity and experience that cannot be contained or bound within covers. And a literary text isn't created by an individual operating in a vacuum. Nothing stops a powerful producer from cutting a scene a director or screenwriter thought important, or an actor from improvising well beyond an author's stage directions, or a writer from revising an already published poem. These varied creative forces need not lead to crucial critical problems; after all, most people are focused on the actual text they encounter, not an idealized text someone thinks they "should" have. Throughout this book, we've been primarily interested in the literary experience, not the physical objects of literary study.

Yet it's also true that if we are oblivious to textual issues, we may fail to appreciate important aspects of an artist's craft. We may also remain insensitive to complex external forces that contribute to the shaping of a particular work. This chapter emphasizes critical issues concerning the production and reproduction of a text. We'll reflect upon how people have used—revised, abridged, and translated—literary texts and films. We'll explore how those uses matter. And we'll examine the underlying theoretical implications of choices we routinely (and often unconsciously) make as readers.

## TEXTS AND TECHNOLOGY

Many people have observed that the development of the personal computer, of the Internet, and of the World Wide Web make our age the "information age." It's often said that what is unfolding now compares in significance to the invention of movable type in the fifteenth century. Gutenberg's printing of the Bible had enormous implications. The ability to produce and distribute texts in great numbers changed notions of literacy and upset established bases of power. In arts, the primacy of spoken or performed works was overtaken by our modern notion of literature, which gave the printed word a privileged place.

In many ways, the computer further emphasizes the printed word. But some things about how words can be arranged and displayed have changed. A book (as we noted previously) makes us turn pages. We read in a linear way, even when authors call into question notions of linear time or sequence. Words in an electronic space allow fresh design possibilities. Writers working in cyberspace are liberated from the physical demands of paper and binding. An electronic manuscript can mix forms of presentation (moving images,

As dramatic as recent developments in textual production may seem, one could argue that there is still nothing new. Many writers who worked decades, even centuries, before the first director's track ever appeared on a DVD have included forewords, prefaces, introductions, afterwords, postscripts, footnotes, and so on that frame the presentation of the main narrative in ways that keep readers conscious of the crafted nature of the text and of the presence of the author within the act of storytelling. In the earliest days of film, images were sped up or run backward to achieve comic effects. As film matured as an art, directors employed styles of editing that made audiences aware of film as film (see Chapter 9). **Split-screen** techniques, for example, may be used to remind viewers that there is never only one thing happening at any one point in time. So, hypertext could be seen as a new technology for the exploration of ideas and techniques about not strictly linear narrative that surfaced long ago.

sound, and so on). Readers may feel liberated as well. The notion of **hypertext** puts the reader/user in a strong position. Hypertext allows readers to access on a computer screen any variety of linked documents instantly, at any time, and in any order. These developments are now apparent in few significant works. The crafting and appreciation of great electronic manuscripts lie in the future. But some writers have begun to shape works that acknowledge new ways of presenting paper texts. It is fairly easy now, for example, to use multiple fonts, introduce color into a text, experiment with formats, or package a paper text with a CD or DVD. Writers have long challenged the idea that a story must be linear. Today, writers hoping to press the challenge further might choose to address the issue of linearity directly in the design of the page.

# TEXTUAL FORM AND CONDITIONS OF PRODUCTION

There is a cliché often invoked when a good writer turns out an inferior bit of work: "even Homer nods." This cliché suggests that even a great writer can be sleepily inattentive to a line or a word, can "nod off" at one point or another in the writing process. It's a nice little saying, but it's also misleading. Homer, after all, wasn't a writer—at least not in the way we now think of what it is to be a writer. The great epics of ancient Greece were first delivered orally. No one lined up at the local bookstore to get copies of the next new work by Homer. *The Iliad* and *The Odyssey* as we know them were, of course, eventually written down. And the person (or persons) who did that writing had an extraordinary command of language. But the source materials were worked and reworked, revised, improvised, and elaborated upon over many years of oral performances.

Our current notions of poetry, drama, fiction, and film don't then simply represent different forms of presentation that have always been available. These genres can be traced back to specific technologies and changing social conditions. Before print, poets spoke or sung to audiences. Rhythmic devices and rhyming effects were used both to assist the memory of the performer and to sustain attention of a listener. Early printed poems tended to circulate within a very narrow range of society. Live drama could not have arisen without a complex social structure to support it (if there were no theaters or no paying audience, would there be playwrights?). The novel emerged only when there was large middle-class readership; in fact, up until the early nineteenth century, novels were primarily aimed at women who had the time, the education, and the means necessary for sustaining a new form of entertainment and instruction. As for one of the latest "new forms" of entertainment, many observers of the film business believe that the growing popularity of DVDs and "home theaters" will redefine the moviegoing experience.

## Experiencing Literature through Issues of Production

William Blake designed pages as well as wrote poems. The interaction of word and image in his works offers an experience that conventional reprinting with words alone cannot match. One must even consider how and to what extent our interpretation of a given Blake poem may be controlled by the form we have of it. Consider, for example, "A Poison Tree," from *Songs of Experience*.

The tree, in the words of the poem, is a tree of wrath—something that has grown from anger and hatred. It is the product of the speaker's experience. The words deliver a powerful and fairly direct message: be open with your anger, or it will become deadly. But our experience of the whole text is much broader and more subtly nuanced. In Blake's engraving, the fallen "foe" beneath the tree lies with arms open wide. He seems at peace in a sacrificial position. His long hair spreads upon the earth. The broad chest is foregrounded; the lower body melds with the landscape behind. There is an almost sensual quality to the figure; if not for the accompanying poem, the figure could be seen as sleeping. The tree *drawn* on Blake's page seems part of a beautiful landscape. But the poem's title, "A Poison Tree," along with the fairly specific allegorical tree conjured by the words alone, jars against the image of the tree that so gracefully frames the whole composition. Blake had written of innocence and experience as qualities marking the "contrary states of the human soul." Viewing the whole page in this case (text and artwork) suggests he has encompassed that range. To put the point in a different way, the "experience" of the poem's speaker doesn't match Blake's complete vision or our own experience of the whole text. How does Blake's image complicate our sense of his poem?

A POISON TREE.

I was angry with my friend:
I told my wrath, my wrath did end.
I was angry with my foe:
I told it not, my wrath did grow.

And I waterd it in fears,
Night & morning with my tears;
And I sunned it with smiles,
And with soft deceitful wiles.

And it grew both day and night,
Till it bore an apple bright,
And my foe beheld it shine,
And he knew that it was mine.

And into my garden stole,
When the night had veild the pole;
In the morning glad I see;
My foe outstretchd beneath the tree.

# AN ORIENTATION TO CONTEMPORARY CRITICAL THEORY

Reading literature can be a challenge, but reading critical analyses of literature can seem impossible to a person unfamiliar with key ideas and assumptions. Not only is it easy to get lost amid the confusing names that signal the different angles critics take in studying literature and film but it can be hard to know what the angle is. What is this critic's point of view? What assumptions does she or he make about the critical task? If you are to tune into conversations that occur in a college environment, you must acquire some understanding of common theoretical approaches to the literary experience.

## New Criticism and *Auteur* Theory

We can orient ourselves to much current theory by knowing something about a critical movement that emerged in the middle of the twentieth century and that continues to influence much teaching. The name—**new criticism**—seems odd now, given that it's relatively old in context of recent schools of thought, but new criticism is the name that has stuck. The new critics were **formalists**; they argued that literary texts are the sole material of literary study. Literary criticism is *not* (the argument went) a branch of history, biography, psychology, or sociology, but a distinct discipline that must focus upon the structure, style, and language of a particular work of literary art. The "object itself" (a poem, story, or play) became the point of intense study for a generation of critics and scholars. **Explication** (the unfolding, the close reading, the analysis of the text) became the heart—indeed the end goal—of literary study. The best reading was the reading that accounted most fully for the work's complex features.

We've certainly assumed in this book that close attention to a work of art leads to a measure of exploration and discovery; but however valuable new criticism was as a disciplined method of analysis, it was ultimately narrow and arbitrary. The text, as we've suggested, can be in itself a problematic concept. And literature, like all human activities, is dynamic, changing, and messy. Both the strengths and the limitations of new criticism emerged quite clearly in the context of film studies. **Auteur theory** closely paralleled the new criticism (*auteur* is the French word for "author"). *Auteur* criticism assumed that if films were to be considered "art," they needed to be created by an artist (that is, the director). The focus on the director's management of the whole gave the critic a point of analytical focus. It led to serious and rigorous treatment of a film's structure and style. It worked from a sense that a single controlling creative force was shaping the whole work that unfolded. But *auteur* criticism disregarded the social and economic processes that influenced the making of films. It also could not encompass the essentially collaborative nature of filmmaking.

## Deconstruction

The limits of new criticism and *auteur* theory met progressively aggressive challenges beginning in the 1960s. The French philosopher Jacques Derrida, in particular, undermined some of the formalists' most basic assumptions. Derrida pointed out that no word has a fixed or "natural" meaning. He argued that a word takes on meaning only within a complex, arbitrary, and ever-changing structure of words. A word is used to *refer* to something or is *associated* with something; a word must not be mistaken for the thing it stands for and must not be read separate from a system of other words. *Carriage*, for example, can in one text refer to a fancy horse-drawn cart and, in another, to a pushcart for babies. An automobile ad might use the word to suggest a substantial, expensive car. In still other contexts, *carriage* could refer to a loading mechanism for a gun or for the roller on a typewriter. Literary texts exploit (with or without the author's intention) such variable associations. It becomes the job of the critic to unfold a play of possible meanings that reveal multiple, even contrary, messages. For Derrida, to read closely is to deconstruct, not interpret, the text. This line of thinking leads to the notion that literary texts are not great because of their wholeness or consistency (qualities new criticism would emphasize) but because of the irreducibly complex associations that they provoke. **Deconstruction**, then, is not a practice that seeks to make a work coherent or consistent. The deconstructionist would reveal inconsistencies and revel in them.

The American critic J. Hillis Miller attempted to clarify deconstruction's task by calling attention to the following description of Eve in John Milton's *Paradise Lost:*

> She as a veil down to the slender waist
> Her unadorned golden tresses wore
>   Dissheveld, but in wanton ringlets wav'd
> As the vine curls her tendrils, which impli'd
>   Subjection.

Miller notes Eve is at this point in Milton's story a free, yet unfallen part of creation. Her place in nature is defined by her subjection to the authority of Adam and ultimately of God. Her loosely flowing hair is as natural as the growth of the garden that surrounds her. But however much Milton may stress Eve's innocence before the fall, "unadorned golden tresses" and "wanton ringlets" also achieve meaning in the context of a culture that sees a woman's loosely flowing hair as associated with sexuality and sin. It would seem the innocent Eve has already fallen or must necessarily fall by some flaw of her nature. But how can this be in a perfect creation? Even if Milton were to tell us that his description of Eve's hair implies nothing more than "subjection" to God's perfect order ("As the vine curls her tendrils"), should we be convinced by his authority? How can we so limit our understanding of "wanton" or the general luxuriance that dominates Milton's description of nature and of Eve herself? Along these lines, Miller argues that there are associations conveyed by the words in Milton's lines that contradict one another. A rigorous deconstructive reading (unlike the interpretation of a new critic) would expose rather than explain those contradictions. The orthodoxy of Milton's theological system may collapse under such analysis, but from a deconstructionist's perspective *Paradise Lost* is no less a poem for that. The richness of a literary text resides in the very complexity that makes final meaning impossible. To translate this into critical practice, a deconstructionist reading unfolds possible meanings rather than the correct meaning.

As you might imagine, deconstruction became highly controversial. Some people found it liberating. The new critical readings/interpretations that competed with one another for status as conclusive could now be seen as multiple and alternative lines of inquiry. New possibilities were opened and encouraged. Critics became strongly and self-consciously involved in the creative shaping of meaning, because meaning was no longer assumed to be determined by the work of art. But as you might also imagine, many academics found deconstruction profoundly threatening: What do we have left if *meaning* cannot be determined? Did deconstruction send us down a path toward nihilism—the belief in nothing? Many other skeptics also pointed out that deconstruction in practice often led to trivial, self-absorbed, and overcomplicated essays. Still others suggested that deconstruction was merely new jargon for essentially old ideas, many of those ideas very well established.

## New Historicism and Other Historically Grounded Approaches

Deconstruction itself no longer stands at the center of critical disputes. It is not so much that matters have been resolved but that the grounds of discussion have shifted. Deconstruction's influence, for example, now shows in ways critics think of the relationship between history and literature. It is nothing new to observe that much can be learned about a given time by reading the literary works of that time. But in past decades literary artists were given a special status as especially accurate mirrors or as particularly perceptive critics of their age. Advocates of **new historicism** don't give a poem or play a privileged place in the materials that make up a given culture. New historicists see systems of meaning as conditional and shifting depending upon the interests the systems represent. In their view, literary artists are both caught in and contribute to the complex formation of ideas about power. From the perspective of a new historicist, a nineteenth-century American writer wouldn't merely take up the "frontier" as a subject but would participate (perhaps unknowingly) in the formation of his culture's attitude toward the frontier. The very notion of "frontier" is, after all, conditioned by assumptions of forward movement and conquest that make sense only to those who move forward and conquer: the western frontier was no frontier for the Native Americans who lived on it.

New historicism hardly had the chance to grow old before some academics began using the term **cultural poetics** (which accents the blurred distinctions between history, culture, and art); others adopted the term **postcolonial criticism** (which highlights a sense of power/authority imposed by one culture/system over another). **Reader-response criticism** stands as yet another variant of new historicism that reflects the influence of deconstruction. As that name implies, reader-response critics shift emphasis from a text to how people read or use a text; the work of art is studied not through its own inherent qualities but through the way readers of a particular time and place react to it. Any of these approaches can be taken from a distinct point of view. **Feminist criticism**, for example, seeks to gain insights largely obscured or bypassed by the men who have until recent decades dominated critical discussions. Feminists join the varieties of new historicists in assuming that a work of art is a product not only of an author but of a specific culture. The "object of study" has shifted from the "text itself" that the new critics identified to a complex set of social/historical/linguistic contexts.

# WHY WE STUDY THE TEXTS WE STUDY

Many people read novels by Michael Crichton (*Congo, Jurassic Park*, among many), but relatively few people study them in literature classes. The distinction relates to the idea of the **canon**. The canon refers to those works considered appropriate for literary study. They are the durable works that a culture adopts and uses over time. Canonical works have achieved "classic" status. This seems simple enough: great books find a secure place in the canon; books less than great find a temporary place on a sales chart. But value judgments are never as clear as this. Canonical works may indeed be great, but one must acknowledge that ideas of greatness change. And perhaps more important, one must acknowledge that literary/artistic greatness is usually defined by a very particular group of people: mostly college professors. This means that the interests, ethnicity, education, and class of a particular profession have great influence in determining what belongs or doesn't belong in the canon.

Challenges to the canon have been prepared for by the unhinging effects of contemporary critical theory, but this challenge has been even more strongly motivated by broad social changes. Literary theories relate to, but do not motivate, battles regarding the canon. The fact is that today's student and teaching population is more highly varied in age, ethnicity, gender, and race than ever before. The multicultural population has understandably inspired revisions of long-established course offerings and text selections. In fact, our perspective on entire genres or art forms changes as the surrounding world changes. For example, movies were once thought barely worth critical attention; they were seen as popular entertainments, not works of art. Although movies are still popular entertainment, the best of them claim attention and respect. Entire college courses are devoted to film (the change in name from "movie" to "film" or "cinema" suggests the higher status within the university). Film (and film studies) has been around long enough now that we can speak of certain movies/films as canonical.

## Experiencing Literature through Theory

The following two passages are taken from the introduction of two very different (although both very large) anthologies of American literature. The first, *Major Writers of America*, was published in 1962—in the days when the new critics held sway in an institution that was still largely white and male. The second, from *The Heath Anthology of American Literature*, first appeared in 1990 and clearly sounded a challenge to conventional notions of "major" or canonical. The first focuses on concepts of quality that are presumed discernible through rigorous analysis. The second shifts attention to historical context and implies that quality is relative to the interests of the reader. As you read, identify how assumptions that govern the editors' principle of selection are signaled in specific words or phrases. Think too about how the editors define the audience or readership of their textbook. What can you learn about education in the United States or about the place literature takes in that education by reading these passages?

## from Major Writers of America (1962)

... while the canon is at long last becoming established, a realization gradually forces itself upon us that, as the age of discovery and of elementary mapping closes, the era of evaluation opens.... [It] is incumbent upon us to make clear which are the few peaks and which the many low-lying hills.... We must vindicate the study of American literature because primarily the matter is literature, and only secondarily because it is American.

... The first requirement of the design, therefore, was inevitably that the authors so nominated be represented fully enough to testify to their superiority.° ∎

# from The Heath Anthology of American Literature (1990)

... a major principle of selection has been to represent as fully as possible the varied cultures of the United States. American cultures sometimes overlap, sometimes differ, sometimes develop separately, sometimes in interactive patterns. To convey this diversity, we have included what is by far the widest sampling of the work of minority and white women writers available in any anthology of American literature. This selection includes material by 109 women of all races, 25 individual Native American authors (as well as 17 texts from tribal origins), 53 African Americans, 13 Hispanics (as well as 12 texts from earlier Spanish originals and two from French) and 9 Asian Americans. We have included significant selections from Jewish, Italian, and other ethnic traditions. ∎

These two selections represent radically opposed notions of what literary study involves. It's important that you understand that the arguments behind each position influence the education you now experience. Professors, after all, must decide on which texts to assign. Can you sense where your professors fit into the conversation about inclusion/exclusion (or "quality"/context) carried on by the two anthologies?

## A Note to Student Writers: Using Theory to Develop Critical Analysis

Although it is important to reflect upon the theoretical implications that lie behind any paper we write, it is not necessarily good to work consciously from a set theoretical perspective. To think from the start, "now I'm going to write as a deconstructionist," may be putting the cart before the horse. The cognitive activities that writing in response to a complex subject inevitably prompts should not be scripted in advance. It is better to discover you've deconstructed a poem than to insist that deconstructing poetry is your job.

We suggest that you attend closely to the prompt your professor offers and begin to write without thinking too much about critical theory. Once you've worked through an

---

° *Major Writers of America* included substantial selections of twenty-eight writers. Only one (Emily Dickinson) was a woman. Dickinson, however, was in the majority on another count: nineteen of the authors included were, like her, from the northeastern United States.

argument very carefully and prepared an essay for submission, you can ask yourself, What characterizes my approach? What assumptions am I making about literary criticism? How do I look upon matters of interpretation or meaning? To what extent have I treated the text as an object of art? To what extent have I seen meaning as conditioned by things "outside" the text? From what perspective is my argument a strong one? If in answering these questions, you achieve a clearer sense of the theoretical underpinnings of your work, you may be able to revise key points effectively. Theory may prove to enrich your reading and strengthen your analysis. But revision and development that bring theory forward happen after careful drafting. Don't allow theory to interfere with your powerful and immediate experience of a text. Don't allow theory to artificially force your writing in any particular direction. And don't assume that imposing a critical vocabulary will make your paper seem more sophisticated.

# ABRIDGING, REVISING, AND REPACKAGING TEXT

For the most part in this book, we've offered "whole" works. But we haven't hesitated to use a fragment from a long novel or poem if we felt that the fragment helped illustrate a point. In relation to the subject of this chapter, it's important to also say that we don't assume that fragments cease to be literature. The passage excerpted from John Milton's *Paradise Lost* (p. 123) no doubt functions fully only in context of the whole poem, yet it reads on its own very well as a short poem. Although we certainly don't want to disregard an author's carefully crafted whole work, it's worth remembering that writers have made or approved abridgments of their own works in various forms (public readings, anthologies, translations, and so on). For that matter, individual readers may well choose to skip a chapter of the most meticulously prepared "critical edition." Such behaviors complicate our sense of what we study when we study literature and film. But these behaviors don't fundamentally change anything that we've addressed in other chapters. Rather than simply dismiss any abridgment as something less than literary, consider how an abridgment functions on its own terms. In other words, understand the limitations of an abridgment, but critically attend to whatever you have before you.

An abridged work normally intends to fairly represent something of the whole from which it is taken. At least, it shouldn't mislead one about the source text. But any substantial change presses a reader to experience a work of art as a new thing. Charles Dickens excerpted sections of his novels for his own dramatic readings. Although he could expect his audience to know the complete novel, the readings inevitably had a strongly focusing effect. From *Oliver Twist*, Dickens selected and strung together passages that told of the murder of Nancy by Bill Sykes. His readings (by all accounts, brilliantly presented) inevitably concentrated attention in such a way as to change the original—or even displace the larger narrative. *Oliver Twist*, for those rapt by Dickens's readings, became an almost unbearably compelling story of a brutal murder. That was hardly the reaction of moviegoers to the musical version that appeared in 1968 (directed by Carol Reed), *Oliver!* Nancy's murder remained an important part of the story, but elaborately staged musical/dance numbers gave the audience some distance from the most dramatic and melodramatic moments. Roman Polanski recently offered his own film version (*Oliver Twist*, 2005) that stripped away some of Dickens's elaborate side stories and concentrated heavily on a child's terrifying progress through a bitterly hard world. As often happens, an original work of art provides the occasion for variations upon a theme. Even though the new works reward attention to their own merits, it becomes necessary to think of film versions of novels or stage productions of plays as interpretations of a text. What does the director choose to foreground? Why does a casting choice matter? How does the look of a film or stage set (dark/light, elaborate/plain) have an effect on our experience of the film or play?

*Oliver Twist* has been subject to very different treatments since its publication.

## Experiencing Literature through Issues of Production and Reproduction of Texts

No author has been subject to more interpretations than Shakespeare. Despite the rigorous efforts to establish the truest texts of his plays, there has never been a time when the texts were strictly honored in performance. Mark Twain has the bogus "king" from *Adventures of Huckleberry Finn* test out an especially corrupt version of "Hamlet's Immortal Soliloquy!!" on an unlettered audience. Twain's comedy doesn't pretend to say anything about Shakespeare, but it does say something about the breadth and variety of ways Shakespeare has been repackaged for innumerable audiences. In other words, it says something about the way people use literature.

**Mark Twain**  (1835–1910)

## from Adventures of Huckleberry Finn (1885)

To be, or not to be; that is the bare bodkin
That makes calamity of so long life;
For who would fardels bear, till Birnam Wood do come to Dunsinane,
But that the fear of something after death
Murders the innocent sleep,                                                                    5
Great nature's second course,
And makes us rather sling the arrows of outrageous fortune
Than fly to others that we know not of.
There's the respect must give us pause:
Wake Duncan with thy knocking! I would thou couldst;                          10
For who would bear the whips and scorns of time,
The oppressor's wrong, the proud man's contumely,
The law's delay, and the quietus which his pangs might take,
In the dead waste and middle of the night, when churchyards yawn
In customary suits of solemn black,                                                         15
But that the undiscovered country from whose bourne no traveler returns,
Breathes forth contagion on the world,
And thus the native hue of resolution, like the poor cat i' the adage,
Is sicklied o'er with care,
And all the clouds that lowered o'er our housetops,                               20
With this regard their currents turn awry,
And lose the name of action.
'Tis a consummation devoutly to be wished. But soft you, the fair Ophelia:
Ope not thy ponderous and marble jaws,
But get thee to a nunnery—go!                                                               25

The king's version manages to mix up sequence and phrasing, misuse words, and interject lines from other sources (most notably *Macbeth*). Twain teases our reverence to texts by making us see how easily and wildly we transform texts over time. For Huck, the king's soliloquy is a privileged discourse that gains its power from being so grandly unlike everyday speech. For educated readers of Twain's novel, the king's speech becomes a kind of game in which one tries to spot all the slips. Inevitably, those readers must think back (perhaps uneasily) on what they do *not* know when an error remains uncaught or is misidentified.

Twain may have left Shakespeare even further behind than Tom Stoppard does in *The Fifteen Minute Hamlet* (p. 282), but Twain and Stoppard together remind us again that every play or filmed version must always be understood as a distinct interpretation of an original work. In fact, every time we read a text, we necessarily interpret it anew. The text doesn't stay the same over successive readings. This may seem like a strange idea, but just reflect upon your own experience in re-reading a poem or a story. Is the second reading just like the first? To take just one example: Reading a Sherlock Holmes story for the first time throws emphasis on the mystery Doyle conjures. Once we know "whodunit," we return to the story and note qualities of character or perhaps admire the complex storytelling strategies Doyle employs.

# TRANSLATIONS, SUBTITLES, AND DUBBING

We don't read or speak Polish, but we've included English translations of several Polish poems in this book (see those by Wislawa Szymborska and Czeslaw Milosz). For practical purposes, we treat these poems (along with all translated works in this book) as we know them in the English language. Our practice requires an obvious concession: a translation is not the same work as the original. Translation isn't merely a matter of trading one word for another equal word. Those of you who know a language other than English know that there are words and phrases that do not easily translate. Specific idioms may in fact be highly regional. And the sounds of one language will not be easily accommodated by another. Romance languages, for example, employ word endings that facilitate rhyming. An English translator approaching Dante is immediately faced with difficult choices: maintaining rhymes in English requires one to sacrifice much flexibility, yet dismissing rhyme changes a fundamental quality of the original poem's sound and rhythm.

A good translator is not simply one who decodes a text but one who grapples creatively with essential qualities of the text—one who seeks to catch and convey the spirit, sense, and tone of the original. A strong command of both languages (and cultures) is essential. Because we don't know Polish, we must trust the expertise and taste of those who have translated Szymborska and Milosz for us. And we feel the trust is merited if it results in a rewarding reading. We are forced to think of a translated poem to some degree as a new, independent work—one inspired by, but not equivalent to, the original piece. If you possess knowledge of a language other than English, we suggest you seek out original works and translations and read them consecutively. What differences do you notice? How does the translation not only translate but *interpret* the original? Do you feel there are any subtle shifts in emphasis from one text to the other? Are there any points at which you feel that the translation has helped you read the original? Or is there anything in the original that you would want to explain to a reader who knew only the translation? Is there something in the translation that strikes you as effective, yet unwarranted by the original?

Issues of translation take on yet still other dimensions in film, for there we do have visual cues that don't depend on words. For that matter, we have sounds (theme music, background noises like the roar of a crowd, the barking of a dog, the ringing of a bell) not tied to a specific language. Sometimes, these elements are so richly textured and suggestive that we feel we experience the film without even keeping up with the subtitles. Other times, however, we're painfully aware of how much we must be missing. There is a clever scene in Sophia Coppola's *Lost in Translation* (2003) that gets at this difficulty. The protagonist, Bob Harris (an aging actor played by Bill Murray) listens without understanding to lengthy instructions offered in an energetic fashion by the director of a television commercial in the making. Bob turns to his translator, who offers the briefest of orders. The exchange that follows comically underscores a serious theme about human communication that runs through the whole film.

TRANSLATOR: He want you to turn, look in camera. OK?

BOB: That's all he said?

TRANSLATOR: Yes. Turn to camera.

BOB: Right. Does he want me to turn from the right or from the left? (*Another lengthy and animated exchange between the director and the translator leaves* BOB *waiting for an answer.*)

TRANSLATOR: Right side. With intensity.

BOB: Is that everything? It seemed he said quite a bit more than that.

Bob is frustrated, for he knows that so many words spoken with such energy in one language cannot be reduced to the few words in the language he understands. He's left groping for something that is surely missing. He's left responding back with the most reductive of phrases: "OK."

Bob's predicament is one many of us have shared in a very specific way while watching a film in a language we do not know. On occasion, after several lengthy lines of spoken dialogue that we cannot follow, we see a scant few words on the screen as subtitles. Like Bob, we believe there must be much we are missing. And it's likely we are right. But we should not give up on foreign films as unwatchable. Once again, we need to remember that we can deal with only what our education and experience allow us to deal with. We don't want to demand of the subtitles something they cannot supply. And in most films, we'll still have a great deal to respond to. In fact, sometimes our deficiencies in language force us to be especially attentive to an actor's physical gestures, expressions, or vocal tones. And we may better appreciate matters of editing, cinematography, or dramatic structure that operate separately from dialogue. If you've ever watched a movie on an airplane flight without purchasing the headphones, you may have had the feeling that much can be learned about the art of film by experiencing a film in silence. So, in dealing with works of art in a foreign language, don't too easily let yourself feel lost in translation.

Watching a dubbed film is another way around language problems. But dubbing presents its own difficulties. We've all seen how the words of one language just don't fit the vocalizations of another language; when the movements of the mouth are out of synch with the sounds we hear, the results are distracting. And there are the poor dubbing jobs in which the physical qualities of a voice simply don't match the physical presence of the person on-screen or voice tones are not matched with the performer's gestures. Dubbing perhaps lends itself best to comedy—oftentimes unintentional comedy. Woody Allen's first full-length film was, in fact, an extended play on bad dubbing. In *What's Up, Tiger Lily?* (1966), Allen simply took a hard-boiled B movie produced in Japan, threw out the original sound track, and imposed his own clumsily dubbed and ridiculous dialogue in English. In some ways, his film made points similar to Twain's appropriation of Hamlet's soliloquy. The ridiculous quality of *What's Up, Tiger Lily?* helps us understand something of the ridiculousness of all inept translations. More important, Allen (like Coppola with *Lost in Translation*) points out the real difficulty of moving from one cultural framework to another.

## MODELING CRITICAL ANALYSIS: TOM STOPPARD, THE FIFTEEN MINUTE HAMLET

William Shakespeare's *Hamlet* is a notoriously unstable text. Even though it is considered to be one of the greatest works by one of the greatest writers, no written record of Shakespeare's original work survives. So, what do we mean when we discuss *Hamlet*? There is evidence that a play fitting *Hamlet's* description was performed in about 1601. In 1603, a version of *Hamlet* appeared in print, apparently based upon an actor's memory of the lines. Some scholars believe that this actor played the minor part of Marcellus, because all of his lines are rendered perfectly, and the text tends to vary considerably from other editions whenever Marcellus is not in the scene. As incomplete and imperfect as this text may be, it can't be dismissed. After all, we have no clearly authoritative alternative. And the 1603 version surely offers insight into the actual production of the play; this is how an original actor experienced *Hamlet*. What the actor from this early production of *Hamlet* thought to record in this first edition may not be a complete text, but it represents what stood out to him—a particular participant from a distant time we seek to recover as best we can.

It's important to remember that the entire process of recording a play in textual form is always problematic. A play is designed to be performed. Unlike a book, a play takes place on a specific stage with a specific set of actors performing to a specific live audience. Even when different productions use the same script (not by any means a given), every performance of the play is different from every other performance simply because it is live theater; actors forget lines or ad lib, the audience laughs in different places, and the weather outside changes the conditions in which this play occurs. Those in charge of a specific production don't necessarily see themselves obligated to the words the author gives them. Would a pared-down version of *Hamlet* command a bigger audience?

Later in 1603 or early in 1604, another version of the play appeared: the second quarto. This one was about twice as long as the previous edition and advertised itself as "according to the true and perfect coppie." If we are to believe this claim, this edition of the text comes from Shakespeare's own copy of the play. This may be a more accurate reflection of what the playwright wrote down, but it may not account for any changes to the play that came about as the play was actually performed. It would be naïve to assume that Shakespeare never revised a play after seeing how it unfolded onstage.

Another version of *Hamlet* appeared in the first complete works of Shakespeare in 1623 the first folio. This script apparently comes from the notes that the playhouse put together (but never used) to prompt actors who forgot their lines in production. It is shorter than the second edition but also includes some material that is not in the longer second edition.

Most modern editions of the play combine material from the second quarto and the first folio; as a result, we usually read a *Hamlet* that is longer than either of these editions. It is striking to realize we have no evidence that this *Hamlet* ever existed in Shakespeare's lifetime. A performance of this "complete" play lasts about four hours, whereas the short first quarto lasts about two. Almost every production of the play edits the version we typically read in some way. Every staged or filmed version of the play must contend with critics who compare text to production and complain that a failure to adhere to the original somehow undermines the integrity of the work. Critics can and should complain, of course, about omissions or revisions that don't make dramatic or thematic sense. In the case of Shakespeare, though, it is problematic to assume that there is a single, true standard to which we can all refer.

Tom Stoppard plays with these critical problems in *The Fifteen Minute Hamlet* by giving us a prologue that catches at bits and pieces of famous lines, a ten-act play that manages to cover essential actions, and then an encore that reduces *Hamlet* further still. Instead of one play in four hours, we have one play performed twice and have what seems a "greatest hits" prologue thrown in for good measure. The effect is a frantic comedy that responds to a long-standing critical problem What is it that makes *Hamlet Hamlet*? Huck Finn listening to "Hamlet's Immortal Soliloquy!!" is satisfied with high-blown phrases that sound grandly important. Theater for Huck is all about posing. He doesn't bother to demand sense. He doesn't even demand plot. Stoppard is asking, What do we demand? Is it plot? Is it the characters? Is it the language? Is it some aura of specialness that is realized in performance? At what point do editorial changes make the play into something different? Something less? In the first quarto, for instance, Hamlet's famous soliloquy begins "to be or not to be, aye there's the point." Is this enough to destroy the play? It is possible that Shakespeare originally wrote the line that way; what does it mean if we say that it doesn't sound Shakespearean?

## Using the Production and Reproduction of Texts to Focus Writing and Discussion

As we study texts, we can keep in mind some general lessons from the various schools of criticism:

- What are the specific details of the language and structure of the text? How is our interpretation rooted in these details?

- How can we unlock meanings within a text rather than look for a single definitive reading?

- What are the historical and cultural contexts of this text? How do these contexts lend to our understanding of this text, and how does this text help us understand these contexts?

- What information do we have about the development of this particular text? How is the version that we are reading different from some original version of the text? How are these differences significant or interesting? Who has been responsible for the different versions? Can we trace some genealogy of the evolution of this text?

## Experiencing Literature through Writing

1. How do the physical properties of a text shape our interpretation of that text? This is a comparative exercise. Find at least two versions of the same text. Blake's poem "A Poison Tree" (p. 314), for instance, looks quite different on the page that he prepared than as it would appear on a page in a typical textbook.

   a. Describe the specific differences that you see.

   b. How are these differences significant?

   c. How do they change the nature of the text? Remember that even a reproduction of Blake's page is out of context here—it is not surrounded by the rest of the pages that he created, and we have not reproduced the size and quality of the paper that Blake originally selected.

2. How is a particular text part of the culture that developed it? This question is one that works nicely for examining different productions of a particular play. Because each production begins with a script that is fairly stable, each difference within the production becomes material for our discussion. How do these differences help us make specific claims about the culture in which this play was produced? We must remember that every artist who is involved in any production has some individual artistic consciousness, but as we look at productions from different eras, we will identify specific details as representative of that era. The various film images of *Oliver Twist* (p. 323) that we have included in this chapter offer an example of the sorts of comparisons that we might make within this question.

3. How does a particular cultural reading of a text contradict our close reading of that text? This is a more complex question, but working to explain the apparent contradiction can result in a very rewarding discussion. In this question, we look for an interpretation of the text that we can support with specific details from within the text. Then, we look at the cultural context of the work. For instance, a text that states "all men are created equal" becomes problematic when juxtaposed with the fact that the author was himself the owner of slaves. The goal in this paper is not simply to point out that there is a contradiction. We must explain why that contradiction is interesting. What does it tell us about this text or this culture that this apparent contradiction might be tolerated?

# 18 An Orientation to Research

## Why Should I Use Sources?

## How Do I Find Them?

## What Material Do I Document?

We have maintained throughout this book that critical writing involves an extension and a deepening of the literary experience. The experience starts with our reading of a literary work or our viewing of a film. But it deepens as we engage with others in conversation. When we come to class, we hear what others have been thinking. We might take some of these ideas in and make them part of our own understanding. We are often prompted to argue and, through argument, more clearly understand our own responses. Perhaps we modify or enlarge our sense of the text or even discover a new set of questions to ask about it. By the end of a good class discussion, our ideas about the work we are studying have become far more complex, far more interesting, and much closer to something that we might want to develop in an essay. The conversation has helped us deepen our literary experience.

When we do research, we are looking for the sort of inspiration and insight that we get from a good class session. With research, though, we have more time to think about our responses. We don't need to respond quickly to participate, as we sometimes do in discussions. In addition, the material that we find will probably be more carefully formulated than anything presented in class; a good article can even model the sort of writing we strive for in our own essays. Still, we don't simply accept the published work of scholars and critics. We modify, contest, enlarge, and apply ideas we come across as readers, just as we do as participants in a discussion. We test reactions of others against our own experience of a work. When we turn to our own writing, we seek to bring the voices of others into the conversation we've joined; we also seek to contribute to that conversation.

## WHY WE USE SOURCES

Some people view writing a "critical essay" as completely different from writing a research paper. The critical essay is seen as the analytical response of an individual; the research essay, as a compilation of opinions. This distinction is built on a big mistake. Analysis isn't done in a vacuum. And research involves much more than mere data gathering; it involves a process of active reading and thinking. So, this chapter should be read as an extension of (not a break from) the chapters that precede it.

False divisions between criticism and research lead writers to weak positions in relation to materials they gather. Sometimes we hear students speak of "plugging in" quotations or "sticking in" some facts; we want to use instead "integrating," "relating," and "weaving in." Good critical writers go beyond a mere display of materials; they see and use their research in the context of an argument they themselves shape. A "good" quotation, a "meaningful" summary, a "relevant" fact can only be good, meaningful, or relevant as it relates to a carefully defined point. We need to use sources, not let sources use us. Writers use research to support their points; to put it another way, research serves a purpose the writer has defined. Either way, the writer is in charge.

It's also important to think specifically about what "support" might mean. In some instances, a writer might enlist the support of a critic whose argument "backs up" the new discussion very directly. In such cases, writers essentially invoke the authority of others to confirm their own insights. But more often, writers define a particular aspect of a larger argument and apply that aspect to a specific point they want to make. Note how the following writer uses insights not only of those who write specifically about the paper's main subject—Nathanael West's *The Day of the Locust*—but of the Shakespearean critic A. C. Bradley. The writer carefully leads into and follows each reference so that none of the references feel out of place in relation to the main point of the passage. The writer has integrated, not "plugged in," research. Note also that the references aren't just to words (quotations) but to ideas as well.

> With the riot at the end of the novel, West releases the potential energy and violence of a city (and perhaps a country) full of broken dreamers. The fantasy of Hollywood has been sold to them and it has disappointed. Nasty, ugly, and completely vacuous, Hollywood, with the machinery of

its vast studios, has pushed its self-perpetuating plaster dream onto America. Kingsley Widmer examines the scope of Hollywood's failure as a dream factory and what it means for the double-crossed.[1] No one is more betrayed than one who has been cheated by false dreams. This representation of Hollywood as the purveyor of a bastardized art form that conveys powerfully corrosive effects (it even corrupts dreams!) is central to understanding West's novel. West ultimately sees Hollywood as the cheater, the force that rips off people who live there. In fact, as Lavonne Mueller notes, *The Day of the Locust* "was originally called The Cheated."[2]

When we conceptualize the novel as a story of "the cheated" rather than the story of Tod [the protagonist], *The Day of the Locust* begins to take on truly tragic proportions. The type of tragedy however is not traditional. As defined by A. C. Bradley, the classic Shakespearean form of tragedy "is pre-eminently the story of one person, the 'hero,' or at most of two, the 'hero' and the 'heroine.'"[3] Bradley goes on to note that the actions of this central character are the source of the tragedy. The stories of each of *The Day of the Locust*'s characters are merely minor tragedies in and of themselves, and their actions have little effect on their fates; but through the patching together of a tapestry of circumstance and torment, West begins to create a sense of communal tragedy. Hollywood has seduced an enormous number of suckers with its empty dream, and the losses are measured in numerous lives wasted.

The writer of the passage has woven in ideas of others into a new fabric. Sometimes, such weaving involves a deliberate kind of counterpointing. In the passage, the writer uses Bradley's definition of Shakespearean tragedy to clarify a quite different kind of tragedy apparent in West's novel. Sometimes, the counterpoint is more blunt; one can support one's own idea by repudiating someone else's. Identifying and making explicit a disagreement can sharpen or emphasize a writer's contribution. Note how the writer of the following passage on H. G. Wells's *The Invisible Man* clarifies the interpretation by strongly rejecting another critic:

Alfred Borrello argues that the scientist Griffin represents a "god-man" in Wells's *The Invisible Man*. Borrello sees Griffin as one "dedicated to research for the good of his species but frustrated by the inability of his

---

[1] Kingsley Widmer, Nathanael West (Boston: Twayne, 1982).

[2] David Madden, ed., Nathanael West: The Cheaters and the Cheated: A Collection of Critical Essays (DeLand: Everett/Edwards, 1973).

[3] A. C. Bradley, Shakespearean Tragedy: Lectures on Hamlet, Othello, King Lear, Macbeth, 3rd rpt. (New York: Palgrave, 1992) 7.

fellowman to accept what lies outside of the familiar."[4] This interpretation completely ignores the signals Wells so carefully builds into Griffin's first person narration. Griffin reveals himself as a totally selfish man. He has no feelings for his father, his fiancé, or his friends. His work absorbs him, but not for the good that work may do; in fact, Griffin never once considers the "good of his species" as Borrello contends. On the contrary, it would seem that Griffin's disregard for the species is exactly what leads him to madness, murder, and death.

The main underlying lessons of the previous two examples is first, to always consider how a given piece may help us build our argument; and second, to always weave sources into the newly constructed fabric of ideas.

## SHAPING A TOPIC

There is, of course, no sense of effective "weaving into" if there is no plan for the design of a new fabric. It's important, therefore, in the early stages of the writing process to think carefully about what constitutes a topic. In the broadest sense, a topic is a subject. It is what a paper is about, what it addresses, what it concerns. That sounds simple enough. But critical writing is never simple. Writers don't pick topics; they *construct* them. Even in response to a specific assignment, a writer must set a topic's limits and establish a topic's significance. Framing the topic is a crucial step in the research process.

A good topic is first of all a doable one. If the scope is too large at the outset, the sheer weight of available materials will become overwhelming. A writer focuses on an aspect of a work; the entire work is too much. For example, *Hamlet* isn't a topic. A topic that might lead somewhere could be "Hamlet's methods of interrogation and detection." A doable topic must also be concretely grounded; it cannot be a large abstraction that remains detached from any particular evidence in a text. One could examine *Hamlet* closely and analyze specific lines or scenes where he questions and investigates. One could look for critical essays that address ways Hamlet searches for truth or seeks to confirm suspicions and so on.

To create and shape a topic, we suggest that you follow these guidelines:

- Be specific. No critical essay "covers" everything about a text; a good essay merely covers what it has promised to cover.
- Focus first on the main text. A topic cannot be cast as a purely abstract issue or as a large, independent historical event or condition. Keep in

---

[4] Alfred Borello, H.G. Wells: Author in Agony (Carbondale: Southern Illinois UP, 1972).

mind the paradox: the grandest ambitions generally result in the smallest papers, both in quality and in length. Grand ambitions are often a disguise for familiar generalities; they prompt summary and statement. However, a particular, concrete observation on a text (how it works, what it says, why it moves us) can help us develop ideas analytically and argumentatively.

- Define key terms. Definition provides a way to get at a precise yet full sense of a subject. Your definition will be much more specific than anything that we might find in any dictionary. What might "interrogation" mean in relation to Hamlet's exchanges with Claudius and Gertrude? Exactly how is it that he plays the detective role given that the ghost has offered clear testimony of the murder in the first act?

- Think of how your topic sets up an argument—a thesis, a contribution to a conversation. Don't settle for writing "about" a topic; press forward to an assertion you need to back up, a point you need to explain.

# HOW TO FIND SOURCES

The writer who has a topic in mind and a sense of how to use information to explore the topic is usually the researcher who enjoys looking for sources. The search for sources is a treasure hunt—a chance to browse through libraries, archives, databases, troves of information. But the sheer wealth of available material in even a modest library can make looking intimidating.

You might think you can avoid the library, given the wealth of material available online. But as mentioned in Chapter 14, each online source has its own kinds of limits. In classrooms around the world, students are generating the same sort of writing that you may be now preparing to create. In the past decade or so, students have been able to post their work online. So, too, have many others with some interest in literature and film (fans, casual readers, independent scholars, and so on). Some of this writing may be quite good, but much of it is still in a fairly early stage of the revision process, and some is quite simply not worth attention. When you do your research, try to find writing that is at least a level or two higher than you think that you are able to produce. You want to learn to use materials that offer a more complex thesis than you might have thought of. Look for a work that uses other sources to create a combination of works different from what you would have put together.

Remember too that carefully chosen sources help establish the authority of your own work. Generally, it is best to pick articles or sources that have been published by a reputable press. Because at least a few people who have professional knowledge in the matter have read the material and have acknowledged that it has some value, the publication indicates that the source might be appropriate for your analysis. There is no avoiding it; you do need to use the library. An important trick here is learning to use your library's online catalogue system as well as the best available databases. Catalogue systems will differ, so do take the time to become familiar with how your library has organized the material it contains. But a few general words of advice will likely apply to most. Any online search can begin by author/title searches when you happen to know author and title. But also test out "key word" searches. This requires a little imagination, but you'll find the misses and hits will help you sharpen ways you define your topic as well as ways others categorize broad topics. Most systems build upon the Library of Congress Subject Headings. You'll begin to note those headings as you experiment with your own key words, but you need not rely on guessing. Most online systems have search commands that allow you to check Library of Congress headings. And don't be afraid to ask librarians for help. They will respond to your general questions and needs in terms of the specific systems in operation at your institution.

Armed with call numbers, you'll need to find the physical book itself. Libraries of higher education generally use the Library of Congress cataloguing system to organize their collections. You will find literary studies in the "P" section of the library. As you browse through the shelves, you can see how the organization works. If you look at a call number, it is fairly simple to determine some useful information about the work. Every book has a unique Library of Congress call number. For instance, *The Complete Works of William Shakespeare*, fourth edition, edited by David Bevington, has the LC number PR2754.B4. The "PR" indicates that this is a work of English literature; "2754" falls within the range of PR2199–3195, which contains works from the English Renaissance (1500–1640). The letter after the period indicates the last name of the author or, in this case, the editor of the text. It is not necessary to memorize any of this information, but it may be useful to have an overview of the "P" section (or languages and literature division) of this system, because it will help you navigate the aisles in the book stacks:

| | |
|---|---|
| P | Language and Literature |
| P | Linguistics |
| PA | Classical Philology (Greek and Latin) |
| PB | Modern European Languages, Celtic Languages |
| PC | Romance Languages |
| PD | Old Germanic and Scandinavian Languages |
| PE | English Language |
| PF | Dutch, Flemish, and German Languages |
| PG | Slavic Languages and Literature |
| PH | Finno-Ugrian, Basque Languages & Literature |
| PJ–PL | Oriental Languages |

| PM | American Indian and Artificial Languages |
| PN | Literature, Literary History and Collections |
| PQ | Romance Literature |
| PR | English Literature |
| PS | American Literature |
| PT | German Literature |
| PZ | Children's Literature |

As you work with this system, you will find sections of the stacks relevant to your search. Browse through those shelves to find books and journals related to your research. Many journals specialize in literary studies. You can find journals that focus on literature in general, on British literature, American literature, literature from different time periods, and literature by a specific author. If you are searching for an idea and you are writing about Shakespeare, browse through a shelf of *Shakespeare Quarterlies*. As you look through the tables of contents (we have reproduced a sample on the next page), you will see the range of articles that scholars have generated just in a single quarter on the subject of this single playwright.

A number of us use libraries that are not rich in these resources. But all schools subscribe to databases that make this library experience available. Although there is an enormous body of material on the web that does not exist on paper in any library, many published articles in volumes on library shelves can be accessed online. Even students at the richest libraries can do much of their research online. In fact, the table of contents in the previous list comes from one of those databases. The important thing is not whether you find material online or in print but that you've found material that has gone through a serious review process and has been published by a scholarly press or organization.

Once you have gathered some materials for review, you'll need to approach them effectively. Read the writing about the literature with the same attention that you read the primary literature.

- Read for understanding—what does the work mean?
- Remember that the author is going to have some main idea—what is that idea?
- In what ways might that idea inspire controversy?
- Does the author mention any others who might disagree with the argument? (Read one or two of these other authors if possible.)
- Can you apply this argument to anything beyond the work in question? For instance, can you see how the argument might apply to another work that you have been reading this term?
- To what extent does the author introduce factual information into the analysis? Does that information have any bearing on your own topic?

# SHAKESPEARE QUARTERLY

Published for the Folger Shakespeare Library
in association with
The George Washington University
by The Johns Hopkins University Press

| VOLUME 57 | 2006 | NUMBER 1 |
|---|---|---|

Table of Contents, *Shakespeare Quarterly* 57 (2006)

Often, you will not learn any new information from reading a piece of criticism. Instead, you are looking for some new insight, some different way of looking at the work that you have been reading. Many times an article will put a work into a different context that you might not have considered before you began your own writing.

# GIVING APPROPRIATE CREDIT: THE ISSUE OF PLAGIARISM

We often value ideas as we value other possessions. Our society considers ownership an important aspect of our relations with things and with other people. We own electronic devices, cars, and houses, and we face anxiety because we would like to own more and don't want anyone to steal what we have. Even the less materialistic like to own the ideas that they have created. If any of us have an idea, no matter how mundane—where to go for dinner, a nice turn of phrase in conversation, a suggestion for some music that we have discovered—we know how annoying it can be to have someone else take the credit for our original thought. Most of us try to give appropriate credit whenever we can. But, as we have been discussing throughout this book, it may be difficult to determine where any idea has been created. We have been thinking about ideas as subjects in the ongoing conversations that we are describing here. Our ideas come from what we read, from what we watch, and from the conversations that we have. With all of these stimuli, it gets increasingly difficult to establish a clear pedigree for every idea that we put to paper. Anyone who writes, though, needs to know when it is necessary to cite sources. Sometimes the rules are pretty obvious.

The poet Neal Bowers was shocked when he read the following poem by David Sumner (Jones).

**David Sumner (Jones)**

## Someone Forgotten (1991)

He is too heavy and careless, my father,
Always leaving me at rest-stops, coffee shops,
Some wide spot in the road. I come out,
Rubbing my hands on my pants or levitating
Two foam cups of coffee, and I can't find him          5
Anywhere, that beat-up Ford gone.

It's the trip itself that blinds him,
black highway like a funeral ribbon
leading to the mesmerizing end,
his hands like Vise Grips on the wheel                        10
and following, until he misses me,
steers wide on the graveled shoulders,
and turns around.
This time he's been gone so long
I've settled in here—married, built a house,                 15
started a family, stopped waiting to see him
pull into the driveway though the wind
sometimes makes a highway roar high up
in the branches,
and I stop whatever I'm doing and look up.                    20

Compare that poem to the following poem that Bowers had written a few
years earlier. Look for the specific similarities. Find the differences. It is
appropriate to evaluate the work here as well—set the differences side by
side—which are the better poetic choices? Can you explain why?

**Neal Bowers** (1948– )

# Tenth-Year Elegy (1990)

Careless man, my father,
Always leaving me at rest stops,
Coffee shops, some wide spot in the road.
I come out, rubbing my hands on my pants
Or levitating two foam cups of coffee,                        5
And can't find him anywhere,
Those banged-up fenders gone.
It's the trip itself that blinds him,
black highway like a chute
leading to the mesmerizing end,                               10
his hands locked dead on the wheel
and following, until he misses me,
steers wide on the graveled shoulders,
turns around.
This time he's been gone so long                             15
I've settled in here—married,
built a house, planted trees for shade,
stopped waiting to see him pull into the drive—

though the wind sometimes makes a high-way roar
high up in the branches, and I stop                                        20
whatever I'm doing and look up.

We should all be able to agree that there is so much similarity between these
two poems that it is not possible that one could have been written without the
other. The fact that most words are the same, that the different words are
synonyms for the words that have been left out, that the line changes don't do
much but disrupt the poetry here suggests that it was inappropriate for David
Sumner (who sometimes calls himself David Jones) to try to claim credit for
this poem. It does not belong to him. The fact that he republished this same
poem multiple times, with different titles and similarly superficial changes
under different names should help convince us that he is the sort of true
plagiarist that all rules against plagiarism were designed to foil. We should be
happy to hear that Bowers wrote up his experiences with this plagiarist and
exposed him to ridicule. What is wrong with what Jones did? He has taken
Bowers's personal remembrance of his father, disfigured the poetry, and
published the mangled result under various aliases. Bowers writes about the
extent to which this violation has infected even his own reminiscences about
his father. The main reason to avoid plagiarism is to avoid this sort of
violation.°

A straightforward definition of **plagiarism** is "intellectual theft—the
unacknowledged (or inadequately acknowledged) use of the words and/or
ideas of another." This leads to a simple moral directive: Do not cheat! But
like many simple directives, this one doesn't always address the real issue.
Most students have no desire to cheat, yet they remain confused and worried
about exactly what professors expect them to document. Something beyond
the plain demand that one do his or her own work is clearly needed, for much
gray lurks about the edges of the definition just offered.

The writing that you do for your classes is a kind of personal expression.
Even though you may feel that it seems more artificial than what you might do
naturally, you are turning in this writing so that you can join and contribute to
conversations about the texts you've been assigned. Your instructor has a
professional obligation to read your work carefully in relation to the work of
other students. Such review (and ultimately assessment) takes considerable
time and energy. If you do the sort of lifting that Jones has done when you turn
in your writing, you are violating the relationship that you have with your
instructor; you've pretended to contribute to a conversation but haven't in fact
offered your own work. You should be aware of how easy it is to see through such
deceptive practices. To anyone who has read student papers for any length of

---

° Neal Bowers, <u>Words for the Taking: The Hunt for a Plagiarist</u> (New York: Norton, 1997).

time, stolen papers in which a few words have been changed from a website or a published source might as well be announced by flashing neon lights.

The best practice for student writers is to acknowledge sources as much as possible within your writing. You will actually be given greater credit for tracing your ideas back to other sources than you will get for simply generating "original" ideas out of thin air. After all, a big part of research is figuring out where ideas have come from, tracing conversations back to their sources, and understanding how the ideas of others can be used to build a new set of ideas.

## Experiencing Literature through Considerations of Plagiarism

One intriguing exercise in this sort of tracing game is the subject of Shakespeare. In many of his plays, Shakespeare borrowed material from sources. Most of his stories were stories that had appeared elsewhere. For instance, much of the historical material in his plays about Rome came from Thomas North's translation of Plutarch's *Lives of the Noble Grecians and Romans*. Here is an excerpt from Plutarch that describes Portia, the wife of the Roman senator Brutus. Brutus has been approached about joining in the conspiracy to murder Julius Caesar, and he is considering whether he believes it to be a moral enterprise, but his reflections are all private. Portia complains that because she is his wife, he should share his concerns with her.

**Plutarch** (ca. 46–127)

## from Lives of the Noble Grecians and Romans

(ca. AD 100, trans. Thomas North, 1579)

This Porcia, being addicted to philosophy, a great lover of her husband, and full of an understanding courage, resolved not to inquire into Brutus's secrets before she had made this trial of herself. She turned all her attendants out of her chamber, and taking a little knife, such as they use to cut nails with, she gave herself a deep gash in the thigh; upon which followed a great flow of blood, and soon after, violent pains and a shivering fever, occasioned by the wound. Now when Brutus was extremely anxious and afflicted for her, she, in the height of all her pain, spoke thus to him: "I, Brutus, being the daughter of Cato, was given to you in marriage, not like a concubine, to partake only in the common intercourse of bed and board, but to bear a part in all your good and all your evil fortunes; and for your part, as regards your care for me, I find no reason to complain; but from me, what evidence of my love, what satisfaction can you receive, if I may not share with you in bearing your hidden griefs, nor to be admitted to any of your counsels that require secrecy and trust? I know very well that women seem to be of too weak a nature to be trusted with secrets; but certainly, Brutus, a virtuous birth and education, and the company of the good and honourable, are of some force to the forming our manners; and I can boast that I am the daughter of Cato, and the wife of Brutus, in which two titles though before I put less confidence, yet now I have tried myself, and find that I can bid defiance to pain." Which words having spoken, she showed him her wound, and related to him the trial that she had made of her constancy; at which he being astonished, lifted up his hands to heaven, and begged the assistance of the gods in his enterprise, that he might show himself a husband worthy of such a wife as Porcia. So then he comforted his wife. ▪

Shakespeare creates a dramatic scene out of these incidents in his play *Julius Caesar* (Act II, Scene 1). Note how he adds a life to Portia's character by developing details within her conversation. She begins with specific incidents that lead to her complaint. Find the specific sections of her speech that contain the ideas and even the words from the Plutarch selection. Think now about any differences between what David Jones has done in his "rewriting" of the Bowers poem and what Shakespeare has done in his rewriting of North's Plutarch.

**William Shakespeare** (1564–1616)

# from Julius Caesar (1599)

PORTIA:  Nor for yours neither. You've ungently, Brutus,
  Stole from my bed: and yesternight, at supper,
  You suddenly arose, and walk'd about,
  Musing and sighing, with your arms across,
  And when I ask'd you what the matter was,
  You stared upon me with ungentle looks;
  I urged you further; then you scratch'd your head,
  And too impatiently stamp'd with your foot;
  Yet I insisted, yet you answer'd not,
  But, with an angry wafture of your hand,
  Gave sign for me to leave you: so I did;
  Fearing to strengthen that impatience
  Which seem'd too much enkindled, and withal

Hoping it was but an effect of humour,
Which sometime hath his hour with every man.
It will not let you eat, nor talk, nor sleep,
And could it work so much upon your shape
As it hath much prevail'd on your condition,
I should not know you, Brutus. Dear my lord,
Make me acquainted with your cause of grief.

BRUTUS:  I am not well in health, and that is all.

PORTIA:  Brutus is wise, and, were he not in health,
He would embrace the means to come by it.

BRUTUS:  Why, so I do. Good Portia, go to bed.

PORTIA:  Is Brutus sick? and is it physical
To walk unbraced and suck up the humours
Of the dank morning? What, is Brutus sick,
And will he steal out of his wholesome bed,
To dare the vile contagion of the night
And tempt the rheumy and unpurged air
To add unto his sickness? No, my Brutus;
You have some sick offence within your mind,
Which, by the right and virtue of my place,
I ought to know of: and, upon my knees,
I charm you, by my once-commended beauty,
By all your vows of love and that great vow
Which did incorporate and make us one,
That you unfold to me, yourself, your half,
Why you are heavy, and what men to-night
Have had to resort to you: for here have been
Some six or seven, who did hide their faces
Even from darkness.

BRUTUS:  Kneel not, gentle Portia.

PORTIA:  I should not need, if you were gentle Brutus.
Within the bond of marriage, tell me, Brutus,
Is it excepted I should know no secrets
That appertain to you? Am I yourself
But, as it were, in sort or limitation,
To keep with you at meals, comfort your bed,
And talk to you sometimes? Dwell I but in the suburbs
Of your good pleasure? If it be no more,
Portia is Brutus' harlot, not his wife.

BRUTUS:  You are my true and honourable wife,
As dear to me as are the ruddy drops
That visit my sad heart

PORTIA: If this were true, then should I know this secret.
    I grant I am a woman; but withal
    A woman that Lord Brutus took to wife:
    I grant I am a woman; but withal
    A woman well-reputed, Cato's daughter.
    Think you I am no stronger than my sex,
    Being so father'd and so husbanded?
    Tell me your counsels, I will not disclose 'em:
    I have made strong proof of my constancy,
    Giving myself a voluntary wound
    Here, in the thigh: can I bear that with patience.
    And not my husband's secrets?
BRUTUS: O ye gods,
    Render me worthy of this noble wife!
    (*Knocking within.*)
    Hark, hark! one knocks: Portia, go in awhile;
    And by and by thy bosom shall partake
    The secrets of my heart.
    All my engagements I will construe to thee,
    All the charactery of my sad brows:
    Leave me with haste.
(*Exit* PORTIA.)

Shakespeare was not writing a paper to be graded for a class; in fact, the *Julius Caesar* that we quote here comes from the text that was published in 1623, about seven years after Shakespeare's death, so we can't hold him responsible for our standards in citation. If this Shakespeare excerpt were a student paper, though, a direct acknowledgment of North's Plutarch would seem essential.

# INTEGRATING SOURCES INTO WRITING: WHAT WE DOCUMENT

Accurate and full citation of sources is an essential part of writing in college. To omit or inadequately cite a source in an academic essay would be to undermine much of your own hard-earned authority. Think again of writing as conversation: a person who borrows the ideas of others without offering the slightest nod of recognition to those others will be seen, at best, as careless; at worst, as rude and dishonest. Thoughtful citation of sources should be understood not only as an ethical obligation but as part of the entire essay's effectiveness.

All citations show our general respect for others who might be part of our conversation. First, we acknowledge our debt to someone who has introduced us to some particular idea. Second, we offer a guide to anyone who might follow our thoughts to show them how they might have access to the thoughts that have influenced us. Precision is important here so that we don't frustrate those who follow our lead. Just as we would not like to chase after some source only to find that the author we are reading was careless enough to list the wrong volume, note the wrong page, or misspell the author's name, we must do all that we can to ensure that our own bibliographic entries are accurate. This is a map to the intellectual treasure that you have discovered. Be diligent as you record the directions. You might want to come back sometime as well.

## Quotation, Paraphrase, and Summary

It's an easy matter to understand that direct quotations must be written as such and cited: that is, place quotation marks around the quoted material—or set off long passages as block quotes—and note the source (specific forms will be displayed as this chapter progresses). But quotations are not the only things that must be documented: ideas require citation as well. When is an idea really someone else's? If plagiarism is intellectual theft, what constitutes protected intellectual property? How much documentation does a reader expect, want, and need?

We can start by illustrating different kinds of borrowings and the credit each requires or encourages. The following passage is from "*Frankenstein* and Comedy" by Philip Stevick:

*Frankenstein*, like early Gothic before it, like Kafka after it, and like a multitude of works of various periods, such a Melville's *Bartleby*, makes itself out of dream images told, but not fully elaborated, into rational and sequential art. The result is a narrative vehicle which allows a large measure of self-exposure, terror, pathos, and psychic pain to coexist with much absurdity, apparent ineptitude, silliness, and the risk that the whole enterprise will be brushed aside by the reader as making no claims on his mature scrutiny.°

Now consider the following two passages that were written with Stevick's work in mind:

1. Like the Gothic novels that preceded it, like Kafka that followed it, and like many other works including Melville's *Bartleby*, Mary Shelley's *Frankenstein* builds itself from dream images that never quite get

---

° Philip Stevick, "Frankenstein and Comedy," The Endurance of Frankenstein: Essays on Mary Shelley's Novel, ed. George Levine and U. C. Knoepflmacher (Berkeley: U of California P, 1979) 221-39.

fully expressed in an orderly or consciously controlled story. The rough narrative that results exposes private terrors of the self, psychic pain, and terror along with sheer nonsense and absurdity. It is no wonder that many mature readers are tempted to dismiss *Frankenstein* as unworthy of serious attention.

2. Philip Stevick maintains that *Frankenstein* seems closer to a dream than to a story. Dreams can be painfully self-revealing; but those same dreams can also be downright silly. Gothic novels and Kafka's stories share these wildly mixed qualities with Mary Shelley's work. Narratives such as these are sometimes difficult to take seriously (Stevick 231).

Passage 1 closely paraphrases Stevick—it follows his paragraph from start to finish and never strays far from the words he uses. It is, in fact, almost exactly the same length as the original. Yet the writer of passage 1 makes no mention of Stevick. A citation (a note or parenthetical reference) to Stevick at the close of passage 1 would be a small step in the right direction, but it would still *not* be enough. Such a note would acknowledge that the writer of the passage has used an idea of Stevick, but it would not spell out how heavily Stevick had been used. This first passage is an example of an inappropriate paraphrase; it would be considered plagiarism.

It's useful to make a distinction between two words that are often used as synonyms: **paraphrase** and **summary**. Think of a paraphrase of another writer's text as a superficial revision of that text; the writer of a paraphrase stays close to the logic, language, and length of the original passage (as illustrated in passage 1). In contrast, think of a summary of another's text as a thorough rewriting of that text (a rewriting wholly in your own language) in as brief a form as your purpose will allow. Paraphrase as defined here should *always* be avoided. If you feel you need to stay very close to the words of your source, quote those words exactly and be sure your reader sees it as a quotation. If you do not need to stay close to the words of the original, convey as briefly as possible the essential idea and signal your debt to that idea.

Passage 2 more effectively summarizes Stevick's original paragraph. It remains close to the original, but it is tightly focused. It is not stuck on the particular words and phrases of the original (close paraphrase sometimes suggests that the writer doesn't understand the original well enough to confidently separate from it). Stevick's name also leads off passage 2—a good idea when the summary runs beyond a sentence or two. The parenthetical reference at the end of this passage gives the reader a clear sense of Stevick's contribution. The summary is neatly framed by the first mention of Stevick and the closing parenthetical reference. A reader who came across passage 2 in a critical paper would understand the degree of indebtedness that is expressed.

## Distinct Insights and Common Observations

Any full summary or particular use of Stevick's insights must give credit to Stevick. But what happens when one reads Stevick yet uses nothing in particular that would easily be identified as distinctly his? Consider this third passage that only vaguely echoes Stevick:

3. *Frankenstein* evokes the disturbing and mixed sensations of dreams: terror, confusion, anxiety. The most absurd images in the novel (or in a dream) must be understood as part of a wider fear.

These two sentences move far away from the original and might not seem to owe Stevick any recognition. Not only is this passage significantly shorter than the original but it is wholly rewritten. Indeed, it doesn't borrow anything from Stevick that a good reader could not get from the novel itself. If this is summary at all, it is the barest sort. In effect, this third passage reduces the distinct contributions of Stevick to a very general, much-discussed level. Many critics before and after Stevick have associated *Frankenstein* with dreams. Why should Stevick get any special credit here for what seems a common insight? The writer has chosen to give him none.

You *must* cite distinct contributions or insights but need not credit observations that many writers have shared in common. But you could move beyond such a grudging attention to rules and consider a more generous policy. Citations, after all, do not merely serve to protect you from charges of plagiarism; citations have a positive purpose as well. Strange as it may seem, academic readers are interested in citations. A note at the end of the third passage would gracefully inform these readers of Stevick's article; it would display the writer's research without diminishing in any way the writer's own contribution. Indeed, if Stevick were found to be an especially significant voice in the conversation about *Frankenstein*, then the writer might want to mention him. This could be done quite easily:

Stevick observes that *Frankenstein* evokes the disturbing and mixed sensations of dreams: terror, confusion, anxiety. The most absurd images in the novel (or in a dream) must be understood as part of a wider fear (Stevick 231).

These options posed by the third example illustrate the fact that rules cannot always suffice; good judgment about what the audience wants, along with a sense of fairness, comes into play when deciding whether to cite a source or not.

## Common Knowledge

You do not need to cite material that is **common knowledge**. But there may be some confusion about this deceptively simple rule, for *common knowledge* does not mean "what most people know"; in the context of academic writing, *common knowledge* means "knowledge that the readership could acquire or confirm from any one of several sources." For example, most people do not know that Edith Wharton's *The Age of Innocence* received a Pulitzer Prize in fiction in 1921. But a writer would not need to cite a source for this bit of information. Any academic reader could, if necessary, check for its accuracy without the slightest difficulty; in source after source, the information will be the same: Edith Wharton's *The Age of Innocence* did receive a Pulitzer Prize in fiction in 1921.

As always, sound judgment and good faith must help you through less clear-cut examples. For even seemingly plain facts should be cited when they invite controversy, depend upon interpretation, or are not widely established. A professor might want to know, for example, where a student discovered that the Pulitzer Prize advisory board overrode the recommendations of the nominating jury in awarding William Styron's *The Confessions of Nat Turner* the Pulitzer in 1968. This is not a disputed point, nor is it something that a particular scholar "discovered"; but not many references to Styron's award are this detailed. Such facts are not easily checked and should therefore be documented.

# HOW TO CITE

Questions about the form of documentation often cause students more anxiety than the substance of their papers. This is both unfortunate and unnecessary. In literary studies, the Modern Language Association (MLA) has established guidelines for writers of research papers. With a little time and patience you can master the essential forms of citation. The following section displays model forms (based on the *MLA Handbook for Writers of Research Papers*, Sixth Edition) that you can use as checkpoints in preparing a research paper.

## Parenthetical References in the Text

Debts are signaled in a text by parenthetical references (not numbered notes).° A sentence in a paper about Tolstoy that uses an idea from Yi-Fu

---

° The traditional format for citations is the footnote. The superscripted numbers, lines at the bottom of the page, and the abbreviated Latin were all part of the indoctrination process to separate true scholars from the mere dabbler. Anyone who could construct a typed manuscript that successfully accommodated a footnote deserved a higher degree. Now that we all use word-processing programs that can easily create elegant footnoting for us, the practice of using a footnote for every citation has been largely abandoned, especially for the types of academic papers that you will be producing. Generally, footnotes are places where an author can include additional informational details that are not essential to the main argument of the paper.

Tuan's *Space and Place* might look like any one of the following:

Yi-Fu Tuan notes that Tolstoy's sense of space subtly registers "profound political and moral commitments" (57–58).

Tolstoy's sense of space subtly registers "profound political and moral commitments" (Tuan 57–58).

Yi-Fu Tuan claims that Tolstoy's sense of space registers deeply felt commitments (57–58).

The information within parentheses at the end of each sentence indicates that a discussion of Tolstoy's sense of space appears on pages 57 and 58 in a book or article by Tuan. Tuan's name does not appear within the parentheses in the first and third examples because the sentence itself makes it clear that Tuan is referred to. Information about Tuan's book will appear in a separate section: a "works cited" list.

## The Works Cited List

The Works Cited list starts on a separate page at the end of the essay (such a list must *not* be subdivided by theme or types of research materials). There, under "Tuan, Yi-Fu," the reader will find full bibliographic information on the work cited in the text:

Tuan, Yi Fu. Space and Place: The Perspective of Experience.
    Minneapolis: U of Minnesota P, 1977.

Throughout the list, entries are alphabetized based upon the first word in the entry. The following examples model common bibliographic forms. Note that there is an underlying structure among the entries that refers to books or parts of books. All begin with the name of the author of the piece cited (last name first). All include full titles and complete publishing information. Names of editors or translators are placed after the title and before the publishing information.

### A book by a single author

Bonca, Teddi Chichester. Shelley's Mirrors of Love: Narcissism,
    Sacrice, and Sorority. Albany: State U of New York P, 1999.

Moore, Rod Val. Igloo among Palms. Iowa City: U of Iowa P, 1994.

The content and the order here (as in all entry forms) are the important elements. Included are the author's name (last name first), the book's title, the place of publication, the publisher (note that for University Press, the abbreviation UP is standard form), and the year of publication. On the first line, the last name is flush on the left margin, and any subsequent lines are indented five spaces. All citations in MLA format must be double-spaced.

### A book by more than one author

Gilbert, Sandra M., and Susan Gubar. The Madwoman in the Attic: The Woman Writer and the Nineteenth-Century Literary Imagination. New Haven: Yale UP, 1979.

Note here that the second author's name is not in reverse order; there is no need to put her last name first because the listing is not alphabetized under her name. Use a comma between the names.

### An article in an edited collection

Glatthaar, Joseph T. "Black Glory: The African-American Role In Union Victory." Why the Confederacy Lost. Ed. Gabor S. Boritt. Oxford: Oxford UP, 1992. 133-62.

The author's name is listed first, then the title of the article (in quotation marks), followed by the title of the book in which it is collected (italicized or underlined), the editor of the book, the place of publication, publisher, and year of publication. Note that the pages placed at the end of the entry denote where the article begins and ends in the book. The parenthetical reference in the text of the paper itself would specify only the pages relevant to the point being made.

### A translated book

Foucault, Michel. Discipline and Punish: The Birth of the Prison. Trans. Alan Sheridan. New York: Pantheon, 1977.

### Literary texts, editions

Collins, Billy. "Thesaurus." The Literary Experience. Ed. Bruce Beiderwell and Jeffrey Wheeler. Boston: Wadsworth, 2008. 109-92.

Dickens, Charles. Great Expectations. Edited by Edgar Rosenberg. New York: Norton, 1999.

Griffin Wolff, Cynthia. Introduction. Ethan Frome. By Edith Wharton. New York: Signet, 1986.

Stein, Gertrude. "Three Portraits of Painters." <u>Selected Writings
    of Gertrude Stein</u>. Ed. Carl Van Vechten. New York: Vintage, 1972.
    327-35.

Zimmerman, Mary. "Metamorphoses." <u>The Literary Experience</u>. Ed.
    Bruce Beiderwell and Jeffrey Wheeler. Boston: Wadsworth, 2008.
    1548-80.

Sometimes you will need to cite a periodical article. These entries will
differ from entries for books, but the most common forms are not complicated.

**An article from an academic journal**

Rader, Ralph W. "The Dramatic Monologue and Related Lyric Forms."
    <u>Critical Inquiry</u> 3 (1976): 131-51.

List the author's name, followed by the title of the article (in quotation
marks), the title of the journal (italicized or underlined) in which it appears,
the volume number of the journal, the year of publication, and the inclusive
pages. Most academic journals paginate continuously throughout a volume. A
volume represents the collected issues of single year (usually four issues). The
first issue of the year starts on page 1. The second issue starts on the page
following the last page of the previous issue, and so on throughout the year.
This makes it unnecessary to note which issue the article appears in. But if
each issue of a volume begins at page 1, simply cite the volume number as
above, then add a period and the issue number:

Tafoya, Eddie. "Born in East L.A.: Cheech as the Chicano Moses."
    <u>Journal of Popular Culture</u> 26.4 (1993): 123-29.

In your research, it is very likely that you will find this information in a
database rather than by looking in an actual journal. It is still essential that
you record the information that we have included here, but you must also
include information about the database that you have used, including the date
that you accessed the information:

Dobson, Hugh. "Mr. Sparkle Meets the Japanese Yakuza: Depictions
    of Japan in <u>The Simpsons</u>." <u>Journal of Popular Culture</u> 39.1 (2006):
    44-68. <u>Project Muse</u>. UCLA Lib., Los Angeles. 15 July 2006
    <http://www.muse.jhu.edu>.

**A newspaper article**

Heffley, Lynne. "L.A. Critics are Crazy for <u>Crazy, Tavern</u>."
    <u>Los Angeles Times</u> 8 Mar. 1994, valley ed.: F1.

If a specific edition is listed in the masthead, include that after the date (not all editions of the same paper contain the same material). If no edition is listed in the masthead of the paper's first page, place the colon after the date and before the section and page number of the article cited.

### An article from a weekly or monthly magazine

Gopnik, Adam. "The Big One: Historians Rethink the War to End All Wars." The New Yorker 23 Aug. 2004: 78–85.

Many magazines and newspapers have their own websites on which they post material that appears in their printed publications. Here is a listing for a short story that appears in this format:

Munro, Alice. "The View from Castle Rock." The New Yorker 29 Aug. 2005. 6 Dec. 2006 <http://www.newyorker.com>.

### A review

Appelo, Tim. Rev. of Three Tall Women, by Edward Albee. The Nation 14 Mar. 1994: 355–56.

The review above was not titled. Note the description of the contents in place of the missing title. Of course, if there is a title, use it. If you find the article online, include information about the database that you used to access it:

Ebert, Roger. "Throbbing Pain Overwhelms Pleasures in Basic Instinct 2." Chicago Sun-Times 31 Mar. 2006: NC29. ProQuest. Long Beach City College Lib., Long Beach. 23 Apr. 2006 <http://www.proquest.umi.com>.

### A film

The Purple Rose of Cairo. Dir. Woody Allen. Perf. Jeff Daniels, Danny Aiello, and Mia Farrow. Orion, 1985.

Works Cited

Bonca, Teddi Chichester. Shelley's Mirrors of Love: Narcissism, Sacrifice, and Sorority. Albany: State U of New York P, 1999.

Dickens, Charles. Great Expectations. Ed. Edgar Rosenberg. New York: Norton, 1999.

Dobson, Hugh. "Mr. Sparkle Meets the Japanese Yakuza: Depictions of Japan in The Simpsons." Journal of Popular Culture 39.1 (2006): 44–68. Project Muse. UCLA Lib., Los Angeles. 15 July 2006 <http://www.muse.jhu.edu>.

Ebert, Roger. "Throbbing Pain Overwhelms Pleasures in Basic Instinct 2." Chicago Sun-Times 31 Mar. 2006: NC29. ProQuest. Long Beach City College Lib., Long Beach. 23 Apr. 2006 <http://www.proquest.umi.com>.

Foucault, Michel. Discipline and Punish: The Birth of the Prison. Trans. Alan Sheridan. New York: Pantheon, 1977.

Gilbert, Sandra M., and Susan Gubar. The Madwoman in the Attic: The Woman Writer and the Nineteenth-Century Literary Imagination. New Haven: Yale UP, 1979.

Gopnik, Adam. "The Big One: Historians Rethink the War to End All Wars." The New Yorker 23 Aug. 2004: 78–85.

Munro, Alice. "The View from Castle Rock." The New Yorker 29 Aug. 2005. 6 Dec. 2006 <http://www.newyorker.com>.

The Purple Rose of Cairo. Dir. Woody Allen. Perf. Jeff Daniels, Danny Aiello, and Mia Farrow. Orion, 1985.

Rader, Ralph W. "The Dramatic Monologue and Related Lyric Forms." Critical Inquiry 3 (1976): 131–51.

Stein, Gertrude. "Three Portraits of Painters." Selected Writings of Gertrude Stein. Ed. Carl Van Vechten. New York: Vintage, 1972. 327–35.

Tuan, Yi Fu. Space and Place: The Perspective of Experience. Minneapolis: U of Minnesota P, 1977.

Zimmerman, Mary. "Metamorphoses." The Literary Experience. Ed. Bruce Beiderwell and Jeffrey Wheeler. Boston: Wadsworth, 2008. 1548–80.

Inevitably, we find works that do not fit into the general categories outlined here. Remember that these citation rules are entirely systematic, that it is possible to figure out the appropriate format even if your specific instance is not covered precisely.

Many databases that you will use in your school's library have a special function that will let you download information about each source in MLA format. This is a useful tool for gathering most of the bibliographic information that you need, but it will not complete the Works Cited page for you. Most databases will leave blank spaces that you need to fill in yourself. You must look closely at each entry to ensure that it conforms to the style that we have described in this section.

## Using Research to Focus Writing and Discussion

- What issues are of interest to me as I read this work?
- What ideas have I found in this article?
- How does this article point to a larger critical conversation that I might want to join?
- How have I given credit to every source I have used in this paper (and at the same time, how have I indicated the research that I have done to develop my ideas)?
- Where have I given full and accurate citation of my sources? A writer can join a critical conversation only by acknowledging other participants in the conversation.
- Have I displayed every quotation as a quotation and cited it appropriately? Distinct ideas, contested or little-known facts, and particular insights must also be cited, even if they are cast in the writer's own words. A careless writer might mistake notes from another source as an original thought. Even though this might be an easy mistake to make, it is never acceptable.
- Have I avoided including extended paraphrases? Remember that we are writing our own papers, not summaries of articles. It is important to return again and again to our own point, to show how this outside information is relevant to the current discussion.

# Appendix

## STUDENT MODEL ESSAY COLLECTION

Each of the essays on the following pages engages a literary text closely. Each grounds an argument in the evidence the text offers. Each may lead you back to your own reading with a richer sense of how the poem, play, or story works. But our main purpose here is not to supply still more critical commentary on texts. We want you to read these works from the perspective of a practicing (and perhaps inexperienced) critical writer. These essays then are offered as models of thoughtful critical analysis. Although we've stressed the importance of process throughout our book, it seems reasonable to display what product might result. After all, you'll be asked to write critically, and you'll be evaluated on your command of that task.

To learn from these models, you'll need to read carefully and actively. No model can or should provide a simple formula for success. How do these authors establish or define a topic? How do they signal the significance of their approach? How and why do they use the examples that they use? Do they explain carefully? How do they shape and follow an argument? Do you find the argument provocative or convincing? You'll also need to consider how you can achieve some of the qualities evident in these pieces (or how you can surpass any weaknesses you detect). How can you practice and build upon the strategies evident here as you write in response to a literary text?

We begin with the paper on "Harlem" by Langston Hughes by high-lighting general organizational and argumentative qualities evident in some fashion in most critical essays. Observe a few very basic features as you read the model essay below:

- The title of the paper serves a purpose; it informs the reader of the broadly drawn subject (in effect, "this paper is about Hughes's 'Harlem'") and hints at the writer's insight regarding the subject (this poem moves from thinking to doing).

- The essay opens with a broad description of an important aspect of the poem and, thereby, establishes a topic.

- The essay moves toward an argument (the third, fourth, and fifth sentences) as the topic is more narrowly defined.

- The first paragraph ends with a thesis. The analysis will have a point to make, an argument to develop.

- The paragraphs that follow include evidence from the text to back up the thesis. Those paragraphs slow down our reading or unfold the text in relation to the thesis.

- The thesis serves as a controlling or leading idea; the writer's notion of how Hughes builds pressure, intensity, or tension can be charted in the first sentence of each paragraph. These sentences also provide a full sense of transition from one point to the next.

In the papers that follow the one on "Harlem," we call attention to more particular features evident in the specific model.

## STUDENT MODEL ESSAY
## LANGSTON HUGHES, HARLEM

Smith 1

Leslie Smith
Professor Jones
EN 112
September 25, 2006

From Thoughts to Deed in
Hughes's "Harlem"
Langston Hughes's "Harlem" opens by asking a
big question that generates a number of what may seem
very uncertain responses. The only sentence in the
poem, after all, that does not end with a question mark
begins with a "maybe." But "Harlem" ultimately

moves well beyond uncertainty. The question that ends
the poem builds forcefully from the questions that
precede it. Indeed, it seems more like a statement
that implies a soon-to-be-realized event. In
"Harlem," Hughes transforms passive speculation
into a feeling of concrete and immediate action.

In the first stanza (or verse paragraph), which
responds to the initial question ("What happens to a
dream deferred?"), Hughes offers a series of similes
as tentative possibilities. All are unpleasant
possibilities. The likeness he draws makes us taste
and smell frustration. Hughes links an abstract
feeling to physical sensations, but the similes keep
us aware of the mind's intellectual play. Similes,
after all, clearly announce with "like" or "as"
comparisons of things we don't usually place side by
side; we are asked if a dream might dry up "like" a
raisin, ooze "like" a sore, smell "like" spoiled
meat, or crystallize "like" old syrup. The very fact
that these possibilities are grouped together in one
stanza strengthens the sense that they exist as
possibilities. The speaker is thinking over feelings
associated with deferred dreams; no one of those
feelings seems any more likely or powerful than any
other.

The collective force of these possibilities
taken altogether, however, generates some sense of
increasing intensity through sheer repetition. The

four questions that pose themselves in such vivid physical images of death and decay come to a full stop at the end of the stanza. It seems that this line of possibilities must be exhausted, as dry and stuck as crusted sugar on the top of a syrup bottle.

The thinking process marked by similes and questions gathers great potential force in the next two lines; these lines are set off from the rest of the poem and express the burden of passive speculation. Again the possible result of deferring dreams is cast in the form of a simile. And again, there is a tentative quality to the idea. The "maybe" that begins the sentence keeps the reader in a state of uncertainty that seems appropriate for a poem largely about uncertainty. But here the separation of one possibility from the others as a group indicates that this feeling of weight is an inevitable result of the collected frustration. And for the first time, the tentative quality is not directly expressed as a question.

These shifts mark an increasing pressure in this two-line stanza. The pressure logically anticipates a breaking point. The first responses concerned taste and smell, but here the feeling is of sheer heaviness. At some point, something must happen. By setting off this simile in its own little stanza, Hughes makes the reader pause fully over it and sense the burden of oppression. And by separating this one simile, Hughes

Smith 4

builds a greater sense of focus. No more are we
quickly listing a series of possibilities. We are, on
the contrary, moving to a point that seems too heavy
to bear.

The closing line also ends with a question mark,
but clearly we have arrived at something much closer
to a flat statement of fact. We sense that this idea
carries with it the force of an impending action.
Hughes emphasizes the final line first of all by
separating it from the rest of the poem. We have
moved from the series of the first full stanza to
the heaviness of the two-line load, to the focus of
a single short line. Furthermore, that line is
italicized. Its final word rhymes precisely with
the last word of the line that precedes it (the other
rhymes in the poem chime in on alternate lines). This
nearness and the precision of this rhyme emphasize a
kind of abrupt decisiveness.

But perhaps the most dramatic change in mood
from tentative thoughts to substantial deeds is
marked by a shift from simile to metaphor; in this
final line, Hughes drops the "like" that has kept
us speculating about possibilities. The final idea is
expressed through metaphor. A deferred dream will not
result in something "like" an explosion. Rather, it
is a bomb that <u>will</u> explode. Hughes ends the poem by
suggesting that violent revolution builds from
frustration.

# STUDENT MODEL ESSAY
# SUSAN GLASPELL, TRIFLES

A major theme of Susan Glaspell's *Trifles* can be used to underscore an essential concern of critical writers: small things matter, or to put it another way, the "big picture" may obscure the significance of specifics. The paper that follows attends to small things to demonstrate how Glaspell leads the audience to sympathize with a character who never actually appears on the stage. For example, the writer notes Glaspell's title and explains how that title signals the play's central irony. The writer also pays attention to how the setting (the cold and depressing farmhouse) serves to clue us in on the quality of the lives lived there. So before moving to the first line of dialogue, a case is being made about how Glaspell controls the way we respond to her characters and to the distinct tone of specific words (think, for example, of the attitude behind the District Attorney's reference to Mrs. Peters as a "housekeeper").

Marquez 1

Joseph Marquez
Professor Wheeler
EN 101
October 9, 2006

Glaspell's Control of the Audience's
Sympathy in Trifles

Susan Glaspell's Trifles doesn't take long to
get to a point where many murder stories end: the
audience knows almost immediately "whodunit." The
audience also knows "why" in a general sense (the
murdered man was cruel to his wife). The only mystery

Marquez 2

involves the specific motive the District Attorney
needs to discover so that he can aggressively pursue
the case against his suspect, but this mystery
doesn't really move the action forward. This play
is more about character than plot. Ironically,
the audience cares most about a murderer who never
appears onstage, never speaks in her own voice, and
never says a word in her own defense. Glaspell makes
the absent Mrs. Wright the emotional center of the
play.

The title of the play strongly directs the
audience's sympathy. The "trifles" suggest a
profound difference between the men who have power
and the women who have no power. The County Attorney
thinks that trifles are the concern of women. As a
man, he believes he has really important matters
to busy himself with. But as the action unfolds,
we become aware that significance is a matter of
imagination, sympathy, and intelligence. These are
qualities that the male officials or authorities in
this play do not possess.

The County Attorney, for example, is looking for
something big but completely misses many leads. He
abruptly cuts off Hale, the man who found the body,
just as Hale begins to comment upon the relationship
Mr. and Mrs. Wright shared. He also assumes that the
dreary quality of the home (ill kept and gloomy)
reflects directly upon the character of the

"housekeeper," not upon the quality of life she had been forced to live. The Sheriff registers nothing beyond the County Attorney's narrow emotional limits; he merely reinforces the sense that authority either breeds insensitivity or grows from insensitivity.

The women who come along with the County Attorney and the Sheriff supply a clear counterpoint. They are, no less than Mrs. Wright, subject to the condescending attitudes of those in charge. The official investigators find it amusing that Mrs. Hale and Mrs. Peters notice small things when something as important as a murder has happened. They seem to think that attention to small things indicates a woman's inability to deal with big concerns. The audience feels distant from this rude and self-satisfied attitude and sympathizes with the women.

Mrs. Hale and Mrs. Peters are the first characters the audience sides with, but Glaspell employs dramatic irony to extend sympathy to Mrs. Wright. The County Attorney and the Sheriff are totally oblivious to what the audience and the women know about Mrs. Wright's married life. The gloomy farmhouse does not reflect bad housekeeping but a miserable, cramped, and lonely existence. It is clear early on that Mr. Wright has controlled that existence. He doesn't want a phone because he doesn't want human contact. According to Mr. Hale (an apparently sensitive man, but not one in power),

Marquez 4

Wright never cared about what his wife might think or
want. Wright doesn't want to talk to his wife any more
than he wants to talk to anyone.

For a time, Glaspell keeps the audience a small
step ahead of Mrs. Hale and Mrs. Peters. They are
in a way also controlled by the men around them. The
women do not easily refute the assumptions the men
make about their value. Mrs. Peters is, in fact,
apologetic about the men's rudeness. She accepts
their self-importance on their terms: "Of course
they've got awful important things on their minds."
Just at this point the audience is once again strongly
cued to look for the importance of small things.
Mrs. Hale notices the sewing Mrs. Wright had left
unfinished and observes that the good stitching
abruptly turns ragged. This small detail is evidence
that Mrs. Wright became powerfully upset at a
particular time. But Mrs. Hale keeps the insight to
herself. Significantly, Mrs. Hale resews the bad
portions to cover for Mrs. Wright. This act reveals
the depth of her sympathy for the accused woman and
the contempt she begins to feel for the Sheriff and
the County Attorney.

From this point on, the audience participates
with Mrs. Hale in her defiance of authority. And the
stakes in that defiance grow ever higher, for the
motif of the singing and silence brings Mrs. Wright
forward as the real victim. Mrs. Hale had already

remembered Mrs. Wright as the youthful Minnie Foster.
Minnie once dressed in "pretty clothes," acted in
a "lively" manner, and sang in the church choir;
but that was thirty years ago (enough time for great
rage to build over the loss of joy). After Mrs. Hale
notices and repairs the ragged sewing, Mrs. Peters
comes across the empty birdcage with the broken door:
"Someone must have been rough with it." Mrs. Hale
pursues her chain of memories: Mrs. Wright "used to
sing real pretty."

All singing is in the past tense. Minnie Foster,
Mrs. Hale tells us, was "like a bird." But the Wright
home is marked by silence. The contrast foreshadows
the dead bird the women discover in Mrs. Wright's
sewing box. Its symbolic meaning is clear; Minnie
Foster was like the singing bird, but John Wright had
silenced her just as he had killed the bird. Mrs.
Wright must have seen her fate in the dead bird and
lashed out in her sense of loss.

All is in place in the closing scene for the
audience to identify with the women's efforts to
protect Mrs. Wright from further injustice. The
audience is aligned in particular with the poised and
able Mrs. Hale. Her final action (snatching the box
from the stunned Mrs. Peters just before the officials
arrive) speaks eloquently of her complete empathy
with Mrs. Wright. By this final point, it is an empathy
the audience shares with her.

# STUDENT MODEL ESSAY
# ERNEST HEMINGWAY,
# HILLS LIKE WHITE ELEPHANTS

The essay that follows responds to Ernest Hemingway's "Hills Like White Elephants." Notice that the author shapes a fairly specific approach to the story: the way Hemingway establishes a perspective on his characters through their response to the environment. This kind of focus is essential; a writer cannot take on everything about any work. But notice, too, that the author does not artificially restrict the topic. Insights about point of view, imagery, symbol, metaphor, and plot all support the thesis. Finally, observe how the author weaves in (and documents) relevant ideas of other critics.

Wright 1

Robin Wright

Professor Beiderwell

FN 110

October 16, 2006

Setting and Character in "Hills Like
White Elephants"
Ernest Hemingway's "Hills Like White
Elephants" conveys in clipped dialogue and spare
descriptions a conflict between an American man and
his girlfriend, Jig. It would seem that the objective
narrator gives the reader only the most impersonal
glimpse at their relationship. Even the specific
issue that generates the conflict, abortion, is only
suggested indirectly. Yet Hemingway strongly guides

the reader's sympathies. He contrasts the perspectives of his two main characters on the surrounding environment in order to define their moral substance.

The story opens with the couple seated in a shaded area at a train station; they stare across a hot, dry land. This is not a comfortable moment for either of them. When Jig states that the barren hills look like white elephants, the American retorts that he has never seen one. His answer is abrupt, and the girl's comment, "No, you wouldn't have," sets off a round of arguments. Something is going on here besides a dispute over the color of the mountain range.

After much frustrating, strained, and indirect discussion, the girl gets up and walks to the end of the station. From there she looks to the opposite side. By the river she sees trees, lush growth, and fields of grain. Her vision stands in sharp contrast to the dried landscape of the hills that were viewed from the other side.

Jig's fresh vision provides perspective on the man's persistent advice: "They just let the air in and then it's all perfectly natural" (726). The man presses Jig to have an abortion without any regard for what she may feel. His selfish manner hurts her more than the advice itself. He simply does not see the

Wright 3

green world that she sees. Nor does he have a clue
as to what Jig feels about the state of their
relationship.

Jig and the reader understand what the American
man misses. Mary Dell Fletcher argues that Jig's
vision of the river Ebro aligns her with the forces of
life:

> The life giving landscape is now
> associated in Jig's mind with ... a
> fruitful life where natural relations
> culminate in new life and spiritual
> fulfillment, not barrenness and
> sterility, as represented by the dry
> hills. (17)

Fletcher may overestimate the importance
Hemingway lends abortion itself; Hemingway seems
more interested in a feeling than he is in the
morality of a specific decision. But the contrasting
attitudes toward abortion do reveal the general
conflict Jig identifies in relation to her lover. One
thing is clear: she feels lonely because she realizes
how remote the man is from her.

By conveying the differing perceptions these
characters have of the landscape, Hemingway helps
the reader see each character fully. Gary Brenner
notes that Hemingway's use of the setting allows
readers to "overhear" the dialogue correctly and

note Jig's "depth of character and [the man's] shallowness" (198). Once we pick up the cues from the ways the characters see the world, we become alert to even the subtlest signs of the man's controlling tendencies and Jig's more vital being. The following dialogue illustrates the point:

> "Doesn't it mean anything to you? We could get along."
>
> "Of course it does. But I don't want anyone but you. I don't want anyone else. And I know it's perfectly simple." (728)

The man first claims that the child means something but quickly shifts the plural pronoun "we" to the singular forms "I" and "you" (Smiley 9). He refuses to accept the implications of Jig's use of the plural pronoun.

This profound separation is also made plain in the images Hemingway employs to mark off physical spaces. The bead curtain in the bar, for example, forms a barrier between the man (who stays inside) and Jig (who steps outside and reflects upon the landscape). The curtain emphasizes the perceptual differences between Jig and her lover: the image of the curtain becomes, in effect, a metaphor of all that divides them in their relationship.

The man's self-absorption is something Jig comes to understand and accept. She sees things between her

Wright 5

and her lover plainly; there is no reason for her to talk to a man who cannot listen. The climax of the story marks her absolute recognition of the state her relationship has come to: "Would you please please please please please please please stop talking" (728). In light of this obvious anger, Jig's terse words at the story's conclusion must be read as ironic:

> "Do you feel better?" he asked.
>
> "I feel fine," she said. "There's nothing wrong with me. I feel fine." (728)

Obviously, she does not feel "fine," but she recognizes what is wrong. She has gained insight about herself and the man who has been her lover and understands very well that the man will not achieve any similar insight.

Jig even knows that the man will not understand the implications of her statement. He will take these words straight because he wants to believe that everything is fixed or "fine." The mysterious smile that precedes Jig's final words indicates her superior understanding. Perhaps this superior level of insight explains why it is that only Jig has a name; her lover is merely "the American." Everything is broken between these two characters, and only she and alert readers of Hemingway's story are in on that knowledge.

Wright 6

Works Cited

Brenner, Gerry. "A Semiotic Inquiry into Hemingway's 'A Simple Inquiry.'" Hemingway's Neglected Short Fiction. Ed. Susan F. Beegel. Ann Arbor: UMI Research P, 1989. 195-205.

Fletcher, Mary Dell. "Hemingway's 'Hills Like White Elephants.'" The Explicator 38 (1980): 16-18.

Hemingway, Ernest. "Hills Like White Elephants." The Complete Short Stories of Ernest Hemingway: The Finca Vigia Edition. New York: Simon, 1987. 211-14.

## STUDENT MODEL ESSAY
## EDNA ST. VINCENT MILLAY, I, BEING BORN A WOMAN AND DISTRESSED

A woman writing (or at least publishing) a love sonnet in the sixteenth century would be a near impossibility. Things did not change much for generations. Given this background, one might understand how a woman writing a love sonnet in the early twentieth century would be conscious of the gender assumptions the form had acquired over time. Such a woman might, for example, write a sonnet that critiques the gender assumptions that sonnets had long perpetuated. The brief essay reprinted here arises from the context of this conversation on the sonnet and socially defined gender roles. The essay specifically addresses Edna St. Vincent Millay's sonnet "I, Being Born a Woman and Distressed."

Note how the writer pays close attention to the function of rhyme and how the rhyme scheme signals an underlying tension in the piece. Note also that the writer doesn't just say that Millay employs a conversational tone but explains how and for what purpose Millay creates a conversational tone. Notice also how the writer uses specific terms aptly (for example, *enjambs*, *turn*, *caesura*, *complication*).

Greene 1

Hunter Greene
Professor Smith
EN 102
October 30, 2006

Millay's Self-Assertive Sonnet
    Edna St. Vincent Millay must have read many love
sonnets by men and heard many proclamations of love by
men. She must have become tired of such romantic
expressions. Millay lived in an age when women were
still usually portrayed as passive objects of men's
desire. "I, Being Born a Woman and Distressed"

suggests that she found these portraits one-sided, presumptuous, and stifling. Millay defies conventional ways of defining courtship roles by writing a sonnet about sexual desires from a woman's frank, self-assured perspective.

Millay raises in the octave what would be in the context of her time a shocking problem: the female speaker admits to experiencing sexual desires that occasionally overpower her rational faculties. Millay enjambs many of her lines to achieve a conversational tone, but the inner war between brain and body is highlighted by an intricate rhyme scheme that is not characteristic of everyday conversation. The "a" rhymes suggest qualities of thought or reason: "kind," "find," "designed," "mind." The "b" rhymes communicate physical, passionate impressions: "distressed," "zest," "breast," "possessed." The caesura before "possessed" (the last word of the octave) emphasizes the speaker's problem: the speaker feels desire but confesses that her desire often leaves her vulnerable.

The turn in this sonnet, however, is decidedly away from possession. The full pause that closes the octave allows the speaker to catch her breath and assert herself against any mistaken ideas the man (the implied audience) may have about her frank admission. The speaker does not regret her feelings but forcefully spells out what the audience should not think: don't think I have strong feelings still, she states; don't think I have any pity for anything you might feel now; don't even think I'm interested in anything about you. Millay's speaker strongly dismisses any romantic, soft conventions of love even as she admits to the power of her own sexual nature.

Conventional poetic ideas of how a woman should act, or what a woman should feel, have of course been established and perpetuated by men. Millay's speaker dismisses male attitudes in general and her former lover in particular; the split personified by "stout blood" and "staggering brain" is only one temporary, internal breakdown. It does not mean that she will feel anything like enduring love, respect, or even interest in the future for the object of the passion.

The complication that loomed so large in the octave is thus put in perspective in the sestet. The speaker accepts her passion and will neither apologize for it nor be forever ruled by it. Men have, after all, had the liberty of that "love them and leave them" attitude all along. Millay announces the final dismissal. She emphasizes the resolution by telling the man that she will "make it plain."

The final two lines make the message very plain indeed; in fact, these lines seem very unpoetic: "I find this frenzy insufficient reason / For conversation when we meet again" (13-14). Millay

Greene 4

conveys a mundane, spoken quality (the enjambment
here is important); the word choice seems cold
("insufficient reason"); and no marked rhythm is
discernible. But the matter-of-fact, conversational
tone these lines express is in perfect accord with
the poem's logic. The speaker acquires control by
claiming her feelings and expressing her desires
without apology.

# Glossary

**Abstract:**     Describing an idea, concept, theme, or feeling as opposed to a thing or person. In literary texts, as in analytical essays, abstractions must occasionally be grounded by particular examples. See **concrete.**

**Absurd:**     Characteristic of a vision in which meaning is drained from life. An absurdist work challenges the way we make sense of the world or the way we lend significance to events.

**Aerial view:**     See **high-angle shot.**

**Allegory:**     Serves to convey meaning through a narrative in which abstract notions are embodied and given life by concrete characters and actions. Usually, allegories set forth a lesson. See **didactic work.**

**Alliteration:**     Refers to the repetition of consonant sounds in words. For example, *woke to black flak.*

**Allusion:**     A reference within a text to some other text or bit of knowledge outside the text. Allusion involves the author's play upon what is assumed the reader's literary experience; a brief reference in one work to a passage or scene from another work is an allusion.

**Ambiguity:**     Uncertainty or multiplicity of meaning. Ambiguity involves suggestive qualities of expression as opposed to plainly directive statements. Ambiguity may also arise from statements in a single text that seem on the surface to possess contradictory implications or intents.

**Analogy:**     A comparison used to make a point. An analogy uses the likeness of two things to build a forceful argument. If the comparison seems strained or if it does not apply clearly to the point made, the analogy breaks down.

**Anapest:**     An anapest (anapestic foot) consists of two unaccented syllables followed by one accented syllable.

**Antagonist:**     The character set in opposition to the **protagonist.**

**Antistrophe:**     In classical drama, a part of the choral ode. While singing, the chorus would dance. According to some analysts, for the **strophe,** the chorus would move from left to right; for the antistrophe, they moved from right to left back to the original position. The two movements are identical in meter. See **strophe.**

**Apostrophe:**     Refers to the speaker's direct address to an absent person or to some abstract idea or spirit.

**Assonance:**   Consists of a similarity in vowel sounds, but the final consonants differ: *date/lake*. See **rhyme.**

**Atmosphere:**   Feelings invoked in the reader or viewer through **setting.** Gothic works are said to be heavily atmospheric.

**Auteur** theory:   Closely parallels notions of **new criticism.** *Auteur* theory identifies the director of a film as the creative center (*auteur* is French for "author"). Such a focus on the choices of a single maker gave critics a point of analytical focus. But this focus necessarily disregarded the essentially collaborative nature of filmmaking.

**Author:**   See **poet.**

**Background:**   The physical elements against which characters are set. In Caspar David Friedrich's *Woman in the Morning Light* (p. 60), the rolling hills, spacious fields, and rising sun are the background. Background can also suggest information supplied about a situation or a character from outside the immediate narrative. For example, in *Oedipus the King* the **chorus,** along with Oedipus's opening speech, supply information about the past and Oedipus's current situation that helps us understand the action that unfolds.

**Blank verse:**   Unrhymed verse in a prevailing **iambic pentameter.** Blank verse lends itself to serious subjects of lofty speech.

**Blending:**   The thorough mixture of genres. The *Buffy the Vampire Slayer* episode "Once More, with Feeling" adopts many conventions of a traditional material but also plays out as a horror story; elements of comedy and tragedy unfold together as well in this episode.

**Cacophony:**   A style marked by harsh, grating, hard sounds. Opposite of **euphony.**

**Caesura:**   A pause within a line of poetry. The word may be used to suggest a pause in any text that has built some sense of rhythm. A caesura may suggest a shift in mood, a turn to another subject, a characteristic of common speech, or any number of effects. Oftentimes, a caesura serves to foreground a word, idea, or moment.

**Canon:**   Refers to a body of works deemed (by experts/scholars) as worthy of critical study, as literature or art. Canonical works are seen as those works that a culture adopts and uses over time.

**Catharsis:**   The release of strong emotions (pity and fear) inspired by **tragedy.** Catharsis is presented by Aristotle as purgation or a cleansing. The audience feels the terror associated with a tragic end yet finds in the action an affirmation of values or life.

**Character:**   A person in a literary text/film/dramatic production.

**Characterization:**   The method of creating **character.** Authors may, for example, create character through **dialogue,** description, or narration (revealing character through actions).

**Chorus:**   A form of commentary in dramatic works that helps an audience contextualize, interpret, or judge the action that unfolds. In classical Greek drama, the chorus was sung by a group onstage in a highly formalized fashion.

**Cliché:**   An expression that has been greatly overused and through overuse has lost its original force or meaning.

**Climax:**   The turning point in a narrative. The point to which **tension** builds and at which must be released.

**Closed ending:**   An ending in which all the questions raised in the plot are answered. The reader senses that things have been neatly pulled together in a way that strongly ends the narrative. Detective stories typically are tightly closed.

**Colloquial:**   Casual language that reflects common usage and informal conversation. The language of everyday life.

**Comedy:**   At the simplest level, a work that ends in marriage (and thereby implies happiness, resolution, stability, continuity, and so on). Although comedies offer some sense of fulfillment, that fulfillment may be of a small sort. See **high comedy** and **farce.**

**Comic relief:**   A form of mixing comic elements in the midst of a **tragedy.** Comic relief diminishes tragedy. The term is often misused, for most such mixing of comic with tragic provides no relief. Indeed, a surprising disruption of the comic into a tragic action may well intensify—not diminish—the action.

**Common knowledge:**   *Not* what most people know, *but* what a reader or writer could acquire or confirm from any one of several accessible sources. Most people, for example, don't know the date of George Washington's death. But that date is common knowledge: several people could go to the library or look on the Internet and find the same information.

**Complication:**   A problem, difficulty, or question raised in a literary text. See **sonnet.**

**Composition:**   In film, the arrangement of objects within a frame seen from a particular **point of view;** more broadly, the arrangement of all elements within a single **scene** (lighting, movement, and so on). Composition can also refer to the arrangement of parts in a poem, play, fiction, or essay.

**Concrete:**   Relating to some thing or person that has a physical presence, to something we can touch, see, or hear, to something we know through our senses. See **abstract.**

**Concrete poetry:**   Poetry that is graphically set so that it takes the shape on the page of the thing it describes; in other words, the lines of the poem illustrate their own subject matter. Sometimes called **shape poetry.**

**Conflict:**   That which creates the **tension** that moves a narrative forward to its **climax.** Conflict arises from opposing forces. A character might be set in conflict with another character, or perhaps a social condition, or nature itself. A conflict could even grow from a single character's inner struggle.

**Connotation:**  What a word suggests that lies beyond what a word means in the strictest sense. Connotations may be complex, varied, and subtle, for they arise from a wide range of ever-changing associations. Compare **denotation.**

**Consonance:**  Strikes a similarity in the sounds of the final stressed consonant, but the preceding vowel sounds differ: *date/rite*. See **rhyme.**

**Context:**  Information from outside the text relevant to understanding the text. For example, it is important to know that Tennyson was Poet Laureate of Great Britain when he wrote "The Charge of the Light Brigade" (p. 252). He wrote, then, in an official position, not to question why the soldiers were asked to fight and die but to celebrate the fact that they did fight and die. The context for our own contemporary reading of this poem has changed dramatically.

**Contextual** or **situational irony:**  Contextual irony arises from circumstances or from coincidence (for example, a homeless person arrested for vagrancy on the street in front of a governmental housing and urban development office). See **irony.**

**Convention:**  An element that has become familiar through our reading or viewing experience.

**Couplet:**  A verse paragraph made up of two lines. See **stanza.**

**Cultural poetics:**  See **new historicism.**

**Dactyl** (dactylic foot):  Consists of an accented syllable followed by two unaccented syllables.

**Deconstruction:**  Posited notion that meaning is not fixed within a text but is both created and undone by a complex and ever-changing structure of words. Whereas new criticism sought a "best" or most complete reading of a text, deconstruction sought to revel in inconsistencies.

**Deep focus:**  In film/photography, a technique that allows all objects to remain clear—even those objects distant from the camera. Deep focus creates a sense of density, fullness, and sometimes activity; it does not direct or hold a viewer's attention to a particular place on the screen. See **shallow focus.**

**Denotation:**  The literal meaning of a word. The leading definition of a word one would find in a contemporary dictionary. Compare **connotation.**

**Denouement:**  Often suggests not only action that follows the **climax** but the explanation or resolution of what has happened. Denouement suggests an untying of a knot. See **falling action.**

**Depth of field:**  In film/photography, an extended range of focus. See **deep focus.**

**Detached observer:**  An observer who is not an active participant in the action he or she relates.

**Dialogue:**     Conversation between characters. Authors may through dialogue create the impression that characters reveal themselves in speech directly to the reader.

**Diction:**     Word choice. See **colloquial.**

**Didactic work:**     Literature intended to teach, to instruct readers in points of moral or social significance.

**Displacement:**     The overlaying of one generic mode upon another. See **blending.**

**Disruption:**     A break from what is expected; a deviation from an established **convention.** A familiar element that is revised or even reversed in a text; for example, Clint Eastwood disrupts the conventions of a western when he has his main character ride off not into the sunset but into a dark, rainy night.

**Dramatic irony:**     Dramatic irony signals a distinction between what a character knows and what an audience understands. In other words, dramatic irony arises at moments when the audience knows more than the character or characters that are part of the action. See **irony.**

**Dramatic monologue:**     A work in which a single speaker addresses an audience within a dramatic situation. Robert Browning's "My Last Duchess" (p. 76) is an especially good example of a dramatic monologue.

**Dynamic character:**     Character who changes over the course of a story. The change might be fundamental (the result, for example, of a transformative experience) or might be superficial (the result of new information).

**Editing:**     In film, the selecting, arranging, and organizing of **shots** to create desired effects. More broadly still, editing involves the integration of sound and image.

**End rhyme:**     Rhyme that falls at the end of the poetic line, the most common place for rhyming words.

**End stop:**     A full stop at the end of a poetic line.

**English** or **Shakespearean sonnet:**     A lyric poem of fourteen lines that lends itself to a tightly developed problem/response structure. The English sonnet often repeats the **complication** over the first twelve lines (three **quatrains**) and saves the **resolution** for the final two lines (**couplet**). See **sonnet.**

**Enjambment:**     Literally, a striding over. Enjambment involves the running of one poetic line into the next without pause. A line that strides over is enjambed.

**Epic simile:**     An extended and highly elaborate **simile.** Essentially, an epic simile carries on at length after the word *like* or *as* that introduces it.

**Episode:**     Suggests a single, continuous, and brief action that either stands alone or could be detached from a larger narrative.

**Episodic narrative/Episodic novel:**     An extended fiction made up of a **sequence** of episodes.

**Epode:** In classical drama, the third part of the ode (after the **strophe** and **antistrophe**), which completed the movement of the chorus with singing in unison at the center of the stage or altar. See **strophe** and **antistrophe**.

**Euphemism:** A deliberately indirect expression. A euphemism may arise from a sense of delicacy, politeness, or respect. Sometimes, however, a euphemism is employed to avoid truth or responsibility (for example, "collateral damage").

**Euphony:** A style marked by smooth, pleasing sounds. Opposite of **cacophony**.

**Expectations:** The result of a reader's previous literary experience. Someone, for example, who has seen many romantic comedies comes to expect the feuding couple to somehow realize at some point that they really can't live without each other. In conventional romantic comedies, the couple will indeed get together at the end—no matter how many misunderstandings they have along the way. In conventional works, expectations are met or satisfied.

**Explication:** Literally, an unfolding. Explication involves the close reading or analysis of a text. Through explication, one seeks to understand how a work achieves meaning and power, as well as what the meaning is. Explication can be thought of as a kind of slow-motion reading.

**Exposition:** A type of composition that centers on explanation (as opposed to argumentation, description, or narration). In relation to narrative works, exposition functions to introduce or contextualize the action that will unfold.

**Extrametrical:** Something that occurs within a **metric line** of poetry, like a pronounced pause, that is not accounted for by simple **scansion**.

**Extreme high-level shot:** See **high-angle shot**.

**Eye-level shot:** In film/photography, a **shot** taken from the same height as the subject. Such shots put the viewer on the same level as the subject.

**Fable:** A short story, usually with an explicit or implicit **moral,** that conveys some general truth through a fictional example. Talking animals are a frequent convention of the fable.

**Falling action:** The action that follows the **climax.** The action that releases **tension** built into the narrative and moves toward the work's conclusion. See **denouement**.

**Falling meter:** A **foot** in which the accent falls on the first syllable.

**Farce:** A form of **comedy** that sustains no **tension** that arises from the emotional complexities of **character**. A farce builds upon silly actions that require only superficial **resolution**. The complexities in farce are situational; complexities do not grow from depth or complexity of character. Television's *Seinfeld* is a good modern example of farce.

**Feminine rhyme:**   A rhyme of two syllables, the second unstressed. Also called a double rhyme. Such rhymes tend to create a light, quick effect.

**Feminist criticism:**   Seeks to gain insights largely obscured or bypassed by the men who have until recent decades dominated critical discussions. Feminists along with **new historicists** assume that a work of art (or a work of criticism for that matter) is a product not only of an author but of a specific culture.

**Figurative language:**   Any language that is used in ways that deviate from standard significance, order, or meaning.

**Figure of thought:**   See **trope.**

**Filmic rhythm:**   Patterns of movement, **composition,** and sound that work together in a film for a particular effect.

**First-person narrator:**   A story told from the perspective of one inside the story; that is to say, the narrator speaks as "I." A first-person narrator may be the **protagonist** of the story, but does not necessarily have that role. Dr. Watson in "A Scandal in Bohemia," for example, reports what he sees and hears of Sherlock Holmes's adventure, but Holmes himself is the protagonist.

**Flashback:**   A return in a narrative to an action that occurred in the past (that is, before the present action of the story).

**Flat character:**   A term used to describe a one-dimensional character. The term is often used negatively, but it is important to remember that characters have to be viewed in relation to how they function in the whole work. See **stock character.**

**Foil:**   A minor character that functions in a narrative to highlight characteristics of more significant and complex characters.

**Foot:**   The combination of one stressed and one or more unstressed syllables that constitutes the recurring rhythmic unit within the larger pattern of a poetic line.

**Foreground:**   In film, that which is in front of the screen, closest to the audience; usually the space where the main action occurs. Foreground also signifies the front of the stage in a dramatic production. More broadly, foreground (used as a verb) may suggest the way an author has highlighted an element for the reader/viewer to note as important.

**Foreshadowing:**   A hint about what will follow—a scene that prepares for action that is to come. In Edgar Allan Poe's "The Fall of the House of Usher," the crack in the foundation that the narrator notices as he first sees the house foreshadows the final collapse of the house.

**Formalist:**   See **new criticism.**

**Formula:**   The strict adherence in all elements of a work to the established **expectations** of readers/viewers. See **convention.**

**Fragment:**   A partial action. An action that suggests something larger left unexplored or unstated. A fragment could be a piece of a whole text, but it could also be an artistic device used to create feelings of mystery, for example, or to comment upon the impossibility of wholeness.

**Frame:**  The smallest element of a film: a single photograph that, strung together with many other photos in **sequence,** creates the illusion of movement. Frame can also suggest the boundary that surrounds the image. In a literary context, frame may also refer to the way a narrative or argument is set up or introduced. For example, Ursula K. Le Guin frames "The Ones Who Walk Away from Omelas" by inviting readers to create their own fantasy paradise. Once readers imagine that perfect world, Le Guin presents the terrible conditions required of such perfection. Conversely, in the film *The Wizard of Oz* the fantasy is framed by the mundane black-and-white world of Kansas.

**Free verse:**  Poetry that is not marked by any regular metrical scheme or pattern of rhyme. Free verse may achieve coherence through repeated images or through purposeful variation of line length.

**Full** or **perfect rhyme:**  Consists of the sameness of sounds in accented vowels and any consonants that follow: *date/fate*. See **rhyme.**

**Genre:**  Literary/artistic type or kind. Genre suggests the grouping of individual works into larger categories. The grouping can be made in various ways. For the sake of convenience, for example, a teacher might treat poems, prose narratives, plays, and films as genres. But it is usually best to define genres on the basis of more particular **expectations** an audience brings to a work.

**Haiku:**  A poetic form borrowed from a Japanese tradition. Haikus contain three unrhymed lines. The brevity serves to intensify emotions that find expression in what is usually a highly specific image.

**Hero/heroine:**  Sometimes considered the same as **protagonist,** but that word more strictly signals the character's function to lead the action. Hero/ heroine usually implies a moral prominence (the most admirable or sympathetic character in the narrative, the strongest force for good).

**Hexameter:**  A line of poetry made up of six feet. See **metric line.**

**High-angle shot:**  In film/photography, a **shot** taken from above the subject. A high-angle shot may be used to give the viewer a sense of power over the subject. Think, for example, of seeing a fallen boxer from the perspective of the boxer's opponent. An extreme high-level shot or an aerial view extends the logic of such shots further still by exaggerating the angle between camera above and subject below.

**High comedy:**  Develops from the emotional substance of complex **characters.** Oftentimes, high comedies press toward tragic possibilities that are barely averted. They also genuinely suffer for the mistakes they make before achieving happiness at the end.

**Hyperbole:**   Deliberate overstatement, exaggeration.

**Hypertext:**   Allows readers to access on a screen any variety of linked documents instantly, at any time, in any order. Hypertext is not bound to a text laid out on a page.

**Iamb:**   A metrical unit within a poetic line. An iamb consists of two syllables, the first unstressed and the second stressed. The iamb might consist of one word with multiple syllables (aTTEMPT) or multiple words (in LOVE).

**Iambic:**   The most common standard rhythmic unit (**foot**) in English poetry. See **iamb.**

**Iambic pentameter:**   A line consisting of ten syllables marked by prevailing **iambs.**

**Identification:**   The effect of close sympathy and understanding with a character in a literary work. If we identify with a character, we see something of ourselves in the character.

**Impersonal narrator:**   See **objective narrator** or **third-person narration.**

**Impressionism:**   The invocation of an immediate, subjective feeling created by the conditions of a particular moment. An impressionist painter, for example, doesn't paint an idealized object but an object in specific conditions of light (not a church, but a church seen from a certain angle at a particular time of day in specific weather conditions).

**Incident:**   A specific, small action that usually takes place within a more extended narrative.

**Internal rhyme:**   Rhyme that occurs within a poetic line as opposed to the end of the line.

**Introspection:**   A personal willingness to consider and reflect upon ideas that may seem to conflict or that may prove uncomfortable.

**Intrusive narrator:**   A narrator who breaks into the story in order to offer judgment or guidance to the reader or to comment on the unfolding action.

**Irony:**   A literary device that plays upon a gap between appearance and reality. Irony requires us to hold up two possible meanings simultaneously and to appreciate how the implied meaning overrides what seems apparent on the surface. There are many different types of irony. **Contextual irony** arises from circumstances or from coincidence (for example, a homeless person arrested for vagrancy on the street in front of a governmental housing and urban development office). **Dramatic irony** signals a distinction between what a character knows and what an audience understands. In other words, dramatic irony arises at moments when the audience knows more than the character or characters that are part of the action. **Verbal irony** (perhaps the most common ironic mode) suggests a deliberate play upon the difference between what is said and what is meant. **Sarcasm** is an especially blunt and aggressive form of verbal irony.

**Italian** or **Petrarchan sonnet:**   A lyric poem made up of fourteen lines that lends itself to a tightly developed problem/response structure. It builds the **complication** (problem, question) in the first eight lines (**octave**), and the **resolution** (response, answer) is delivered after the **turn** in the final six lines (**sestet**). See **sonnet.**

**Juxtaposition:**   A rhetorical technique of putting two (or more) things next to each other; the resulting contrast or similarity makes us see both objects differently than we saw them when each stood alone.

**Limited narrator:**   See **limited omniscient narrator** and **third-person narration.**

**Limited omniscient narrator:**   A narrator who knows most things but cannot relate selected bits of information or insight. See **third-person narration.**

**Line break:**   The point at which a line of poetry breaks; the end of a line of poetry.

**Low-angle shot:**   In film/photography, a **shot** taken from below the subject. A low-angle shot may be used to place the viewer in a weak position. For example, in the film *Rear Window*, Hitchcock uses a low-angle shot to have us look up at the murderer who is about to attack the wheelchair-bound hero. The viewer is, in effect, put in the wheelchair and feels the threat of the attacker.

**Low comedy:**   A comedy that involves **characters** of little emotional or intellectual substance.

**Masculine rhyme:**   A rhyme in which the rhyming syllable falls on the stressed and final syllable.

**Metaphor:**   A joining of two qualities or things to create new meaning. For example, the phrase "love is a red rose" fuses two essentially unlike things to communicate something about the quality of love. Usually, metaphors build upon one concrete thing (like a rose) and an abstraction (like love). **Similes**, unlike metaphor, signal a comparison as opposed to a fusion (love is *like* a red rose).

**Meter:**   The regular and therefore discernible rhythmic pattern of sounds that can be charted in poetry line by line.

**Metric line:**   A line of poetry measured by the number of feet that compose it. The most common lines are **trimeter** (three feet), **tetrameter** (four feet), **pentameter** (five feet), and **hexameter** (six feet). See **iamb.**

**Milieu:**   A French word that literally means "center" or "middle" and is used to designate particular social, temporal, and physical surroundings.

**Mise en scène:**   A French term that indicates what is put into the scene. Mise en scène originally referred to the staging of plays: the arrangement and inclusion of furniture, backdrops, stray items, and props that make up the environment within which characters act. Film critics use the term to describe what is captured in a shot. The concept applies to any work of art that places objects in a scene. It's important to remember that if an item is in a scene, it's there because the author/director put it there.

**Montage:**  From the French verb "to assemble." In film criticism, refers to a style of editing that uses sudden **juxtapositions** of images, surprising cuts, and radical shifts in **perspective.** Literary critics may use the word to describe dramatic contrasts of images, voices, or **genres.**

**Moral:**  An explicit lesson oftentimes stated at the end of a narrative. An overt message signaled by the **author.** See **didactic work.**

**Motif:**  A recurring element (an image, a key word, a **symbol,** a phrase, and so on) in a work of literature, film, or music. A motif may be analyzed in context of a group of works (that is, as a familiar element repeated in many different texts) or may be seen to operate within a single text.

**Multiple plots:**  The weaving together of two or more plots in a single work; multiple plots suggest complexity or density of experience.

**New criticism:**  A school of criticism that emerged in the middle of the twentieth century and continues to influence much teaching of literature and film. New critics were **formalists:** they argued that literary texts are the sole material of literary study. Literary criticism was seen as a distinct discipline that focused on the structure, style, and language of particular works.

**New historicism:**  Views systems of meaning as conditional and shifting depending upon the interests the system represents. Literary artists are not free of the assumptions of power that are encoded in language. New historicism has also been called **cultural poetics** and **postcolonial criticism.** The former term puts emphasis on the cultural context that produces literary texts; the latter term calls attention to the ways in which language functions within a system of power.

**Objective narrator:**  A narrator who reports from the outside what can be seen but makes no effort to get inside the minds of any character (sometimes called an **impersonal narrator**). See **third-person narration.**

**Octave:**  A **stanza** of eight lines. An octave often constitutes the first part of an **Italian sonnet.** See **sonnet** and **sestet.**

**Ode:**  Once structured in three parts that reflected their origins as public poems, performed by a **chorus** that moved in one direction as it delivered the first part (the strophe), moved in the opposite direction as it voiced the second part (the antistrophe), and stood still as it came to the final section (the epode). Those conventions of form and performance have worn away. Now odes are characterized more by elements of mood and subject; they are substantial poems of a meditative cast—serious and dignified.

**Omniscient narrator:**  A narrator who knows everything about the characters' actions and thoughts. See **third-person narration.**

**Open ending:**  An ending that prompts the reader to think, question, or project beyond the narrative. A reader might wonder after reading an open-ended novel, for example, what will happen to a character or might be left thinking about the implications of an action.

**Pace:**   The relative speed of an unfolding action, presentation, or argument.

**Paradox:**   An expression that seems to contradict itself but that actually realizes something genuine and deeply coherent. Paradox demands that we question common assumptions or understandings. Blake often plays upon paradox in his *Songs of Innocence* and *Songs of Experience* (p. 417–418; 419–420).

**Paraphrase:**   Involves a superficial revision of the original text; the writer of a paraphrase stays close to the logic, length, and language of the original. See **summary.**

**Parody:**   A comic imitation of a serious work or **genre.** Mel Brooks has made a career of making parodies of successful films or film genres (*Robin Hood* becomes *Men in Tights; Star Wars* becomes *Space Balls;* classic westerns become *Blazing Saddles,* and so on). **Self-parody** suggests an unintentional revelation of empty and tired formulas. Some critics would argue that Michael Bay's action films have descended into self-parody.

**Particular:**   The specific and concrete illustration/image as opposed to the general and **abstract** idea. Authors often use the particular in order to ground more ambitious ideas and feelings—and make those ideas and feelings vivid and convincing. Note for example, Czeslaw Milosz's "A Song on the End of the World" (p. 256).

**Pastoral:**   Marked by setting in the quiet countryside amid a gently cultivated nature. Pastorals once had elaborate conventions (shepherds living the simple life upon nature's bounty), but the word has come to signal broader qualities: a peaceful and uncomplicated life away from the city can be called pastoral.

**Pentameter:**   A line of poetry made up of five feet. See **metric line.**

**Personification:**   Projecting animate (human or animal) qualities on an inanimate thing.

**Perspective:**   See **point of view.**

**Plagiarism:**   The inappropriate use of the words or ideas of another writer. Plagiarism is a form of theft. In its most extreme form, plagiarism involves lifting directly from a prior source and passing off the work as original. But inadequately acknowledged **summary** and/or an extended **paraphrase** (as opposed to straight copying) can also be deemed plagiarism and be subject to disciplinary or legal action.

**Plot:**   A meaningful fabric of action. Plot suggests structure (a beginning, middle, and end). It suggests not only *what happened* but also *how what happened was conveyed.*

**Poet:**   The source of the word suggests "maker." Poet can, of course, simply mean one who makes poetry. But oftentimes, the word is used more broadly. It can be important to distinguish the poet or **author** (the maker of any text you read) from the **speaker** or narrator (a voice created by the poet/author).

**Poetic diction:**   The notion that the poetic words are necessarily different from everyday words.

**Point of view:**   Strictly speaking, the point from which one sees. More broadly, point of view signals narrative perspective—the way a story is related. Thinking in terms of point of view involves considering who tells the story as well as how the teller's interests, personality, motives, and background influence what is observed and reported.

**Postcolonial criticism:**   See **new historicism.**

**Postmodernism:**   A highly self-conscious mode of expression that calls attention to the artifice of a work of art—the fictionality of a work of fiction. Postmodernism can be playful, but it also blurs distinctions between real and imagined in ways that challenge our conventional ways of understanding. *Pulp Fiction* has been called a postmodern film. The stories of Borges have also been called postmodern.

**Prosody:**   The study of **meter** and verse.

**Protagonist:**   From the Greek, "the first one to battle." The main or leading **character.** Although the protagonist is usually the **hero** of a story, the terms are not synonymous. See **antagonist.**

**Pyrrhic:**   A foot that consists of two consecutive unstressed syllables; a **variant** or **substitution** of a standard rhythmic unit. That is, a pyrrhic foot may break a pattern, but it cannot be the pattern (a line cannot be made up of only unstressed syllables).

**Quatrain:**   A verse paragraph made up of four lines. See **stanza.**

**Reader-response criticism:**   A variant of **new historicism.** Reader-response critics shift emphasis from a text to how people read/use a text; the work of art is studied not through its own inherent qualities but through the way readers of a particular time and place react to it.

**Realism:**   A mode of depiction that builds on close, accurate attention to specific historical and social conditions. Realism is a constructed illusion; it involves the author's efforts to convince the reader of the reality of a particular vision.

**Reflexive plot** (also reflexive or **self-conscious narrative**):   A story in which the way a story is constructed becomes the very thing we are forced to think about. For example, the film *Memento* makes questions of narration central to its theme. A self-conscious narrator is aware of the artfulness of the story he or she tells.

**Refrain:**   A phrase, line, or **stanza** that recurs regularly throughout a poem or song.

**Reliable narrator:**  A narrator who offers accurate information and a credible interpretation of action. A narrator who establishes and rewards trust.

**Repetition:**  A means to foreground an image or theme.

**Resolution:**  A satisfying explanation; the part of a **plot** in which problems are addressed. In a long Victorian novel, for example, the resolution might involve a final word on how all the characters turn out (who gets married and has children, who dies miserable and alone, and so on). In a **sonnet,** resolution suggests a response to the **complication** set forth in the first part of the poem.

**Rhetorical figure:**  Uses a word or words in an unusual context or sequence but does not radically change the customary meaning of the word or words. See **trope.**

**Rhyme:**  Consists of the similarity of the last stressed vowel of one word with the last stressed vowel of another. **Full** or **perfect rhyme** consists of the sameness of sounds in accented vowels and any consonants that follow: *date/fate*. **Assonance** also consists of a similarity in vowel sounds, but the final consonants differ: *date/lake*. **Consonance** strikes a similarity in the sounds of the final stressed consonant, but the preceding vowel sounds differ: *date/rite*. Such examples are often called **slant rhymes** or **off-rhymes.**

**Riddle poem:**  A poem that leaves its subject unstated, that invites or requires readers to supply the missing subject. Emily Dickinson's "[A Route of Evanescence]," for example, describes something that it doesn't name: a hummingbird. Part of the fun is guessing the subject from the evidence supplied. See also Dickinson's "[I like to see it lap the Miles—]."

**Rising action:**  The building part of a narrative that establishes, sustains, and intensifies a **conflict.**

**Rising meter:**  A **foot** in which the accent falls on the last syllable.

**Round character:**  A term used to describe characters that possess a complex psychology. A term used in opposition to **flat character.**

**Sarcasm:**  An especially blunt and aggressive form of **verbal irony.** See **irony.**

**Scan:**  To define by close metrical analysis the rhythmic pattern of poetic lines.

**Scansion:**  The metrical analysis of a line of poetry.

**Scene:**  In a dramatic work, may simply indicate the entrance and/or exit of characters from the stage. More broadly understood, a scene is an action within a larger narrative that has some thematic or dramatic function. A scene may be defined by mood, function, or place. It may convey a particular **conflict** that is subordinate to the larger conflict of the entire narrative.

**Self-conscious narrative:**  See **reflexive plot.**

**Self-parody:**   Self-parody suggests an unintentional revelation of empty and tired formulas. See **parody.**

**Sequence:**   A series of actions or a list of points with no necessary logic; sequence alone implies no more than one thing after another.

**Sestet:**   A **stanza** of six lines. A sestet often constitutes the second and final part of an Italian sonnet. See **sonnet.**

**Sestina:**   A highly complicated, fixed poetic form. The sestina consists of six **sestets** (thirty-six lines) and a concluding **tercet** (three lines). The six words that close the first sestet must also appear (not necessarily in the same order) at the ends of the other sestets and then must appear in the final tercet. The **repetition** serves to foreground or develop **themes** and feelings central to the whole.

**Setting:**   The total environment within which narrative actions take place. The characters' living conditions as well as the time and place in which they live constitute setting.

**Shallow focus:**   In film/photography, a technique that brings a specific plane into clear focus and leaves the rest of the picture blurry. A director might use shallow focus to get us to look closely at the face of one character. See **deep focus.**

**Shape poem:**   See **concrete poetry.**

**Shot:**   A single length of film that communicates a continuous action on the screen.

**Shot analysis:**   A means to comprehend how a film communicates meaning and power. In shot analysis, one breaks a film down and assesses the relationship of shot to shot.

**Simile:**   A comparison that links two things with *like* or *as*. Langston Hughes employs a series of similes in "Harlem" to answer the question "what happens to a dream deferred": for example, it may dry up *like* a raisin. See **metaphor.**

**Sincere:**   The antithesis of **irony**; the perfect correspondence between words and intended meaning. But it is important to remember that sincerity in a literary text may be a device used by an author as opposed to a quality the author actually possesses.

**Slant rhyme** or **off-rhyme:**   Rhyme in which the sounds of the final stressed consonant are similar, but the preceding vowel sounds differ: *date/rite*. See **consonance** and **rhyme.**

**Sonnet:**   A lyric poem of fourteen lines that lends itself to a tightly developed problem/response structure. The sonnet's opening section is often called the **complication;** the second part, the **resolution.** The brief transition that gives us pause just between these two parts is called the **turn.** The two most common forms are the **Italian** (or **Petrarchan**) sonnet and **English** (or **Shakespearean**) sonnet. The Italian sonnet builds the complication (problem, question, and so on) in the first eight lines (octave), and the resolution (response, answer, and so on) is delivered after the turn in the final six lines (sestet). The English sonnet often repeats the complication over the first twelve lines (three quatrains) and saves the resolution for the final two lines (couplet).

**Speaker:**   Distinct from **poet** or **author.** The speaker is the voice created by the poet/author of a text. Robert Browning is the author/poet of "My Last Duchess," but the speaker is the duke (a character Browning has created).

**Split-screen:**   A film-editing technique in which the screen space is split so that two or more film sequences run simultaneously next to each other. One of the more famous of these sequences shows a man and a woman talking on the phone with each other. Although they are in different places, the split screen allows us to see both sides of the conversation.

**Spondee** or **spondaic foot:**   Consists of two consecutive stressed syllables. A spondee is a **variant** or **substitution** of a standard rhythmic unit. That is, a spondee may break a pattern, but it cannot be the pattern (a line cannot be made up of only stressed syllables).

**Staging:**   The elements that concern the physical production of a dramatic work: lighting, sound effects, costumes, mise-en-scène, and so on.

**Stanza:**   A verse paragraph organized by a pattern of rhyme. The most common forms are the **couplet** (two lines), **tercet** (three lines), and **quatrain** (four lines). See also **octave** and **sestet.**

**Stanzaic structure:**   The shape of a **stanza,** marked and knit together by a pattern of **rhyme.** Sometimes called **rhyme scheme.**

**Static character:**   Character who does not change over the course of a story.

**Stock character:**   Simple or **flat character** that is wholly defined by a familiar type or characteristic (for example, Nelson, the schoolyard bully in *The Simpsons* is a stock character).

**Stream of consciousness:**   Direct access to the thoughts and feelings of a character as those thoughts and feelings unfold.

**Strophe:**   In classical drama, a part of the choral ode. While singing, the chorus would dance. According to some analysts, for the strophe, they would move from left to right; for the **antistrophe,** they would move from right to left back to the original position. The two movements are identical in meter. See **antistrophe.**

**Subplot:**   A secondary plot that runs parallel to the main plot. Subplots complement (reinforce, complicate, and deepen) the main plot. There may be more than one subplot in an extended narrative. See **multiple plots.**

**Substitution:**   A break in the prevailing rhythmic pattern of a poetic line; a **foot** (oftentimes a **spondaic** or **pyrrhic** foot) that interrupts a pattern. Substitutions (also called **variants**) may be used to draw attention to a word or phrase. Substitutions/variants might be used to speed or slow the pace of a line.

**Summary:**    Often used interchangeably with **paraphrase,** but a clear distinction between the two is useful. Paraphrase involves a superficial revision of the original text; the writer of a paraphrase stays close to the logic, length, and language of the original. Summary suggests a thorough rewriting and significant compression of the original. Whereas a summary may be appropriate when the source and the extent of the debt are clearly signaled and cited, an extended paraphrase should always be avoided.

**Symbol:**    A type of **trope** in which an object or image comes to represent something more than or other than the object or image alone.

**Synchronicity:**    Events that coincide in time and appear to be related but have no discoverable causal connection.

**Synesthesia:**    The conflation or cross association of two or more of the five senses. For example, hearing a beautiful piece of music might lead one to feel a particular touch (perhaps a piercing pain or a soft caress).

**Synecdoche:**    A figure of speech in which a part represents the whole (for example, all hands on deck).

**Tension:**    A feeling (suspense, doubt, worry, puzzlement, and so on) that is sustained and released/resolved in a work. These feelings do not need to be the broadly drawn **conflicts** that press forward a narrative; many of Emily Dickinson's short poems, for example, are built upon a tension between highly specific words/images and cosmic associations/suggestions.

**Tercet:**    A verse paragraph made up of three lines. See **stanza.**

**Tetrameter:**    A line of poetry made up of four feet. See **metric line.**

**Theme:**    A recurrent idea or feeling woven through a text. Although themes may be explicit (as in a moral to a **fable**), they are more often suggestive and open ended. See **motif.**

**Thesis:**    An assertion that guides an argument, a main point, or a leading insight. A strong, clearly defined thesis underlies the development of a critical essay.

**Third-person narration:**    A story told from outside; that is, the narrator refers to all characters as "he," "she," or "they." There are varied forms of third-person narration. An **omniscient narrator** knows everything about the characters' actions and thoughts. A **limited omniscient narrator** (as the name would suggest) knows most things but cannot relate selected bits of information or insight. Such a limited narrator might, for example, be able to report on the thoughts of all characters but one. An **objective narrator** (sometimes called an **impersonal narrator**) reports from the outside what can be seen but makes no effort to get inside the minds of any character.

**Tragedy:**    At the simplest level, a work that ends in death. More particularly, tragedy involves a powerful sense of lost promise.

**Trimeter:**    A line of poetry made up of three feet. See **metric line.**

**Trochee:** (trochaic foot) Consists of two syllables, the first stressed and the second unstressed.

**Trope:** From the Greek for a "turn" or "turning." Tropes use words to turn from conventional understanding; they significantly alter or enlarge meaning. A trope is also called a **figure of thought** (as opposed to a **rhetorical figure**). **Metaphor, simile,** and **personification** are all tropes. A sarcastic statement (**sarcasm**) is also a trope (if one says, "thanks a lot" in response to an insult, no genuine thanks is intended).

**Turn:** Suggests a transition space between the **complication** and the **resolution** in a **sonnet.** More broadly, a turn can suggest a sudden movement against a main line of development in any literary work. It also suggests a break from the usual sense of a word or phrase. See **trope.**

**Understanding:** Grasping a key thought or feeling in a text. Understanding is distinct from knowing. Knowing suggests certainty and completeness (for example, we know Emily Dickinson is an American poet who lived in the nineteenth century). Conversely, one can attain a level of understanding or achieve an insight about an aspect of a text.

**Universal:** The belief that some ideas transcend historical or social **context** and apply across generations and cultures.

**Unreliable narrator:** A narrator who provides false leads or misinterprets important actions. Readers are forced to consider how the entire situation (not just what is related) help establish a fair view of what unfolds.

**Variant:** See **substitution.**

**Verbal irony:** Perhaps the most common ironic mode; suggests a deliberate play upon the difference between what is said and what is meant. See **irony.**

**Villanelle:** A fixed and especially complex poetic form. A villanelle consists of nineteen lines. The first fifteen are made up of a series of five **tercets** (rhymed *aba*); a **quatrain** closes the poem (*abaa*). Dylan Thomas's "Do Not Go Gentle into That Good Night" (p. 152) is a famous example.

**Visual image:** The realization in words of something seen.

# Credits

This page constitutes an extension of the copyright page. We have made every effort to trace the ownership of all copyrighted material and to secure permission from copyright holders. In the event of any question arising as to the use of any material, we will be pleased to make the necessary corrections in future printings. Thanks are due to the following authors, publishers, and agents for permission to use the material indicated.

## TEXT CREDITS

**Chinua Achebe** "Dead Man's Path" copyright © 1972, 1973 by Chinua Achebe, from *Girls at War and Other Stories*. Used by permission of Doubleday, a division of Random House, Inc. and Emma Sweeney Agency.

**Douglas Adams** excerpt from *The Hitchhiker's Guide to the Galaxy* by Douglas Adams. Copyright © 1979 by Douglas Adams. Reprinted by permission of Harmony Books, a division of Random House, Inc.

**Margaret Atwood** "Siren Song" from *Selected Poems: 1965–1975 and 1966–1984* by Margaret Atwood. Copyright © 1976, 1990 by Margaret Atwood. Reprinted by permission of Houghton Mifflin Company and Oxford University Press. All rights reserved; "you fit into me" from *Selected Poems: 1965–1975* by Margaret Atwood. Copyright © 1976 by Margaret Atwood. Reprinted by permission of Houghton Mifflin Company. All rights reserved. Permission granted by House of Anansi for "you fit into me" from *Power Politics* by Margaret Atwood.

**Dick Barnes** "Up Home Where I Come From" from *A Word Like Fire*. Copyright © 2005 Dick Barnes, Other Press, LLC. Used with permission.

**Wendell Berry** "The Vacation" from *Selected Poems of Wendell Berry*. Copyright © 1998 by Wendell Berry. Reprinted by permission of Counterpoint, a member of Perseus Books, LLC.

**Neal Bowers** "Tenth Year Elegy" from *Words for the Taking: The Hunt for a Plagiarist*. Copyright © 1997 Neal Bowers. Reprinted by permission.

**Bulwer-Lytton Fiction Contest Winners** used courtesy of the Bulwer-Lytton Fiction Contest, Department of English, San Jose State University. All rights reserved.

**Yosa Buson** poetry from *Haiku Master Buson*, translated by Yuki Sawa and Edith Marcombe Shiffert. English translation copyright © 1978 by Yuki Sawa. Reprinted with the permission of White Pine Press, Buffalo, NY.

**Cathy Song** "Picture Bride" from *Picture Bride*. Copyright © 1983 Cathy Song. Reprinted by permission of Yale University Press.
**Gary Soto** "Oranges" from *New and Selected Poems*. Copyright © 1995 by Gary Soto. Reprinted by permission of Chronicle Books, LLC, San Francisco.
**Tom Stoppard** *The Fifteen Minute Hamlet: A Play*. Copyright © 1968 Tom Stoppard.
**Robert Sward** "For Gloria on Her 60th Birthday, Or Looking for Love in Merriam-Webster" from *Four Incarnations: New and Selected Poems, 1957–1991*. Copyright © 1991 by Robert Sward. Reprinted with the permission of Coffee House Press, Minneapolis, MN.
**Wislawa Szymborska** "ABC," and "The Courtesy of the Blind" from *Monologue of a Dog*. Copyright © 2002 by Wislawa Szymborska. English translation copyright © 2006 by Harcourt, Inc. Reprinted by permission of the publisher.
**Henry Taylor** "After a Movie," from *Understanding Fiction: Poems 1986–1996*. Copyright © 1996 by Henry Taylor. Reprinted by permission of Louisiana State University Press.
**Dylan Thomas** "Do Not Go Gentle into That Good Night" by Dylan Thomas from *The Poems of Dylan Thomas*. Copyright © 1952 by Dylan Thomas. Reprinted by permission of New Directions Publishing Corp.
**James Thurber** "The Girl and the Wolf" from *Fables for Our Time*. Copyright © 1940 by James Thurber. Copyright renewed © 1968 by Helen Thurber and Rosemary A. Thurber. Reprinted by arrangement with Rosemary A. Thurber and The Barbara Hogenson Agency.
**Richard Wilbur** "A Fire Truck" from *Advice to a Prophet and Other Poems*. Copyright © 1975 and renewed 2003 by Richard Wilbur, reprinted by permission of Harcourt, Inc.
**William Carlos Williams** "The Red Wheelbarrow" from *Collected Poems: 1909–1939, Volume I* by William Carlos Williams. Copyright © 1938 by New Directions Publishing Corp. Reprinted by permission of New Directions Publishing Corp.
**W. B. Yeats** "The Folly of Being Comforted" reprinted with the permission of Scribner, an imprint of Simon & Schuster Adult Publishing Group, from *The Collected Works of W. B. Yeats, Volume I: The Poems, Revised*, edited by Richard J. Finneran (New York: Scribner, 1927).

# IMAGE CREDITS

**Chapter 1. 2:** top Edouard Boubat/Rapho/H.P.P. **7:** top center, Erich Lessing/Art Resource, NY **14:** top, Summit Entertainment/ The Kobal Collection
**Chapter 2. 27:** top, Bettman/Corbis **28:** top center, Bettman/Corbis
**Chapter 3. 43:** center left, Corbis; center right, MGM/The Kobal Collection **51:** bottom center, Mary Evans Picture Library/The Image Works
**Chapter 4. 56:** bottom, Stapleton Collection/Corbis **57:** bottom center, Erich Lessing/Art Resource, NY **58:** top, Piero Sanpaolesi, BRUNELLESCHI. Florence, S. Barbera, 1962, figure C, opposite page 52 **60:** bottom center, Foto Marburg/Art Resource, NY; top center, Photo: Elke Walford. Bildarchiv Preussischer Kulturbesitz/Art Resource, NY **66:** bottom, Everett Collection; top, © Jerry Tavin/Everett Collection **67:** top, Everett Collection; bottom, Prana-Film/The Kobal Collection **70:** bottom, Bettmann/Corbis **73:** bottom center, © The Lane Collection Courtesy, Museum of Fine Arts, Boston
**Chapter 5. 80:** bottom, Lake Country Museum/Corbis **84:** bottom, Bettmann/Corbis **90:** top, Sketch by Luc Desportes, used with permission; sketch and film still reproduced with the permission of Jean-Pierre Jeunet **90:** bottom, Sketch by Luc Desportes, used with permission; sketch and film still reproduced with the permission of Jean-Pierre Jeunet **91:** bottom, Universal/The Kobal Collection/Mill Film
**Chapter 6. 97:** bottom center, Everett Collection
**Chapter 7. 116:** top left, Onne van der Wal/Corbis **116:** top right, Onne van der Wal/Corbis **116:** center, Onne van der Wal/Corbis **116:** bottom center, The Museum of Modern Art, New York, NY. Digital Image © The Museum of Modern Art/Licensed by SCALA /Art Resource, NY **119:** bottom center, Fox Searchlight Pictures/The Kobal Collection/Wallace, Merie W. **121:** top center, Hulton-Deutsch Collection/Corbis **125:** bottom, Focus Features/The Kobal Collection/Sato, Yoshio; top, Miramax/ Dimension Films/The Kobal Collection/Tursi, Mario **129:** bottom center, Photograph by Rollie McKenna. Copyright © 2006 The Estate of Rosalie Thorne McKenna **130:** top, RKO/The Kobal Collection
**Chapter 8. 142:** top, Touchstone/The Kobal Collection/Moseley, Melissa
**Chapter 9. 160:** bottom, 20th Century Fox/The Kobal Collection **161:** top, 20th Century Fox/The Kobal Collection **167:** top, © Miramax/ Everett Collection **168:** bottom, Photo by Margaret Bourke-White//Time

Life Pictures/Getty Images **172:** bottom, Photo by Dirck Halstead//Time Life Pictures/Getty Images; top, Photo by Taro Yamasaki/Time Life Pictures/Getty Images
**Chapter 10. 192:** bottom center, Photo by Margaret Bourke-White/Time Life Pictures/Getty Images **193:** top, copyright © Walt Disney Co./ Courtesy Everett/Everett Collection
**Chapter 11. 199:** bottom, 20th Century Fox/The Kobal Collection/ Kirkland, Douglas
**Chapter 12. 217:** top center, From TOOTLE by Gertrude Crampton and Tibor Gergeley, copyright 1945, renewed 1972 by Random House, Inc. Used by permission of Golden Books, an imprint of Random House Children's Books, a division of Random House, Inc. **220:** top, Corbis **221:** bottom center, Bettmann/Corbis **222:** top center, 89.PA.32, The J. Paul Getty Museum, Los Angeles **229:** top center, Corbis Sygma
**Chapter 13. 237:** bottom center, Clarita Natoli/moreguefile.com **243:** top, Bettmann/Corbis; bottom left, Blue Lantern Studio/Corbis; center right, Chris Hellier/Corbis; bottom right, Royalty-Free/Corbis **244:** bottom left, Bettmann/Corbis; center right, Bettmann/Corbis; bottom right, James Leynes/Corbis; top, John Springer Collection/Corbis
**Chapter 14. 255:** bottom, Zoetrope/United Artists/The Kobal Collection **260:** bottom, Warner Bros/First National/The Kobal Collection **262:** bottom right, © Private Collection/The Bridgeman Art Library **268:** center, Hieroglyphic line for "The Third Bank of the River" (A Terceira Margem Do Rio), from João Guimarães Rosa, Primeiras Estœrias, Editora Nova Fronteira, Rio de Janeiro, Brazil
**Chapter 15. 276:** bottom center, Scala/Art Resource, NY **278:** center, Bettmann/Corbis; bottom center, Corbis Sygma
**Chapter 16. 300:** bottom center, Photo by Kevin Winter/Getty Images **304:** top left, Bettmann/Corbis; top right, Bettmann/Corbis **305:** bottom, Paramount/The Kobal Collection **306:** bottom center, Warner Bros/The Kobal Collection
**Chapter 17. 314:** Yale Center for British Art, Paul Mellon Collection, USA/The Bridgeman Art Library **322:** bottom center, Private Collection/ Ken Walsh/The Bridgeman Art Library **323:** top, John Springer Collection/Corbis; bottom, R.P. Productions/Runteam Ltd/The Kobal Collection/Ferrandis, Guy
**Chapter 18. 338:** Shakespeare Quarterly 57:1 (2006), Table of Contents Page. © Folger Shakespeare Library. Reprinted with permission of The Johns Hopkins University Press.

# Index of First Lines of Poetry

# Index of Authors and Titles

Italics indicate a title of a work of art, film, or literature.